CONGRESSIONAL POLICIES, PRACTICES AND PROCEDURES

CONGRESSIONAL OVERSIGHT: AN OVERVIEW, A MANUAL AND SELECT DEVELOPMENTS

CONGRESSIONAL POLICIES, PRACTICES AND PROCEDURES

Additional books in this series can be found on Nova's website under the Series tab.

Additional E-books in this series can be found on Nova's website under the E-books tab.

CONGRESSIONAL POLICIES, PRACTICES AND PROCEDURES

CONGRESSIONAL OVERSIGHT: AN OVERVIEW, A MANUAL AND SELECT DEVELOPMENTS

JAMIE C. HOWELL
EDITOR

Nova Science Publishers, Inc.
New York

For permission to use material from this book please contact us:
Telephone 631-231-7269; Fax 631-231-8175
Web Site: http://www.novapublishers.com

NOTICE TO THE READER

The Publisher has taken reasonable care in the preparation of this book, but makes no expressed or implied warranty of any kind and assumes no responsibility for any errors or omissions. No liability is assumed for incidental or consequential damages in connection with or arising out of information contained in this book. The Publisher shall not be liable for any special, consequential, or exemplary damages resulting, in whole or in part, from the readers' use of, or reliance upon, this material. Any parts of this book based on government reports are so indicated and copyright is claimed for those parts to the extent applicable to compilations of such works.

Independent verification should be sought for any data, advice or recommendations contained in this book. In addition, no responsibility is assumed by the publisher for any injury and/or damage to persons or property arising from any methods, products, instructions, ideas or otherwise contained in this publication.

This publication is designed to provide accurate and authoritative information with regard to the subject matter covered herein. It is sold with the clear understanding that the Publisher is not engaged in rendering legal or any other professional services. If legal or any other expert assistance is required, the services of a competent person should be sought. FROM A DECLARATION OF PARTICIPANTS JOINTLY ADOPTED BY A COMMITTEE OF THE AMERICAN BAR ASSOCIATION AND A COMMITTEE OF PUBLISHERS.

LIBRARY OF CONGRESS CATALOGING-IN-PUBLICATION DATA
Available upon request

ISBN 978-1-61728-477-9

Published by Nova Science Publishers, Inc. ✢ New York

CONTENTS

Preface		**vii**
Chapter 1	Congressional Oversight: An Overview *Walter J. Oleszek*	**1**
Chapter 2	Congressional Oversight Manual *Frederick M. Kaiser, Walter J. Oleszek, T.J. Halstead, Morton Rosenberg and Todd B. Tatelman*	**19**
Chapter 3	Congressional Oversight of Intelligence: Current Structure and Alternatives *Frederick M. Kaiser*	**145**
Chapter 4	Sensitive Covert Action Notifications: Oversight Options for Congress *Alfred Cumming*	**173**
Chapter 5	Congressional Oversight and Related Issues Concerning International Security Agreements Concluded by the United States *Michael John Garcia and R. Chuck Mason*	**189**

PREFACE

A fundamental objective of congressional oversight is to hold executive officials accountable for the implementation of delegated authority. This objective is especially important given the huge expansion of executive influence in the modern era. Given the role and scope of the federal establishment, the importance of Congress's review function looms large in checking and monitoring the delegated authority that it grants to federal departments and agencies. This book highlights the reasons for expansion of the federal government; discusses the definition and purpose of oversight; reviews oversight techniques and identifies several incentives and disincentives to the conduct of congressional oversight.

Chapter 1- A fundamental objective of congressional oversight is to hold executive officials accountable for the implementation of delegated authority. This objective is especially important given the huge expansion of executive influence in the modern era. If the Founding Fathers returned to observe their handiwork, they would likely be surprised by such developments as the creation of a "presidential branch" of government (the Office of Management and Budget, the National Security Council, and the like) and the establishment of so many federal departments and agencies. From three departments in 1789 (State, Treasury, and War, renamed Defense in 1947), a dozen more have been added to the cabinet. The newest creation in 2002, is the Department of Homeland Security (DHS). Formed from the merger of 22 separate executive branch units, it employs roughly 180,000 people.

Clearly, given the role and scope of the federal establishment, the importance of Congress's review function looms large in checking and monitoring the delegated authority that it grants to federal departments and agencies. The goals of this chapter, then, are essentially six-fold: (1) highlight several reasons for the expansion of the federal government; (2) discuss a few definitions of oversight; (3) spotlight three essential purposes of oversight; (4) comment upon a few oversight laws and rules; (5) review several important oversight techniques; and (6) identify several incentives and disincentives to the conduct of congressional oversight. The report concludes with summary observations.

Chapter 2- The *Congressional Oversight Manual* was developed about 30 years ago following a three-day December 1978 Workshop on Congressional Oversight and Investigations. The workshop was organized by a group of House and Senate committee aides from both parties and the Congressional Research Service (CRS) at the request of the bipartisan House leadership. The *Manual* was produced by CRS with the assistance of a number of House committee staffers. In subsequent years, CRS sponsored and conducted various oversight seminars for House and Senate staff and updated the *Manual* as circumstances warranted. The last revision occurred in 2004. Worth noting is the bipartisan recommendation of the House members of the 1993 Joint Committee on the Organization of Congress (Rept. No. 103-413, Vol. I):

> [A]s a way to further enhance the oversight work of Congress, the Joint Committee would encourage the Congressional Research Service to conduct on a regular basis, as it has done in the past, oversight seminars for Members and congressional staff and to update on a regular basis its *Congressional Oversight Manual*.

Over the years, CRS has assisted many Members, committees, party leaders, and staff aides in the performance of the oversight function, that is, the review, monitoring, and supervision of the implementation of public policy. Understandably, given the size, reach, cost, and continuing growth of the modern executive establishment, Congress's oversight role is even more significant — and more demanding — than when Woodrow Wilson wrote in his classic *Congressional Government* (1885): "Quite as important as lawmaking is vigilant oversight of administration." Today's lawmakers and congressional aides, as well as commentators and scholars, recognize that Congress's work, ideally, should not end when it passes legislation. Oversight is an integral way to make sure that the laws work and are being administered in an effective, efficient, and economical manner. In light of this destination, oversight can be viewed as one of Congress's principal responsibilities as it grapples with the complexities of the 21st century.

To revise a document of this size and scope requires the contributions of many people. Five CRS specialists, listed on the title page, were responsible for organizing and writing this version of the *Manual*. In addition, other CRS personnel assisted in the preparation and publication of this chapter, along with staff of the Congressional Budget Office (CBO) and the Government Accountability Office (GAO).

Chapter 3- Interest in congressional oversight of intelligence has risen again recently in Congresses, in part because of disputes over reporting to Congress by Intelligence Community (IC) components on sensitive matters, including developments generated by the wars in Iraq and Afghanistan. The changes in the oversight structure proposed by the 111th Congress, however, reflect long-term concerns and considerations. For instance, the House Democratic majority had pledged in the 110th Congress to enact the remaining recommendations from the U.S. National Commission on Terrorist Attacks Upon the United States, commonly known as the 9/11 Commission, which called for a transformation of Congress's oversight structure. The commission's unanimous report in 2004, covering many issues, set the stage for reconsideration of the problems affecting Congress's structure in this area. The panel concluded that congressional oversight of intelligence was "dysfunctional" and proposed two distinct solutions. These were (1) creation of a joint committee on intelligence (JCI), modeled after the defunct Joint Committee on Atomic Energy (JCAE), with authority to report legislation to each chamber; or (2) enhanced status and power for the existing select committees on intelligence, by making them standing committees and granting both authorization and appropriations power.

Proposals to create a joint committee on intelligence date to 1948 and the early years of the Cold War, when the Central Intelligence Agency (CIA) and Director of Central Intelligence (DCI) were established. Similar recommendations have emerged in the meantime, although the lion's share were made before separate Intelligence Committees were established in the House (1977) and Senate (1976). The numerous proposals for a JCI, which would end the two existing intelligence panels, moreover, vary in their specifics and raise competing viewpoints over practical matters and matters of principle.

Chapter 4- Legislation enacted in 1980 gave the executive branch authority to limit advance notification of especially sensitive covert actions to eight Members of Congress—the "Gang of Eight"—when the President determines that it is essential to limit prior notice in order to meet extraordinary circumstances affecting U.S. vital interests. In such cases, the executive branch is permitted by statute to limit notification to the chairmen and ranking minority members of the two congressional intelligence committees, the Speaker and minority leader of the House, and Senate majority and minority leaders, rather than to notify the full intelligence committees, as is required in cases involving covert actions determined to be less sensitive.

Congress, in approving this new procedure in 1980, during the Iran hostage crisis, said it intended to preserve operational secrecy in those "rare" cases involving especially sensitive covert actions while providing the President with advance consultation with the leaders in Congress and the leadership of the intelligence committees who have special expertise and responsibility in intelligence matters. The intent appeared to some to be to provide the President, on a short-term basis, a greater degree of operational security as long as sensitive operations were underway. In 1991, in a further elaboration of its intent following the Iran-Contra Affair, congressional report language stated that limiting notification to the Gang of Eight should occur only in situations involving covert actions of such extraordinary sensitivity or risk to life that knowledge of such activity should be restricted to as few individuals as possible.

In its mark-up of H.R. 2701, the FY2010 Intelligence Authorization Act, the House Permanent Select Committee on Intelligence (HPSCI) replaced the Gang of Eight statutory provision, adopting in its place a statutory requirement that each of the intelligence committees establish written procedures as may be necessary to govern such notifications. According to committee report language, the adopted provision vests the authority to limit such briefings with the committees, rather than the President.

Chapter 5- The United States is a party to numerous security agreements with other nations. The topics covered, along with the significance of the obligations imposed upon agreement parties, may vary. Some international security agreements entered by the United States, such as those obliging parties to come to the defense of another in the event of an attack, involve substantial commitments and have traditionally been entered as treaties, ratified with the advice and consent of the Senate. Other agreements dealing with more technical matters, such as military basing rights or the application of a host country's laws to U.S. forces stationed within, are entered more routinely and usually take a form other than treaty (i.e., as an executive agreement or a nonlegal political commitment).

Occasionally, the substance and form of a proposed security agreement may become a source of dispute between Congress and the executive branch. In November 2007, the Bush Administration announced its intention to negotiate a long-term security agreement with Iraq that would have committed the United States to provide security assurances to Iraq, and contemplated a long-term presence by U.S. forces in Iraq. This announcement became a source of congressional interest, in part because of statements by Administration officials that such an agreement would not be submitted to the legislative branch for approval. Congressional concern appeared to dissipate when U.S.-Iraq negotiations culminated in an agreement that did not contain a long-term binding security commitment by the United States, but instead called for the withdrawal of U.S. forces from Iraq by December 31, 2011.

It is likely that future disputes will arise between the political branches regarding the entering or implementation of international security agreements. Regardless of the form a security arrangement may take, Congress has several tools to exercise oversight regarding the negotiation, form, conclusion, and implementation of the agreement by the United States.

In: Congressional Oversight An Overview, A Manual and... ISBN: 978-1-61728-477-9
Editor: Jamie C. Howell

Chapter 1

CONGRESSIONAL OVERSIGHT: AN OVERVIEW*

Walter J. Oleszek

SUMMARY

A fundamental objective of congressional oversight is to hold executive officials accountable for the implementation of delegated authority. This objective is especially important given the huge expansion of executive influence in the modern era. If the Founding Fathers returned to observe their handiwork, they would likely be surprised by such developments as the creation of a "presidential branch" of government (the Office of Management and Budget, the National Security Council, and the like) and the establishment of so many federal departments and agencies. From three departments in 1789 (State, Treasury, and War, renamed Defense in 1947), a dozen more have been added to the cabinet. The newest creation in 2002, is the Department of Homeland Security (DHS). Formed from the merger of 22 separate executive branch units, it employs roughly 180,000 people.

Clearly, given the role and scope of the federal establishment, the importance of Congress's review function looms large in checking and monitoring the delegated authority that it grants to federal departments and agencies. The goals of this chapter, then, are essentially six-fold: (1) highlight several reasons for the expansion of the federal government; (2) discuss a few definitions of oversight; (3) spotlight three essential purposes of oversight; (4) comment upon a few oversight laws and rules; (5) review several important oversight techniques; and (6) identify several incentives and disincentives to the conduct of congressional oversight. The report concludes with summary observations.

* This is an edited, reformatted and augmented edition of a United States Congressional Research Service publication, Report R41079, dated February 22, 2010.

Introduction

A fundamental objective of congressional oversight is to hold executive officials accountable for the implementation of delegated authority. This objective is especially important given the huge expansion of executive influence in the modern era. If the Founding Fathers returned to observe their handiwork, they would likely be surprised by such developments as the creation of a "presidential branch" of government (the Office of Management and Budget, the National Security Council, and the like) and the establishment of so many federal departments and agencies. From three departments in 1789 (State, Treasury, and War, renamed Defense in 1947), a dozen more have been added to the cabinet. The newest creation, in 2002, is the Department of Homeland Security (DHS). Formed from the merger of 22 separate executive branch units, it employees roughly 180,000 people.

Contemporary presidents have expressed some concern about the size and reach of the national government. In his 1981 inaugural address, for instance, President Ronald Reagan declared that "government is not the solution to our problem, government is the problem." Fifteen years later, in his State of the Union address, President Bill Clinton exclaimed, "The era of big government is over." Needless to say, the era of big government is back, if it ever went away.

Under presidents of both parties, the national government continues to grow. The administration of Republican President George W. Bush witnessed substantial governmental growth, partially triggered by new domestic security, law enforcement, and military requirements after the September 11, 2001, terrorist attacks. As journalist David S. Broder concluded, President Bush presided over one of the largest expansions of government in history. "He has created a mammoth Cabinet department [DHS], increased federal spending, imposed new federal rules on local and state governments, and injected federal requirements into every public school in America."[1] President Bush also initiated the Troubled Asset Relief Program (TARP)—a major governmental intervention in the private sector—as part of the Emergency Economic Stabilization Act (P.L. 110-343). TARP was authorized to purchase up to $700 billion in "troubled" real estate and other assets following a nationwide financial meltdown in numerous business enterprises.[2]

Democratic President Barack Obama took office in the midst of the most serious national economic crisis since the Great Depression. Regularly, the news media spotlighted such stories as the hikes in joblessness, home foreclosures, or plant closings. As a result, the government intervened dramatically in the marketplace. Trillions of dollars were committed to revive the ailing economy and prevent the recession from spiraling downward into another depression. "Not since Lyndon B. Johnson," wrote a congressional journalist, has a president like Obama "moved to expand the role of government so much on so many fronts—and with such a sense of urgency."[3]

In short, the probabilities of any major retrenchment or rollback in the role and scope of the federal government seem remote. Hence the importance of Congress exercising its implicit constitutional prerogative to check the delegated authority that it grants to federal departments and agencies. The goals of this chapter, then, are essentially six-fold: (1) highlight several reasons for the expansion of the role and reach of government; (2) discuss a few definitions of oversight; (3) spotlight three essential purposes of oversight; (4) comment upon a few oversight laws and rules; (5) review several important oversight techniques; and

(6) identify several incentives and disincentives to the conduct of congressional oversight. The report concludes with summary observations.

THE ROLE AND REACH OF GOVERNMENT

"The role of government in a free society must be a matter of continuous negotiation among members of the public," wrote Princeton Professor Michael Walzer.[4] This fundamental idea is the essence of self-government by the people through their elected representatives. From the beginning, our Founding Fathers argued about the role of the national government. Their basic argument continues to this day. Two schools of thought emerged during this early period, one articulated by Thomas Jefferson and the other by Alexander Hamilton.

Jefferson was an advocate of limited government: "That government governs best that governs least." Government closest to the people—state and local units—is to be preferred, according to Jefferson, to a robust and remote national government. As Jefferson said in his March 4, 1801, inaugural address:

> Still one thing more, fellow-citizens—a wise and frugal Government, which shall restrain men from injuring one another, shall leave them otherwise free to regulate their own pursuits of industry and improvement, and shall not take from the mouth of labor the bread it has earned. This is the sum of good government, and this is necessary to close the circle of our felicities.[5]

President Jefferson, however, was not reluctant to use the government to double the size of the country with the Louisiana Purchase.

Jefferson's rival, Alexander Hamilton, favored a strong national government and an energetic chief executive as essential if the new nation was to survive and prosper. A proponent of the implied powers of government, Hamilton wrote in *Federalist No. 31*: "A government ought to contain in itself every power requisite to the full accomplishment of the objects committed to its care, and to the complete execution of the trust for which it is responsible, free from every other control but a regard to the public good and to the sense of the people." Hamilton's philosophy, in brief, was that the national government could be a positive instrument for addressing common problems that no individual or locality could resolve by itself, such as maintaining a strong defense against foreign adversaries or creating a national currency. As Abraham Lincoln put it, "Government is people coming together collectively to do that which they could not do as well, or at all, individually."[6]

Fast forward to the contemporary era and it appears evident that the Hamiltonian view has largely prevailed over the Jeffersonian perspective. To be sure, Jefferson's ideas of limited government and states' rights resonate powerfully with millions of Americans including lawmakers, analysts, scholars, and others. Yet their actions often belie their words. Today's yeoman farmers might say they dislike or even resent big government, but they strongly support farm subsidies. Many people, it seems, are ideologically conservative but operationally liberal. On the one hand, they may emotionally view government as a necessary evil, but personally they support federal programs that benefit them, and even welcome the government's expansion in various areas (security from terrorist attacks, protection of the environment, and so on).

The fundamental reality is that the national government has taken on increasingly numerous functions and responsibilities throughout American history. The 20th century—from the Progressive era to World War I, from the New Deal to the Great Society—witnessed a huge increase in the size and power of government. Its expansion was driven by a number of factors.

Domestic and international crises have expanded the reach of the government. Wars, for example, threaten the nation itself, and the government often accrues new and expanded prerogatives to protect the country.[7] The intelligence community, as an example, grew rapidly during the Cold War as the United States of America faced a major threat from a nuclear-armed superpower rival: the Soviet Union. The internationalization of numerous domestic issues—trade, the environment, immigration, drug trafficking, and more—often requires a federal response for their resolution.

Complexity is another factor the promotes governmental growth. New issues and problems constantly arise that call for governmental action, such as food safety or national preparedness in the event of an epidemic or pandemic (H1N1, the swine flu virus, for instance). Many national programs, moreover, are crosscutting—that is, more than one federal agency, jurisdiction, and, in some cases, international organizations are engaged in policy implementation—which adds to the complexness of determining how or what the government is doing. To be sure, a nation with over 300 million people creates a variety of federal issues (civil rights, financial turmoil, high unemployment, and so on). Even when issues have been traditionally under the purview of states and localities, such as education, it does not mean that they are exclusively state and local responsibilities. In brief, a host of military, economic, and social challenges, along with many other factors (industrialization, globalization, scientific and technological developments, public demand, and more), all contributed to the large expansion in the size and reach of the federal government.

Given today's large federal establishment, congressional oversight is more important than ever in ensuring that the federal government functions economically, efficiently, and effectively. The American public's traditional and usually healthy skepticism about concentrating power in government underscores the legislative review function's significant role in holding federal agencies and officials accountable for their actions and decisions. To determine the quantity and quality of legislative oversight is not an easy assignment, however.

Definitions of Oversight

Different definitions of oversight influence perspectives on the adequacy of the review function. Oversight has two basic *dictionary* meanings. First, it denotes some form of legislative "supervision" or "watchfulness" of delegated authority to executive branch entities and officials. It is this general definition that orients the focus of this chapter. The second meaning of oversight implies a "failure to notice"—something that is overlooked or inadvertently omitted. Ironically, the two definitions may sometimes overlap one another. As Speaker Thomas P. O'Neill, D-Mass. (1977-1987), once exclaimed: Members "like to create and legislate, but we have shied from both the word and deed of oversight."[8] A Senator offered a related observation about the need for more overseeing rather than overlooking. Congress has "delegated so much authority to the executive branch of government, and we ought to devote more time to oversight then we do."[9]

Scholars have advanced a number of definitions of oversight that go beyond the meanings provided in dictionaries. For example, one political scientist wrote: '"Oversight,' strictly speaking refers to review after the fact. It includes inquiries about policies that are or have been in effect, investigations of past administrative actions, and the calling of executive officers to account for their financial transactions."[10] Another political scientist provided an expanded definition: "Legislative oversight is behavior by legislators and their staffs, individually or collectively, which results in an impact, intended or not, on bureaucratic behavior."[11] A third scholar offered a narrower definition: "I define [oversight] as congressional review of the actions of federal departments, agencies, and commissions, and of the programs and policies they administer, including review that takes place during program and policy implementation as well as afterward."[12]

The absence of consensus on a precise definition means that it is difficult quantitatively to know how much oversight Congress is performing, largely through its committees and subcommittees. Oversight is a ubiquitous activity on Capitol Hill that occurs in various ways, forums, and activities. It is subsumed in many hearings, meetings, or informal settings that may not be labeled as "oversight." Indeed, the review function is a byproduct of many congressional activities—committee meetings on legislation, the confirmation process, casework, informal Member and staff meetings with executive officials, legislative communications with administrative leaders, and so on. Thus, questions about whether Congress does enough oversight are difficult to answer because of methodological limitations (time and resources, for instance) in measuring its frequency comprehensively and systematically. Moreover, how "oversight is defined affects what oversight one finds."[13] Suffice it to say that undercounting surely characterizes the amount of oversight carried out by Congress primarily through the work of its committees, Members, staff aides, and legislative support units, such as the Government Accountability Office (GAO).

Worth raising is a related matter: What constitutes effective or quality oversight? The traditional method of exercising congressional oversight is through committee hearings and investigations into executive branch operations. For more than 200 years, Congress has conducted investigations of varying types and with varying results. Along the way, there have been abuses and excesses—for example, the 1954 Army-McCarthy hearings about communists in government—and successes and accomplishments. For instance, the World War II Truman Committee's (after Senator and later President Harry S Truman) investigation of the war mobilization effort, including waste and fraud in defense procurement, was viewed by many as a large success.

Although people may disagree on what constitutes "quality" oversight, there are a number of components that appear to foster effective oversight. They include (1) a committee chair who is committed to doing oversight on a sustained basis; (2) the involvement of committee members in an activity that might take weeks or months of time and resources; (3) bipartisanship: more is likely to be achieved when both parties work together rather than against each other; (4) an experienced professional staff with investigatory skills; (5) preparation and documentation in advance of public hearings; (6) coordination with other relevant committees of jurisdiction; and (7) follow-through to ensure that any recommendations of the committee are acted upon. Helpful, too, is a cooperative Administration. Absent cooperation, committees may need to use compulsory processes (subpoena and contempt) to obtain pertinent reports and documents and the testimony of key witnesses.[14]

Major Purposes of Oversight

Oversight is an implicit constitutional obligation of the Congress. According to Historian Arthur Schlesinger, Jr., the framers believed it was not necessary to make specific reference to "oversight" in the Constitution. "[I]t was not considered necessary to make an explicit grant of such authority," wrote Schlesinger. "The power to make laws implied the power to see whether they were faithfully executed."[15] The Constitution also granted Congress an array of formal powers—the purse strings, lawmaking, impeachment, among others—to hold the president and the administration accountable for their actions or inactions. In short, oversight plays a key role in our system of checks and balances.

There is a large number of overlapping purposes associated with oversight. This array can be divided into three basic types: programmatic, political, and institutional. *Programmatic* purposes include such objectives as making sure agencies and programs are working in a cost-effective and efficient manner; ensuring executive compliance with legislative intent; evaluating program performance; improving the economy of governmental performance; investigating waste, fraud, and abuse in governmental programs; reviewing the agency rulemaking process; acquiring information useful in future policymaking; or determining whether agencies or programs are fulfilling their statutory mission.[16]

There are also *political* purposes associated with oversight, such as generating favorable publicity for lawmakers, winning the electoral support of constituents and outside groups, or rebutting criticisms of favorite programs or agencies. After all, oversight occurs in an ever-present political context in which Congress's relationship with administrative entities can range from cooperation to conflict. There are, moreover, inherent constitutional and political tensions between Congress and the President even during periods of unified government (one party in charge of the House, Senate, and White House). Partisan and inter-branch conflicts are not uncommon in the conduct of the legislative review function.

In addition, there are *institutional* oversight purposes that merit special mention, because they serve to protect congressional prerogatives and strengthen the American public's ability to evaluate and reevaluate executive activities and actions. Three institutional purposes include checking the power of the executive branch; investigating how a law is being administered; and informing Congress and the public.

Checking the Executive Branch

One of the most dramatic developments of the modern era, as noted earlier, is the huge expansion of executive entities. Little surprise that some scholars refer to "the administrative state"—the plethora of federal departments, agencies, commissions, and boards.[17] The rise of the administrative state has produced a policymaking rival to the Congress. Administrators do more than simply "faithfully execute" the laws according to congressional intent (which may be vague). Federal agencies are filled with knowledgeable career and noncareer specialists who, among other things, write rules and regulations that have the force of law; enforce the rules via investigations and inquiries; formulate policy initiatives for Congress and the White House; interpret statutes in ways that may expand their discretionary authority or undermine legislative intent; and shape policy development by "selling" their ideas to lawmakers and committees via the hearings process, the issuance of agency reports, and in other ways. The large role of the executive branch, whose activities affect nearly every citizen's life, underscores the critical role of oversight in protecting the policymaking prerogatives of Congress and holding administrative entities accountable for their actions and decisions.

Investigating the Administration of Laws

Congressional oversight ideally involves the continuous review by the House and Senate, especially through their committee structures, of how effectively and efficiently the executive branch is carrying out legislative mandates. The "continuous watchfulness" precept—an obligation statutorily assigned to the standing committees by the Legislative Reorganization Act of 1946—implied that Congress would henceforth participate actively in administrative decisionmaking, in line with the observation that "administration of a statute is, properly speaking, an extension of the legislative process."[18]

Oversight, in brief, is crucial to the lawmaking process. Only by investigating how a law is being administered can Congress discover deficiencies in the original statute and make necessary adjustments and refinements. As a Senator stated, "We must do more than write laws and decide policies. It is also our responsibility to perform the oversight necessary to insure that the administration enforces those laws as Congress intended."[19]

Informing Congress and the Public

A central function of representative government, wrote two Senators, is "to allow a free people to drag realities out into the sunlight and demand a full accounting from those who are permitted to hold and exercise power."[20] Dragging "realities out" is how Congress shines the spotlight of public attention on many significant issues, allowing lawmakers and the American people to make informed judgments about executive activities and actions. Woodrow Wilson, in his 1885 classic titled *Congressional Government*, declared that Congress's informing function "should be preferred even to its legislative [lawmaking] function." He explained:

> Unless Congress have and use every means of acquainting itself with the acts and dispositions of the administrative agents of government, the country must be helpless to learn how it is being served; and unless Congress both scrutinize these things and sift them by every form of discussion, the country must remain in embarrassing, crippling ignorance of the very affairs which it is most important it should understand and direct.[21]

Oversight Laws and Rules

To encourage, promote, and prod the legislative branch to do more oversight, the House and Senate have enacted an array of laws and rules that help to complement its many techniques (see "Oversight Techniques" section below) for monitoring executive branch performance. Mention of a few laws and rules illustrates Congress's continuing interest in strengthening its own procedures for oversight, as well as obtaining oversight-related information from the executive branch. Two statutes worth briefly noting for illustrative purposes are the Government Performance and Results Act of 1993 (GPRA, or the Results Act) and the Congressional Review Act of 1996 (CRA).

Selected Laws

The Results Act aims to promote more cost-effective federal spending by requiring agencies to set strategic goals—for example, a statement of their basic missions and the resources required to achieve those objectives—and to prepare annual performance plans and annual performance reports, which are submitted to Congress and the President. GPRA strengthens legislative oversight by enhancing committees' ability to hold agencies accountable for the implementation of their performance goals and actual outcomes; to evaluate the budget requests of various agencies, and to reduce or eliminate unnecessary overlap and duplication among federal agencies that implement similar policy areas.[22] For example, various lawmakers have urged an overhaul of the food inspection structure, because there are "at least 15 government agencies [that] have a hand in making sure food is safe under at least 30 different laws." The administrative reality, exclaimed a House Appropriations subcommittee chair, is that there is "no one person, no individual today who is responsible for food safety."[23] The chair's observation was underscored by a House majority leader when he held up a pizza box: "If this were a cheese pizza, it would be inspected by the [Food and Drug Administration]. If it were a pepperoni pizza, it would be inspected by the [Department of Agriculture]. We definitely have a great deal of duplication here."[24]

The Congressional Review Act enables Congress to review and disapprove agency rules and regulations. Under the CRA, agencies must submit their major rules to the House, Senate, and Government Accountability Office (GAO) before they can take effect.[25] The act provides for expedited procedures in the Senate (but not the House) if a lawmaker introduces a joint resolution of disapproval. "To be eligible for consideration under the terms of the Act, a disapproval resolution must be submitted in either house within 60 days after Congress receives the rule."[26] This law, however, has been little used by Congress to block agency rules. Since the law went into effect, only one rule has been rejected (an ergonomics rule in March 2001) despite nearly 50,000 rules that have become effective.[27] Various interpretive ambiguities, such as whether the act allows disapproval of parts of a rule or only its entirety, account in part for its limited use. Analysts also acknowledge that the law contains a potential flaw: The President can veto the joint resolution of disapproval—"which is likely if the underlying rule is developed during his administration."[28] Congress is unlikely to override the President's veto given the two-thirds vote required of each chamber. Still, the law is available to either chamber to express its views about agency rulemaking. Congress, to be sure, can repeal rules by passing statutes, including appropriations measures that include provisions "designed to prevent or restrict the development, implementation, or enforcement" of certain rules or types of rules.[29]

Chamber Rules

The two chambers, especially the larger House, have a number of formal oversight rules. For example, the House has a rule requiring all standing committees to prepare at the start of each Congress an oversight plan that, among other things, ensures to the maximum extent feasible that "all significant laws, programs, or agencies within its jurisdiction are subject to review every 10 years" (House Rule X, clause 2). At the start of the 111th Congress (2009-2011), the House amended its rules "to require each standing committee to hold at least three hearings per year on waste, fraud, and abuse [in the programs and agencies] under each respective committee's jurisdiction." Committees, moreover, are obligated to hold a hearing if "an agency's financial statements are not in order" and if a program under the panel's jurisdiction is "deemed by GAO to be at high risk for waste, fraud, and abuse."[30]

The Senate, too, has a number of rules that address oversight. Committee reports accompanying each bill or joint resolution must contain an evaluation of their regulatory impact, including "a determination of the amount of additional paperwork that will result from the regulations to be promulgated pursuant to the bill or joint resolution" (Senate Rule XXVI, clause 11). The Senate assigned comprehensive oversight authority to certain standing committees (see Rule XXV) for specific policy areas, such as oceans policy or energy and resources development. The Senate chair who authored the rule explained its purposes.

> Standing committees are directed and permitted to undertake investigations and make recommendations in broad policy areas—for example, nutrition, aging, environmental protection, or consumer affairs—even though they lack legislative jurisdiction over some aspects of the subject. Such oversight authority involves subjects that generally cut across the jurisdictions of several committees. Presently, no single committee has a comprehensive overview of these policy areas. [This rule change] corrects that. It assigns certain committees the right to undertake comprehensive review of broad policy issues.[31]

The House has a similar rule which it calls "special oversight." For instance, the Committee on Homeland Security is authorized to "review and study on a continuing basis all Governmental activities relating to homeland security" (House Rule X, clause 3) even though some of those activities fall within the legislative jurisdiction of other standing committees.

Oversight Techniques

In carrying out its oversight responsibilities, Congress must be able to choose from a variety of techniques to hold agencies accountable, so that if one technique proves to be ineffective, committees and Members can employ others singly or in combination. Most of these techniques are utilized by the committees of Congress: standing, subcommittee, select, or special. In no particular order, they include such oversight methods as the10 discussed briefly below.

Hearings and Investigations

A traditional method of congressional oversight is hearings and investigations into executive branch operations.[32] Legislators need to know how effectively federal programs are working and how well agency officials are responding to legislative or committee directives. And they want to know the scope and intensity of public support for government programs to assess the need for statutory changes. Although the terms "hearings" and "investigations" overlap ("investigative hearings," for example) and they may look alike in their formal setting and operation, a shorthand distinction is that hearings focus generally on the efficiency and effectiveness of federal agencies and programs. Investigations, too, may address programmatic efficiency and effectiveness, but their primary focus—triggered by widespread public interest and debate—is often on allegations of wrongdoing, lack of agency preparedness or competence, fraud and abuse, conflicts of interest, and the like. Famous examples include investigations so well-known that a few words are often enough to trigger the attentive public's recollection, such as the 1972 Watergate break-in, the 1987 Iran-Contra affair, or the Hurricane Katrina debacle of 2005.

The Authorizing Process

Congress can pass authorizing legislation that establishes, continues (a reauthorization), or abolishes (a de-authorization) a federal agency or program. It can enact "statutes authorizing the activities of the departments, prescribing their internal organization and regulating their procedures and work methods."[33] Once an agency or program is created, the reauthorization process, which typically occurs on an annual or multiyear cycle, can be an important oversight tool. As a House member observed during debate on a bill to require the annual reauthorization of the Federal Communications Commission (FCC):

> Our subcommittee hearings disclosed that the FCC needs direction, need guidance, needs legislation, and needs leadership from us in helping to establish program priorities. Regular oversight through the reauthorization process, as all of us know in Congress, is necessary, and nothing brings everybody's attention to spending more forthrightly than when we go through the reauthorization process.[34]

Significant issues are often raised during the authorization or reauthorization process. Lawmakers may ask such questions as: Can the agency be made smaller? If this program or agency did not exist, would it be created today? Should functions that overlap several agencies be merged or consolidated? What fundamental changes need to be made in how the department operates?

The Appropriations Process

Congress probably exercises its most effective oversight of agencies and programs through the appropriations process. As James Madison wrote in *The Federalist Papers* No. 58: "The power of the purse may, in fact, be regarded as the most complete and effectual weapon with which any constitution can arm the immediate representatives of the people, for obtaining a redress of every grievance, and for carrying into effect every just and salutary measure." By cutting off or reducing funds, Congress can effectively abolish agencies or curtail federal programs. For example, in its various committee reports to accompany FY2010 appropriations measures, the House Appropriations Committee includes "a three-part list of terminations, program reductions and White House initiatives that have been denied."[35] By increasing funds, appropriators can build up neglected program areas. In either case, the appropriating panels in each chamber have formidable power to shape ongoing federal agencies and programs. A noted, congressional budget expert remarked that the appropriating process as an oversight method is comparable to a Janus (after the mythical Roman god)-like weapon: "The stick of spending reductions in case agencies cannot satisfactorily defend their budget requests and past performance, and the carrot of more money if agencies produce convincing success stories or the promise of future results."[36]

Inspectors General

Congress has created statutory offices of inspectors general (IGs) in nearly 70 major federal entities and departments. The IGs, for example, are located in all fifteen cabinet departments, the Central Intelligence Agency (CIA), and the independent regulatory commissions. Granted substantial independence by the Inspectors General Act of 1978, as amended in 1988 and again in 2008, these officials are authorized to conduct investigations and audits of their agencies to improve efficiency, end waste and fraud, discourage mismanagement, and strengthen the effectiveness and economy of agency operations. Appointed in various ways—in most cases either by the President subject to Senate confirmation or by agency heads—IGs report their findings and recommendations to (1) the Attorney General in cases of suspected violations of federal criminal law, (2) semiannually to the agency head, who must transmit the IG report to Congress within thirty days with no changes to the report but with his or her suggestions; and (3) in the case of "particularly serious or flagrant problems," immediately to the agency head who must send the report to Congress within seven days unaltered but with his or her recommendations.[37] Inspectors generals, said a Senator, are "the government's first line of defense against fraud."[38]

Congress also has created special inspectors generals (SIGs) who have responsibility for auditing and investigating specific programs. For example, there is a SIG for Iraq Reconstruction (SIGIR) another SIG for Afghanistan Reconstruction (SIGAR), and still another SIG for the Troubled Asset Relief Program (SIGTARP).[39]

Whether regular or special, IGs strive to keep Congress fully and currently informed about agency activities, problems, and program performance through such practices as the issuance of periodic reports and testimony before House and Senate committees.

Government Accountability Office

The Government Accountability Office (GAO), formerly titled the General Accounting Office until the name change in 2004, was established by the Budget and Accounting Office of 1921. With about 3,100 employees, GAO functions as Congress's investigative arm, conducting financial and program audits and evaluations of executive activities, operations, and programs. For example, in one study, GAO reported "that 19 of 24 Federal agencies … could not fully explain how they had spent taxpayer money appropriated by Congress."[40] The head of GAO is the Comptroller General (CG), who is nominated by the President (following a recommendation process involving the bipartisan leaders of the House and Senate) and subject to the advice and consent of the Senate for a non-renewable 15-year term.

The GAO conducts field investigations of administrative activities and programs, prescribes accounting standards for the executive branch, prepares policy analyses, adjudicates bid protests, makes recommendations for legislative action, evaluates programs, and provides legal opinions on government actions and activities. The office submits hundreds of reports to Congress annually, describing ways to root out waste and mismanagement in executive branch programs and to promote program performance. One of its traditional reports to Congress is on government programs and activities that are "high risk," that is, they require significant improvements in their operations and performance.[41]

Reporting Requirements

Numerous laws require executive agencies to submit reports periodically, and as required by specific events or certain conditions, to Congress and its committees. As one scholar explained:

> Reporting requirements are provisions in laws requiring the executive branch to submit specified information to Congress or committees of Congress. Their basic purpose is to provide data and analysis Congress needs to oversee the implementation of legislation and foreign policy by the executive branch.[42]

Generally the report requirement encourages self-evaluation by the executive branch and promotes agency accountability to Congress. Reporting requirements involve weighing Congress's need for information and analysis to conduct evaluations of agencies and programs against the imposition of burdensome or unnecessary obligations on executive entities. (Recall, too, that IGs regularly report to Congress.)

Senate Confirmation Process

High-ranking public officials are chosen by the President "by and with the Advice and Consent of the Senate," in accord with the Constitution. In general, the Senate gives the President considerable latitude in selecting cabinet heads, nominees to regulatory boards and commissions, and other significant executive branch positions. Nomination hearings establish a public record of the policy views of nominees, on which they could be called to account at a later time. Committees, for example, might ask agency nominees to discuss their plans for addressing the high-risk programs under their jurisdiction that GAO identified as being vulnerable to waste, fraud, and abuse. Committees may also extract pledges from nominees that they will testify at hearings when requested to do so, with the implicit acknowledgement that otherwise the appointee's name might not be reported for consideration to the full Senate. They can also inquire into nominees' previous government experience and other pertinent matters.

Program Evaluation

Program evaluation is an approach to oversight that uses social science and management methodology, such as surveys, cost-benefit analyses, and efficiency studies, to assess the effectiveness of ongoing programs. This type of analysis is often conducted by the GAO, IGs, and the agencies themselves. President Obama has stressed the importance of measuring the effectiveness of government programs. "All programs—from Medicare to small-business loans—will be judged based on their progress in meeting certain quantifiable goals developed with input from agencies, Congress, management experts and the public," he said.[43] Peter Orszag, the director of the Office of Management and Budget (OMB), added: "Rigorous, independent program evaluation can be a key resource in determining whether government programs are achieving their intended outcomes as well as possible and at the lowest possible cost."[44]

Casework

Each lawmaker's office handles thousands of requests each year from constituents seeking help in dealing with executive agencies. The requests range from inquiries about lost Social Security checks or delayed pension payments to disaster relief assistance and complicated tax appeals to the Internal Revenue Service. "Constituents perceive casework in nonpolitical terms," wrote two scholars. "They *expect* their representatives to provide [this service]."[45] Casework, an ombudsman-like function, has the positive effect of bringing quirks in the administrative machinery to Members' attention. Solutions to an individual constituent's problems can suggest legislative remedies on a broader scale.[46] On occasion, constituents' casework requests may be used in oversight hearings by Members to highlight and lend support to a problem or shortcoming in the operations of a program or agency.

Impeachment and Removal

The ultimate check on the executive (and judicial) branch is impeachment and removal from office, and it is vested exclusively in Congress. Article II, section 4, of the Constitution states: "The President, Vice President, and all Civil Officers of the United States, shall be removed from office on Impeachment for, and Conviction of, Treason, Bribery, or other high

Crimes and misdemeanors." The House has the authority to impeach an official by majority vote. (Impeachment is the formal lodging of charges against an official.) House trial managers then prosecute the case before the Senate, where a two-thirds vote is required for conviction. The process of impeachment and removal is complex and cumbersome; as a result, it has been employed in over 200 years only in a limited number of instances involving executive branch officials, judges, and Presidents.[47]

Incentives and Disincentives

Despite the importance of oversight, "pass it and forget it" lawmaking sometimes occurs on Capitol Hill. This reality is not to suggest that committees and subcommittees fail to hold regular oversight hearings and meetings, often aimed at rooting out government waste and abuse and, more broadly, monitoring the executive branch. Instead, there are various institutional and other developments that have limited the ability of committees and lawmakers to carry out their "continuous watchfulness" function in a continual manner. There are, in brief, various *disincentives* and *incentives* associated with the conduct of oversight. Three will be spotlighted in each category for illustrative purposes.

Disincentives

First, there are time and energy limits. Workload-packed legislative schedules, constant campaign fund-raising, weekly travel back-and-forth to Members' districts or states, periodic meetings with constituents visiting Washington, or print and media interviews are among the factors that combine to reduce constant attention to oversight. The term *lawmaker*, moreover, suggests where many Members prefer to spend much of their time. As former Speaker Newt Gingrich, R-GA (1995-1999) put it: "This is the city [Washington, DC] which spends almost all of its energy trying to make the right decisions and almost none of its energy focusing on how to improve implementing the right decisions. And without implementation, the best ideas in the world simply don't occur."[48]

Second, unified government could act as a disincentive to assertive and aggressive oversight of administrative departments and agencies, especially during an era of partisan polarization. As one senior House Republican said of President George W. Bush's Administration: "Our party controls the levers of government. We're not about to go out and look beneath a bunch of rocks to try and cause heartburn. Unless they really screw up, we're not going to go after them."[49] Added another experienced GOP lawmaker: "We ended up functioning like a parliament, not a Congress. We confused wanting a joint agenda with not doing oversight."[50]

Third, the policy or political payoff might be minimal at best or counterproductive at worst. Oversight can be unglamorous, tedious, technical, and long-term work that achieves few results. "To do it right," said a Republican Senator, "you have to hear an endless stream of witnesses, review numerous records, and at the end of it you may find an agency was doing everything right. It is much more fun to create a new program."[51] Moreover, lawmakers recognize that hard-hitting investigations might arouse the ire of numerous constituents and special interests, which could jeopardize their chance of winning reelection.

Incentives

One of the principal incentives that encourages legislative oversight of the executive branch is divided government (one party in charge of one or both chambers or Congress, the other party in control of the White House). Political and substantive issues are important factors that prompt heightened interest in oversight. Politically, as former Representative Lee Hamilton, D-IN, noted, when Democrats controlled the House during the first two years of the Clinton administration, no subpoenas were issued to executive officials by the panel with broad oversight jurisdiction. However, when Republicans captured control of the House, that same committee handed out "well over a thousand subpoenas to Clinton administration officials."[52]

Substantively, policy disagreements between the President and the congressional majority party also contribute to the amount and scope of oversight. As one scholar concluded:

> [P]olicy divergence is most likely to occur under divided government, so the majority party in Congress will want to constrain the agencies under the president's control. In addition, members of the majority party may believe they can benefit from using oversight to emphasize policy differences between their party and the president's party, and if in the case of such hearings and investigations they embarrass a president and his agency, this is not an insignificant [political] side benefit.[53]

Electoral incentives are another factor that can motivate lawmakers to oversee the bureaucracy. The opportunity to assist constituents in their dealings with federal agencies or to receive favorable publicity back home for resolving flaws or inequities in executive programs is a potential electoral bonus for members of Congress. Committee and subcommittee chairs "seek a high pay off—in attention from the press and other agencies—when selecting federal programs to be their oversight targets."[54] Electoral support from constituents, combined with press and media attention, are likely to prompt additional oversight activity by committees and lawmakers.

A third incentive for more oversight is large public concern about various issues (surging federal deficits, for instance) or events (a terrorist incident, for example). Numerous analysts and studies emphasize that the nation faces short- and long-term fiscal challenges. Growing citizen concern about the urgency of this issue could provoke committees to devote considerable resources to scrutinizing federal programs for waste and inefficiency, even eliminating or scaling back agencies or programs that are duplicative or not working. The money saved might then be used more productively. To be sure, a specific event can also prompt oversight. The unsuccessful 2009 Christmas Day attempt to blow up an airplane reportedly triggered no fewer than eight House and Senate committee hearings and investigations "to explore the intelligence, homeland security and foreign policy ramifications of the failed attack" by a Nigerian-born terrorist.[55]

CONCLUDING OBSERVATIONS

There is no doubt that Congress has significant authority to oversee the executive branch. Control of the purse strings, enactment of laws, the conduct of investigations, or the Senate's confirmation role are among the principal levers of power available to the legislative branch to hold executive officials accountable for the implementation of federal policies and programs. In carrying out its oversight responsibilities, Congress engages in different, often overlapping, types or models of review: for example, programmatic versus political, adversarial versus cooperative, formal (hearings) versus informal (staff meetings with agency officials), or "police patrol" versus "fire alarm." Police patrol oversight is akin to "the cop on the beat": pro-active, regular, and systematic review of administrative performance by House and Senate committees. Fire alarm oversight is reactive; it occurs when outside events or public interest triggers episodic reviews of the executive branch.[56]

Significantly, Congress may be obtaining some extra police patrol assistance through the combination of technology and civic-minded individuals or groups. A rather new oversight trend is the "public as watchdog," or, stated differently, the "democratization" of the review function. There are many groups, such as the Project on Government Oversight (POGO) or The Heritage Foundation, bloggers, and websites devoted to monitoring federal expenditures and activities. For example, websites such as Recovery.gov (initiated and maintained by a task force of federal inspectors general) or StimulusWatch.org (an independent website developed by volunteers) enable interested individuals to monitor projects that receive money from more than $800 billion economic stimulus package enacted during the first session of the 111th Congress.

President Obama has made transparency and open government one of his top priorities. One result is that federal agencies are posting more of their information and data online so citizens who visit the sites can assess how their dollars are being spent or how well agencies are managing their various projects. As the government's chief information officer stated, the new-found transparency "will elicit a more informed public oversight to help guide federal policies and programs."[57] A better informed public is likely to make their evaluations of federal programs and expenditures known to congressional lawmakers. The blogosphere, in short, adds millions of extra eyes to oversight of government spending and activities.

Ultimately, Congress will decide how best to pursue its oversight responsibility. Much will depend on the context of the times, the willingness of Members and their staff to watch and assess the executive branch, and Congress's relationship with the incumbent Administration. This relationship may range from cooperation to confrontational, but it is principally Congress that can ensure that executive policies reflect the values of the American people, anticipate long-range trends, and meet the challenges of an every-changing nation and world.

End Notes

[1] David S. Broder, "So, Now Bigger Is Better?" *The Washington Post*, January 12, 2003, p. B1.

[2] CRS Report R41001, *Redirecting Troubled Asset Relief Program (TARP) Funds to Other Uses*, by Marc Labonte, Edward V. Murphy, and Baird Webel.

[3] Janet Hook, "Obama's Budget Is the End Of An Era," *Los Angeles Times*, February 27, 2009, online edition.

[4] Michael Walzer, "The Popular Patron," *The New Republic*, April 9, 1984, p. 35.
[5] James D. Richardson, *A Compilation of the Messages and Papers of the Presidents*, vol. I (New York: Bureau of National Literature, Inc., 1897), p. 311.
[6] Quoted in Vic Hallard, "In Defense of Legislatures," *The Council of State Governments*, February 1996, p. 9.
[7] See, for example, Robert Higgs, *Crisis and Leviathan: Critical Episodes in the Growth of American Government* (New York: Oxford University Press, 1987).
[8] *Workshop on Congressional Oversight and Investigations*, H. Doc. No. 96-117 (Washington: GPO, 1979), p.3.
[9] Geoff Earle, "Dems Did Oversight Better, Says Grassley," *The Hill*, May 13, 2004, p. 2.
[10] Joseph P. Harris, *Congressional Control of Administration* (Garden City, NY: Anchor Books, 1964), p. 9.
[11] Morris S. Ogul, *Congress Oversees the Bureaucracy: Studies in Legislative Supervision* (Pittsburgh, PA.: University of Pittsburgh Press, 1976), p. 11.
[12] Joel D. Aberbach, *Keeping a Watchful Eye: The Politics of Congressional Oversight* (Washington, DC: The Brookings Institution, 1990), p. 2.
[13] Ogul, *Congress Oversees the Bureaucracy*, p. 7.
[14] See Todd B. Tatelman, "Congress's Contempt Power: Three Mechanisms for Enforcing Subpoenas," *Government Information Quarterly*, vol. 25, January 2008, pp. 592-624.
[15] Arthur M. Schlesinger, Jr. and Roger Burns, eds., *Congress Investigates: A Documented History, 1792-1974*, vol. 1 (New York: Chelsea House, 1975), p. xix.
[16] See CRS Report RL30240, *Congressional Oversight Manual*, by Frederick M. Kaiser et al.
[17] Lawrence C. Dodd and Richard L. Schott, *Congress and the Administrative State* (New York: John Wiley and Sons, 1979).
[18] David B. Truman, *The Governmental Process* (New York: Knopf, 1953), p. 439.
[19] *Congressional Record*, vol. 129, June 21, 1983, p. 16523.
[20] Senators William S. Cohen and George J. Mitchell, *Men of Zeal, A Candid Inside Story of the Iran-Contra Hearings* (New York: Viking, 1988), p. 305.
[21] Woodrow Wilson, *Congressional Government* (Boston: Houghton Mifflin, 1885), p. 303.
[22] CRS Report RS20257, *Government Performance and Results Act: Brief History and Implementation Activities*, by Genevieve J. Knezo, and CRS Report 97-1059, *Government Performance and Results Act: Performance-related Requirements Included in Laws and in Committee Report Language During the 104th Congress*, by Genevieve J. Knezo and Bill Heniff Jr.
[23] "U.S. Food Inspection Is An Alphabet Soup," *The Examiner*, February 25, 2009, p. 14. In January 2010, President Obama appointed Michael R. Taylor, a food expert, to serve as deputy commissioner of the Food and Drug Administration with responsibility "to address the nation's fractured food system." Gardinder Harris, "New Official Named With Portfolio to Unite Agencies and Improve Food Safety," *New York Times*, January 14, 2010, p. A20.
[24] Jennifer Kabbany, "Armey Targets Waste in Federal Agencies," *The Washington Times*, February 12, 1999, p. A6.
[25] A Congressional Research Service report found that various federal agencies since 1999 had failed to provide notice to Congress or the Government Accountability Office of more than a 1,000 final rules, as required by the Congressional Review Act. See CRS Report R40997, *Congressional Review Act: Rules Not Submitted to GAO and Congress*, by Curtis W. Copeland.
[26] See CRS Report RL31160, *Disapproval of Regulations by Congress: Procedure Under the Congressional Review Act*, by Richard S. Beth.
[27] See CRS Report RL30116, *Congressional Review of Agency Rulemaking: An Update and Assessment of The Congressional Review Act after a Decade*, by Morton Rosenberg.
[28] CRS Report RL32240, *The Federal Rulemaking Process: An Overview*, by Curtis W. Copeland.
[29] CRS Report RL34354, *Congressional Influence on Rulemaking and Regulation Through Appropriations Restrictions*, by Curtis W. Copeland.
[30] *Congressional Record*, vol. 155, January 14, 2009, p. H268.
[31] *Congressional Record*, vol. 123, February 1, 1977, p. 2897.
[32] There are numerous U.S. Supreme Court decisions that bolster and buttress Congress's investigatory power. For example, in the 1957 case of *Watkins v. United States* (354 U.S. 178), the majority opinion stated that the "power of the Congress to conduct investigations is inherent in the legislative process. That power is broad. It encompasses inquiries concerning the administration of existing laws as well as proposed or possibly needed statutes."
[33] Harris, *Congressional Control of Administration*, p. 284.
[34] Louis Fisher, "Annual Reauthorizations: Durable Roadblocks to Biennial Budgeting," *Public Budgeting and Finance*, spring 1983, p. 38. The annual defense authorization process might be the most noteworthy example of the authorizing process as an oversight tool.
[35] David Rogers, "Democrats Make Show of Budget Cuts," *Politico*, June 23, 2009, p. 1.

[36] *Workshop on Congressional Oversight and Investigations*, H. Doc. No. 96-217 (Washington, DC: GPO, 1979), p. 19. The budget expert was Professor Allen Schick of the University of Maryland and The Brookings Institution. Appropriations bills must be signed by the President before they can become law.

[37] See CRS Report 98-379, *Statutory Offices of Inspector General: Past and Present*, by Frederick M. Kaiser.

[38] Sen. Charles Grassley, "The Federal Government Needs an IG in Chief," *Politico*, July 22, 2009, p. 30.

[39] CRS Report R40099, *The Special Inspector General for the Troubled Asset Relief Program (SIGTARP)*, by Vanessa K. Burrows.

[40] *Congressional Record*, 109th Congress, 2nd Session, June 27, 2006, p. H4675.

[41] See Government Accountability Office, *High Risk Series; An Update*, GAO-09-271, January 2009.

[42] Ellen C. Collier, "Foreign Policy by Reporting Requirement," *Washington Quarterly*, Winter 1988, p. 75.

[43] Elisse Castelli, "How Does Your Program Measure Up?" *Federal Times*, May 18, 2009, p. 1.

[44] Ralph Lindeman, "OMB Announces Initiative to Improve Evaluations of Programs in Budget Process," *Daily Report for Executives*, October 8, 2009, p. A-1.

[45] John R. Johannes and John C. McAdams, "Entrepreneurs or Agent: Congressmen and the Distribution of Casework, 1977-1978," *Western Political Quarterly*, September 1987, p. 549.

[46] CRS Report RL33209, *Casework in a Congressional Office: Background, Rules, Laws, and Resources*, by R. Eric Petersen.

[47] CRS Report 98-186, *Impeachment: An Overview of Constitutional Provisions, Procedure, and Practice*, by Elizabeth B. Bazan and Anna C. Henning.

[48] Tichakorn Hill, "Gingrich: Government's Problem Is 'Gotcha' Culture," *Federal Times*, July 18, 2005, p. 12.

[49] David Nather, "Congress as Watchdog: Asleep on the Job?" *CQ Weekly*, May 22, 2004, p. 1190. See also Thomas E. Mann and Norman J. Ornstein, *The Broken Branch* (New York: Oxford University Press, 2006).

[50] Ronald Brownstein, "Treating Oversight as an Afterthought Has Its Costs," *Los Angeles Times*, November 19, 2006, online edition.

[51] *Congress Speaks: A Survey of the 100th Congress* (Washington, DC: Center for Responsive Politics, 1988), p. 163.

[52] Lee H. Hamilton, *Strengthening Congress* (Bloomington, IN: Indiana University Press, 2009), p. 25.

[53] Charles R. Shipan, "Congress and the Bureaucracy," in Paul Quirk and Sarah Binder, eds., *The Legislative Branch* (New York: Oxford University Press, 2005), p. 437.

[54] Richard Cohen, "King of Oversight," *Government Executive*, September 1988, p. 17.

[55] Tim Starks and Caitlin Webber, "Bombing Attempt Generates Wave of Probes," *CQ Today*, January 13, 2009, 1.

[56] See Matthew D. McCubbins and Thomas Schwartz, "Congressional Oversight Overlooked: Police Patrols versus Fire Alarms," *American Journal of Political Science*, February 1984, pp. 165-179.

[57] Elise Castelli, "Transparency, Public Input to Guide IT Policies," *Federal Times*, January 11, 2010, p. 13. See CRS Report RL34718, *The Federal Funding Accountability and Transparency Act: Implementation and Proposed Amendments*, by Garrett Hatch.

In: Congressional Oversight An Overview, A Manual and... ISBN: 978-1-61728-477-9
Editor: Jamie C. Howell

Chapter 2

CONGRESSIONAL OVERSIGHT MANUAL*

Frederick M. Kaiser, Walter J. Oleszek, T.J. Halstead, Morton Rosenberg and Todd B. Tatelman

SUMMARY

The *Congressional Oversight Manual* was developed about 30 years ago following a three-day December 1978 Workshop on Congressional Oversight and Investigations. The workshop was organized by a group of House and Senate committee aides from both parties and the Congressional Research Service (CRS) at the request of the bipartisan House leadership. The *Manual* was produced by CRS with the assistance of a number of House committee staffers. In subsequent years, CRS sponsored and conducted various oversight seminars for House and Senate staff and updated the *Manual* as circumstances warranted. The last revision occurred in 2004. Worth noting is the bipartisan recommendation of the House members of the 1993 Joint Committee on the Organization of Congress (Rept. No. 103-413, Vol. I):

> [A]s a way to further enhance the oversight work of Congress, the Joint Committee would encourage the Congressional Research Service to conduct on a regular basis, as it has done in the past, oversight seminars for Members and congressional staff and to update on a regular basis its *Congressional Oversight Manual*.

Over the years, CRS has assisted many Members, committees, party leaders, and staff aides in the performance of the oversight function, that is, the review, monitoring, and supervision of the implementation of public policy. Understandably, given the size, reach, cost, and continuing growth of the modern executive establishment, Congress's oversight role is even more significant — and more demanding — than when Woodrow Wilson wrote in his classic *Congressional Government* (1885): "Quite as important as lawmaking is vigilant

* This is an edited, reformatted and augmented edition of a United States Congressional Research Service publication, Report RL30240, dated May 1, 2007.

oversight of administration." Today's lawmakers and congressional aides, as well as commentators and scholars, recognize that Congress's work, ideally, should not end when it passes legislation. Oversight is an integral way to make sure that the laws work and are being administered in an effective, efficient, and economical manner. In light of this destination, oversight can be viewed as one of Congress's principal responsibilities as it grapples with the complexities of the 21st century.

To revise a document of this size and scope requires the contributions of many people. Five CRS specialists, listed on the title page, were responsible for organizing and writing this version of the *Manual*. In addition, other CRS personnel assisted in the preparation and publication of this chapter, along with staff of the Congressional Budget Office (CBO) and the Government Accountability Office (GAO).

I. Purposes, Authority, and Participants

Throughout its history, Congress has engaged in oversight of the executive branch — the review, monitoring, and supervision of the implementation of public policy. The first several Congresses inaugurated such important oversight techniques as special investigations, reporting requirements, resolutions of inquiry, and use of the appropriations process to review executive activity. Contemporary developments, moreover, have increased the legislature's capacity and capabilities *to check on and check the Executive.* Public laws and congressional rules have measurably enhanced Congress's implied power under the Constitution to conduct oversight.

Despite its lengthy heritage, oversight was not given explicit recognition in public law until enactment of the Legislative Reorganization Act of 1946. That act required House and Senate standing committees to exercise "*continuous watchfulness*" over programs and agencies within their jurisdiction.

Since the late 1960s, according to such scholars as political scientist Joel Aberbach, Congress has shown increasing interest in oversight for several major reasons. These include the expansion in number and complexity of federal programs and agencies; increase in expenditures and personnel, including contract employees; the rise of the budget deficit; and the frequency of divided government, with Congress and the White House controlled by different parties. Major partisan disagreements over priorities and processes also heighten conflict between the legislature and the executive.

Oversight occurs in virtually any congressional activity and through a wide variety of channels, organizations, and structures. These range from formal committee hearings to informal Member contacts with executive officials, from staff studies to support agency reviews, and from casework conducted by Member offices to studies prepared by non-congressional entities, such as statutory commissions and offices of inspector general.

Purposes

Congressional oversight of the Executive is designed to fulfill a number of purposes:

A. Ensure Executive Compliance with Legislative Intent

Congress, of necessity, must delegate discretionary authority to federal administrators. To make certain that these officers faithfully execute laws according to the intent of Congress, committees and Members can review the actions taken and regulations formulated by departments and agencies.

B. Improve the Efficiency, Effectiveness, and Economy of Governmental Operations

A large federal bureaucracy makes it imperative for Congress to encourage and secure efficient and effective program management, and to make every dollar count toward the achievement of program goals. A basic objective is strengthening federal programs through better managerial operations and service delivery. Such steps can improve the accountability of agency managers to Congress and enhance program performance.

C. Evaluate Program Performance

Systematic program performance evaluation remains a relatively new and still-evolving technique in oversight. Modern program evaluation uses social science and management methodologies, such as surveys, cost-benefit analyses, and efficiency studies, to assess the effectiveness of ongoing programs.

D. Prevent Executive Encroachment on Legislative Prerogatives and Powers

Beginning in the late 1960s, many commentators, public policy analysts, and legislators argued that Presidents and executive officials overstepped their authority in various areas such as impoundment of funds, executive privilege, war powers, and the dismantling of federal programs without congressional consent. Increased oversight — as part of the checks and balances system — was called for to redress what many in the public and Congress saw to be an executive arrogation of legislative prerogatives.

E. Investigate Alleged Instances of Poor Administration, Arbitrary and Capricious Behavior, Abuse, Waste, Dishonesty, and Fraud

Instances of fraud and other forms of corruption, the breakdown of federal programs, incompetent management, and the subversion of governmental processes arouse legislative and public interest in oversight.

F. Assess Agency or Officials' Ability to Manage and Carry out Program Objectives

Congress's ability to evaluate the capacity of agencies and managers to carry out program objectives can be accomplished in various ways. For example, numerous laws require agencies to submit reports to Congress; some of these are regular, occurring annually or semi-annually, for instance, while others are activated by a specific event, development, or set of conditions. The report requirement may promote self-evaluation by the agency. Organizations outside of Congress, such as offices of inspector general and study commissions, also advise Members and committees on how well federal agencies are working.

G. Review and Determine Federal Financial Priorities

Congress exercises some of its most effective oversight through the appropriations process, which provides the opportunity to review recent expenditures in detail. In addition, most federal agencies and programs are under regular and frequent reauthorizations — on an annual, two-year, four-year, or other basis —giving the authorizing committees the same opportunity. As a consequence of these oversight efforts, Congress can abolish or curtail obsolete or ineffective programs by cutting off or reducing funds or it may enhance effective programs by increasing funds.

H. Ensure That Executive Policies Reflect the Public Interest

Congressional oversight can appraise whether the needs and interests of the public are adequately served by federal programs, and thus lead to corrective action, either through legislation or administrative changes.

I. Protect Individual Rights and Liberties

Congressional oversight can help to safeguard the rights and liberties of citizens and others. By revealing abuses of authority, for instance, oversight hearings can halt executive misconduct and help to prevent its recurrence, either directly through new legislation or indirectly by putting pressure on the offending agency.

J. Other Specific Purposes

The general purposes of oversight — and what constitutes this function — can be stated in more specific terms. Like the general purposes, these unavoidably overlap because of the numerous and multifaceted dimensions of oversight. A brief list includes:

1. review the agency rulemaking process;
2. monitor the use of contractors and consultants for government services;
3. encourage and promote mutual cooperation between the branches;
4. examine agency personnel procedures;
5. acquire information useful in future policymaking;
6. investigate constituent complaints and media critiques;
7. assess whether program design and execution maximize the delivery of services to beneficiaries;
8. compare the effectiveness of one program with another;
9. protect agencies and programs against unjustified criticisms; and
10. study federal evaluation activities.

THOUGHTS ON OVERSIGHT AND ITS RATIONALE FROM . . .

James Wilson (The Works of James Wilson, 1896, vol. II, p. 29), an architect of the Constitution and Associate Justice on the first Supreme Court:

The house of representatives . . . form the grand inquest of the state. They will diligently inquire into grievances, arising both from men and things.

Woodrow Wilson (Congressional Government, 1885, p. 297), perhaps the first scholar to use the term "oversight" to refer to the review and investigation of the executive branch:

Quite as important as legislation is vigilant oversight of administration.

It is the proper duty of a representative body to look diligently into every affair of government and to talk much about what it sees. It is meant to be the eyes and the voice, and to embody the wisdom and will of its constituents.

The informing function of Congress should be preferred even to its legislative function.

John Stuart Mill (Considerations on Representative Government, 1861, p. 104), British utilitarian philosopher:

. . . the proper office of a representative assembly is to watch and control the government; to throw the light of publicity on its acts; to compel a full exposition and justification of all of them which any one considers questionable . . .

Authority to Conduct Oversight

A. United States Constitution

The Constitution grants Congress extensive authority to oversee and investigate executive branch activities. The constitutional authority for Congress to conduct oversight stems from such explicit and implicit provisions as:

1. *The power of the purse.* The Constitution provides that "No Money shall be drawn from the Treasury, but in Consequence of Appropriations made by Law." Each year the Committees on Appropriations of the House and Senate review the financial practices and needs of federal agencies. The appropriations process allows the Congress to exercise extensive control over the activities of executive agencies. Congress can define the precise purposes for which money may be spent, adjust funding levels, and prohibit expenditures for certain purposes.

2. *The power to organize the executive branch.* Congress has the authority to create, abolish, reorganize, and fund federal departments and agencies. It has the authority to assign or reassign functions to departments and agencies, and grant new forms of authority and staff to administrators. Congress, in short, exercises ultimate authority over executive branch organization and generally over policy.

3. *The power to make all laws for "carrying into Execution" Congress's own enumerated powers as well as those of the executive.* Article I grants Congress a wide range of powers, such as the power to tax and coin money; regulate foreign and interstate commerce; declare war; provide for the creation and maintenance of armed forces; and establish post offices. Augmenting these specific powers is the so-called "Elastic Clause," which gives Congress the authority "To make all Laws which shall be necessary and proper for carrying into Execution the foregoing Powers, and all other Powers vested by this Constitution in the Government of the United States, or in any Department or Officer thereof." Clearly, these provisions grant broad authority to regulate and oversee departmental activities established by law.

4. *The power to confirm officers of the United States*. The confirmation process not only involves the determination of a nominee's suitability for an executive (or judicial) position, but also provides an opportunity to examine the current policies and programs of an agency along with those policies and programs that the nominee intends to pursue.

5. *The power of investigation and inquiry.* A traditional method of exercising the oversight function, an implied power, is through investigations and inquiries into executive branch operations. Legislators often seek to know how effectively and efficiently programs are working, how well agency officials are responding to legislative directives, and how the public perceives the programs. The investigatory method helps to ensure a more responsible bureaucracy, while supplying Congress with information needed to formulate new legislation.

6. *Impeachment and removal.* Impeachment provides Congress with a powerful, ultimate oversight tool to investigate alleged executive and judicial misbehavior, and to eliminate such misbehavior through the convictions and removal from office of the offending individuals.

THE SUPREME COURT ON CONGRESS'S POWER TO OVERSEE AND INVESTIGATE

McGrain v. *Daugherty*, 273 U.S. 135, 177, and 181-182 (1927):

Congress, investigating the administration of the Department of Justice during the Teapot Dome scandal, was considering a subject "on which legislation could be had or would be materially aided by the information which the investigation was calculated to elicit." The "potential" for legislation was sufficient. The majority added, "We are of [the] opinion that the power of inquiry — with the process to enforce it — is an essential and appropriate auxiliary to the legislative function."

Eastland v. *United States Servicemen's Fund*, 421 U.S. 491, 509 (1975):

Expanding on its holding in *McGrain*, the Court declared, "To be a valid legislative inquiry there need be no predictable end result."

B. Principal Statutory Authority

A number of laws directly augment Congress's authority, mandate, and resources to conduct oversight, including assigning specific duties to committees. Among the most important, listed chronologically, are

1. *1912 Anti-Gag Legislation and Whistleblower Protection Laws for Federal Employees.*
    a. The 1912 act countered executive orders, issued by Presidents Theodore Roosevelt and William Howard Taft, which prohibited civil service employees from communicating directly with Congress.

b. It also guaranteed that "the right of any persons employed in the civil service . . . to petition Congress, or any Member thereof, or to furnish information to either House of Congress, or to any committee or member thereof, shall not be denied or interfered with." 37 Stat. 555 (1912) codified at 5 U.S.C. § 7211 (1994).
c. The Whistleblowers Protection Act of 1978, as amended, makes it a prohibited personnel practice for an agency employee to take (or not take) any action against an employee that is in retaliation for disclosure of information that the employee believes relates to violation of law, rule or regulation or which evidences gross mismanagement, waste, fraud or abuse of authority (5 U.S.C. § 2302 (b) (8)). The prohibition is explicitly intended to protect disclosures to Congress: "This subsection shall not be construed to authorize the withholding of information from the Congress or the taking of any personnel action against an employee who disclosures information to the Congress."
d. Intelligence Community Whistleblower Protection Act (P.L. 105-272) establishes special procedures for personnel in the Intelligence Community, to transmit urgent concerns involving classified information to inspectors general and the House and Senate Select Committees on Intelligence.
e. Section 818 of the Treasury, Transportation et al. Appropriations Act of 2005, P.L. 109-115, 119 Stat. 2500, prohibits the payment of the salary of any officer or employee of the Federal Government who prohibits or prevents or attempts or threatens to prohibit or prevent, any other Federal officer or employee from having direct oral or written communication or contact with any Member, committee or subcommittee. This prohibition applies irrespective of whether such communication was initiated by such officer or employee or in response to the request or inquiry of such Member, committee or subcommittee. Further, any punishment or threat of punishment because of any contact or communication by an officer or employee with a Member, committee, or subcommittee is prohibited under the provisions of this act.
f. Section 820 of the Treasury, Transportation et al. Appropriations Act of 2005, P.L. 109-115, 119 Stat. 2500, prohibits the expenditure of any appropriated funds for use in implementing or enforcing agreement in Standard Forms 312 and 4414 of the Government or any other non-disclosure policy form, or agreement if such policy, form, or agreement that does not contain a provision that states that the restrictions are consistent with and do not supercede, conflict with, or otherwise alter the employee obligation, rights and liabilities created by E.O. 12958; 5 U.S.C. § 7211 (Lloyd-LaFollette Act); 10 U.S.C.§ 1034 (Military Whistleblower Act); 5 U.S.C. § 2303 (b)(8) (Whistleblower Protection Act); 50 U.S.C. § 421 et seq. (Intelligence Identities Protection Act); and 18 U.S.C. §§ 641, 793, 794, 798, and 952 and 50 U.S.C. § (783)(b).

2. *1921 Budget and Accounting Act Establishing the General Accounting Office (GAO), renamed the Government Accountability Office in 2004.*
   a. Insisted that GAO *"shall be independent of the executive* departments and under the control and direction of the Comptroller General of the United States." (Emphasis added.) 42 Stat. 23 (1921)

b. Granted authority to the Comptroller General to "*investigate, at the seat of government or elsewhere*, all matters relating to the receipt, disbursement, and application of public funds." (Emphasis added.) 42 Stat. 26 (1921)

3. *1946 Legislative Reorganization Act*
   a. Mandated House and Senate committees to exercise *"continuous watchfulness"* of the administration of laws and programs under their jurisdiction. (Emphasis added.) 60 Stat. 832 (1946)
   b. Authorized for the first time in history, *permanent professional and clerical staff* for committees. 60 Stat. 832 (1946)
   c. Authorized and directed the *Comptroller General* to make administrative management analyses of each executive branch agency. 60 Stat. 837 (1946)
   d. Established the Legislative Reference Service, renamed the Congressional Research Service by the 1970 Legislative Reorganization Act (see below), as a separate department in the Library of Congress and called upon the Service "to advise and assist any committee of either House or joint committee in the analysis, appraisal, and evaluation of any legislative proposal . . . and *otherwise to assist in furnishing a basis for the proper determination of measures* before the committee." (Emphasis added.) 60 Stat. 836 (1946)

4. *1968 Intergovernmental Cooperation Act*
   a. Required that House and Senate committees having jurisdiction over *grants-in-aid* conduct studies of the programs under which grants-in-aid are made. 82 Stat. 1098 (1968)
   b. Provided that studies of these programs are to determine whether: (1) their purposes have been met, (2) their objectives could be carried on without further assistance, (3) they are adequate to meet needs, and (4) any changes in programs or procedures should be made. 82 Stat. 1098 (1968)

5. *1970 Legislative Reorganization Act*
   a. Revised and rephrased in more explicit language the oversight function of House and Senate standing committees: ". . . each standing committee shall *review and study, on a continuing basis, the application, administration, and execution* of those laws or parts of laws, the subject matter of which is within the jurisdiction of that committee." (Emphasis added.) 84 Stat. 1156 (1970)
   b. Required most House and Senate committees to issue *biennial* oversight reports. 84 Stat. 1156 (1970)
   c. Strengthened the *program evaluation* responsibilities and other authorities and duties of the Government Accountability Office. 84 Stat. 1168-1171 (1970)
   d. Redesignated the Legislative Reference Service as the *Congressional Research Service*, strengthening its *policy analysis* role and expanding its other responsibilities to Congress. 84 Stat. 1181-1185 (1970)
   e. Recommended that House and Senate committees ascertain whether *programs* within their jurisdiction could be *appropriated for annually*. 84 Stat. 1174-1175 (1970)

f. Required most House and Senate committees to include in their committee reports on legislation *five-year cost estimates* for carrying out the proposed program. 84 Stat. 1173-1174 (1970)
g. *Increased by two the number of permanent staff for each standing committee, including provision for minority party hirings*, and provided for hiring of *consultants* by standing committees. 84 Stat. 1175-1179 (1970)

6. *1972 Federal Advisory Committee Act*
   a. Directed House and Senate committees to make a *continuing review* of the activities of each advisory committee under its jurisdiction. 86 Stat. 771 (1972)
   b. The studies are to determine whether: (1) such committee should be abolished or merged with any other advisory committee, (2) its responsibility should be revised, and (3) it performs a necessary function not already being performed. 86 Stat. 771 (1972) (Advisory committee charters and reports can generally be obtained from the agency or government organization being advised.)

7. *1974 Congressional Budget Act, as amended*
   a. *Expanded* House and Senate committee *authority for oversight*. Permitted committees to appraise and evaluate programs themselves "or by contract, or (to) require a Government agency to do so and furnish a report thereon to the Congress." 88 Stat. 325 (1974)
   b. Directed the Comptroller General to "*review and evaluate the results of Government programs and activities*," on his own initiative, or at the request of either House or any standing or joint committee and to assist committees in analyzing and assessing program reviews or evaluation studies. (Emphasis added.) Authorized GAO to establish an Office of Program Review and Evaluation to carry out these responsibilities. 88 Stat. 326 (1974)
   c. Strengthened GAO's role in *acquiring fiscal, budgetary, and program-related information*. 88 Stat. 327-329 (1974)
   d. Required any House or Senate legislative committee report on a public bill or resolution to include an *analysis* (prepared by the Congressional Budget Office) providing an *estimate and comparison of costs* which would be incurred in carrying out the bill during the next and following four fiscal years in which it would be effective. 88 Stat. 320 (1974)
   e. Established House and Senate Budget Committees and the Congressional Budget Office. The CBO director is authorized to "*secure information, data, estimates, and statistics directly* from the various departments, agencies, and establishments" of the government. 88 Stat. 302 (1974)

8. *Other noteworthy statutory provisions*

   Separate from expanding its own authority and resources directly, Congress has strengthened its oversight capabilities *indirectly*, by, for instance, establishing study commissions to review and evaluate programs, policies, and operations of the government. In addition, Congress has created various *mechanisms, structures, and procedures within the executive* that improve the executive's ability to monitor and control its own operations and, at the same time, provide additional information and oversight-related analyses to Congress. These statutory provisions include

a. Establishing offices of inspector general in all cabinet departments, larger agencies and numerous boards, commissions, and government corporations — *Inspector General Act of 1978*, as amended, 5 U.S.C. Appendix 3
b. Establishing chief financial officers in all cabinet departments and larger agencies — *Chief Financial Officers Act of 1990*, 107 Stat. 2838 (1990)
c. Improving the government's ability to manage its programs — *Federal Managers' Financial Integrity Act of 1982*, 96 Stat. 814-815 (1982)
d. Improving the efficiency, effectiveness, and equity in the exchange of funds between the federal government and state governments — *Cash Management Improvement Act of 1990,* 104 Stat. 1058 (1990)
e. Increasing efficiency, effectiveness, and accountability within the government — *Government Performance and Results Act of 1993,* 107 Stat. 285-296 (1993)
f. Improving the executive's stewardship of federal resources and accountability — *Government Management and Reform Act of 1994*, 108 Stat. 3410 (1994)
g. Controlling federal paperwork requirements — *Paperwork Reduction Act of 1995*, 109 Stat. 163 (1995)
h. Establishing the position of chief information officer in federal agencies to provide relevant advice for purchasing the best and most cost-effective information technology available — *Information Technology Improvement Act*, 110 Stat. 679 (1996)
i. Establishing uniform audit requirements for state and local governments and nonprofit organizations receiving federal financial assistance — *Single Audit Act of 1984*, as amended, 98 Stat. 2327 (1984) and 110 Stat. 679 (1996)
j. Creating a mechanism, the Congressional Review Act by which Congress can review and disapprove virtually any federal rule or regulation — *Small Business Regulatory Enforcement Fairness Act of 1996*, 110 Stat. 857-874 (1996), codified at 5 U.S.C. §§ 801-808 (2000)

C. Responsibilities in House and Senate Rules

1. *House Rules*
   a. House rules grant the *Committee on Government Reform* a comprehensive role in the conduct of oversight (Rule X, clause 4). For example, pertinent review findings and recommendations of this committee are to be considered by the authorizing committees, if presented to them in a timely fashion. In addition, the authorizing committees are to indicate on the cover of their reports on public measures that they contain a summary of such findings when that is the case (Rule XIII, clause 3).
   b. The Committee on Government Reform has *additional* oversight duties to
      (1) review and study on a continuing basis, the operation of government activities at all levels to determine their economy and efficiency (Rule X, clause 3);
      (2) receive and examine reports of the Comptroller General and submit recommendations thereon to the House (Rule X, clause 4);

(3) evaluate the effects of laws enacted to reorganize the legislative and executive branches of the government (Rule X, clause 4);
(4) study intergovernmental relationships between the United States and states, municipalities, and international organizations of which the United States is a member (Rule X, clause 4); and
(5) *report an oversight agenda*, not later than March 31 of the first session of a Congress, based upon oversight plans submitted by each standing committee and after consultation with the Speaker of the House, the majority leader, and the minority leader. The oversight agenda is to include the oversight plans of each standing committee together with any recommendations that it or the House leadership group may make to ensure the most effective coordination of such plans (Rule X, clause 2).

c. House rules mandate or provide authority for other oversight efforts by *standing committees*:
(1) Each standing committee (except Appropriations and Budget) shall review and study on a *continuing basis* the application, administration, and execution of all laws within its legislative jurisdiction (Rule X, clause 2).
(2) Committees have the authority to *review the impact of tax policies* on matters that fall within their jurisdiction (Rule X, clause 2).
(3) Each committee (except Appropriations and Budget) has a responsibility for futures research and forecasting (Rule X, clause 2).
(4) Specified committees have *special oversight authority* (i.e., the right to conduct comprehensive reviews of specific subject areas that are within the legislative jurisdiction of other committees). Special oversight is akin to the broad oversight authority granted the Committee on Government Reform, by the 1946 Legislature Reorganization Act, except that special oversight is generally limited to named subjects (Rule X, clause 3).
(5) Each standing committee having more than 20 members shall establish an oversight subcommittee, or require its subcommittees, if any, *to conduct oversight* in their jurisdictional areas; a committee that establishes such a subcommittee may add it as a sixth subcommittee, beyond the usual limit of five (Rule X, clauses 2 and 5).
(6) Committee reports on measures are to include *oversight findings* separately set out and clearly identified (Rule XIII, clause 3).
(7) Costs of stenographic services and transcripts for *oversight hearings* are to be paid "from the applicable accounts of the House" (Rule XI, clause 1).
(8) *Each standing committee is to submit its oversight plans* for the duration of a Congress by February 15 of the first session to the Committee on Government Reform and the Committee on House Administration. Not later than March 31, the Government Reform Committee must report an oversight agenda (discussed above). In developing such plans, each standing committee must, to the extent feasible (Rule X, clause 2):
(a) consult with other committees of the House that have jurisdiction over the same or related laws, programs, or agencies within its jurisdiction, with the objective of ensuring that such laws, programs, or agencies are reviewed in the same Congress and that there is a maximum of

coordination between such committees in the conduct of such reviews; and such plans shall include an explanation of what steps have been and will be taken to ensure such coordination and cooperation;

(b) give priority consideration to including in its plans the review of those laws, programs, or agencies operating under permanent budget authority or permanent statutory authority; and

(c) have a view toward ensuring that all significant laws, programs, or agencies within its jurisdiction are subject to review at least once every 10 years.

(9) *Each committee* must submit to the House, not later than January 2 of each odd-numbered year, *a report on the activities of that committee* for the Congress (Rule XI, clause 1):

(a) Such report must include *separate sections summarizing the legislative and oversight activities* of that committee during that Congress.

(b) The *oversight section* of such report must include a summary of the oversight plans submitted by the committee at the beginning of the Congress, a summary of the actions taken and recommendations made with respect to each such plan, and a summary of any additional oversight activities undertaken by that committee, and any recommendations made or actions taken thereon.

d. *The Speaker*, with the approval of the House, is given additional authority to "appoint *special ad hoc oversight committees* for the purpose or reviewing specific matters within the jurisdiction of two or more standing committees." (Emphasis added.) (Rule X, clause 2)

2. Senate Rules

a. Each standing committee (except for Appropriations and Budget) must *review and study on a continuing basis, the application, administration, and execution of all laws within its legislative jurisdiction* (Rule XXVI, clause 8).

b. "*Comprehensive policy oversight*" responsibilities are granted to specified standing committees. This duty is similar to special oversight in the House. The Committee on Agriculture, Nutrition, and Forestry, for example, is authorized to "study and review, on a comprehensive basis, matters relating to food, nutrition, and hunger, both in the United States and in foreign countries, and rural affairs, and report thereon from time to time (Rule XXV, clause 1a)."

c. All standing committees, except Appropriations, are required to prepare *regulatory impact evaluations* in their committee reports accompanying each public bill or joint resolution (Rule XXVI, clause 11). The evaluations are to include:

(1) an estimate of the numbers of individuals and businesses to be affected;

(2) a determination of the measure's economic impact and effect on personal privacy; and

(3) a determination of the amount of additional paperwork that will result.

d. The Committee on Homeland Security and Government Affairs has the following *additional oversight duties* (Rule XXV, clause 1k):

(1) review and study on a continuing basis the operation of government activities at all levels to determine their economy and efficiency;

(2) receive and examine reports of the Comptroller General and submit recommendations thereon to the Senate;
(3) evaluate the effects of laws enacted to reorganize the legislative and executive branches of the government; and
(4) study intergovernmental relationships between the United States and states, municipalities, and international organizations of which the United States is a member.
(5) On March 1, 1948 of the 80th Congress, the Senate adopted S. Res. 189, which established the Permanent Subcommittee on Investigations of the then titled Committee on Government Operations. The Subcommittee was an outgrowth of the famous 1941 Truman Committee (after Senator Harry Truman) which investigated fraud and mismanagement of the nation's war program. The Truman Committee ended in 1948, but the chairman of the Government Operations Committee made the functions of the Truman panel one of his subcommittees: the Permanent Subcommittee on Investigations. Since then this subcommittee has investigated scores of issues, such as government waste, fraud, and inefficiency.

Congressional Participants in Oversight

A. Members and Committees

1. *Members*. Oversight is generally considered a committee activity. However, both casework and other project work conducted in a Member's personal office can result in findings about bureaucratic behavior and policy implementation; these, in turn, can lead to the adjustment of agency policies and procedures and to changes in public law.
   (a) *Casework* — responding to constituent requests for assistance on projects or complaints or grievances about program implementation provides an opportunity to examine bureaucratic activity and operations, if only in a selective way.
   (b) Sometimes *individual Members* will conduct their own investigations or ad hoc hearings, or direct their staffs to conduct oversight studies. Individual Members have no authority to issue compulsory process or conduct official hearings. The Government Accountability Office or some other legislative branch agency, a specially created task force, or private research group might be requested to conduct an investigation of a matter for a Senator or Representative.
2. *Committees*. The most common and effective method of conducting oversight is through the committee structure. Throughout their histories, the House and Senate have used their standing committees as well as select or special committees to investigate federal activities and agencies along with other matters.
   (a) The House Committee on *Government Reform* and the Senate Committee on *Homeland Security and Governmental Affairs*, which have oversight jurisdiction over virtually the entire federal government, have been vested with broad investigatory powers over government-wide activities.
   (b) The House and Senate Committees on *Appropriations* have similar responsibilities when reviewing fiscal activities.

(c) Each *standing* committee of Congress has oversight responsibilities to review government activities within their jurisdiction. These panels also have authority on their own to establish oversight and investigative *subcommittees*. The establishment of such subcommittees does *not preclude* the *legislative* subcommittees from conducting oversight.

(d) Certain House and Senate committees have *"special oversight"* or "*comprehensive policy oversight*" of designated subject areas as explained in the previous subsection.

B. Staff of Member Offices and Committees

1. *Personal Staff.* Constituent letters, complaints, and requests for projects and assistance frequently bring problems and deficiencies in federal programs and administration to the attention of Members and their personal office staffs. The casework performed by a Member's staff for constituents can be an effective oversight tool.
   (a) Casework can be an important vehicle for pursuing both the oversight and legislative interests of the Member. The Senator or Representative and the staff may be attuned to the *relationship* between *casework* and the *oversight* function. This is facilitated by a regular exchange of ideas among the Member, legislative aides, and caseworkers on problems brought to the office's attention by constituents, and of possible legislative initiatives to resolve those problems.
   (b) If casework is to be useful as an oversight technique, *effective staffing and coordination are needed.* Casework and legislative staffs maximize service to their Member's constituents when they establish a relationship with the staff of the subcommittees and committees that handle the areas of concern to the Member's constituents. Through this interaction, the panel's staff can be made aware of the problems with the agency or program in question, assess how widespread and significant they are, determine their causes, and recommend corrective action.
   (c) *Office procedures* enable staff in some offices to identify cases that represent a situation in which *formal* changes in agency procedure could be an appropriate remedy. Prompt congressional inquiry and follow up enhance this type of oversight. Telephone inquiries reinforced with written requests tend to ensure agency attention.
2. *Committee Staff.* As issues become more complex and Members' staffs more overworked, professional staffs of committees can provide the expert help required to conduct oversight and investigations. Committee staff typically have the experience and expertise to conduct effective oversight for the committees and subcommittees they serve. Committees may also call upon *legislative support agencies* for assistance, hire *consultants*, or *"borrow" staff* from federal departments.

   Committee staff, in summary, occupy a central position in the conduct of oversight. The informal contacts with executive officials at all levels constitute one of Congress's most effective devices for performing its "continuous watchfulness" function.

C. Congressional Support Agencies and Offices

1. Of the agencies in the legislative branch, three directly assist Congress in support of its oversight function. (See "Section V" below for further detail on each):
   (a) Congressional Budget Office (CBO),
   (b) Congressional Research Service (CRS) of the Library of Congress, and
   (c) Government Accountability Office (GAO), formerly the General Accounting Office.
2. Additional offices that can assist in oversight are
   (a) House General Counsel's Office,
   (b) House Parliamentarian's Office,
   (c) House Clerk's Office,
   (d) Senate Legal Counsel's Office, and
   (e) Senate Historian's Office and Senate Library

SELECTED READINGS

Aberbach, Joel D. Keeping a Watchful Eye: The Politics of Congressional Oversight. Washington: Brookings Institution, 1990. JK585.A63

Congressional Oversight: Methods and Techniques. Committee Print, Prepared for the Subcommittee on Oversight Procedures of the Senate Committee on Government Operations by the Congressional Research Service and the General Accounting Office, 94th Congress, 2nd session. Washington: GPO, 1976.

Ehlke, Richard. Congressional Access to Information From the Executive: A Legal Analysis. CRS Report 86-50A, March 10, 1986.

Fisher, Louis. Constitutional Conflicts between Congress and the President. Lawrence, Kansas: University Press of Kansas, 1997, 4th Revised Edition. KF4565.F57 1997

Foreman, Christopher H. Signals from the Hill: Congressional Oversight and the Challenge of Social Regulation. New Haven: Yale University Press, 1988. JK585.F68

Hamilton, James. The Power to Probe: A Study of Congressional Investigations. New York: Vintage Books, 1976.

Harris, Joseph P. Congressional Control of Administration. Washington: Brookings Institution, 1964. JK1061.H3

History of the United States House of Representatives, 1789-1994. H.Doc. 103-324, 103rd Congress, 2nd session. Washington: GPO, 1994. Chapter XI, "Oversight," pp. 233-266.

Kaiser, Frederick M. Congressional Oversight. CRS Report 97-936, January 2, 2001.

——. Congressional Oversight of the Presidency. Annals, vol. 499, September 1988, pp. 75-89.

Leading Cases on Congressional Investigatory Power (Compiled by the Joint Committee on Congressional Operations). Committee Print, 94th Congress, 2nd session. Washington: GPO, 1976.

Maskell, Jack H. and Morton Rosenberg. Congressional Intervention in the Administrative Process: Legal and Ethical Considerations. CRS Report RL32113, September 25, 2003.

Mayhew, David R. Divided We Govern: Party Control, Lawmaking, and Investigations, 1946-1990. New Haven: Yale University Press, 1991. JK2261.M36

McCubbins, Mathew D. and Thomas Schwartz. Congressional Oversight Overlooked: Police Patrol Versus Fire Alarms. American Journal of Political Science, vol. 2, February 1984, pp. 165-79.

National Academy of Public Administration. Panel on Congress and the Executive. Beyond Distrust: Building Bridges Between Congress and the Executive. Washington: NAPA, 1992.

Ogul, Morris S. Congress Oversees the Bureaucracy: Studies in Legislative Supervision. Pittsburgh: University of Pittsburgh Press, 1976. JK585.048

Oleszek, Walter J. Congressional Procedures and the Policy Process, 6th ed. Washington: Congressional Quarterly Press, 2004. Chapter 10, Legislative Oversight. KF4937.O44

——. A Perspective on Congress's Oversight Function. CRS Report RL32617, September 30, 2004.

Ornstein, Norman F. and Thomas E. Mann. When Congress Checks Out. Foreign Affairs, vol. 85, 2006, pp. 67-80,

Rosenberg, Morton. Congress's Prerogative Over Agencies and Agency Decisionmakers: The Rise and Demise of the Reagan Administration's Theory of the Unitary Executive. George Washington Law Review, vol. 57, January 1989, pp. 627-703.

——. Congressional Review of Agency Rulemaking: An Update and Assessment of the Congressional Review Act After Ten Years. CRS Report RL30116, March 29, 2006.

——. Investigative Oversight: An Introduction to the Law, Practice and Procedure of Congressional Inquiry. CRS Report 95-464 A, April 7, 1995.

Rosenbloom, David H. Building a Legislative-Centered Public Administration: Congress and the Administrative State, 1946-1999. Tuscaloosa, Ala.: The University of Alabama Press, 2000. KF1601.R58

Schlesinger, Arthur M. and Roger Bruns, eds. Congress Investigates: A Documented History, 1792-1974 (5 vols.) New York: Chelsea House Publishers, 1975. JK1123.A2S34

Study on Federal Regulation: Congressional Oversight of Regulatory Agencies. Senate Doc. 95-26, 95th Congress, 1st session. Washington: GPO, 1977.

U.S. General Accounting Office. Investigators' Guide to Sources of Information. GAO Report OSI-97-2. Washington: GAO, 1997.

West, William F. Controlling the Bureaucracy: Institutional Constraints in Theory and Practice. Armonk, New York and London, England: M.E. Sharpe: 1995. JK421.W44

II. Oversight Coordination and Processes

A persistent problem for Congress in conducting oversight is coordination among committees, both within each chamber as well as between the two houses. As the final report of the House Select Committee on Committees of the 93rd Congress noted, "Review findings and recommendations developed by one committee are seldom shared on a timely basis with another committee, and, if they are made available, then often the findings are transmitted in a form that is difficult for Members to use." Despite the passage of time, this statement remains relevant today. Oversight coordination between House and Senate committees is also uncommon; and it occurs primarily in the aftermath of perceived major policy failures or prominent inter-branch conflicts, as with the Iran-contra affair (1986) and the 9/11 terrorist attacks (2001-2002).

Intercommittee cooperation on oversight can prove beneficial for a variety of reasons. It should, for example, minimize unnecessary duplication and conflict and inhibit agencies from playing one committee off against another. There are formal and informal ways to achieve oversight coordination among committees.

Oversight Coordination

A. General Techniques of Ensuring Oversight Coordination Include

1. The House and Senate can establish select or special committees to probe issues and agencies, to promote public understanding of national concerns, and to coordinate oversight of issues that overlap the jurisdiction of several standing committees.
2. House rules require the findings and recommendations of the Committee on Government Reform to be considered by the authorizing committees if presented to them in a timely fashion. Such findings and recommendations are to be published in the authorizing committees' reports on legislation. House rules also require the oversight plans of committees to include ways to maximize coordination between and among committees that share jurisdiction over related laws, programs, or agencies.

B. Specific Means of Ensuring Oversight Coordination Include

1. Joint oversight hearings on programs or agencies.
2. Informal agreement among committees to oversee certain agencies and not others. For example, the House and Senate Committees on Commerce agreed to hold oversight hearings on certain regulatory agencies in alternate years.
3. Consultation between the authorizing and appropriating committees. The two Committees on Commerce have worked closely and successfully with their corresponding appropriations subcommittees to alert those panels to the authorizing committees' intent with respect to regulatory ratemaking by such agencies as the Federal Communications Commission.

Oversight Processes

A. The Budget Process

1. The Congressional Budget and Impoundment Control Act of 1974, as amended, enhanced the legislative branch's capacity to shape the federal budget. The act has major institutional and procedural effects on Congress:
   a. *Institutionally*, Congress created three new entities:
      (1) the Senate Committee on the Budget;

   (2) the House Committee on the Budget; and
   (3) the Congressional Budget Office.

   b. *Procedurally*, the act established methods that permit Congress to:
      (1) determine budget policy as a whole;
      (2) relate revenue and spending decisions;
      (3) determine priorities among competing national programs; and
      (4) ensure that revenue, spending, and debt legislation are consistent with the overall budget policy.

2. The new budget process coexists with the established authorization and appropriation procedures and significantly affects each.
   a. On the *authorization side*, the Budget Act requires committees to submit their budgetary "views and estimates" for matters under their jurisdiction to their Committee on the Budget within six weeks after the President submits a budget.
   b. On the *appropriations side*, new contract and borrowing authority must go through the appropriations process. Subcommittees of the Appropriations Committees are assigned a financial allocation that determines how much may be included in the measures they report, although less than one-third of federal spending is subject to the annual appropriations process. (The tax and appropriations panels of each house also submit budgetary views and estimates to their respective Committee on the Budget.)
   c. In deciding spending, revenue, credit, and debt issues, Congress is sensitive to trends in the overall composition of the annual federal budget (expenditures for defense, entitlements, interest on the debt, and domestic discretionary programs).
3. In short, the Budget Act has the potential of strengthening oversight by enabling Congress better to relate program priorities to financial claims on the national budget. Each committee, knowing that it will receive a fixed amount of the total to be included in a budget resolution, has an incentive to scrutinize existing programs to make room for new programs or expanded funding of ongoing projects or to assess whether programs have outlived their usefulness.

B. The Authorization Process

1. Through its authorization power, Congress exercises significant control over any government agency.
2. The entire authorization process may involve a host of oversight tools —hearings, studies, and reports — but the key to the process is the *authorization statute*.
   a. An authorization statute creates and shapes government programs and agencies and it contains the statement of legislative policy for the agency.
   b. Authorization is the *first* lever in congressional exercise of the power of the purse; it usually allows an agency to be funded, but it does *not* guarantee financing of agencies and programs. Frequently, authorizations establish dollar ceilings on the amounts that can be appropriated.
3. The authorization-reauthorization process is an important oversight tool.
   a. Through this process, Members are educated about the work of an agency and given an opportunity to direct the agency's effort in light of experience.
   b. Expiration of an agency's program provides an excellent chance for in-depth oversight:

(1) In recent decades, there has been a mix of permanent and periodic (annual or multi-year) authorizations, although some reformers are now pressing for *biennial budgeting* (acting on a two-year cycle for authorizations, appropriations, and budget resolutions).

(2) Periodic authorizations improve the likelihood that an agency will be scrutinized systematically.

4. In addition to formal amendment of the agency's authorizing statute, the authorization process gives committees an opportunity to exercise informal, nonstatutory controls over the agency.
   a. Knowledge by an agency that it must come to the legislative committee for renewed authority increases the influence of the committee.
   b. This condition helps to account for the appeal of short-term authorizations.
   c. *Non-statutory controls* used by committees to exercise direction over the administration of laws include statements made in:
      (1) committee hearings;
      (2) committee reports accompanying legislation;
      (3) floor debates; and
      (4) committee contacts and correspondence with the agency.
5. If agencies fail to comply with these informal directives, the authorization committees can apply sanctions or move to convert the informal directive to a statutory command.

C. The Appropriations Process

1. The appropriations process is one of Congress's most important forms of oversight.
   a. Its strategic position stems from the constitutional requirement that "no Money shall be drawn from the Treasury, but in Consequence of Appropriations made by Law."
   b. Congress's power of the purse allows the House and Senate Committees on Appropriations to play a prominent role in oversight.
2. The oversight function of the Committees on Appropriations derives from their responsibility to examine and pass on the budget requests of the agencies as contained in the President's Budget.
   a. The decisions of the committees are conditioned on their assessment of the agencies' need for their budget request as indicated by past performance.
   b. In practice, the entire record of an agency is fair game for the required assessment.
   c. This comprehensive overview and the "carrot and stick" of the appropriations recommendations make the committees significant focal points of congressional oversight and is a key source of their power in Congress and in the federal government generally.
3. Enacted appropriations legislation frequently contains at least five types of *statutory controls* on agencies:
   a. Such legislation specifies the *purpose* for which funds may be used.
   b. It defines the specified *funding level* for the agency as a whole as well as for programs and divisions within the agency.
   c. It sets *time limits* on the availability of funds for obligation.

   d. Appropriations legislation may contain *limitation* provisions. For example, in appropriating $350 million to the Environmental Protection Agency for research and development, Congress added this condition: "Provided, That not more than $55,000,000 of these funds shall be available for procurement of laboratory equipment, supplies, and other operating expenses in support of research and development." 108 Stat. 2319 (1994).
   e. Appropriations measures and committee reports also stipulate how an agency's budget can be *reprogrammed* (shifting funds within an appropriations account; see box below).
4. *Nonstatutory controls* are a major form of oversight. Legislative language in committee reports and in hearings, letters to agency heads, and other communications give detailed instructions to agencies regarding committee expectations and desires. Agencies are not legally obligated to abide by non-statutory recommendations, but failure to do so may result in a loss of funds and flexibility the following year. Agencies ignore nonstatutory controls at their peril (see box).

> The conference report for the Omnibus Consolidated and Emergency Supplemental Appropriations for FY1999 provides guidelines for the reprogramming and transfer of funds for the Treasury and General Government Appropriations Act, 1999. Each request from an agency to the review committee "shall include a declaration that, as of the date of the request, none of the funds included in the request have been obligated, and none will be obligated, until the Committees on Appropriations have approved the request." H. Rept. No. 105-825, p. 1472 (1998).

D. The Investigatory Process

1. Congress's power of investigation is *implied* in the Constitution.
   a. Numerous Supreme Court decisions have upheld the legislative branch's right of inquiry, provided it stays within its legitimate legislative sphere.
   b. The roots of Congress's authority to conduct investigations extend back to the British Parliament and colonial assemblies.
   c. In addition, the Framers clearly perceived the House of Representatives to function as a "grand inquest." Since the Framers expected lawmakers to employ the investigatory function, based upon parliamentary precedents, it was unnecessary to invest Congress with an explicit investigatory power.
   d. From time to time, legal questions have been raised about the investigative authority of Congress. However, numerous Supreme Court decisions have upheld the legislative branch's right of inquiry, provided it serves a legitimate legislative interest.
2. Investigations and related activities may be conducted by:
   a. individual Members;
   b. committees and subcommittees;
   c. staff or outside organizations and personnel under contract; or
   d. congressional support agencies.
3. Investigations serve several purposes:
   a. they help to ensure honesty and efficiency in the administration of laws;
   b. they secure information that assists Congress in making informed policy judgments; and

c. they may aid in informing the public about the administration of laws.

[See Section III for greater detail and analysis]

E. The Confirmation Process

By establishing a public record of the policy views of nominees, congressional hearings allow lawmakers to call appointed officials to account at a later time. Since at least the Ethics in Government Act of 1978, which encouraged greater scrutiny of nominations, Senate committees are setting aside more time to probe the qualifications, independence, and policy predilections of presidential nominees, seeking information on everything from physical health to financial assets. Confirmation can assist in oversight in several ways.

1. The Constitution provides that the President "shall nominate, and by and with the *Advice and Consent of the Senate*, shall appoint Ambassadors, other public Ministers and Consuls, Judges of the supreme court, and all other Officers of the United States, whose Appointments are not herein otherwise provided for, and which shall be established by Law." (Emphasis added.)
   a. The consideration of appointments to executive branch leadership positions is a major responsibility of the Senate and especially of Senate committees.
   b. Panels review the qualifications of nominees for public positions.
2. The confirmation hearing provides a forum for the discussion of the policies and programs the nominee intends to pursue; this is a classic opportunity for senatorial oversight and influence. The confirmation process as an oversight tool can be used to:
   a. provide policy direction to nominees;
   b. inform nominees of congressional interests; and
   c. extract future commitments.
3. Once a nominee has been confirmed by the Senate, oversight includes following up to ensure that the nominee fulfills any commitments made during confirmation hearings. Subsequent hearings and committee investigations can explore whether such commitments have been kept.
4. *Recess Appointments*. The Constitution provides that the President "shall have Power to fill up all Vacancies that may happen during the Recess of the Senate, by granting Commissions which shall expire at the End of their next Session." When Presidents relied on this power to circumvent Senate confirmation, Congress responded with legislation that prohibits, with certain exceptions, the payment of salaries to recess appointees. 54 Stat. 751 (1940); 5 U.S.C. § 5503 (2004). Also, in the annual Treasury, Transportation, Housing and Urban Development Appropriations Act, Congress enacts an additional funding restriction on recess appointees (see box).

> No part of any appropriation for the current fiscal year contained in this or any other Act shall be paid to any person for the filling of any position for which he or she has been nominated after the Senate has voted not to approve the nomination of said person. 114 Stat. 2763A-157, sec. 609 (2000).

5. *Vacancies Act*. In addition to making recess appointments, Presidents make other temporary or interim appointments. Since 1795, Congress has legislated limits on the

time a temporary officer may occupy a vacant advice and consent position. In 1868, Congress established a procedure for filling vacancies in advice and consent positions through the Vacancies Act. When the head of an executive department dies, resigns, or is sick or absent, the next in command may perform the duties until a successor is appointed or the absence ceases. The President may also direct someone else (previously appointed with the advice and consent of the Senate) to perform the duties. These acting officials, under the Vacancies Act, were restricted by law to a period of not to exceed 30 days. That limit was violated with such frequency that Congress in 1988 increased it to 120 days. 102 Stat. 988, sec. 7 (1988); 5 U.S.C. §§ 3345-48 (2004).

The Justice Department took the position that some executive officials were not restricted by the Vacancies Act and could serve beyond the 120-day period. Under that interpretation, the Administration selected Bill Lann Lee to head the Justice Department's Civil Rights Division, and argued that he could serve longer than had he been a recess appointee. Congress responded by passing legislation in 1998 to make the Vacancies Act the exclusive vehicle for temporarily filling vacant advice and consent positions. The new Vacancies Act, included in the FY1999 Omnibus Consolidated and Emergency Supplemental Appropriations Act (P.L. 105-277), rejects the Justice Department position and established procedures for the appointment of executive officials who temporarily hold an office. With various exceptions, the 120-day period has been replaced by a 210-day period.

F. The Impeachment Process

1. The impeachment power of Congress is a unique oversight tool, reserved for unusual circumstances and as a technique of last resort when conventional forms of oversight fail. Impeachment applies also to the judiciary. Impeachment offers Congress:
   a. a constitutionally mandated method for obtaining information that might otherwise not be made available by the executive; and
   b. an implied threat of punishment for an executive official whose conduct exceeds acceptable boundaries.
2. Impeachment procedures differ from those of conventional congressional oversight.
   a. The most significant procedural differences center on the *roles* played by each house of Congress.
   b. The House of Representatives has the sole power to impeach. A majority is required to impeach.
   c. If the House votes to impeach, the person is tried by the Senate, which has the sole power to try an impeachment. A two-thirds majority is required to convict and remove the individual. Should the Senate deem it appropriate in a given case, it may, by majority vote, impose an additional judgment of disqualification from further federal offices of honor, trust, or profit.
   d. In *Nixon v. United States*, 506 U.S. 226 (1993), the Supreme Court held nonjusticiable a constitutional challenge to the use by the Senate in an impeachment proceeding of a 12-member committee appointed to take testimony and gather evidence. Such a committee makes no recommendations as to the ultimate question before the Senate. Nor does the committee rule on questions of relevancy, materiality, and competency. Rather, it reports a certified copy of the

transcript of the proceedings before the committee and any evidence received by the committee to the full Senate for its consideration. The full Senate may take further testimony or evidence, or it may hold the entire trial in open Senate. In either event, the full Senate determines whether to convict on one or more of the articles of impeachment involved and, upon conviction, decides the appropriate judgment to be imposed.

3. The impeachment process is cumbersome and infrequently used. The House has voted to impeach in 17 cases, 16 of which have reached the Senate, and 15 of which have gone to a vote on one or more articles of impeachment. Seven cases, all pertaining to federal judges, have resulted in conviction and removal; two of these also resulted in disqualification. The most recent impeachment trial was that of President Clinton in 1998-99; the most recent judicial impeachment trials were those of Judges Claiborne, Hastings, and Nixon in 1986, 1988 and 1989, respectively. A number of issues were addressed in the Clinton impeachment trial and other past impeachment proceedings, although the answers to some still remain somewhat ambiguous. For example:
   a. An impeachment may be continued from one Congress to the next, although the procedural steps vary depending upon the stage in the process.
   b. The Constitution defines the grounds for impeachment as "Treason, Bribery, or other high Crimes and Misdemeanors." However, the meaning and scope of "high Crimes and Misdemeanors" remains in dispute and depends on the interpretation of individual legislators.
   c. The Constitution provides for impeachment of the "President, Vice President, and all civil Officers of the United States." While the outer limits of the "civil Officers" language are not altogether clear, past precedents suggest that it covers at least federal judges and executive officers subject to the Appointments Clause.
   d. Members of the House and Senate are not subject to impeachment because they are not "civil officers." William Blount, a U.S. Senator from Tennessee, was impeached by the House in 1797, but the Senate chose to *expel* him instead of conducting an impeachment trial.

SELECTED READINGS

The Budget Process

Fisher, Louis. Presidential Spending Power. Princeton, N.J.: Princeton University Press, 1975. 345 p. HJ257.2.F57

Keith, Robert and Allen Schick. Manual on the Federal Budget Process. CRS Report 98-720, August 25, 1998.

Schick, Allen. Congress and Money. Washington, D.C.: Urban Institute, 1980. 604 p. HJ2051.S34

Wilmerding, Lucius, Jr. The Spending Power: A History of the Efforts of Congress to Control Expenditures. New Haven, Conn.: Yale University Press, 1943. 317 p. HJ2013.U5W5

Authorization and Appropriation Processes

Devins, Neal E. “Regulation of Government Agencies Through Limitation Riders,” Duke Law Journal, v. 1987, 1987:456.

Fisher, Louis. “Annual Authorizations: Durable Roadblocks to Biennial Budgeting,” Public Budgeting & Finance, v. 3, Spring 1983: 24.

——. “The Authorization-Appropriation Process in Congress: Formal Rules and Informal Practices,” Catholic University Law Review, v. 29, 1979: 51.

Fenno, Richard F., Jr. The Power of the Purse. Boston, Mass.: Little, Brown, 1966. 704 p. JK1074.F4

LeBoeuf, Jacques B. “Limitations on the Use of Appropriations Riders by Congress to Effectuate Substantive Policy Changes,” Hastings Constitutional Law Quarterly, v. 19, Winter 1992: 457.

LeLoup, Lance T. “Appropriations Politics in Congress: The House Appropriations Committee and the Executive Agencies,” Public Budgeting & Finance, v. 4, Winter 1984: 78.

U.S. General Accounting Office, Office of the General Counsel. Principles of Federal Appropriations Law. Vols. I, II, and III. 2004.

The Investigatory Process [See Section III]

The Confirmation Process

Carter, Stephen L. The Confirmation Mess: Cleaning Up the Federal Appointments Process. New York: Basic Books, 1994. 252 p. JK736.C37

Fisher, Louis. Recess Appointments of Federal Judges. CRS Report RL3112, September 5, 2001.

Gerhardt, Michael J. The Federal Appointments Process. Durham and London: Duke University Press, 2000. 400 p. JK731.G47

——. “Toward a Comprehensive Understanding of the Federal Appointments Process,” Harvard Journal of Law and Public Policy, v. 21, no. 4, 1998: 468.

Harris, Joseph P. The Advice and Consent of the Senate: A Study of the Confirmation of Appointments by the United States Senate. Berkeley, Cal.: University of California Press, 1953. 457 p. JK1274.H3

Hogue, Henry. “The Law: Recess Appointments to Article III Courts,” Presidential Studies Quarterly, v. 34, 2004: 656.

Haynes, George H. The Senate of the United States: Its History and Practice. Boston, Mass.: Houghton Mifflin Co., 1938. 2 vols. 1118 p. JK1161.H28

Kim, Haeryon. “Congressional Influence on the FCC: An Analysis of Confirmation Hearings for Commission Chairmen, 1969-1989,” Communications and the Law, v. 15, 1993: 37.

Mackenzie, G. Calvin. The Politics of Presidential Appointments. New York: The Free Press, 1981. 298 p. JK736.M33

Palmer, Betsy. 9/11 Commission Recommendations: The Senate Confirmation Process for Presidential Nominees. CRS Report RL32551, August 30, 2004.

Rosenberg, Morton. The New Vacancies Act: Congress Acts to Protect the Senate's Confirmation Prerogative. CRS Report 98-892, November 2, 1998.

Ross, William G. "The Senate's Constitutional Role in Confirming Cabinet Nominees and Other Executive Officials," Syracuse Law Review, vol. 48, 1998: 1123.

The Impeachment Process

Bazan, Elizabeth B. Impeachment: An Overview of Constitutional Provisions, Procedure, and Practice. CRS Report 99-186, February 27, 1998.

Black, Charles L., Jr. Impeachment: A Handbook. New Haven, Conn.: Yale University Press, 1974. 80 p. LC 73-92315

Bushnell, Eleanor. Crimes, Follies, and Misfortunes: The Federal Impeachment Trials. Urbana, Ill.: University of Chicago Press, 1992. 380 p. KF8781.B87

Gerhardt, Michael J. The Federal Impeachment Process: A Constitutional and Historical Analysis. Princeton, N.J.: Princeton University Press, 1996. 233 p. KF4958.G47

Labowitz, John R. Presidential Impeachment. New Haven: Yale University Press, 1978. 257 p. KF5075.L33

Maskell, Jack. Censure of the President by the Congress. CRS Report 98-343, December 8, 1998.

Posner, Richard A. An Affair of State: The Investigation, Impeachment, and Trial of President Clinton. Cambridge, Mass.: Harvard University Press, 1999. 276 p. KF5076.C57P67

Rae, Nicol C. and Colton C. Campbell. Impeaching Clinton: Partisan Strife on Capitol Hill. Lawrence: University Press of Kansas, 2004. 234 p. E886.2.R435

Rehnquist, William H. Grand Inquests: The Historic Impeachments of Justice Samuel Chase and President Andrew Johnson. New York: William Morrow and Co., 1992. 303 p. E302.6C4R44

U.S. Congress. "Impeachment: Selected Materials," Committee on the Judiciary, House of Representatives, 93rd Congress, 1st session, October 1973. 718 p.

——. "Impeachment: Selected Materials on Procedure," Committee on the Judiciary, House of Representatives, 93rd Congress, 2nd session, January 1974. 900 p.

——. "Constitutional Grounds for Impeachment: Modern Precedents," Committee on the Judiciary, House of Representatives, 105th Congress, 2nd session, Ser. No. 9, November 1998. 94 p.

——. "Impeachment: Selected Materials," Committee on the Judiciary, House of Representatives, 105th Congress, 2nd session, Ser. No. 10, November 1998. 1854 p.

III. INVESTIGATIVE OVERSIGHT

Congressional investigations, often adversarial and confrontational, sustain and vindicate Congress's role in our constitutional scheme of separated powers. The rich history of congressional investigations, from the failed St. Clair expedition in 1792 through Teapot Dome, Watergate, Iran-Contra, and Whitewater, has established, in law and practice, the nature and contours of congressional prerogatives necessary to maintain the integrity of the legislative role in that constitutional scheme.

This section provides a brief overview of some of the more common legal, procedural, and practical issues that committees face in the course of an investigation. Following a summary of the case law developing the scope and limitations of the power of inquiry, the essential tools of investigative oversight —subpoenas, staff interviews and depositions, grants of immunity, and the contempt power — are described. Next, some of the special problems of investigating the executive branch are detailed, with particular emphasis on claims of presidential executive privilege and agency assertions of common law testimonial privileges. The section concludes with a discussion of the role of the minority in the investigatory process.

A. The Legal Basis for Oversight

Numerous Supreme Court precedents recognize a broad and encompassing power in Congress to engage in oversight and investigation that would reach all sources of information necessary for carrying out its legislative function. In the absence of a countervailing constitutional privilege or a self-imposed statutory restriction upon its authority, Congress and its committees have plenary power to compel information needed to discharge its legislative function from executive agencies, private persons, and organizations. Within certain constraints, the information so obtained may be made public.

Although there is no express provision of the Constitution that specifically authorizes Congress to conduct investigations and take testimony for the purposes of performing its legitimate functions, numerous decisions of the Supreme Court have firmly established that the investigatory power of Congress is so essential to the legislative function as to be implied from the general vesting of legislative power in Congress.[1] Thus, in *Eastland v. United States Servicemen's Fund*, the Court explained that "[t]he scope of its power of inquiry . . . is as penetrating and far-reaching as the potential power to enact and appropriate under the Constitution."[2] In *Watkins v. United States,* the Court described the breadth of the power of inquiry: "The power of the Congress to conduct investigations is inherent in the legislative process. That power is broad. It encompasses inquiries concerning the administration of existing laws as well as proposed or possibly needed statutes."[3] The Court went on to emphasize that Congress's investigative power is at its peak when the subject is alleged waste, fraud, abuse, or maladministration within a government department. The investigative power, it stated, "comprehends probes into departments of the Federal Government to expose corruption, inefficiency, or waste."[4]

But while the congressional power of inquiry is broad, it is not unlimited. The Supreme Court has admonished that the power to investigate may be exercised only "in aid of the legislative function"[5] and cannot be used to expose for the sake of exposure alone. The *Watkins* Court underlined these limitations: "There is no general authority to expose the private affairs of individuals without justification in terms of the functions of the Congress . . . nor is the Congress a law enforcement or trial agency. These are functions of the executive and judicial departments of government. No inquiry is an end in itself; it must be related to, and in furtherance of, a legitimate task of the Congress."[6] Moreover, an investigating committee has only the power to inquire into matters within the scope of the authority delegated to it by its parent body.[7] But once having established its jurisdiction and authority and the pertinence of the matter under inquiry to its area of authority, a committee's investigative purview is substantial and wide-ranging.

B. The Tools of Oversight

1. The Subpoena Power

The power of inquiry, with the accompanying process to enforce it, has been deemed "an essential and appropriate auxiliary to the legislative function."[8] A properly authorized subpoena issued by a committee or subcommittee has the same force and effect as a subpoena issued by the parent House itself. To validly issue a subpoena, individual committees or subcommittees must be delegated this authority. Senate Rule XXVI(1) and House Rule XI(2)(m)(1) presently empower all standing committees and subcommittees to require the attendance and testimony of witnesses and the production of documents. Special or select committees must be specifically delegated that authority by Senate or House resolution. The rules or practices of standing committees may restrict the issuance of subpoenas only to full committees or in certain instances allow issuance by a committee chairman alone, with or without the concurrence of the ranking minority member.[9]

Congressional subpoenas are most frequently served by the U.S. marshal's office or by committee staff, or less frequently by the Senate or House Sergeants-At- Arms. Service may be effected anywhere in the United States. The subpoena power reaches aliens in the United States. Securing compliance of United States nationals and aliens living in foreign countries presents more complex problems.

A witness seeking to challenge the legal sufficiency of a subpoena has only limited remedies to raise objections. The Supreme Court has ruled that courts may not enjoin the issuance of a congressional subpoena, holding that the Speech or Debate Clause of the Constitution[10] provides "an absolute bar to judicial interference" with such compulsory process.[11] As a consequence, a witness's sole remedy generally is to refuse to comply, risk being cited for contempt, and then raise the objections as a defense in a contempt prosecution.

Challenges to the legal sufficiency of subpoenas must overcome formidable judicial obstacles. The standard to be applied in determining whether the congressional investigating power has been properly asserted was articulated in *Wilkinson v. United States*:[12] (1) the committee's investigation of the broad subject matter area must be authorized by Congress; (2) the investigation must be pursuant to "a valid legislative purpose;" and (3) the specific inquiries must be pertinent to the broad subject matter areas which have been authorized by the Congress. As to the requirement of "valid legislative purpose," the Supreme Court has made it clear that Congress does not have to state explicitly what it intends to do as a result of an investigation.[13] (See model subpoena at Appendix A.)

2. Staff Depositions

Committees normally rely on informal staff interviews to gather information preparatory to investigations hearings. However, with more frequency in recent years, when specially authorized, congressional committees have utilized staff-conducted depositions as a tool in exercising the investigatory power. Staff depositions afford a number of significant advantages for committees engaged in complex investigations. Staff depositions may assist committees in obtaining sworn testimony quickly and confidentially without the necessity of Members devoting time to lengthy hearings that may be unproductive because witnesses do not have the facts needed by the committee or refuse to cooperate. Depositions are conducted in private and may be more conducive to candid responses than would be the case at a public hearing. Statements made by witnesses that might defame or even tend to incriminate third parties can be verified before they are repeated in an open hearing. Depositions can prepare a committee for the questioning of witnesses at a hearing or provide a screening process that can obviate the need to call some witnesses. The deposition process also allows questioning of witnesses outside of Washington, D.C., thereby avoiding the inconvenience of conducting field hearings requiring the presence of Members.

Moreover, Congress has enhanced the efficacy of the staff deposition process by re-establishing the applicability of 18 U.S.C. § 1001 to false statements made during congressional proceedings, including the taking of depositions.[14]

Certain disadvantages may also inhere. Unrestrained staff may be tempted to engage in tangential inquiries. Also, depositions present a “cold record” of a witness’s testimony and may not be as useful for Members as in-person presentations.

At present, neither house of Congress has rules that expressly authorize staff depositions. On a number occasions such specific authority has been granted pursuant to Senate and House resolutions.[15] When granted, a committee will normally adopt procedures for taking depositions, including provisions for notice (with or without a subpoena), transcription of the deposition, the right to be accompanied by counsel, and the manner in which objections to questions are to be resolved.

3. Congressional Grants of Immunity

The Fifth Amendment to the Constitution provides in part that “no person ... shall be compelled in any criminal case to be a witness against himself....” The privilege against self-incrimination is available to a witness in a congressional investigation.[16] When a witness before a committee asserts this testimonial constitutional privilege, the committee may, upon a two-thirds vote of the full committee, obtain a court order that compels and grants immunity against the use of testimony and information derived from that testimony in a subsequent criminal prosecution. The witness may still be prosecuted on the basis of other evidence. Grants of immunity have figured prominently in a number of major congressional investigations, including Watergate (John Dean and Jeb Magruder) and Iran-Contra (Oliver North and John Poindexter). The decision to grant immunity involves a number of complex issues (see box below), but is ultimately a political decision that Congress makes. As observed by Iran-Contra Independent Counsel Lawrence E. Walsh, “[t]he legislative branch has the power to decide whether it is more important perhaps even to destroy a prosecution than to hold back testimony they need. They make that decision. It is not a judicial decision or a legal decision but a political decision of the highest importance.”[17]

GRANTING IMMUNITY

In determining whether to grant immunity to a witness, a committee might wish to consider, on the one hand, its need for the witness's testimony in order to perform its legislative, oversight, and informing functions, and on the other, the possibility that the witness' immunized congressional testimony could jeopardize a successful criminal prosecution. If a witness is prosecuted after giving immunized testimony, the burden is on the prosecutor to establish that the case was not based on the witness's previous testimony or evidence derived therefrom. Kastigar v. United States, 406 U.S. 441, 460 (1972).

Appellate court decisions reversing the convictions of key Iran-Contra figures Lt. Colonel Oliver North and Rear Admiral John Poindexter appear to have made the prosecutorial burden substantially more difficult, if not insurmountable, in high-profile cases. Despite extraordinary efforts by the independent counsel and his staff to avoid being exposed to any of North's or Poindexter's immunized testimony, and the submission of sealed packets of evidence to the district court to show that the material was obtained independently of any immunized testimony to Congress, the appeals court in both cases remanded the cases for a further determination whether the prosecution had directly or indirectly used immunized testimony. Upon remand in both cases, the independent counsel moved to dismiss the prosecutions upon his determination that he could not meet the strict standards set by the appeals court in its decisions. *See United States* v. *North*, 910 F. 2d 843 (D.C. Cir.), *modified*, 920 F. 2d 940 (D.C. Cir. 1990), *cert denied*, 500 U.S. 941 (1991); *United States* v. *Poindexter*, 951 F. 2d 369 (D.C. Cir. 1991). It is unclear whether a consequence of the ruling was to engender a reluctance on the part of committees to issue immunity grants. Since the enactment of the 1970 statute, congressional committees have obtained approximately 345 immunity orders. Of these, almost half (165) were obtained in connection with the 1978 investigation into the assassinations of President Kennedy and Martin Luther King, Jr. Since 1990, House committees have obtained 31 immunity orders, and Senate committees have obtained 20.

C. Enforcement of the Investigative Power

1. The Contempt Power

While the threat or actual issuance of a subpoena normally provides sufficient leverage to ensure compliance, it is through the contempt power, or its threat, that Congress may act with ultimate force in response to actions that obstruct the legislative process in order to punish the contemnor and/or to remove the obstruction. The Supreme Court early recognized the power as an inherent attribute of Congress's legislative authority, reasoning that if it did not possess this power, it "would be exposed to every indignity and interruption that rudeness, caprice or even conspiracy may mediate against it."[18]

There are three different kinds of contempt proceedings. Both the House and Senate may cite a witness for contempt under their inherent contempt power or under a statutory criminal contempt procedure. The Senate also has a third option, enforcement by means of a statutory civil contempt procedure.[19]

(a) Inherent Contempt

Under the inherent contempt power, the individual is brought before the House or Senate by the Sergeant-at-Arms, tried at the bar of the body, and can be imprisoned. The purpose of the imprisonment or other sanction may be either punitive or coercive. Thus, the witness can be imprisoned for a specified period of time as punishment, or for an indefinite period (but not, at least in the case of the House, beyond the adjournment of a session of the Congress) until he agrees to comply. The inherent contempt power has been recognized by the Supreme Court as inextricably related to Congress's constitutionally-based power to investigate.[20] Between 1795 and 1934 the House and Senate utilized the inherent contempt power over 85 times, in most instances to obtain (successfully) testimony and/or documents. The inherent contempt power has not been exercised by either House in over 70 years. This appears to be because it has been considered too cumbersome and time-consuming to hold contempt trials at the bar of the offended chamber. Moreover, some have argued that the procedure is ineffective because punishment can not extend beyond Congress's adjournment date.

(b) Statutory Criminal Contempt

Congress recognized the problem raised by its inability to punish a contemnor beyond the adjournment of a congressional session. In 1857, Congress enacted a statutory criminal contempt procedure as an alternative to the inherent contempt procedure that, with minor amendments, is codified today at 2 U.S.C. §§192 and 194. A person who has been subpoenaed to testify or produce documents before the House or Senate or a committee and who fails to do so, or who appears but refuses to respond to questions, is guilty of a misdemeanor, punishable by a fine of up to $100,000 and imprisonment for up to one year. A contempt citation must be approved by the subcommittee, the full committee, and the full House or Senate (or by the presiding officer if Congress is not in session). After a contempt has been certified by the President of the Senate or the Speaker of the House, it is the "duty" of the U.S. Attorney "to bring the matter before the grand jury for its action."

The criminal contempt procedure was rarely used until the twentieth century, but since 1935 it has been essentially the exclusive vehicle for punishment of contemptuous conduct. Prior to Watergate, no executive branch official had ever been the target of a criminal contempt proceeding. Since 1975, however, 10 cabinet-level or senior executive officials have been cited for contempt for failure to produce subpoenaed documents by either a subcommittee, a full committee, or by a House.[21] In each instance there was substantial or full compliance with the document demands before the initiation of criminal proceedings. However, following the vote of contempt of EPA Administrator Anne Gorsuch Burford, but before the contempt citation was forwarded to the United States Attorney for grand jury action, the Department of Justice raised the question whether Congress could compel the U.S. Attorney to submit the citation for grand jury consideration. The documents in question were turned over to Congress before the issue was litigated in court. The question of the duty of the U.S. Attorney under section 192 to enforce contempt of Congress citations remains unresolved and has left some uncertainty as to the efficacy of the use of criminal contempt proceedings against executive branch officials.

(c) Civil Contempt

As an alternative to both the inherent contempt power of each house and criminal contempt, a civil contempt procedure is available in the Senate. Upon application of the Senate, the federal district court issues an order to a person refusing, or threatening to refuse, to comply with a Senate subpoena. If the individual still refuses to comply, he may be tried by the court in summary proceedings for contempt of court, with sanctions imposed to coerce compliance. Civil contempt can be more expeditious than a criminal proceeding, and it also provides an element of flexibility, allowing the subpoenaed party to test legal defenses in court without necessarily risking a criminal prosecution. Civil contempt is not authorized for use against executive branch officials refusing to comply with a subpoena except in certain limited circumstances.[22] Since 1979, the Senate has authorized the Office of Senate Legal Counsel to seek civil enforcement of a document subpoena at least 6 times, the last in 1995. None have been against executive branch officials.

2. Perjury and False Statements Prosecutions

(a) Testimony under Oath

A witness under oath before a congressional committee who willfully gives false testimony is subject to prosecution for perjury under section 1621 of title 18 of the United States Code. The false statement must be "willfully" made before a "competent tribunal" and involve a "material matter." For a legislative committee to be competent for perjury purposes a quorum must be present.[23] The problem has been ameliorated in recent years with the adoption of rules establishing less than a majority of members as a quorum for taking testimony, normally two members for House committees[24] and one member for Senate committees.[25] The requisite quorum must be present at the time the alleged perjurious statement is made, not merely at the time the session convenes. No prosecution for perjury will lie for statements made only in the presence of committee staff unless the committee has deposition authority and has taken formal action to allow it.

(b) Unsworn Statements

Most statements made before Congress, at both the investigatory and hearing phases of oversight, are unsworn. The practice of swearing in all witnesses at hearings is infrequent. Prosecutions may be brought to punish congressional witnesses for giving willfully false testimony not under oath. Under 18 U.S.C. § 1001, false statements by a person in "any investigation or review, conducted pursuant to the authority of any committee, subcommittee, commission or office of the Congress, consistent with applicable rules of the House and Senate" are punishable by a fine of up to $250,000 or imprisonment for not more than five years, or both.

D. Executive Privilege and Common Law Testimonial Privileges

Presidential claims of a right to preserve the confidentiality of information and documents in the face of legislative demands have figured prominently, though intermittently, in executive-congressional relations since at least 1792, when President Washington discussed with his cabinet how to respond to a congressional inquiry into the military debacle that befell General St. Clair's expedition.[26] The vast majority of these interbranch disputes have been resolved through political negotiation and accommodation, thus, few have reached the courts for substantive resolution.[27] In fact, it was not until the Watergate-related lawsuits in the 1970's seeking access to President Nixon's tapes that the existence of a presidential confidentiality privilege was judicially established as a necessary derivative of the President's status in our constitutional scheme of separated powers. Of the seven court decisions involving interbranch information access disputes,[28] three have involved Congress and the Executive[29] but only one of these resulted in a decision on the merits.[30] One other case, involving legislation granting custody of President Nixon's presidential records to the Administrator of the General Services Administration, also determined several pertinent executive privilege issues.[31]

The *Nixon* and post-Watergate cases established the broad contours of the presidential communications privilege. Under those precedents, the privilege, which is constitutionally rooted, could be invoked by the President when asked to produce documents or other materials or information that reflect presidential decisionmaking and deliberations that he believes should remain confidential. If the President does so, the materials become presumptively privileged. The privilege, however, is qualified, not absolute, and can be overcome by an adequate showing of need. Finally, while reviewing courts have expressed reluctance to balance executive privilege claims against a congressional demand for information, they have acknowledged they will do so if the political branches have tried in good faith but failed to reach an accommodation.

However, until the Court of Appeals for the District of Columbia Circuit's 1997 ruling in *In re Sealed Case (Espy),*[32] and its 2004 ruling in *Judicial Watch Inc. v. Department of Justice,*[33] these judicial decisions had left important gaps in the law of presidential privilege which increasingly became focal points, if not the source, of interbranch confrontations. Among the more significant issues left open included whether the President has to have actually seen or been familiar with the disputed matter; whether the presidential privilege encompasses documents and information developed by, or in the possession of, officers and employees in the departments and agencies of the Executive Branch; whether the privilege encompasses all communications with respect to which the President may be interested or is it confined to presidential decisionmaking and, if so, is it limited to any particular type of presidential decisionmaking; and precisely what kind of demonstration of need must be shown to justify release of materials that qualify for the privilege. The unanimous panel in *In re Sealed Case* authoritatively addressed each of these issues in a manner that may have drastically altered the future legal playing field in resolving such disputes. The ruling in the *Judicial Watch* case reinforces that likelihood.[34]

1. The Presidential Communications Privilege

In rare instances the executive response to a congressional demand to produce information may be an assertion of presidential executive privilege, a doctrine which, like Congress's powers to investigate and cite for contempt, has constitutional roots. No decision of the Supreme Court has yet resolved the question whether there are any circumstances in which the executive branch can refuse to provide information sought by the Congress is on the basis of executive privilege. Indeed, most such disputes are settled short of litigation through employment of the political process and negotiations,[35] and the few that reach a judicial forum find the courts highly reluctant to rule on the merits. However, in *United States v. Nixon* (1974), involving a judicial subpoena issued to the President at the request of the Watergate special prosecutor,[36] the Supreme Court found a constitutional basis for the doctrine of executive privilege in "the supremacy of each branch within its own assigned area of constitutional duties" and in the separation of powers. Although it considered presidential communications to be "presumptively privileged," the Court rejected the President's contention that the privilege was absolute, thereby precluding judicial review whenever it is asserted. The Court held that the judicial need for the tapes outweighed the President's "generalized interest in confidentiality." The Court was careful to limit the scope of its decision, noting that "we are not here concerned with the balance between the President's generalized interest in confidentiality . . . and congressional demands for information."[37]

In *In re Sealed Case (Espy)*, involving a grand jury subpoena for documents to the White House Counsel's Office during an independent counsel's investigation of allegations of improprieties by the Secretary of Agriculture, an appeals court elaborated on several important issues left unresolved by *Nixon* and other Watergate-related cases: the precise parameters of the presidential executive privilege; how far down the chain of command the privilege reaches; whether the President has to have seen or had knowledge of the existence of the documents for which he claims privilege; and what showing is necessary to overcome a valid claim of privilege. The court held that the presidential communications privilege extended to communications authored by or solicited and received by presidential advisers that involved information regarding governmental operations that ultimately call for direct decision making by the President, but he does not have to actually have seen the documents for which he claims privilege. However, the privilege was held to be confined to White House staff, and not staff in agencies, and then only to White House staff that has "operational proximity" to direct presidential decision making. The claim of privilege may be overcome by a demonstration that each discrete group of subpoenaed materials likely contains important evidence, and that the evidence was not available with due diligence elsewhere, a showing which the court held the independent counsel had made.[38] In *Espy* the appeals court held that the independent counsel had met his burden and ordered the disclosure of the disputed documents.

The District of Columbia Circuit's 2004 decision in *Judicial Watch, Inc. v. Department of Justice*[39] appears to lend substantial support to the above-expressed understanding of *Espy*. The *Judicial Watch* dispute involved requests by Judicial Watch, Inc. for documents concerning pardon applications and pardon grants reviewed by the Justice Department's Office of the Pardon Attorney and the Deputy Attorney General for consideration by President Clinton.[40] Some 4300 documents were withheld on the grounds that they were protected by the presidential communications and deliberative process privileges. The district court held that because the materials sought had been produced for the sole purpose of advising the President on a "quintessential and non-delegable Presidential power" — the exercise of the President's constitutional pardon authority — the extension of the presidential communications privilege to internal Justice Department documents which had not been "solicited and received" by the President or the Office of the President was not warranted.[41] The appeals court reversed, concluding that "internal agency documents that are not solicited and received by the President or his Office are instead protected against disclosure, if at all, by the deliberative process privilege." [42]

Guided by the analysis of the *Espy* ruling, the panel majority emphasized that the "solicited and received" limitation "is necessitated by the principles underlying the presidential communications privilege, and a recognition of the dangers of expanding it too far."[43] *Espy* teaches, the court explained, that the privilege may be invoked only when presidential advisers in close proximity to the President who have significant responsibility for advising him on non-delegable matters requiring direct presidential decisionmaking have solicited and received such documents or communications or the President has received them himself. In rejecting the Government's argument that the privilege should be applicable to all departmental and agency communications related to the Deputy Attorney General's pardon recommendations for the President, the panel majority held that:

> such a bright-line rule is inconsistent with the nature and principles of the presidential communications privilege, as well as the goal of serving the public interest. ... Communications never received by the President or his Office are unlikely to "be revelatory of his deliberations ... nor is there any reason to fear that the Deputy Attorney General's candor or the quality of the Deputy's pardon recommendations would be sacrificed if the presidential communications privilege did not apply to internal documents. ... Any pardon documents, reports or recommendations that the Deputy Attorney General submits to the Office of the President, and any direct communications the Deputy or the Pardon Attorney may have with the White House Counsel or other immediate Presidential advisers will remain protected. ... It is only those documents and recommendations of Department staff that are not submitted by the Deputy Attorney General for the President and are not otherwise received by the Office of the President, that do not fall under the presidential communications privilege.[44]

Indeed, the *Judicial Watch* panel makes it clear that the *Espy* rationale would preclude cabinet department heads from being treated as being part of the President's immediate personal staff or as some unit of the Office of the President:

> Extension of the presidential communications privilege to the Attorney General's delegatee, the Deputy Attorney General, and his staff, on down to the Pardon Attorney and his staff, with the attendant implication for expansion to other Cabinet officers and their staffs, would, as the court pointed out in *In re Sealed Case*, pose a significant risk of expanding to a large swatch of the executive branch a privilege that is bottomed on a recognition of the unique role of the President.[45]

The *Judicial Watch* majority took great pains to explain why *Espy* and the case before it differed from the Nixon and post-Watergate cases. According to the court, "[u]ntil *In re Sealed Case*, the privilege had been tied specifically to direct communications of the President with his immediate White House advisors."[46] The *Espy* court, it explained, was for the first time confronted with the question whether communications that the President's closest advisors make in the course of preparing advise for the President and which the President never saw should also be covered by the presidential privilege. The *Espy* court's answer was to "espouse[ ] a 'limited extension' of the privilege' 'down the chain of command' beyond the President to his immediate White House advisors only," recognizing "the need to ensure that the President would receive full and frank advice with regard to his non-delegable appointment and removal powers, but was also wary of undermining countervailing considerations such as openness in government.... Hence, the [*Espy*] court determined that while 'communications authored or solicited and received' by immediate White House advisors in the Office of the President could qualify under the privilege, communications of staff outside the White House in executive branch agencies that were not solicited and received by such White House advisors could not."[47]

The situation before the *Judicial Watch* court tested the *Espy* principles. While the presidential decision involved — exercise of the President's pardon power — was certainly a non-delegable, core presidential function, the operating officials involved, the Deputy Attorney General and the Pardon Attorney, were deemed to be too remote from the President and his senior White House advisors to be protected. The court conceded that functionally those officials were performing a task directly related to the pardon decision but concluded that an organizational test was more appropriate for confining the potentially broad sweep that would result from a functional test; under the latter test, there would be no limit to the coverage of the presidential communications privilege. In such circumstances, the majority concluded, the lesser protections of the deliberative process privilege would have to suffice.[48] The appeals court ordered the disclosure of 4300 withheld documents.

Since the Kennedy Administration, executive policy directives establish that presidential executive privilege may be asserted only by the President personally. The latest such directive, issued by President Reagan in November 1982, and still in effect, requires that when agency heads believe that a congressional information request raises substantial questions of executive privilege they are to notify and consult with the attorney general and the counsel to the President. If the matter is deemed to justify invocation of the privilege, it is reported to the President who makes his decision (See Reagan memo at Appendix B).

However, a memorandum of September 28, 1994, from White House Counsel Lloyd Cutler to all department and agency general counsels modified the Reagan policy by requiring agency heads directly to notify the White House Counsel of any congressional request for "any document created in the White House . . . or in a department or agency, that contains deliberations of, or advice to or from, the White House" that may raise privilege issues. The White House counsel is to seek an accommodation and, if that does not succeed, he is to consult the attorney general to determine whether to recommend invocation of privilege to the President. The President then determines whether to claim privilege, which is then communicated to the Congress by the White House Counsel. Thus, it would appear that decision making with respect to claims of presidential privilege is now fully centralized in the White House, but that the President must still personally assert the claim. (See Cutler memo at Appendix C.) The current Bush Administration has not taken a public position on the Reagan memorandum or the Cutler modification, but President Bush's sole assertion of executive privilege in December 2001 was issued over his signature.

The current Bush Administration, through presidential signing statements[49] and opinions of the Department of Justice's Office of Legal Counsel (OLC), has articulated a legal view of the breadth and reach of presidential constitutional prerogatives that, if applied to information and documents often sought by congressional committees, would stymie such inquiries.[50] In OLC's view, under the precepts of executive privilege and the unitary executive, Congress may not bypass the procedures the President establishes to authorize disclosure to Congress of classified, privileged, or even non-privileged information by vesting lower-level officers or employees with a right to disclose such information without presidential authorization. Thus, OLC has declared that, "right of disclosure" statutes "unconstitutionally limit the ability of the President and his appointees to supervise and control the work of subordinate officers and employees of the Executive Branch."[51]

The OLC assertions of these broad notions of presidential prerogatives are unaccompanied by any authoritative judicial citations and, as indicated in the above discussion, recent appellate court rulings cast considerable doubt on the broad claims of privilege posited by OLC. Taken together, *Espy* and *Judicial Watch* arguably have effected important qualifications and restraints on the nature, scope and reach of the presidential communications privilege. As established by those cases, and until reviewed by the Supreme Court, to appropriately invoke the privilege the following elements appear to be essential:

1. The protected communication must relate to a "quintessential and non-delegable presidential power." *Espy* and *Judicial Watch* involved the appointment and removal and the pardon powers, respectively. Other core, direct presidential decisionmaking powers include the Commander-in-Chief power, the sole authority to receive ambassadors and other public ministers, the power to negotiate treaties, and the power to grant pardons. It would arguably not include decisionmaking with respect to laws that vest policymaking and implementation authority in the heads of departments and agencies or which allow presidential delegations of authority.
2. The communication must be authored or "solicited and received" by a close White House advisor (or the President). The judicial test is that an advisor must be in "operational proximity" with the President. This effectively means that the scope of the presidential communications privilege extends only to the boundaries of the White House and the Executive Office complex.
3. The presidential communications privilege remains a qualified privilege that may be overcome by a showing of need and unavailability of the information elsewhere by an appropriate investigating authority. The *Espy* court found an adequate showing of need by the Independent Counsel; while in *Judicial Watch*, the court found the privilege did not apply and the deliberative process privilege was unavailing.

2. Common-Law Testimonial Privileges

More common are claims by departments and agencies (and at times by the White House), and by private persons, that common law testimonial privileges, such as the attorney-client, work-product, and deliberative-process privileges, afford a shield to congressional investigative inquiries. Although there has never been a definitive Supreme Court ruling on the question, the strong constitutional underpinnings of the legislative investigatory power, long-standing congressional practice, and recent appellate court rulings casting doubt on the viability of common-law privilege claims by executive officials in the face of grand jury investigations, support the position that committees may determine, on a case-by case basis, whether to accept a claim of privilege.

Thus it is well established by congressional practice that acceptance of a claim of attorney-client, work product, or other common law testimonial privilege before a committee rests in the sound discretion of that committee. Such common-law privileges cannot be claimed as a matter of right by a witness, and a committee can deny them simply because it believes it needs the information sought to be protected in order to accomplish its legislative functions.[52] In actual practice, all committees that have denied claims of privilege have engaged in a process of weighing considerations of legislative need, public policy, and the statutory duties of congressional committees to engage in continuous oversight of the application, administration, and execution of the laws that fall within its jurisdiction, against any possible injury to the witness. Committees, among other factors, have considered whether a court would have recognized the claim in the judicial forum.[53] Moreover, the conclusion that recognition of nonconstitutionally based privileges is a matter of congressional discretion is consistent with both traditional British parliamentary and the Congress's historical practice.[54]

The legal basis for Congress's prerogative in this area is based upon its inherent constitutional prerogative to investigate, which has been long recognized by the Supreme Court as extremely broad and encompassing, and which is at its peak when the subject is fraud, abuse, or maladministration within a government department.[55] Common-law privileges are, on the other hand, judicially-created exceptions to the normal principle of full disclosure in the adversary process, which are to be narrowly construed and have been confined to the judicial forum. These privileges have no constitutional basis.[56] Recent appellate court rulings have cast substantial doubt whether executive branch officials may claim attorney-client, work product or deliberative process privileges in the face of investigative demands of a grand jury.[57]

While no court has as yet recognized the inapplicability of common law testimonial privileges in congressional proceedings,[58] an advisory opinion directly addressing the issue,[59] by Legal Ethics Committee of the District of Columbia Bar in February 1999 provides substantial support for the longstanding congressional practice. The occasion for the ruling arose as a result of an investigation of a Subcommittee of the House Commerce Committee into the circumstances surrounding the planned relocation of the Federal Communications Commission to the Portals office complex.[60] During the course of the inquiry, the Subcommittee sought certain documents from the Portals developer, Mr. Franklin L. Haney. Mr. Haney's refusal to comply resulted in subpoenas for those documents to him and the law firm representing him during the relocation efforts. Haney and the law firm asserted attorney-client privilege in their continued refusal to comply. The law firm sought an opinion from the D.C. Bar's Ethics Committee as to its obligations in the face of the subpoena and a possible contempt citation, but the Bar Committee notified the firm that the question was novel and that no advice could be given until the matter was considered in a plenary session of the committee.[61] The firm continued its refusal to comply until the Subcommittee cited it for contempt, at which time the firm proposed to turn over the documents if the contempt citation was withdrawn. The subcommittee agreed to the proposal.[62]

Subsequently, on February 16, 1999, the D.C. Bar's Ethics Committee issued an opinion vindicating the action taken by the firm. The Ethics Committee, interpreting D.C. Rule of Professional conduct 1.6(d)(2)(A),[63] held that an attorney faced with a congressional subpoena that would reveal client confidences or secrets

> has a professional responsibility to seek to quash or limit the subpoena on all available, legitimate grounds to protect confidential documents and client secrets. If, thereafter, the Congressional subcommittee overrules these objections, orders production of the documents and threatens to hold the lawyer in contempt absent compliance with the subpoena, then, in the absence of a judicial order forbidding the production, the lawyer is permitted, but not required, by the D.C. Rules of Professional Conduct to produce the subpoenaed documents. A directive of a Congressional subcommittee accompanied by a threat of fines and imprisonment

pursuant to federal criminal law satisfies the standard of "required by law" as that phrase is used in D.C. Rule of Professional conduct 1.6(d)(2)(A).

The D.C. Bar opinion urges attorneys to press every appropriate objection to the subpoena until no further avenues of appeal are available, and even suggests that clients might be advised to retain other counsel to institute a third-party action to enjoin compliance,[64] but allows the attorney to relent at the earliest point when he is put in legal jeopardy. The opinion represents the first (and thus far the only) bar in the nation to directly and definitively address the merits of the issue. It is likely to arouse a controversial and sensitive debate,[65] particularly if congressional committees choose to subpoena client documents from attorneys as a matter of course.

Assertions of deliberative process privilege by agencies have not been uncommon in the past. In essence it is argued that congressional demands for information as to what occurred during the policy development process of an agency would unduly interfere, and perhaps "chill," the frank and open internal communications necessary to the quality and integrity of the decisional process. It may also be grounded on the contentions that it protects against premature disclosure of proposed policies before they are fully considered or actually adopted by the agency, and to prevent the public from confusing matters merely considered or discussed during the deliberative process with those on which the decision was based. However, as with claims of attorney-client privilege and work product immunity discussed previously, congressional practice has been to treat their acceptance as discretionary with the committee. Moreover, a recent appellate court decision underlines the understanding that the deliberative process privilege is a common law privilege of agencies that is easily overcome by a showing of need by an investigatory body, and other court rulings and congressional practice have recognized the overriding necessity of an effective legislative oversight process.

The 1997 appeals court ruling in *In re sealed Case (Espy)*,[66] discussed previously, is of special note. The case involved, *inter alia*, White House claims of executive and deliberate process privileges for documents subpoenaed by an independent counsel. At the outset of the appeals court's unanimous ruling it carefully distinguished between the "presidential communications privilege" and the "deliberative process privilege." Both, the court observed, are executive privileges designed to protect the confidentiality of executive branch decisionmaking. But the deliberative process privilege applies to executive branch officials generally, is a common law privilege which requires a lower threshold of need to be overcome, and "disappears altogether when there is any reason to believe government misconduct has occurred."[67] The court's recognition of the deliberative process privilege as a common law privilege which, when claimed by executive department and agency officials, is easily overcome, and which "disappears" upon the reasonable belief by an investigating body that government misconduct has occurred, may severely limit the common law claims of agencies against congressional investigative demands. A demonstration of need of a jurisdictional committee would appear to be sufficient, and a plausible showing of fraud, waste, abuse or maladministration would be conclusive.

E. Investigative Oversight Hearings

1. Jurisdiction and Authority

A congressional committee is a creation of its parent house and only has the power to inquire into matters within the scope of the authority that has been delegated to it by that body. Thus, the enabling rule or resolution which gives the committee life is the charter that defines the grant and limitations of the committee's power. In construing the scope of a committee's authorizing charter, courts will look to the words of the rule or resolution itself, and then, if necessary, to the usual sources of legislative history such as floor debate, legislative reports, past committee practice, and interpretation. Jurisdictional authority for "special" investigations may be given to a standing committee, a joint committee of both houses, or a special subcommittee of a standing committee, among other vehicles. In view of the specificity with which Senate and House rules now confer jurisdiction on standing committees, as well as the care with which most authorizing resolutions for select committees have been drafted in recent years, sufficient models exist to avoid a successful judicial challenge by a witness that his noncompliance was justified by a committee's overstepping its delegated scope of authority.

2. Rules Applicable to Hearings

House Rule XI(2) and Senate Rule XXVI(2) require that committees adopt written rules of procedure and publish them in the *Congressional Record*. The failure to publish has resulted in the invalidation of a perjury prosecution.[68] Once properly promulgated, such rules are judicially cognizable and must be strictly observed. The House and many individual Senate committees require that all witnesses be given a copy of a committee's rules.

Both the House and the Senate have adopted rules permitting a reduced quorum for taking testimony and receiving evidence. House hearings may be conducted if at least two members are present; most Senate committees permit hearings with only one member in attendance. Although most committees have adopted the minimum quorum requirement, some have not, while others require a higher quorum for sworn rather than unsworn testimony. For perjury purposes, the quorum requirement must be met at the time the allegedly perjured testimony is given, not at the beginning of the session. Reduced quorum requirement rules do not apply to authorizations for the issuance of subpoenas. Senate rules require a one-third quorum of a committee or subcommittee while the House requires a quorum of a majority of the members, unless a committee delegates authority for issuance to its chairman.[69]

Senate and House rules limit the authority of their committees to meet in closed session. A House rule provides that testimony "shall" be held in closed session if a majority of a committee or subcommittee determines it "may tend to defame, degrade, or incriminate any person." Such testimony taken in closed session is normally releasable only by a majority vote of the committee. Similarly, confidential material received in a closed session requires a majority vote for release.

3. Conducting Hearings

The chair usually makes an opening statement. In the case of an investigative hearing, it is an important means of defining the subject matter of the hearing and thereby establishing the pertinence of questions asked the witnesses. Not all committees swear in their witnesses; a few committees require that all witnesses be sworn. Most committees leave the swearing of witnesses to the discretion of the chair. If a committee wishes the potential sanction of perjury to apply, it should, in accordance with the statute, administer an oath and swear its witnesses, though it should be noted that false statements not under oath are also subject to criminal sanctions.

A witness does not have a right to make a statement before being questioned but that opportunity is usually accorded. Committee rules may prescribe the length of such statements and also require written statements be submitted in advance of the hearing. Questioning of witnesses may be structured so that members alternate for specified lengths of time. Questioning may also be conducted by staff. Witnesses may be allowed to review a transcript of their testimony and to make nonsubstantive corrections.

The right of a witness to be accompanied by counsel is recognized by House rule and the rules of Senate committees. The House rule limits the role of counsel as solely "for the purpose of advising them concerning their constitutional rights." Some committees have adopted rules specifically prohibiting counsel from "coaching" witnesses during their testimony.[70] A committee has complete authority to control the conduct of counsel. Indeed, House Rule XI(2)(k)(4) provides that "[t]he chairman may punish breaches of order and decorum, and of professional ethics on the part of counsel, by censure or exclusion from the hearings; and the Committee may cite the offender for contempt." Some Senate committees have adopted similar rules.[71] There is no right of cross-examination of adverse witnesses during an investigative hearing. Witnesses are entitled to a range of constitutional protections (see box).

Constitutional Rights of Witnesses

It is well established that the protections of the Bill of Rights extend to witnesses at legislative inquiry and thus may pose significant limitations on congressional investigations. The Fifth Amendment provides that "no person . . . shall be compelled in any criminal case to be a witness against himself." The privilege protects a witness against being compelled to testify subject to a grant of immunity (see pages 35 and 36) but not against a subpoena for existing documentary evidence. However, where compliance with a subpoena *duces tecum* would constitute an implicit testimonial authentication of the documents produced, the privilege may apply. There is no particular formulation of words necessary to invoke the privilege. All that is required is that the witness's objection be stated in a manner that the committee may reasonably expected to understand as an attempt to invoke the privilege.

Although the First Amendment, by its terms, is expressly applicable only to *legislation* that abridges freedom of speech, press, or assembly, the Court has held that the amendment also restricts Congress in conducting investigations. In the leading case involving the application of First Amendment rights in a congressional investigation, *Barenblatt v. United States*, the Court held that "where first amendment rights are asserted to bar government interrogation resolution of the issue always involves a balancing by the courts of the competing private and public interests at stake in the particular circumstances shown." 360 U.S. 109, 162 (1959). Thus, unlike the Fifth Amendment privilege against self-incrimination, the First Amendment does not give a witness an absolute right to refuse to respond to congressional demands for information.

Dicta in opinions of the Supreme Court indicate that the Fourth Amendment's prohibition against unreasonable searches and seizures is applicable to congressional committees. It appears that there must be probable cause for the issuance of a congressional subpoena. The Fourth Amendment protects a congressional witness against a subpoena that is unreasonably broad or burdensome.

F. Specialized Investigations

Oversight at times occurs through specialized, temporary investigations of a specific event or development. These are often dramatic, high profile endeavors, focusing on scandals, alleged abuses of authority, suspected illegal conduct, or other unethical behavior. The stakes are high, possibly even leading to the end of individual careers of high ranking executive officials. Indeed, congressional investigations can induce resignations, firings, and impeachment proceedings and question major policy actions of the executive, as with these notable occasions: the Senate Watergate Committee investigation into the Nixon Administration in the early 1970s; the Church and Pike select committees' inquiries in the mid-1970s into intelligence agency abuses; the 1981 select committee inquiry into the ABSCAM scandal; the 1987 Iran-contra investigation during the Reagan Administration; the multiple investigations of scandals and alleged misconduct during the Clinton Administration; and the Hurricane Katrina probe in 2005 during the Bush Administration. As a consequence, interest — in Congress, the executive, and the public — is frequently intense and impassioned.

PROMINENT SELECT INVESTIGATIVE COMMITTEES

Senate Watergate Committee (1973-74), S.Res. 60, 93rd Congress, 1st session.

"To establish a select committee of the Senate to conduct an investigation and study of the extent, if any, to which illegal, improper, or unethical activities were engaged in by any persons, acting individually or in combination with others, in the presidential election of 1972, or any campaign, canvass, or other activity related to it."

House Select Committee on the Iran-Contra Affair (1987), H.Res. 12, 100th Congress, 1st session.

"The select committee is authorized and directed to conduct a full and complete investigation and study, and to make such findings and recommendations to the House as the select committee deems appropriate," regarding the sale or transfer of arms, technology, or intelligence to Iran or Iraq; the diversion of funds realized in connection with such sales and otherwise, to the anti-government forces in Nicaragua; the violation of any law, agreement, promise, or understanding regarding the reporting to and informing of Congress; operational activities and the conduct of foreign and national security policy by the staff of the National Security Council; authorization and supervision or lack thereof of such matters by the President and other White House personnel; the role of individuals and entities outside the government; other inquiries regarding such matters, by the Attorney General, White House, intelligence community, and Departments of Defense, Justice, and State; and the impact of such matters on public and international confidence in the United States Government.

1. These investigative hearings may be *televised* in the contemporary era, and often result in *extensive news media coverage*.
2. Such investigations may be undertaken by *different organizational arrangements*. These include temporary select committees, standing committees and their subcommittees, specially created subcommittees, or specially commissioned task forces within an existing standing committee.
3. Specially created investigative committees usually have a *short life span* (e.g., six months, one year, or at the longest until the end of a Congress, at which point the panel would have to be reapproved if the inquiry were to continue).
4. The investigative panel often has to *employ additional and special staff*—including investigators, attorneys, auditors, and researchers — because of the added work load and need for specialized expertise in conducting such investigations and in the subject matter. Such staff can be hired under contract from the private sector, transferred from existing congressional offices or committees, transferred from the congressional support agencies, or loaned by executive agencies, including the Federal Bureau of Investigation. The staff would require appropriate security clearances if the inquiry looked into matters of national security.
5. Such special panels have often been vested with investigative authorities not ordinarily available to standing committees. Staff deposition authority is the most commonly given, but given the particular circumstances, special panels have been vested with the authority to obtain tax information, to seek international assistance in information gathering efforts abroad, and to participate in judicial proceedings (see **Table 1**).

Table 1. Special Investigative Authorities of Selected Investigating Committees

	Deposition Authority	International Information Gathering Authority	Tax Information Access Authority	Authority to Participate In Judicial Proceedings
Sen. Select Committee on Watergate[a]	Member/ Staff	No	No	Yes
Nixon Impeachment Proceedings[b]	Member/ Staff	Yes	No	No
Billy Carter Investigation[c]	Staff	No	Yes	No
House Assassinations Inquiry[d]	Member/ Staff	Yes	No	No

Table 1. (Continued)

	Deposition Authority	International Information Gathering Authority	Tax Information Access Authority	Authority to Participate In Judicial Proceedings
Church Committee[e]	Member/ Staff	Yes	No	No
Koreagate[f]	Member/ Staff	Letters Rogatory	No	Yes, by special counsel
ABSCAM (House)[g]	Member	Letters Rogatory	No	Yes, by special counsel
ABSCAM (Senate)[h]	Member/ Staff	No	No	No
Iran-Contra House[i] and Senate[j]	Member/ Staff	Letters Rogatory, Commissions, Depositions	Yes	Yes
Judge Hastings Impeachment[k]	Staff	No	No	No
Judge Nixon Impeachment[l]	Staff	No	No	No
October Surprise[m]	Member/ Staff	Letters Rogatory, Commissions, Depositions	No	Yes
Senate Whitewater(I)[n]	Staff	No	No	No
Senate Whitewater (II)[o]	Staff	Letters Rogatory, Commissions	Yes	No
White House Travel Office[p]	Member/ Staff	No	No	No
House Campaign Finance[q]	Member/ Staff	Letters Rogatory, Commissions	No	No
Senate Campaign Finance[r]	Staff	No	No	No
Select Committee on National Security Commercial Concerns[s]	Member/ Staff	Letters Rogatory, Depositions	Yes	Yes, by House General Counsel
Teamsters Election Investigation[t]	Member/ Staff	No	No	No

Note: More comprehensive compilations of authorities and rules of Senate and House special investigatory committees may be found in Senate Committee on Rules and Administration, "Authority and Rules of Senate Special Investigatory Committees and Other Senate Entities, 1973-97," S.Doc. 105-16, 105th Cong., 1st sess. (1998), and CRS Report 95-949, *Staff Depositions in Congressional Investigations*, by Jay Shampansky., at notes 16 and 18.

a. S.Res. 60 and S.Res. 194, 93rd Cong., (1973).
b. H.Res. 803, 93rd Cong., (1974).
c. 126 Cong. Rec. 19544-46 (1980) (unanimous consent agreement); S.Res. 495, 96th Cong., (1980) (staff deposition authority); S.Res. 496, 96th Cong., (1980) (tax access authority).
d. H.Res. 222, 95th Cong., (1974).
e. S.Res. 21, 94th Cong., (1974).
f. H.Res. 252 and H.Res. 752, 95th Cong., (1977).
g. H.Res. 67, 97th Cong., (1981).
h. S.Res. 350, 97th Cong., (1982).
i. H.Res. 12, 10th Cong., (1987).
j. S.Res. 23, 100th Cong., (1987).
k. H.Res. 320, 100th Cong., (1987).
l. H.Res. 562, 100th Cong., (1988).
m. H.Res. 258, 102nd Cong., (1991).
n. S.Res. 229, 103rd Cong., (1994).
o. S.Res. 120, 104th Cong., (1995).
p. H.Res. 369, 104th Cong., (1996).
q. H.Res. 167, 105th Cong., (1997).
r. S.Res. 54, 105th Cong., (1997)).
s. H.Res. 463, 105th Cong., (1998).
t. H.Res. 507, 105th Cong., (1998).

G. Role of Minority-Party Members In the Investigative Process

The role of members of the minority in the investigatory oversight process is governed by the rules of each house and its committees. While minority members are specifically accorded some rights (e.g., in the House of Representatives, whenever a hearing is conducted on any measure or matter, the minority may, upon the written request of a majority of the minority members to the chairman before the completion of the hearing, call witnesses selected by the minority, and presumably request documents[72]), no House or committee rules authorize either ranking minority members or individual members on their own to institute official committee investigations, hold hearings, or issue subpoenas. Individual members may seek the voluntary cooperation of agency officials or private persons. But no judicial precedent has directly recognized a right in an individual member, other than the chair of a committee,[73] to exercise the authority of a committee in the context of oversight without the permission of a majority of the committee or its chair. Moreover, a 1994 federal district court ruling dismissed the attempt of the then-ranking minority member of the House Banking [now titled Financial Services] Committee to compel disclosure of documents from two agencies under the Freedom of Information Act and the Administrative Procedure Act. The court held that the case was one "in which a congressional plaintiff's dispute is primarily with his or her fellow legislators" and that the ranking minority member's "complaint derives solely from his failure to persuade his colleagues to authorize his request for the documents in question, and that Plaintiff thus has a clear 'collegial remedy' capable of affording him substantial relief."[74]

That court also suggested that the possibility that a "collegial remedy" for the minority exists already, pointing to 5 U.S.C. § 2954, under which small groups of members of the House Government Reform and Senate Governmental Affairs Committees can request information from executive agencies without the need of formal committee action.[75] However, the precise scope and efficacy of this provision is uncertain and a recent federal district court opinion cases doubt on its enforceability by a court.

5 U.S.C. § 2954 is derived from section 2 of the Act of May 29, 1928,[76] which originally referred not to the current committees generally overseeing government agency operations but their predecessors, the House and Senate Committees on Expenditures in the Executive Departments. The principal purpose of the 1928 act, embodied in its first section, was to repeal legislation that required the submission to the Congress of some 128 reports, many of which had become obsolete in part, and which, in any event, were deemed at the time to have no value, serve no useful purpose, and were not printed by the House of Representatives.[77]

Section 2 of the 1928 Act contains the language that has been codified in 5 U.S.C. § 2954. The legislative history, is somewhat mixed on the purpose of that language. The Senate report indicated a limited purpose: to make "it possible to require any report discontinued by the language of this bill to be resubmitted to either House upon its necessity becoming evident to the membership of either body."[78] The House report agreed on that point, but added: "If any information is desired by any Member or Committee upon a particular subject that information can be better secured by a request made by an individual Member or Committee, so framed as to bring out the special information desired."[79]

It is uncertain, then, on how closely 5 U.S.C. § 2954 is tied to the 128 reports abolished by section 1 of the 1928 legislation.[80] Moreover, the provision lacks an explicit enforcement component. Agency refusals to comply would not be subject to existing contempt processes, and the outcome of a civil suit to compel production on the basis of the provision is problematic despite the *Leach* court's suggestion. Further, the provision applies only to the named committees; thus members of all other committees would still face the *Leach* problem. Finally, even members of the named committees are still likely to have to persuade a court that their claim is more than an intramural dispute, that a court has jurisdiction to hear the suit, and that committee members have standing to sue within the narrow parameters set by the Supreme Court in *Raines* v. *Byrd*.[81]

The first attempt to secure court enforcement of a document demand under section 2954 was brought in 2001 in a federal district court.[82] That case involved a request of 16 minority party members of the House Government Reform Committee for information from the Secretary of Commerce for data concerning the 2000 census. The congressional plaintiffs sought declaratory and injunctive relief, arguing that the plain language of section 2954 unambiguously directs agency compliance with information requests and that while resort to the legislative history of the provision is not necessary in such clear language situations, that history is supportive. In addition, the plaintiffs argued that they were entitled to judicial relief because of the agency's direct and particularized rejection of an entitlement specifically granted to them by law. The government argued that because the case had arisen out of a political dispute between Congress and the Executive concerning access to information, the court should refrain from hearing the case in accordance with the doctrine of equitable discretion. Alternatively, the government argued that section 2954 should be construed, in light of its legislative history, and to avoid doubts about its constitutionally, as preserving Congress' access to the information formerly contained in the reports abolished by section 1 of the 1928 Act, but not as guaranteeing an unqualified right of access to information possessed by the executive branch. The district court rejected these arguments and ordered release of the requested census data. The government thereafter moved for reconsideration, raising for the first time the questions whether plaintiffs, as individual legislators, lacked standing under the Supreme Court's ruling in *Raines* v. *Byrd* to sue for institutional injuries and whether the plaintiffs had a right of action under section 2954, the Administrative Procedure Act, or the Mandamus statute to bring suit against the Executive Branch for access to information. The court declined to consider these arguments on the ground that the government could have presented them in support of its original motion to dismiss but did not do so.[83]

On appeal to the Ninth Circuit, the case was argued together with a separate Freedom of Information Act (FOIA) suit for the same census data brought by two Washington State legislators. After oral argument, the appeals court withdrew the submission of *Waxman* v. *Evans*, deferring the case pending its decision in the FOIA suit. The appeals court ruled in favor of the plaintiffs in the FOIA case on October 8, 2002,[84] and on December 6, 2002, declared that the action in *Waxman* was mooted by its FOIA decision and issued an order reversing and vacating the district court's decision, and remanding the case to the district court with instructions to dismiss.[85] On motion of the plaintiffs, the court of appeals modified this order on January 9, 2003, striking its reversal of the district court's ruling, but leaving in effect its order to vacate and dismiss.

A second attempt to secure judicial enforcement of a section 2954 document demand in the same district court was recently rejected. *Waxman* v. *Thompson*,[86] is a suit by 19 Members of the House Government Reform Committee to compel release by the Department of Health and Human Services (HHS) of cost estimates prepared by its Office of Actuary during congressional consideration of Medicare reform legislation in 2003. In addition to asserting a right of access under section 2954, the congressional plaintiffs allege a violation of 5 U.S.C. § 7211, which provides that "[t]he right of employees . . . to furnish information to either House of Congress, or to a committee or member thereof, may not be interfered with or denied." The government opposed the claims, raising the issues of standing under *Raines* v. *Byrd*, jurisdiction of the court to enforce either statute, and the doctrine of equitable discretion.

On July 24, 2006, the district court, applying the guiding principles established by the Supreme Court in the 1997 decision in *Raines v. Byrd*, ruled that the congressional plaintiffs did not have standing to sue.[87] *Raines* involved a challenge to the constitutionality of the Line-Item Veto Act of 1996 by six Members of Congress who had voted against it, alleging that it unconstitutionally diminished the Member's voting power by authorizing the President to "cancel" certain spending and tax measures after he signed them into law, without complying with the requirements of bicameral passage and presentment to the President. In *Raines*, the Supreme Court held that the Member plaintiffs lacked standing because their complaint did not establish that they had suffered an injury that was personal, particularized, and concrete. The Court distinguished between a personal injury to a private right and an institutional or official one, and was of the view that a congressional plaintiff may have standing in a suit against the executive if it is alleged that the plaintiff has suffered either a personal injury (e.g., loss of Member's seat) on an institutional one that is not "abstract or widely dispersed," but amounts to Member vote nullification. The Court concluded that the plaintiffs in *Raines* had alleged an institutional injury that damaged all Members (a reduction of legislative and political power), rather than a personal injury to a private right, which would be more particularized and concrete.[88]

Bound by the Supreme Court's precedent, the district court concluded that when the Secretary refused to produce the documents requested pursuant to section 2954, plaintiffs did not suffer a personal injury as that term is defined by *Raines*. Rather, Congress, on whose behalf the plaintiffs acted, suffered an institutional injury; namely, that its ability to assess the merits of the bill in question was impeded or impaired. Such an injury is precisely of the type that, under *Raines*, deprives individual legislators of standing to sue. Quoting *Raines*, the court noted that the plaintiffs were "not ... singled out for specifically unfavorable treatment as opposed to other Members of their respective bodies," and cannot "claim that they have been deprived of something to which they are *reasonably* entitled," since the alleged injury "runs (in a sense) with the Member's seat, a seat which the Member holds (it might be quite arguably be said) as trustees of his constituents, not as prerogatives of personal power." A violation of section 2954, the court concluded, therefore raises no personal or particularized injury to the plaintiffs, but at most a type of institutional injury which necessarily damages all Members of Congress and both Houses of Congress equally. The plaintiffs' right to request and receive information from the executive branch pursuant to section 2954 would cease once they were no longer in Congress or no longer a member of the House Committee on Government Reform. The right that is asserted, the court observed, runs with their congressional and committee seats, and is not personal to them. The court also noted that no jurisdictional committee has specifically requested that the documents be produced either by an official request or by a subpoena, nor does the legislative history of the provision imply an intent to delegate authority to the requisite number of Members to seek to enforce its provisions judicially.

The rules of the Senate provide substantially more effective means for individual minority-party members to engage in "self-help" to support oversight objectives than afforded their House counterparts. Senate rules emphasize the rights and prerogatives of individual Senators and, therefore, minority groups of Senators.[89] The most important of these rules are those that effectively allow unlimited debate on a bill or amendment unless an extraordinary majority votes to invoke cloture.[90] Senators can use their right to filibuster, or simply the threat of filibuster, to delay or prevent the Senate from engaging in legislative business. The Senate's rules also are a source of other minority rights that can directly or indirectly aid the minority in gaining investigatory rights. For example, the right of extended debate applies in committee as well as on the floor, with one crucial difference: the Senate's cloture rule may not be invoked in committee. Each Senate committee decides for itself how it will control debate, and therefore a filibuster opportunity in a committee may be even greater than on the floor. Also, Senate Rule XXVI prohibits the reporting of any measure or matter from a committee unless a majority of the committee is present, another point of possible tactical leverage. Even beyond the potent power to delay, Senators can promote their goals by taking advantage of other parliamentary rights and opportunities that are provided by the Senate's formal procedures and customary practices, such as are afforded by the processes dealing with floor recognition, committee referrals, and the amending process.[91]

Selected Readings

Beard, Glenn A. Congress v. The Attorney-Client Privilege: A "Full and Frank" Discussion, American Criminal Law Review, v. 35, 1997: 119.

Berger, Raoul. Congressional Subpoenas to Executive Officials. Columbia Law Review, v. 75, 1975: 865.

Berger, Raoul. Executive Privilege: A Constitutional Myth. Cambridge: Harvard University Press, 1974.

Brand. Stanley M. Battle Among the Branches: The Two Hundred Year War. North Carolina Law Review, v. 65, 1987: 901.

Brand, Stanley M. and Connelly, Sean. Constitutional Confrontations: Preserving a Prompt and Orderly Means By Which Congress May Enforce Investigative Demands Against Executive Branch Officials. Catholic University Law Review, v. 36, 1986: 71.

Bush, Joel D. Congressional Executive Access Disputes: Legal Standards and Political Settlements. Journal of Law and Politics, v. 9, Summer 1993: 719.

Clavelaux, Ronald L. The Conflict Between Executive Privilege and Congressional Oversight: The Gorsuch Controversy. Duke Law Journal, v. 1983, No. 6: 1333.

Cole, Lance. The Fifth Amendment and Compelled Production of Personal Documents after United States v. Hubbell — New Protection for Private Papers? American Journal of Criminal Law, v. 29, Spring 2002: 123.

Devins, Neal. Congressional-Executive Information Disputes: A Modest Proposal — Do Nothing. Administrative Law Review, vol. 48, Winter 1996: 109.

Dimock, Marshall E. Congressional Investigating Committees. Baltimore: Johns Hopkins University Press, 1929. JK1123.A2E2

Fisher, Louis. Congressional Access to Executive Branch Information: Legislative Tools. CRS Report RL30966. May 17, 2001.

——. Congressional Investigations: Subpoenas and Contempt Power. CRS Report RL31836. April 2, 2003.

——. The Politics of Executive Privilege. Durham, N.C.: Carolina Academic Press, 2004. 272 p. JK468.S4F57

Ghio, R.S. The Iran-Contra Prosecutions and the Failure of Use Immunity. Stanford Law Review, v. 45, 1992: 229.

Grabow, John C. Congressional Investigations: Law and Practice. New Jersey: Prentice Hall Law and Business, 1988. KF4942.G73

Hamilton, James. The Power to Probe: A Study in Congressional Investigations. New York: Vintage Books, 1976. KF4942.H34

Iraola, Roberts. Congressional Oversight, Executive Privilege, and Requests for Information Relating to Federal Criminal Investigations and Prosecutions. Iowa Law Review, v. 87, 2002: 1559.

Hamilton, James and Grabow John C. A Legislative Proposal for Resolving Executive Privilege Disputes Precipitated by Congressional Subpoenas. Harvard Journal Legislation, v. 21, Winter 1984: 145.

Moreland, Allen B. Congressional Investigations and Private Persons. Southern California Law Review, v. 40, Winter 1967: 189.

Peterson, Todd D. Prosecuting Executive Branch Officials For Contempt Of Congress. New York University Law Review, v. 66, 1991: 563.

——. Congressional Oversight of Open Criminal Investigations. Notre Dame Law Review, v. 75, 2002: 1373.

Relyea, Harold and Shampansky, Jay. Presidential Advisors' Testimony Before Congressional Committees: An Overview. CRS Report RL31351. October 6, 2004.

Roberts, John C. Are Congressional Committees Constitutional? Radical Textualism, Separation of Powers, and the Enactment Process, and the Enactment Process. Case Western Rescue Law Review, v. 52, 2001: 489.

Rosenberg, Morton. Investigative Oversight: An Introduction to the Law, Practice and Procedure of Congressional Inquiry. CRS Report 95-464 A, April 7, 1995.

——. Presidential Claims of Executive Privilege: History, Law, Practice and Recent Developments. CRS Report RL30319, September 21, 1999.

Rosenthal, Paul C. and Grossman, Robert S. Congressional Access to Confidential Information Collected by Federal Agencies. Harvard Journal of Legislation, v. 15, 1977: 74.

Rozell, Mark J. Executive Privilege: Presidential Power, Secrecy, and Accountability. Lawrence: University Press of Kansas, 2002 (2d edition, revised). JK468.S4 R67

Schlesinger, Arthur M., Jr., and Bruns, Rogers (eds.). Congress Investigates: 1792-1974. New York: Chelsea House Publishers. 1975 (5 Vols.). JK 1123.A2 S34

Shampansky, Jay R. Staff Depositions in Congressional Investigations. CRS Report 95-949 A, December 3, 1999.

——. Congress' Contempt Power. CRS Report 86-83A, February 28, 1986.

Shane, Peter M. Legal Disagreement and Negotiation in a Government of Laws: The Case of Executive Privilege Claims Against Congress. Minnesota Law Review, v. 71, February 1987: 461.

Shane, Peter M. Negotiation for Knowledge: Administrative Responses to Congressional Demands For Information. Administrative Law Review, v. 44, Spring 1992: 197.

Sklamberg, Harold. Investigation Versus Protection: The Constitutional Limits on Congress' Power to Immunize Witnesses. North Carolina Law Review, v. 78: November 1999: 153.

Stathis, Stephen W. Executive Cooperation: Presidential Recognition of the Investigative Authority of Congress and the Courts. Journal of Law and Politics, v. 3, Fall 1986: 187.

Taylor, Telford. Grand Inquest: The Story of Congressional Investigations. New York: Simon and Schuster, 1995. KF4942.T38

Tiefer, Charles. Congressional Oversight of the Clinton Administration and Congressional Procedure. Administrative Law Review, v. 50, 1998: 199.

——. The Law: President Bush's First Executive Privilege Claim: The FBI/Boston Investigation. Presidential Studies Quarterly, v. 33, March 2003: 201.

Vermeule, Adrian. The Constitutional Law of Congressional Procedure. University of Chicago Law Review, v. 71, Spring 2004: 361.

Walsh, Lawrence E. The Independent Counsel and the Separation of Powers. Houston Law Review, v. 25, January 1988: 1.

Wald, Patricia and Siegel, Jay. The D.C. Circuit and the Struggle for Control of Presidential Information. Georgetown Law Journal, v. 90, March 2002: 737.

Wright, Ronald F. Congressional Use of Immunity Grants After Iran-Contra. Minnesota Law Review, v. 80, December 1995: 407.

APPENDIX A. ILLUSTRATIVE SUBPOENA

Subpena Duces Tecum

By Authority of the House of Representatives of the Congress of the United States of America

To ..Custodian of Documents International Brotherhood of Teamsters..................

You are hereby commanded to produce the things identified on the attached schedule before the Subcommittee on Oversight and Investigations. Committee on ...Education and the Workforce.............................

of the House of Representatives of the United States, of which the Hon. Pete Hoekstra..........

.... is chairman, by producing such things in Room ...B-346A... of the

.........Rayburn.............. Building ...., in the city of Washington, on

.........March 17, 1998......, at the hour of ....5:00 p.m...............

To .Any staff member or agent of the Committee on Education and the Workfor of the age of 18 years or older or to any United States Marshal to serve and make return.

Witness my hand and the seal of the House of Representatives

of the United States, at the city of Washington, this

.....10th..... day of ......March................, 19..98..

Peter Hoekstra

The Honorable Pete Hoekstra *Chairman.*

Attest:

Robin H Carle

Clerk.

Subpena for..Custodian of Documents....

International Brotherhood of Teamsters

25 Louisiana Avenue, N.W. ....

Washington, D.C. 20001 ....

before the Committee on the Education....

and the Workforce, Subcommittee on

Oversight and Investigations ....

Served....... ....

....

....

....

....

....

.............................**House of Representatives**

GENERAL INSTRUCTIONS

1. In complying with this Subpoena, you are required to produce all responsive documents that are in your possession, custody, or control, whether held by you or your past or present agents, employees, and representatives acting on your behalf. You are also required to produce documents that you have a legal right to obtain, documents that you have a right to copy or have access to, and documents that you have placed in the temporary possession, custody, or control of any third party. No records, documents, data or information called for by this request shall be destroyed, modified, removed or otherwise made inaccessible to the Committee.
2. In the event that any entity, organization or individual denoted in this subpoena has been, or is also known by any other name than that herein denoted, the subpoena shall be read to also include them under that alternative identification.
3. Each document produced shall be produced in a form that renders the document susceptible of copying.
4. Documents produced in response to this subpoena shall be produced together with copies of file labels, dividers or identifying markers with which they were associated when this subpoena was served. Also identify to which paragraph from the subpoena that such documents are responsive.
5. It shall not be a basis for refusal to produce documents that any other person or entity also possesses non-identical or identical copies of the same document.
6. If any of the subpoenaed information is available in machine-readable form (such as punch cards, paper or magnetic tapes, drums, disks, or core storage), state the form in which it is available and provide sufficient detail to allow the information to be copied to a readable format. If the information requested is stored in a computer, indicate whether you have an existing program that will print the records in a readable form.
7. If the subpoena cannot be complied with in full, it shall be complied with to the extent possible, which shall include an explanation of why full compliance is not possible.
8. In the event that a document is withheld on the basis of privilege, provide the following information concerning any such document: (a) the privilege asserted; (b) the type of document; (c) the general subject matter; (d) the date, author and addressee; and (e) the relationship of the author and addressee to each other.
9. If any document responsive to this subpoena was, but no longer is, in your possession, custody, or control, identify the document (stating its date, author, subject and recipients) and explain the circumstances by which the document ceased to be in your possession, or control.
10. If a date set forth in this subpoena referring to a communication, meeting, or other event is inaccurate, but the actual date is known to you or is otherwise apparent from the context of the request, you should produce all documents which would be responsive as if the date were correct.
11. Other than subpoena questions directed at the activities of specified entities or persons, to the extent that information contained in documents sought by this

subpoena may require production of donor lists, or information otherwise enabling the re-creation of donor lists, such identifying information may be redacted.

12. The time period covered by this subpoena is included in the attached Schedule A.
13. This request is continuing in nature. Any record, document, compilation of data or information, not produced because it has not been located or discovered by the return date, shall be produced immediately upon location or discovery subsequent thereto.
14. All documents shall be Bates stamped sequentially and produced sequentially.
15. Two sets of documents shall be delivered, one set for the Majority Staff and one set for the Minority Staff. When documents are produced to the Subcommittee, production sets shall be delivered to the Majority Staff in Room B346 Rayburn House Office Building and the Minority Staff in Room 2101 Rayburn House Office Building.

General Definitions

1. The term "document" means any written, recorded, or graphic matter of any nature whatsoever, regardless of how recorded, and whether original or copy, including, but not limited to, the following: memoranda, reports, expense reports, books, manuals, instructions, financial reports, working papers, records notes, letters, notices, confirmations, telegrams, receipts, appraisals, pamphlets, magazines, newspapers, prospectuses, interoffice and intra office communications, electronic mail (E-mail), contracts, cables, notations of any type of conversation, telephone call, meeting or other communication, bulletins, printed matter, computer printouts, teletypes, invoices, transcripts, diaries, analyses, returns, summaries, minutes, bills, accounts, estimates, projections, comparisons, messages, correspondence, press releases, circulars, financial statements, reviews, opinions, offers, studies and investigations, questionnaires and surveys, and work sheets (and all drafts, preliminary versions, alterations, modifications, revisions, changes, and amendments of any of the foregoing, as well as any attachments or appendices thereto), and graphic or oral records or representations of any kind (including without limitation, photographs, charts, graphs, microfiche, microfilm, videotape, recordings and motion pictures), and electronic, mechanical, and electric records or representations of any kind (including, without limitation, tapes, cassettes, discs, and recordings) and other written, printed, typed, or other graphic or recorded matter of any kind or nature, however produced or reproduced, and whether preserved in writing, film, tape, disc, or videotape. A documents bearing any notation not a part of the original text is to be considered a separate document. A draft or non-identical copy is a separate document within the meaning of this term.
2. The term "communication" means each manner or means of disclosure or exchange of information, regardless of means utilized, whether oral, electronic, by document or otherwise, and whether face to face, in a meeting, by telephone, mail, telexes, discussions, releases, personal delivery, or otherwise.
3. The terms "and" and "or" shall be construed broadly and either conjunctively or disjunctively to bring within the scope of this subpoena any information which might

otherwise be construed to be outside its scope. The singular includes plural number, and vice versa. The masculine includes the feminine and neuter genders.

4. The term "White House" refers to the Executive Office of the President and all of its units including, without limitation, the Office of Administration, the White House Office, the Office of the Vice President, the Office of Science and Technology Policy, the Office of Management and Budget, the United States Trade Representative, the Office of Public Liaison, the Office of Correspondence, the Office of the Deputy Chief of Staff for Policy and Political Affairs, the Office of the Deputy Chief of Staff for White House Operations, the Domestic Policy Council, the Office of Federal Procurement Policy, the Office of Intergovernmental Affairs, the Office of Legislative Affairs, Media Affairs, the National Economic Council, the Office of Policy Development, the Office of Political Affairs, the Office of Presidential Personnel, the Office of the Press Secretary, the Office of Scheduling and Advance, the Council of Economic Advisors, the Council on Environmental Quality, the Executive Residence, the President's Foreign Intelligence Advisory Board, the National Security Council, the Office of National Drug Control, and the Office of Policy Development.

March 10, 1998
Custodian of Documents
International Brotherhood of Teamsters
25 Louisiana Avenue, N.W.
Washington, D.C. 20001

SCHEDULE A

1. All organizational charts and personnel rosters for the International Brotherhood of Teamsters ("Teamsters" or "IBT"), including the DRIVE PAC, in effect during calendar years 1991 through 1997.
2. All IBT operating, finance, and administrative *manuals* in effect during calendar years 1991 through 1997, including, but not limited to those that set forth (1) operating policies, practices, and procedures; (2) internal financial practices and reporting requirements; and (3) authorization, approval, and review responsibilities.
3. All annual audit reports of the IBT for the years 1991 through 1996 performed by the auditing firm of Grant Thornton.
4. All IBT annual reports to its membership and the public for years 1991 through 1997, including copies of IBT annual audited financial statements certified to by independent public accountants.
5. All books and records showing receipts and expenditures, assets and liabilities, profits and losses, and all other records used for recording the financial affairs of the IBT including, journals (or other books of original entry) and ledgers including cash receipts journals, cash disbursements journals, revenue journals, general journals, subledgers, and workpapers reflecting accounting entries.
6. All Federal Income Tax returns filed by the IBT for years 1991 through 1997.

7. All minutes of the General Board, Executive Board, Executive Council, and all Standing Committees, including any internal ethics committees formed to investigate misconduct and corruption, and all handouts and reports prepared and produced at each Committee meeting.
8. All documents referring or relating to, or containing information about, any contribution, donation, expenditure, outlay, in-kind assistance, transfer, loan, or grant (from DRIVE, DRIVE E&L fund, or IBT general treasury) to any of the following entities/organizations:
    a. Citizen Action
    b. Campaign for a Responsible Congress
    c. Project Vote
    d. National Council of Senior Citizens
    e. Vote Now '96
    f. AFL-CIO
    g. AFSCME
    h. Democratic National Committee
    i. Democratic Senatorial Campaign Committee ("DSCC")
    j. Democratic Congressional Campaign Committee ("DCCC")
    k. State Democratic Parties
    l. Clinton-Gore ' 96
    m. SEIU
9. All documents referring or relating to, or containing information about any of the following individuals/entities:
    a. Teamsters for a Corruption Free Union
    b. Teamsters for a Democratic Union
    c. Concerned Teamsters 2000
    d. Martin Davis
    e. Michael Ansara
    f. Jere Nash
    g. Share Group
    h. November Group
    i. Terrence McAuliffe
    j. Charles Blitz
    k. New Party
    l. James P. Hoffa Campaign
    m. Delancy Printing
    n. Axis Enterprises
    o. Barbara Arnold
    p. Peter McGourty
    q. Charles McDonald
    r. Theodore Kheel
10. All documents referring or relating to, or containing information on about, communications between the Teamsters and the White House regarding any of the following issues:
    a. United Parcel Service Strike
    b. Diamond Walnut Company Strike
    c. Pony Express Company organizing efforts
    d. Davis Bacon Act
    e. NAFTA Border Crossings

f. Ron Carey reelection campaign
g. IBT support to 1996 federal election campaigns.
i. All documents referring or relating to, or containing information about, communications between the Teamsters and the Federal Election Commission.

12. All documents referring or relating to, or containing information about, communications between the Teamsters and the Democratic National Committee, DSCC, or DCCC.
13. All documents referring or relating to, or containing information about, communications between the Teamsters and the Clinton-Gore # 96 Campaign Committee.
14. All documents referring or relating to, or containing information about, policies and procedures in effect during 1996 regarding the approval of expenditures from the IBT general treasury, DRIVE E&L fund, and DRIVE PAC.
15. All documents referring or relating to, or containing information about the retention by the IBT of the law firm Covington & Burling and/or Charles Ruff.
16. All documents referring or relating to, or containing information about work for the IBT performed by the firm Palladino & Sutherland and/or Jack Palladino.
17. All documents referring or relating to, or containing information about work for the IBT performed by Ace Investigations and/or Guerrieri, Edmund, and James.
18. All documents referring or relating to, or containing information about IBT involvement in the 1995-1996 Oregon Senate race (Ron Wyden vs. Gordon Smith).
19. All documents referring or relating to, or containing information about, Ron Carey's campaign for reelection as general president of the Teamsters.
20. All documents referring or relating to, or containing information about organization, planning, and operation of the 1996 IBT Convention.
21. All documents referring or relating to, or containing information about the following:
    a. Trish Hoppey
    b. John Latz
    c. any individual with the last name of "Golovner".
    d. Convention Management Group.
22. All documents referring or relating to, or containing information about the Household Finance Corporation.
23. All documents referring or relating to, or containing information about, any "affinity credit card" program or other credit card program sponsored by or participated in by the IBT.
24. A list of all bank accounts held by the International Brotherhood of Teamsters including the name of the bank, account number, and bank address.
25. All documents referring or relating to, or containing information about, payments made by the IBT to any official or employee of the Independent Review Board.
26. Unless otherwise indicated, the time period covered by this subpoena is between January 1991 and December 1997.

APPENDIX B. THE WHITE HOUSE

November 4, 1982

Memorandum for the Heads of Executive Departments and Agencies

Subject: Procedures Governing Responses to Congressional Request for Information

The policy of this administration is to comply with Congressional Requests for information to the fullest extent consistent with the constitutional and statutory obligations of the Executive Branch. While this Administration, like its predecessors, has an obligation to protect the confidentiality of some communications, executive privilege will be asserted only in the most compelling circumstances, and only after careful review demonstrates that assertion of the privilege is necessary. Historically, good faith negotiations between Congress and the executive branch has minimized the need for invoking executive privilege, and this tradition of accommodation should continue as the primary means of resolving conflicts between the Branches. To ensure that every reasonable accommodation is made to the needs of Congress, executive privilege shall not be invoked without specific Presidential authorization.

The Supreme Court has held that the Executive Branch may occasionally find it necessary and proper to preserve the confidentiality of national security secrets, deliberative communications that form a part of the decision-making process, or other information important to the discharge of the Executive Branch's constitutional responsibilities. Legitimate and appropriate claims of privilege should not thoughtlessly be waived. However, to ensure that this Administration acts responsibly and consistently in the exercise of its duties, with due regard for the responsibilities and prerogatives of Congress, the following procedures shall be followed whenever Congressional requests for information raise concerns regarding the confidentiality of the information sought:

1. Congressional requests for information shall be complied with as promptly and as fully as possible, unless it is determined that compliance raises a substantial question of executive privilege. A "substantial question of executive privilege" exists if disclosure of the information requested might significantly impair the national security (including the conduct of foreign relations), the deliberative processes of the Executive Branch or other aspects of the performance of the Executive Branch's constitutional duties.
2. If the head of an executive department or agency ("Department Head") believes, after consultation with department counsel, that compliance with a Congressional request for information raises a substantial question of executive privilege, he shall promptly notify and consult with the Attorney General through the Assistant Attorney General for the Office of Legal Counsel, and shall also promptly notify and consult with the Counsel to the President. If the information requested of a department or agency derives in whole or in part or from information received from another department or agency, the latter entity shall also be consulted as to whether disclosure of the information raises a substantial question of executive privilege.

3. Every effort shall be made to comply with the Congressional request in a manner consistent with the legitimate needs of the Executive Branch. The Department Head, the Attorney "General and the Counsel to the President may, in the exercise of their discretion in the circumstances, determine that executive privilege shall not be invoked and release the requested information.
4. If the Department Head, the Attorney General or the Counsel to the President believes, after consultation, that the circumstances justify invocation of executive privilege, the issue shall be presented to the President by the Counsel to the President, who will advise the Department Head and the Attorney General of the President's decision.
5. Pending a final Presidential decision on the matter, the Department Head shall request the Congressional body to hod its request for the information in abeyance. The Department Head shall expressly indicate that the purpose of this request is to protect the privilege pending a Presidential decision, claim of privilege.
6. If the President decides to invoke executive privilege, the Department Head shall advise the requesting Congressional body that the claim of executive privilege is being made with the specific approval of the President.

Any questions concerning these procedures or related matters should be addressed to the Attorney General, through the Assistant Attorney General for the Office of Legal Counsel, and to the Counsel to the President.

Ronald Reagan

APPENDIX C. THE WHITE HOUSE

September 28, 1994

Memorandum for All Executive Department and Agency General Counsels

From: Lloyd N. Cutler, Special Counsel to the President

Subject: Congressional Requests to Departments and Agencies for Documents Protected by Executive Privilege

The policy of this Administration is to comply with congressional requests for information to the fullest extent consistent with the constitutional and statutory obligations of the Executive Branch. While this Administration, like its predecessors, has an obligation to protect the confidentiality of core communications, executive privilege will be asserted only after careful review demonstrates that assertion of the privilege is necessary to protect Executive Branch prerogatives.

The doctrine of executive privilege protects the confidentiality of deliberations within the White House, including its policy councils, as well as communications between the White House and executive departments and agencies. Executive privilege applies to written and oral communications between and among the White House, its policy councils and Executive Branch agencies, as well as to documents that describe or prepares for such communications (e.g. "talking points"). This has been the view expressed by all recent White House Counsels. In circumstances involving communications relating to investigations of personal wrongdoing by government officials, it is our practice not to assert executive privilege, either, in judicial proceedings or in congressional investigations and hearings. Executive privilege must always be weighed against other competing governmental interests, including the judicial need to obtain relevant evidence, especially in criminal proceedings, and the congressional need to make factual findings for legislative and oversight purposes.

In the last resort, this balancing is usually conducted by the courts. However, when executive privilege is asserted against a congressional request for documents, the courts usually decline to intervene until after the other two branches have exhausted the possibility of working out a satisfactory accommodation. It is our policy to work out such an accommodation whenever we can, without unduly interfering with the President's need to conduct frank exchange of views with his principal advisors.

Historically, good faith negotiations between Congress and the Executive Branch have minimized the need for invoking executive privilege.

Executive privilege belongs to the President, not individual departments or agencies. It is essential that all requests to departments and agencies for information of the type described above be referred to the White House Counsel before any information is furnished. Departments and agencies receiving such request should therefore follow the procedures set forth below, designed to ensure that this Administration acts responsibly and consistently with respect to executive privilege issues, with due regard for the responsibilities and prerogatives of Congress:

First, any document created in the White House, including a White House policy council, or in a department or agency, that contains the deliberations of, or advice to or from, the White House, should be presumptively treated as protected by executive privilege. This is so regardless of the document's location at the time of the request or whether it originated in the White House or in a department or agency.

Second, a department or agency receiving a request for any such document should promptly notify the White House Counsel's Office, and direct any inquiries regarding such a document to the White House Counsel's Office.

Third, the White House Counsel's Office, working together with the department or agency (and, where appropriate, the Department of Justice), will discuss the request with appropriate congressional representatives to determine whether a mutually satisfactory recommendation is available.

Fourth, if efforts to reach a mutually satisfactory accommodation are unsuccessful, and if release of the document would pass a substantial question of executive privilege, the Counsel to the President will consult with the Department of Justice and other affected agencies to determine whether to recommend that the President invoke the privilege.

We believe this policy will facilitate the resolution of issues relating to disclosures to Congress and maximize the opportunity for reaching mutually satisfactory accommodations with Congress. We will of course try to cooperate with reasonable congressional requests for information in ways that preserve the President's ability to exchange frank advice with his immediate staff and the heads of the executive departments and agencies.

IV. Selected Oversight Techniques

Many oversight techniques are self-explanatory. There are several techniques, however, for which explanation or elaboration may prove helpful for a better understanding of their utility.

A. Determine Laws, Programs, Activities, Functions, Advisory Committees, Agencies, and Departments Within Each Committee's Jurisdiction

A basic step in oversight preparation is to determine the laws, programs, activities, functions, advisory committees, agencies, and departments within a committee's jurisdiction. This is essential if a committee is to know the full range of its oversight responsibilities. To accomplish this general goal, House and Senate committees might:

1. Prepare a document, as needed, which outlines for each subcommittee of a standing committee the agencies, laws, programs activities, functions, advisory committees, and required agency reports that fall within its jurisdictional purview.
2. Publish, as needed, a compilation of the all the basic statutes in force within the jurisdiction of each subcommittee or for the committee itself if it has no subcommittees.
3. Request the assistance of the various legislative support agencies (the Congressional Budget Office, the Congressional Research Service, or the Government Accountability Office) in identifying the full range of federal programs and activities under a committee's jurisdiction.

B. Orientation and Periodic Review Hearings with Agencies

1. Oversight hearings (or even "pre-hearings") may be held for the purposes of briefing Members and staff on the organization, operations, and programs of an agency, and determining how an agency intends to implement any new legislation. The hearings can also be used as a way to obtain information on the administration, effectiveness, and economy of agency operations and programs.
2. Agency officials can be noticeably influenced by the knowledge and expectation that they will be called before a congressional committee regularly to account for the activities of their agencies.
3. Such hearings benefit the committee by, for example:
    a. helping committee members keep up-to-date on important administrative developments;
    b. serving as a forum for exchanging and communicating views on pertinent problems and other relevant matters;
    c. providing background information which could assist members in making sound legislative and fiscal judgments;

d. identifying program areas within each committee's jurisdiction that may be vulnerable to waste, fraud, abuse, or mismanagement; and
e. determining whether new laws are needed or whether changes in the administration of existing laws will be sufficient to resolve problems.

4. The ability of committee members during oversight hearings to focus on meaningful issues and to ask penetrating questions will be enhanced if staff have accumulated, organized, and evaluated relevant data, information, and analyses about administrative performance.
   a. Ideally, each standing committee should regularly monitor the application of laws and implementation of programs within its jurisdiction. A prime objective of the "continuous watchfulness" mandate (Section 136) of the Legislative Reorganization Act of 1946 is to encourage committees to take an active and ongoing role in administrative review and not wait for public revelations of agency and program inadequacies before conducting oversight. As Section 136 states in part: "each standing committee of the Senate and House of Representatives shall exercise continuous watchfulness of the execution by the administrative agencies concerned of any laws, the subject matter of which is within the jurisdiction of such committee."
   b. Committee personnel could be assigned to maintain active liaison with appropriate agencies and to record their pertinent findings routinely.
   c. Information compiled in this fashion will be useful not only for regular oversight hearings, but also for oversight hearings called unexpectedly with little opportunity to conduct an extensive background study.
5. It is important that specific letters be directed by the committee to the agency witnesses so that they will be on notice about what they will have to answer. In this way witnesses will be responsive in providing worthwhile testimony at hearings; testify "to the point" and avoid rambling and/or evasive statements; and restrict their use of this kind of answer to questions: "I didn't know you wanted that information."

C. Casework

An important check against bureaucratic indifference or inefficiency is "casework," as noted in Section I. Typically, Members of Congress hear from individual constituents and communities about problems they are having with various federal agencies and departments. As a House member once said:

> Last year, one of my constituents, a 63-year old man who requires kidney dialysis, discovered that he would no longer be receiving Medicare because the Social Security Administration thought he was dead. Like many residents who have problems dealing with the federal bureaucracy, this man contacted my district office and asked for help. Without difficulty, he convinced my staff that he was indeed alive, and we in turn convinced the Social Security Administration to resume sending him benefits.[92]

Casework is important not only in resolving problems that constituents are having with bureaucrats but also in identifying limitations in the law. As a scholar of constituency service explained: "Casework allows ad hoc correction of bureaucratic error, impropriety, and laxity, and can lead a senator or representative to consider changes in laws because of particularly flagrant or persistent problems that casework staff discovered."[93]

D. Audits

1. *Periodic auditing* of executive departments is among the strongest techniques of legislative oversight. Properly utilized, the audit enables Congress to hold executive officers to a strict accounting for their use of public funds and the conduct of their administration.

2. *Government auditing* encompasses more than checking and verifying accounts, transactions, and financial statements. Many federal, state, and some foreign audit agencies are moving in the direction pioneered by Government Accountability Office (GAO), the chief audit agency of Congress of including an evaluation of:
   a. whether claimed *achievements* are *supported* by adequate and reliable evidence and data and are in compliance with legislatively established objectives; and
   b. whether resources are being used efficiently, effectively, and economically.
3. In reviewing the agencies' own evaluations, or in undertaking an initial evaluation, auditors are advised by GAO to ask questions such as the following:
   a. How successful is the program in *accomplishing the intended results*? Could program objectives be achieved at less cost?
   b. Has agency management clearly defined and promulgated the objectives and goals of the program or activity?
   c. Have *performance standards been developed*?
   d. Are *program objectives* sufficiently clear to permit agency management to accomplish effectively the desired program results? Are the objectives of the component parts of the program consistent with overall program objectives?
   e. Are program costs reasonably commensurate with the benefits achieved?
   f. *Have alternative programs or approaches been examined*, or should they be examined to determine whether objectives can be achieved more economically?
   g. Were all studies, such as cost-benefit studies, appropriate for analyzing costs and benefits of alternative approaches?
   h. Is the program producing benefits or detriments that were not contemplated by Congress when it authorized the program?
   i. Is the *information furnished* to Congress by the agency *adequate and sufficiently accurate* to permit Congress to monitor program achievements effectively?
   j. Does top management have *the essential and reliable information* necessary for exercising supervision and control and for ascertaining directions or trends?
   k. Does management have *internal review or audit facilities* adequate for monitoring program operations, identifying program and management problems and weaknesses, and insuring fiscal integrity?
4. In addition to GAO and other governmental audits, Congress may have access to the internal audit reports of agency audit teams.

a. Internal audit reports are designed to meet the needs of *executive* officials.
b. This information is useful in conducting oversight; executive agencies are sometimes reluctant to provide internal audit reports to Congress.
c. A large number of governmental and private organizations conduct audits of expenditures. Every major federal agency, for example, has its own statutory Inspector General and each of the 50 states plus hundreds of local governments have their own audit offices. Many government agencies also contract with public accounting firms to perform financial audits. For assistance in finding audit reports or in learning how to commission audit reports, congressional staff might consult with officials at the GAO, which is the auditing arm of the Congress.

E. Monitoring the *Federal Register*

1. The Federal Register is published daily, Monday through Friday, except official holidays by the Office of the Federal Register, National Archives and Records Administration. It provides a uniform system for making available to the public regulations and legal notices issued by Federal agencies. These include presidential proclamations and executive orders, federal agency documents having general applicability and legal effect, documents required to be published by act of Congress, and other Federal agency documents of public interest. Final regulations are codified by subject in the Code of Federal Regulations.
2. Documents are on file for public inspection in the Office of the Federal Register the day before they are published, unless the issuing agency requests earlier filing. The list of documents on file for public inspection can be accessed via [http://www.nara.gov/fedreg].
3. Regular scrutiny of the Federal Register by committees and staff may help them to identify proposed rules and regulations in their subject areas that merit congressional review as to need and likely effect.
4. The Federal Register is now available and searchable online (see [http://www.acess.gpo.gov/nara]). The Regulatory Information Service Center of the General Services Administration annually issues two publications — the *Unified Agenda of Federal Regulatory and Deregulatory Actions* in April and *The Regulatory Plan and the Unified Agenda of Federal Regulatory and Deregulatory Actions* in October —that provide a wealth of information about proposed and completed regulatory actions of federal agencies. Both documents are available online at [http://reginfo.gov]. Further information about these two publications can be obtained from the center. The center's telephone number is (202) 482-7350 and its e-mail address is RIS@gsa.gov.

F. Special Studies and Investigations by Staff, Support Agencies, Outside Contractors, and Others

1. *Staff Investigations.* The staffs of committees and individual Members play a vital role in the legislative process.
   a. Committee staffs, through field investigations or on-site visits for example, can help a committee develop its own independent evaluation of the effectiveness of laws.
2. *Support Agencies.* The legislative support agencies, directly or indirectly, can assist committees and Members in conducting investigations and reviewing agency performance. (See "Section V" for a discussion of CRS, GAO, and CBO capabilities.)
   a. The Government Accountability Office is the agency most involved in investigations, audits, and program evaluations. It has a large, professional investigative staff and produces numerous reports useful in oversight.
3. *Outside Contractors.* The 1974 Budget Act, as amended, and the Legislative Reorganization Act of 1970 authorize House and Senate committees to enlist the services of individual consultants or organizations to assist them in their work.
   a. A committee might contract with an independent research organization or employ professional investigators for short-term studies.
   b. Committees may also utilize, subject to appropriate approvals, federal and support agency employees to aid them in their oversight activities.
   c. Committees might also establish a voluntary advisory panel to assist them in their work.

G. Communicating with the Media

1. Public exposure of a problem is an effective oversight technique, and will often help bring about a solution to that problem. Public officials often seem much more responsive to correcting deficiencies *after* the issue has been described in widely circulated news stories.
2. Effective communication with the media is based on knowledge and understanding of each of the media forms and the *advantages* and *disadvantages* of each.

   a. Wire Services.
   (1) Timeliness, brevity, and accuracy are the main criteria for dealing with the wire service.
   (2) Personal contact with wire service reporters gets the best results.

   b. Daily Newspapers.
   (1) Obtain information on the operational procedures and deadlines of daily newspapers, and how they are affected by time.
   (2) Since regular news for Monday is usually low, it may be useful to issue statements and releases for "Monday a.m." use.

(3) Saturday usually has the lowest circulation and Sunday has the widest.
(4) Stories for weekend publication should be given to reporters during the middle of the week or earlier.

c. Magazines.

(1) Magazines and other periodicals are generally wider ranging and focus on why something happens, not *what* happened.
(2) Weeklies do not ordinarily respond to Member press conferences and releases in the same manner as the other media; personal meetings and telephone conversations are usually more effective.
(3) *Deadlines Vary*
    (a) Obtain information on operational procedures.
    (b) Weekends are generally production periods for most magazines.

d. Trade Periodicals.

Many of these topically oriented magazines and newsletters are produced by publishing firms which utilize the services of the periodical press galleries in the Capitol.

e. Television.

(1) House and Senate rules identify procedures for radio and television broadcasting of committee hearings. (See House Rule XI and Senate Rule XXVI).
(2) News of a committee's oversight activities may appear in diverse forms on television. For example, it could appear on the networks as a brief report on the morning or evening news, air on a cable news channel, or arise in the course of live House or Senate floor debate telecast over C-SPAN (the Cable Satellite Public Affairs Network).
    Washington-based news organizations may also provide daily television coverage of Congress to independent television stations. Public television and cable news organizations occasionally broadcast live coverage of committee oversight hearings.
(3) To encourage television coverage of a committee's oversight activities, the following checklist might be helpful to staff.
    (a) Alert correspondents and Washington bureau chiefs of upcoming hearings several days in advance via press releases; follow up with personal or telephone notification of certain "must-contact" correspondents.
    (b) Notify the Associated Press, Reuters, and other news services of a scheduled hearing or meeting at least a day in advance. Allow enough lead time to permit inclusion of the committee activity in the wire services' calendar of daily events for the next day.
    (c) If widespread media interest is anticipated, reserve at least a week in advance a hearing room large enough to accommodate television cameras.

(d) Alert interested correspondents or assignment editors when House or Senate floor action is likely on a matter related to the committee's oversight function.
(e) Provide or have available for the media background information on oversight issues awaiting committee action or consideration by the House or Senate.
(f) Consider making committee members readily available for television cameras either before or after any executive sessions (e.g., allowing television crews in briefly at the start to take video footage of the committee, or arranging for a press conference after the committee session).
(g) Videotape, where appropriate committee members discussing topical oversight issues for distribution to interested television stations.
(h) Keep the contact person of each of the network news interview programs ("Meet the Press," etc.) appraised of a committee's oversight activities, and their relevance to topical national issues. Suggest the appearance of committee members on interview programs when a committee oversight issue becomes especially newsworthy.
(i) Be alert to live television interview possibilities for committee members that can be arranged on relatively short notice (e.g., newsmaker interviews on cable news channels).

f. Radio.

(1) Time is of the essence. Radio newsmen want congressional reaction *immediately*, not hours later when the story breaks in the newspaper or on television.
(2) Members who are readily available for quick interviews are frequently broadcast within minutes or the next morning coast-to-coast on hundreds of radio stations. In most cases an interview will be aired repeatedly over a period of several hours.
(3) Congressional offices should contact radio reporters *directly* through the House and Senate press galleries.

g. Press Conferences.

(1) *Time*
- (a) The periods between 10 a.m. and 2 p.m. are often preferable.
- (b) *Early* morning press conferences usually have low attendance because reporters on daily papers do not start work until midmorning.
- (c) Late afternoon press conferences are often unattended because reporters begin to lose news time for that particular day.
- (d) Check with the press galleries. They keep a running log of most scheduled news events and can provide information on possible competition at any time on any day.

(2) *Place*
- (a) Committee rooms are good, but they are frequently in use at the best time for a conference.

(b) A Member's office or the press galleries can be adequate, but keep in mind that the reporters and cameramen need room to operate.

(c) It might be wise to go to the radio-TV galleries after the conference and do a repeat to get electronic coverage.

(3) Notification

(a) Notify the press galleries in *writing* as far in advance as possible.

(b) Also notify the wire services and television networks *directly* at their downtown offices.

(4) Form

(a) A press conference should be viewed as an open house with *everybody* invited and *everybody* welcome.

(b) A brief *opening* statement should be read or summarized. After copies of it have been distributed, the questioning should begin.

(1) Leave plenty of time for questions.

(2) Do not restrict the areas of questioning.

(3) Anticipate the questions and have answers prepared.

(c) The normal time for a routine press conference is about one-half hour.

h. News Releases.

(1) A good news release answers in *one page* or less the questions where, when, who, what, how, why, and, for some topics, how much (e.g., cost) or how many (e.g., beneficiaries).

(2) A good news release should:

(a) contain the name, *telephone number*, and e-mail of your *press contact*;

(b) be for *immediate* release (better than embargo);

(c) quote the Member *directly*;

(d) avoid excessive use of the Member's name;

(e) avoid needless big words, *long* sentences, and *long* paragraphs; and

(f) make the point quickly, clearly, directly, and then end.

i. The Internet and the Media.

(1) Members and committees can use the Internet to communicate with media representatives and constituents to explain their views and positions with respect to oversight activities. The Internet permits lawmakers and committees to rely less on traditional journalistic sources for coverage and more on direct communication with the citizenry.

(2) The Internet can be employed in a variety of ways to mobilize public interest in congressional oversight. For example, lawmakers can conduct on-line discussions with interested citizens or committees can establish their own websites to solicit input from individuals and organizations about executive branch departments and programs.

(3) There are various "bloggers" who now monitor federal spending. A *USA Today* article — "'Blogosphere' Spurs Government Oversight," September 12, 2006, p . 4A — highlights this trend and underscores how more citizen participation in the public realm can promote grater government accountability.

H. Statutory Offices of Inspector General: Establishment and Evolution

Statutory offices of inspector general (OIGs) consolidate responsibility for audits and investigations within a federal agency. Established by public law as permanent, nonpartisan, independent offices, they now exist in more than 60 establishments and entities, including all departments and largest agencies, along with numerous boards and commissions. Under two major enactments — the Inspector General Act of 1978 and its amendments of 1988 — inspectors general (IGs) have been granted substantial independence and powers to carry out their mandate to combat waste, fraud, and abuse. Recent laws have added offices in agencies, funding for special operations, and law enforcement powers to OIGs in establishments. Other initiatives have set up mechanisms to oversee the Gulf Recovery Program, while various legislative proposals have been introduced to increase the IGs' independence and establish new posts.

Responsibilities

The IGs' three principal responsibilities are:

- conducting and supervising audits and investigations relating to the programs and operations of the establishment;
- providing leadership and coordination and recommending policies for activities designed to promote the economy, efficiency, and effectiveness of such programs and operations, and preventing and detecting waste, fraud, and abuse in such programs and operations; and
- providing a means for keeping the establishment head and Congress fully and currently informed about problems and deficiencies relating to such programs and the necessity for and progress of corrective action.

Authority and Duties

To carry out these purposes, IGs have been granted broad authority to: conduct audits and investigations; access directly all records and information of the agency; request assistance from other federal, state, and local government agencies; subpoena information and documents; administer oaths when taking testimony; hire staff and manage their own resources; and receive and respond to complaints from agency employees, whose confidentiality is to be protected. In addition, the Homeland Security Act of 2002 gave law enforcement powers to criminal investigators in offices headed by presidential appointees. IGs, moreover, implement the cash incentive award program in their agency for employee disclosures of waste, fraud, and abuse (5 U.S.C. 4511).

Notwithstanding these powers and duties, IGs are *not* specifically authorized to take corrective action themselves. Along with this, the Inspector General Act prohibits the transfer of "program operating responsibilities" to an IG. The rationale here is that it would be difficult, if not impossible, for IGs to audit or investigate programs and operations impartially and objectively if they were directly involved in carrying them out.

Reporting Requirements

IGs have reporting obligations regarding their findings, conclusions, and recommendations. These include reporting (1) suspected violations of federal criminal law directly and expeditiously to the Attorney General; (2) semiannually to the agency head, who must submit the IG report (along with his or her comments) to Congress within 30 days; and (3) "particularly serious or flagrant problems" immediately to the agency head, who must submit the IG report (with comments) to Congress within seven days. The CIA IG must also report to the Intelligence Committees if the Director or Acting Director is the focus of an investigation or audit. By means of these reports and "otherwise," IGs are to keep the agency head and Congress fully and currently informed. Other means of communication include testifying at congressional hearings; meeting with Members and staff of Congress; and responding to congressional requests for information and reports.

Independence

In addition to having their own powers (e.g., to hire staff and issue subpoenas), the IGs' independent status is reinforced in other ways: protection of their budgets in the larger establishments, qualifications on their appointment and removal, prohibitions on interference with their activities and operations, a proscription on operating responsibilities, and fixing the priorities and projects for their office without outside direction in most cases. One exception to the IGs' rule occurs when a review is required in statute, while another is the contrary: in the few instances when an establishment head prevents or halts an audit or investigation. IGs, of course, may voluntarily conduct a review requested by the agency head, President, or legislators.

Supervision

IGs serve under the "general supervision" of the agency head, reporting exclusively to the head or to the officer next in rank if such authority is delegated. With but a few specified exceptions, neither the agency head nor the officer next in line "shall prevent or prohibit the Inspector General from initiating, carrying out, or completing any audit or investigation, or from issuing any subpoena...." Under the IG Act, the heads of only six agencies — the Departments of Defense, Homeland Security, Justice, and Treasury, plus the U.S. Postal Service and Federal Reserve Board — may prevent the IG from initiating, carrying out, or completing an audit or investigation, or issuing a subpoena, and then only for specified reasons: to preserve national security interests or to protect ongoing criminal investigations, among others. When exercising this power, the department head must transmit an explanatory statement for such action to the House Government Reform Committee, the Senate Homeland Security and Governmental Affairs Committee, and other appropriate congressional panels within 30 days. The CIA IG Act also similarly allows the head to prohibit the inspector general from conducting investigations, audits, or inspections; but he must then notify the House and Senate intelligence panels of his reasons, within seven days.

Appropriations

Presidentially appointed IGs in the larger federal agencies — but not in designated federal entities (DFEs) — are granted a separate appropriations account (a separate budget account in the case of the CIA) for their offices. This prevents agency administrators from limiting, transferring, or otherwise reducing IG funding once it has been specified in law.

Appointment and Removal

Under the Inspector General Act, IGs are to be selected without regard to political affiliation and solely on the basis of integrity and demonstrated ability in accounting, auditing, financial and management analysis, law, public administration, or investigations. The CIA IG, who operates under a different statute, is to be selected under these criteria as well as prior experience in the field of foreign intelligence and in compliance with the security standards of the agency. Presidentially nominated and Senate-confirmed IGs can be removed only by the President. When so doing, he must communicate the reasons to Congress.

However, IGs in the (usually) smaller DFEs are appointed by can be removed by the agency head, who must notify Congress in writing when exercising the power. In the Postal Service, by comparison, the governors appoint the inspector general, one of only two IGs with a set term (seven years) specified in law. The other is in the Capitol Police (five years), who is appointed by and can be removed by the Capitol Police Board. Indirectly, the IG in the Peace Corps also faces an effective limited tenure, because all positions in the entity are restricted to a certain period (from five to 8½ years). Furthermore, the USPS IG is the only one with the qualification that he or she can be removed only "for cause" and then only by the written concurrence of at least seven of the nine governors.

Coordination and Controls

Several presidential orders govern coordination among the IGs and investigating charges of wrongdoing by the IGs themselves and other top echelon officers. The President's Council on Integrity and Efficiency (PCIE) was established in 1981 to coordinate and enhance efforts at promoting integrity and efficiency in government programs and to combat waste, fraud, and abuse (E.O. 12301). Chaired by the Deputy Director of the OMB, the PCIE is composed of the existing statutory IGs plus officials from other relevant agencies. In 1992, the concept was extended to IGs in designated federal entities, through a parallel Executive Council on Integrity and Efficiency (ECIE). Both PCIE and the ECIE now operate under E.O. 12805, issued in 1992. An Intelligence Community Inspectors General Forum — a coordinative body of the inspectors general from the IC agencies along with observers from the FBI and several defense units — also exists. Investigations of alleged wrongdoing by IGs or other high-ranking OIG officials (under the IG act) are governed by a special Integrity Committee, composed of PCIE and ECIE members and chaired by the FBI representative (E.O. 12993), with investigations referred to an appropriate executive agency or to an IG unit.

Establishment

Statutory offices of inspector general been authorized in 63 current federal establishments and entities, including all 15 cabinet departments; major executive branch agencies; independent regulatory commissions; various government corporations and boards; and three legislative branch agencies. All but six of the OIGs — in GPO, LOC, Capitol Police, CIA, ODNI, and the Special Inspector General for Iraq Reconstruction (SIGIR) — are directly and explicitly under the 1978 Inspector General Act. Each office is headed by an inspector general, who is appointed in one of two ways:

(1) 30 are nominated by the President and confirmed by the Senate in the federal establishments, including all departments and the larger agencies under the IG act specifically, plus the CIA under its separate statutory authority (Table 1).
(2) 33 are appointed by the head of the entity in the 28 designated federal entities — usually smaller boards and commissions — and in five other units, where the IGs operate under separate but parallel authority: SIGIR, ONDI, and three legislative agencies (i.e., GPO, LOC, and U.S. Capitol Police) (Table 2).

Table 2. Statutes Authorizing Inspectors General Nominated by the President and Confirmed by the Senate, 1976-Present (current offices are in bold)[a]

Year	Statute	Establishment
1976	P.L. 94-505	Health, Education, and Welfare (now Health and Human Services)
1977	P.L. 95-91	Energy
1978	P.L. 95-452	Agriculture, Commerce, Community Services Administration,[b] Housing and Urban Development, Interior, Labor, Transportation, Environmental Protection Agency, General Services Administration, National Aeronautics and Space Administration, Small Business Administration, Veterans Administration (now the Veterans Affairs Department)
1979	P.L. 96-88	Education
1980	P.L. 96-294	U.S. Synthetic Fuels Corporation[b]
1980	P.L. 96-465	State[c]
1981	P.L. 97-113	Agency for International Development[d]
1982	P.L. 97-252	Defense
1983	P.L. 98-76	Railroad Retirement Board
1986	P.L. 99-399	U.S. Information Agency[b,c]
1987	P.L. 100-213	Arms Control and Disarmament Agency[b,c]
1988	P.L. 100-504	Justice,[e] Treasury, Federal Emergency Management Administration,[b,f] Nuclear Regulatory Commission, Office of Personnel Management
Year	**Statute**	**Establishment**
1989	P.L. 101-73	Resolution Trust Corporation[b]
1989	P.L. 101-193	Central Intelligence Agency[a]
1993	P.L. 103-82	Corporation for National and Community Service
1993	P.L. 103-204	Federal Deposit Insurance Corporation
1994	P.L. 103-296	Social Security Administration
1994	P.L. 103-325	Community Development Financial Institutions Fund[b]
1998	P.L. 105-206	Treasury Inspector General for Tax Administration[g]
2000	P.L. 106-422	Tennessee Valley Authority[h]
2002	P.L. 107-189	Export-Import Bank
2002	P.L. 107-296	Homeland Security[f]

[a] All except the CIA IG are directly under the 1978 Inspector General Act, as amended.

[b] CSA, Synfuels Corporation, USIA, ACDA, RTC, CDFIF, and FEMA have been abolished or transferred.

[c] The State Department IG had also served as the IG for ACDA. In 1998, P.L. 105-277 transferred the functions of ACDA and USIA to the State Department and placed the Broadcasting Board of Governors and the International Broadcasting Bureau under the jurisdiction of the State IG.

[d] The Inspector General in AID may also conduct reviews, investigations, and inspections of the Overseas Private Investment Corporation (22 U.S.C. 2199(e)).

[e] In 2002, P.L. 107-273 expanded the jurisdiction of the Justice OIG to cover all department components, including DEA and the FBI.

[f] P.L. 107-296, which established the Department of Homeland Security, transferred FEMA's functions to it and also granted law enforcement powers to OIG criminal investigators in establishments.

[g] The OIG for Tax Administration in Treasury is the only case where a separate IG, under the 1978 IG Act, exists within an establishment or entity that is otherwise covered by its own statutory IG.

[h] P.L. 106-422, which re-designated TVA as an establishment, also created, in the Treasury Department, a Criminal Investigator Academy to train IG staff and an Inspector General Forensic Laboratory.

Table 3. Designated Federal Entities and Other Agencies with Statutory IGs Appointed by the Head of the Entity or Agency (current offices are in bold)[a]

ACTION[b]	Interstate Commerce Commission[f]
Amtrak	Legal Services Corporation
Appalachian Regional Commission	Library of Congress[aj]
Board of Governors of the Federal Reserve System	National Archives and Records Administration
Board for International Broadcasting[c]	National Credit Union Administration
Coalition Provisional Authority (in Iraq)[a]	National Endowment for the Arts
Commodity Futures Trading Commission	National Endowment for the Humanities
Consumer Product Safety Commission	National Labor Relations Board
Corporation for Public Broadcasting	National Science Foundation
Election Assistance Commission[l]	Office of the Director of National Intelligence[ak]
Equal Employment Opportunity Commission	Panama Canal Commission[g]
Farm Credit Administration	Peace Corps
ACTION[b]	**Interstate Commerce Commission[f]**
Federal Communications Commission	Pension Benefit Guaranty Corporation
Federal Deposit Insurance Corporation[d]	Securities and Exchange Commission
Federal Election Commission	Smithsonian Institution
Federal Home Loan Bank Board[e]	Special Inspector General for Iraq Reconstruction[a]
Federal Housing Finance Board[e]	Tennessee Valley Authority[h]
Federal Labor Relations Authority	United States Capitol Police[aj]
Federal Maritime Commission	United States International Trade Commission
Federal Trade Commission	United States Postal Service[i]
Government Printing Office[a]	

[a] All these agencies — except SIGIR, ODNI, GPO, LOC, and Capitol Police — are considered "designated federal entities" and placed directly under the 1978 IG Act by the 1988 Amendments and subsequent acts. The CPA was dissolved in mid-2004 and its IG was converted to SIGIR.

[b] In 1993, P.L. 103-82 merged ACTION into the new Corporation for National and Community Service.

[c] The BIB was abolished by P.L. 103-236 and its functions transferred to the International Broadcasting Bureau within USIA, which was later abolished and its functions transferred to the State Department.

[d] In 1993, P.L. 103-204 made the IG in FDIC a presidential appointee, subject to Senate confirmation.

[e] In 1989, P.L. 101-73 abolished the FHLBB and placed the new FHFB under the 1988 IG Act.

[f] The ICC was abolished in 1995 by P.L. 104-88.

[g] The Panama Canal Commission, replaced by the Panama Canal Commission Transition Authority, was phased out with the transfer of the Canal to the Republic of Panama (22 U.S.C. 3611).

[h] P.L. 106-422 re-designated TVA as a federal establishment.

[i] In 1996, the U.S. Postal Service Inspector General post was separated from the Chief Postal Inspector. The separated IG is appointed by, and can be removed only by, the governors.

[j] The Legislative Branch Appropriations Act, FY2006 (P.L. 109-55) added IGs to LOC, following the IG Act of 1978 closely, and the Capitol Police, whose IG has specialized responsibilities.

[k] P.L. 108-458 grants the Director of National Intelligence (DNI) full discretion to create and construct an OIG in his Office (based on provisions in the IG Act). This occurred in 2006. ODNI, *Report on the Progress of the DNI in Implementing "the Intelligence Reform Act of 2004,"* May 2006; and House Select Committee on Intelligence, *Intelligence Authorization Act for FY 2007* (H.Rept. 109-411).

[l] P.L. 107-252, the Help America Vote Act of 2002.

Table 4. Tabulation of Existing Federal Establishments, Entities, or Agencies with IGs Authorized in Law

Controlling statute	IGs nominated by President and confirmed by Senate	IGs appointed by head of entity or agency	Total
1978 IG Act, as amended	29	28	57
Other statutes	1[a]	5[b]	6
Total	30	33	63

a. CIA Inspector General.

b. SIGIR, GPO, LOC, U.S. Capitol Police, and ODNI inspectors general.

Recent Initiatives

Initiatives in response to the 2005 Gulf Coast Hurricanes arose to increase OIG capacity and capabilities in overseeing the unprecedented recovery and rebuilding efforts: an initial coordinating team of IGs or deputies from affected agencies has evolved into the Homeland Security Roundtable, chaired by the IG in DHS; a Hurricane Katrina Contract Task Force, established by the Justice Department, includes relevant inspectors general; an official in the DHS office has been designated to direct its effort here; and an additional $15 million for the OIG in Homeland Security was approved (P.L. 109-62). Other proposals include setting up a long-term task force or coordinative mechanism of IGs from relevant agencies and creating an office of inspector general with overarching jurisdiction for gulf recovery programs (H.R. 3737 and 3810, 109th Cong.).

Other suggestions included consolidating DFE OIGs under one or more new presidentially appointed IGs or under a related establishment office (GAO-02-575) and granting law enforcement authority to DFE IGs.

Separate recommendations have arisen in the 110th Congress. H.R. 785 and S. 461 would establish an inspector general for the Judicial Branch, appointed by and removable by the Chief Justice for a renewable four-year term, with authority to investigate and audit matters pertaining to the Judicial Branch. H.R. 3496 would create an IG in the office of the Architect of the Capitol and one in the Washington Metropolitan Area Transit Authority, while another would make the Postal Service IG a presidential appointment (H.R. 22). A far-reaching proposal, advanced to increase the IGs' independence and powers, calls for sending the initial OIG budget requests to Congress and OMB for later comparison with the final amount in the President's budget submission, removing an IG only "for cause," setting a term of office for IGs, establishing a Council of Inspectors General for Integrity and Efficiency in law (thus, replacing the PCIE and ECIE), revising the pay structure for IGs, and granting personnel flexibilities powers to IGs over their own employees (H.R. 2489). Another (S. 680) would increase the pay level for presidentially appointed IGs, set qualifications for the appointment and removal of IGs in designated federal entities, and grant IGs subpoena power in any medium.

I. Reporting, Consultation, and Other Sources of Information

Congressional oversight of the executive is dependent to a large degree upon *information supplied by the agencies being overseen.* In the contemporary era, reporting and prior consultation provisions have increased in an attempt to ensure congressional access to information, statistics, and other data on the workings of the executive. The result is that *approximately 4,000 reports arrive annually* on Capitol Hill. Concerns about unnecessary, duplicative, and wasteful reports, however, have prompted efforts to eliminate these. One such initiative, in part stimulated by earlier recommendations from the Vice President's National Performance Review and from the GAO, resulted in the Federal Reports Elimination and Sunset Acts of 1995 and 1998. Nonetheless, reductions in the number of required reports have not kept pace with new or continuing requirements, such as those identified in the 2001 act to Prevent the Elimination of Certain Reports (P.L. 107-74).

1. Reporting Requirements

Reporting requirements affect executive and administrative agencies and officers, including the President; independent boards and commissions; and federally chartered corporations (as well as the judiciary). These statutory provisions vary in terms of the specificity, detail, and type of information that Congress demands. Reports may be required at periodic intervals, such as semiannually or at the end of a fiscal year, or submitted only if and when a specific event, activity, or set of conditions exists. The reports may also call upon an agency, commission, or officer to

a. make a study and recommendations about a particular problem or concern;

b. alert Congress or particular committees and subcommittees in advance about a proposed or planned activity or operation;
c. provide information about specific on-going or just-completed operations, projects, or programs; or
d. summarize an agency's activities for the year or the prior six months.

EXAMPLES OF REPORTING REQUIREMENTS IN LAW

Initial Requirement in the 1789 Treasury Department Act:

"That it shall be the duty of the Secretary of the Treasury . . . to make report, and give information to either branch of the legislature, in person or in writing (as he may be required), respecting all matters referred to him by the Senate or House of Representatives, or which shall appertain to his office . . . ." 1 Stat. 65-66 (1789)

Reporting on Covert Action in the 1991 Intelligence Oversight Act:

"The President shall ensure that the intelligence committees are kept fully and currently informed of the intelligence activities of the United States, including any significant anticipated intelligence activity . . .

(1) The President shall ensure that any finding [authorizing a covert action] shall be reported to the intelligence committees as soon as possible after such approval and before the initiation of the covert action, except as otherwise provided in paragraph (2) and paragraph (3).

(2) If the President determines that it is essential to limit access to the finding to meet extraordinary circumstances affecting the vital interests of the United States, the finding may be reported to the chairmen and ranking minority members of the intelligence committees, the Speaker and minority leader of the House of Representatives, the majority and minority leaders of the Senate, and such other members of the congressional leadership as may be included by the President.

(3) Whenever a finding is not reported [in advance to the committees], the President shall fully inform the intelligence committees in a timely fashion and shall provide a statement of the reasons for not giving prior notice." 105 Stat. 441-443 (1991)

2. Prior Consultation

In the past, explicit prior consultation provisions were rarely incorporated into law. However, there appears to be an increase in statutory provisions as well as in committee reports that accompany legislation specifying conditions for such discussion (see box).

A provision in the Conference Committee report on the 1978 Ethics in Government Act illustrates this development: "The conferees expect the Attorney General to *consult* with the Judiciary Committees of both Houses of Congress *before* substantially expanding the scope of authority or mandate of the Public Integrity Section of the Criminal Division."

3. Other Significant Sources of Information

A number of general management laws provide for additional sources of information, data, and material that can aid congressional oversight endeavors.

a. **Chief Financial Officers Act of 1990 (104 Stat. 2838).** The CFO act is designed to improve financial management throughout the federal government, through various procedures and mechanisms.
    1. The act created two new posts within OMB, along with a new position of chief financial officer in 23 major federal agencies, including all Cabinet departments; a 24th agency has since been added. Sixteen of these posts are filled by presidential appointees *subject to Senate confirmation*; these are in the 14 Cabinet departments plus the Environmental Protection Agency and the National Aeronautics and Space Administration. The remaining eight CFO positions are in the Agency for International Development, Federal Emergency Management Agency, General Services Administration, National Science Foundation, Nuclear Regulatory Commission, Office of Personnel Management, Small Business Administration, and the Social Security Administration.
    2. The CFO act also provides for improvements in agency systems of accounting, financial management, and internal controls to assure the *issuance of reliable financial information* and to deter fraud, as well as waste and abuse of government resources.
    3. The enactment, furthermore, calls for the production of *complete, reliable, timely, and consistent financial information for use by both the executive and the legislature* in the financing, management, and evaluation of federal programs.

b. **Government Performance and Results Act (107 Stat. 285).** This act — commonly known by the acronym GPRA or the Results Act — requires federal agencies to submit long-range strategic plans and follow-up annual performance plans.
    1. Strategic Plans. The strategic plans specify five-year goals and objectives for agencies, based on their basic missions and underlying statutory or other authority of the agency. These plans, initially required in 1997, were to be developed *in consultation with relevant congressional offices* and with information from "stakeholders" and then *submitted to Congress*.
    2. Annual Performance Plans and Goals. Based on these long-term plans, which may be modified if conditions and agency responsibilities change, the agencies are directed to set annual performance goals and to measure the results of their programs in achieving these goals. The objective of GPRA is to focus on *outcomes* (i.e., the results and accomplishments of a program, such as a decline in the use of illegal drugs for an anti-drug abuse program) rather than outputs (i.e. other measures of agency activity and operations, such as the number of anti-drug agents in the field). The annual plans, which are also *available to Congress*, began with FY1999; the follow-up reports, which began in 2000, are required six months after the end of the fiscal year.

c. **Small Business Regulatory Enforcement Fairness Act of 1996 (110 Stat. 857-874).** Subtitle E of this act established, for the first time, a mechanism by which *Congress can review and disapprove virtually any federal rule or regulation*. It requires that:

1. All agencies promulgating a covered rule must submit a report *to each house of Congress and the Comptroller General,* containing specific information about the rule before it can go into effect.
2. Rules designated by the Office of Management and Budget as "major" may normally not go into effect *until 60 days after submission,* while non-major rules may become effective "as otherwise allowed in law," usually 30 days after publication in the *Federal Register.*
3. All covered rules are subject to *fast-track disapproval by passage of a joint resolution*, even if they have already gone into effect, for a period of at least 60 days. Upon enactment of such a joint resolution, no new rule that is "substantially the same" as the disapproved rule may be issued until it is *specifically authorized by a law* enacted subsequent to the disapproval of the original rule.
4. There can be *no judicial review of actions taken (or not taken) by Congress, the Comptroller General, or OMB*; but the failure of an agency to submit a covered rule for congressional review may be subject to sanction by a federal court.

d. **Paperwork Reduction Act of 1995 (109 Stat. 163).** This most recent version of paperwork reduction legislation builds on a heritage of statutory controls over government paperwork that dates to 1940.

1. Among other things, the current act and its 1980 predecessor more clearly defined the oversight responsibilities of OMB's Office of Information and Regulatory Affairs (OIRA); it is authorized to develop and administer uniform information policies in order to ensure *the availability and accuracy of agency data collection.*
2. Congressional oversight has been strengthened through its subsequent *reauthorizations* and the requirement for *Senate confirmation* of OIRA's administrator.

e. **Federal Managers' Financial Integrity Act (FMFIA) of 1982 (96 Stat. 814).** FMFIA is designed to improve the government's ability to manage its programs by strengthening internal management and financial controls, accounting systems, and financial reports.

1. The internal accounting systems are to be consistent with standards that the *Comptroller General* prescribes, including a requirement that all assets be safeguarded against waste, fraud, loss, unauthorized use, and misappropriation.
2. FMFIA also provides for *ongoing evaluations* of the internal control and accounting systems that protect federal programs against waste, fraud, abuse, and mismanagement.
3. The enactment further mandates that the head of each agency *report annually to the President and Congress* on the condition of these systems and on agency actions to correct any material weakness which the reports identify.
4. FMFIA is also connected to the Chief Financial Officers Act of 1990, which calls upon the director of OMB to submit a financial management *status report to appropriate congressional committees*; part of this chapter is to be a summary of reports on internal accounting and administrative control systems as required by FMFIA.

f. **Cash Management Improvement Act of 1990 (104 Stat. 1058**). This enactment is intended to *improve efficiency, effectiveness, and equity in the exchange of funds* between the federal government and state governments. Its fundamental objective is to prevent either level of government from engaging in cash management practices that allow it to earn interest on cash reserves at the expense of the other.

g. **Information Technology Management Reform Act of 1996 (110 Stat. 679).** This act requires that agencies buy the *best and most cost-effective information technology* available. To do so, the act gave more responsibility to individual agencies, revoking the primary role that the General Services Administration had played previously, and established the position of chief information officer (CIO) in federal agencies to provide relevant advice to agency heads.

h. **Federal Advisory Committee Act.** Congress formally acknowledged the merits of using advisory committees to obtain expert views drawn from business, academic, government, and other interests when it enacted the Federal Advisory Committee Act (FACA) in 1972 (5 U.S.C. Appendix; 86 Stat. 700). Congressional enactment of FACA established the first requirements for the management and oversight of federal advisory committees to ensure impartial and relevant expertise. As required by FACA, the General Services Administration (GSA) administers and provides management guidelines for advisory committees. GSA also submits an annual report to the President and Congress, based on the information provided by the federal agencies concerning the meetings, costs, and membership of advisory committees. During FY2003, GSA reported a total of 953 advisory committees, with 31,385 individuals serving as members during the year. On March 14, 2000, GSA announced the elimination of its annual report on advisory committees, relying instead on its website to make available the detailed reports covering each committee's activities during the fiscal year [http://fido.gov/facadatabase]. GSA also issues an annual summary report for Congress pertaining to advisory committee management and performance.

i. **Federal Information Security Management Act of 2002.** The Federal Information Security Management Act of 2002 (FISMA) replaced what has been commonly referred to as the Government Information Security Reform Act (GISRA),which expired at the end of the 107th Congress. Both GISRA and FISMA represent an effort by Congress to improve federal agency compliance with information security standards and guidelines. Congress put into statute certain requirements, including a directive that federal agencies submit their information security programs to an annual independent review, along with a requirement that the Director of the Office of Management and Budget report the results of these reviews to Congress.

j. **Accountability of Tax Dollars Act of 2002.** The Accountability of Tax Dollars Act (ATDA) of 2002 (P.L. 107-289; 116 Stat. 2049) was intended "to expand the types of Federal agencies that are required to prepare audited financial statements to all executive branch agencies in the federal government." In fact, ATDA brings almost all executive branch agencies under the requirement for preparation of annual audited financial statements that previously applied only to the 24 major departments and agencies covered by the Chief Financial Officers (CFO) Act. Specifically, Section 2(a) changes the list of agencies covered by the audited annual financial statements requirement in 31 U.S.C. § 3515 by deleting the cross-reference to CFO Act agencies and inserting "each covered executive agency."

k. **Federal Financial Management Improvement Act of 1996.** The Federal Financial Management Improvement Act of 1996 (FFMIA) (110 Stat. 3009-389; 31 U.S.C. § 3512 note) incorporates in statute certain financial management system requirements already established as executive branch policy. The law also requires auditors to report on agency compliance with these requirements, and agency heads and management to correct deficiencies within certain time periods. FFMIA reflects an ongoing effort to reform financial management in the federal government. The 1996 law builds upon prior legislation, including the Chief Financial Officers Act of 1990, the Government Performance and Results Act of 1993, and the Government Management Reform Act of 1994.

l. **Unfunded Mandates Reform Act of 1995.** After considerable debate, the Unfunded Mandates Reform Act (P.L. 104-4; 109 Stat. 48-71; 2 U.S.C. §§ 1501-1571) was enacted early in the 104th Congress. Generally, unfunded intergovernmental mandates include responsibilities or duties that federal programs, standards, or requirements impose on governments at other levels without providing for the payment of the costs of carrying out these responsibilities or duties. The intent of the mandate legislation was to limit the ability of the federal government to impose costs on state and local governments through unfunded mandates. The enactment has three components: revised congressional procedures regarding future mandates; new requirements for federal agency regulatory actions; and authorization for a study of existing mandates to evaluate their current usefulness. The primary objective was to create procedures that would retard and spotlight, if not stop, congressional authorization of new unfunded mandates on state and local governments.

m. **Federal Funding Accountability and Transparency Act.** On September 26, 2006, President George W. Bush signed into law the Federal Funding Accountability and Transparency Act (P.L. 109-282; 31 U.S.C. § 6101). This Act requires OMB by 2008 to launch a searchable, free, and public website that will enable anyone to go online to find information that names the recipients and dollar amounts of most federal grants, loans, and contracts. A key concept of the new law is to provide citizens with greater transparency as to how Federal funds are spent and thus be better able to hold public officials accountable for funding decisions.

J. Resolutions of Inquiry

The House of Representatives can call upon the executive for factual information through resolutions of inquiry.

1. This is a *simple resolution*, approved by only the House.
2. Resolutions of inquiry are addressed to either the President or heads of departments and agencies to supply specific factual information to the chamber. The resolutions usually "*request*" the President or "*direct*" administrative heads to supply such information. In calling upon the President for information, especially about foreign affairs, the qualifying phrase — "if not incompatible with the public interest" — is often added.
3. Such resolutions are to ask for facts, documents, or specific information; these devices are *not* to request an opinion or require an investigation (see box).
4. Even when a committee of jurisdiction reports a resolution of inquiry adversely, or succeeds in tabling the resolution on the House floor, it is often the case that the Administration has substantially complied with the resolution.
5. Resolutions of inquiry can be instrumental in triggering other congressional methods of obtaining information, such as through supplemental hearings or the regular legislative process.
6. A resolution of inquiry is privileged and may be considered in the House after it is reported. If the resolution is not reported within 14 legislative days after its introduction, any Member can move to discharge the committee of jurisdiction and bring the resolution to the floor. However, action by a committee within the 14 days to reject the resolution effectively sidetracks House action on the resolution.

RESOLUTIONS OF INQUIRY IN PRACTICE

The initial resolution of inquiry was approved on March 24, 1796, when the House sought documents in connection with the Jay Treaty negotiations:

Resolved, That the President of the United States be requested to lay before this House a copy of the instructions to the minister of the United States, who negotiated the treaty with the King of Great Britain . . . together with the correspondence and other documents relative to the said treaty; excepting such of the said papers as any existing negotiation may render improper to be delivered. (*Journal of the House of Representatives*, 4th Cong., 1st sess., March 24, 1796. p. 480.)

A contemporary illustration occurred on March 1, 1995, when the House adopted H. Res. 80, as amended (104th Cong., 1st sess.), 407-21. The resolution sought information about the Mexican peso crisis at the time and an Administration plan to use up to $20 billion in resources from the Exchange Stabilization Fund to help stabilize the Mexican currency and financial system. The resolution read:

"*Resolved,* That the President, is hereby requested to provide the House of Representatives (consistent with the rules of the House), not later than 14 days after the adoption of this resolution, the following documents in the possession of the executive branch, if not inconsistent with he public interest . . ." The House request then specified the matters that the documents were to cover: The condition of the Mexican economy; consultations between the Government of Mexico, on the one hand, and the U.S. Secretary of the Treasury and/or the International Monetary fund, on the other; market policies and tax policies of the Mexican Government; and repayment agreements between Mexico and the United States; among other things.

K. Limitations and Riders on Appropriations

Congress uses a two-step legislative procedure: authorization of programs in bills reported by legislative committees followed by the financing of those programs in bills reported by the Committees on Appropriations. Congressional rules generally keep the two stages distinct and sequential. Authorizations should not be in general appropriation bills, nor appropriations in authorization measures. However, there are various exceptions to the general principle that Congress should not make policy through the appropriations process. One exception is the practice of permitting "limitations" in an appropriations bill. "Riders" (language extraneous to the subject of the bill) are also added to control agency actions.

1. **Limitations.** Although House rules forbid in any general appropriations bill a provision "changing existing law," certain "limitations" may be admitted. "Just as the House under its rules may decline to appropriate for a purpose authorized by law, so it may by limitation prohibit the use of the money for part of the purpose while appropriating for the remainder of it." Constitution, Jefferson's Manual, and Rules of the House of Representatives, H. Doc. No. 106-320, 106th Cong., 2d Sess. §1053 (2001). Limitations can be an effective device in oversight by strengthening Congress's ability to exercise control over federal spending and to reduce unnecessary or undesired expenditures. Under House Rule XXI, no provision changing existing law can be reported in any general appropriation bill "except germane provisions that retrench expenditures by the reduction of amounts of money covered by the bill" (the Holman rule). Rule XXI was amended in 1983 in an effort to restrict the number of limitations on appropriations bills. The rule was changed again in 1995 by granting the majority leader a central role in determining consideration of limitation amendments. The procedures for limitation in the House are set forth in the *Congressional Record* for January 6, 1999, p. H29. A well-known limitation is the Hyde amendment, which since the 1970s has restricted the use of Medicaid funds to fund abortions for indigent women (see box).

> "None of the funds appropriated under this Act shall be expended for any abortion ... [except] (1) if the pregnancy is the result of an act of rape or incest; or (2) in the case where a woman suffers from a physical disorder, physical injury, or physical illness, including a life-endangering physical condition caused by or arising from the pregnancy itself, that would, as certified by a physician, place the woman in danger of death unless an abortion is performed." Labor-HHS Appropriations Act for fiscal 1998, 111 Stat. 1516, sec. 509 & 510 (1997).

2. **Riders.** Unlike limitations, legislative riders are extraneous to the subject matter of the bill to which they are added. Riders appear in both authorization bills and appropriations bills. In the latter, they may be subject to a point of order in the House on the ground that they are attempts to place legislation in an appropriations bill. In the Senate, Rule XVI prohibits on a point of order the addition to general appropriations bills of amendments that are legislative or non-germane. Both chambers have procedures to waive these prohibitions (see box on pg 103).

(a) No later than six months after the date of enactment of this Act, the Secretary of Homeland Security shall issue interim final regulations establishing risk-based performance standards for security of chemical facilities and requiring vulnerability assessments and the development and implementation of site security plans for chemical facilities: Provided, That such regulations shall apply to chemical facilities that, in the discretion of the Secretary, present high levels of security risk: Provided further, That such regulations shall permit each such facility, in developing and implementing site security plans, to select layered security measures that, in combination, appropriately address the vulnerability assessment and the risk-based performance standards for security for the facility: Provided further, That the Secretary may not disapprove a site security plan submitted under this section based on the presence or absence of a particular security measure, but the Secretary may disapprove a site security plan if the plan fails to satisfy the risk-based performance standards established by this section: Provided further, That the Secretary may approve alternative security programs established by private sector entities, Federal, State, or local authorities, or other applicable laws if the Secretary determines that the requirements of such programs meet the requirements of this section and the interim regulations: Provided further, That the Secretary shall review and approve each vulnerability assessment and site security plan required under this section: Provided further, That the Secretary shall not apply regulations issued pursuant to this section to facilities regulated pursuant to the Maritime Transportation Security Act of 2002, Public Law 107-295, as amended; Public Water Systems, as defined by section 1401 of the Safe Drinking Water Act, Public Law 93-523, as amended; Treatment Works as defined in section 212 of the Federal Water Pollution Control Act, Public Law 92-500, as amended; any facility owned or operated by the Department of Defense or the Department of Energy, or any facility subject to regulation by the Nuclear Regulatory Commission.

(b) Interim regulations issued under this section shall apply until the effective date of interim or final regulations promulgated under other laws that establish requirements and standards referred to in subsection (a) and expressly supersede this section: Provided, That the authority provided by this section shall terminate three years after the date of enactment of this Act.

(c) Notwithstanding any other provision of law and subsection (b), information developed under this section, including vulnerability assessments, site security plans, and other security related information, records, and documents shall be given protections from public disclosure consistent with similar information developed by chemical facilities subject to regulation under section 70103 of title 46, United States Code: Provided, That this subsection does not prohibit the sharing of such information, as the Secretary deems appropriate, with State and local government officials possessing the necessary security clearances, including law enforcement officials and first responders, for the purpose of carrying out this section, provided that such information may not be disclosed pursuant to any State or local law: Provided further, That in any proceeding to enforce this section, vulnerability assessments, site security plans, and other information submitted to or obtained by the Secretary under this section, and related vulnerability or security information, shall be treated as if the information were classified material.

(d) Any person who violates an order issued under this section shall be liable for a civil penalty under section 70119(a) of title 46, United States Code: Provided, That nothing in this section confers upon any person except the Secretary a right of action against an owner or operator of a chemical facility to enforce any provision of this section.

(e) The Secretary of Homeland Security shall audit and inspect chemical facilities for the purposes of determining compliance with the regulations issued pursuant to this section.

(f) Nothing in this section shall be construed to supersede, amend, alter, or affect any Federal law that regulates the manufacture, distribution in commerce, use, sale, other treatment, or disposal of chemical substances or mixtures.

(g) If the Secretary determines that a chemical facility is not in compliance with this section, the Secretary shall provide the owner or operator with written notification (including a clear explanation of deficiencies in the vulnerability assessment and site security plan) and opportunity for consultation, and issue an order to comply by such date as the Secretary determines to be appropriate under the circumstances: Provided, That if the owner or operator continues to be in noncompliance, the Secretary may issue an order for the facility to cease operation, until the owner or operator complies with the order. Department of Homeland Security Appropriations Act, 2007, P.L. 109-295 § 550, 120 Stat. 1355 (2006).

L. Legislative Veto and Advance Notice

Many acts of Congress have delegated authority to the executive branch on the condition that proposed executive actions be submitted to Congress for review and possible disapproval before they can be put into effect. This way of ensuring continuing oversight of policy areas follows two paths: the legislative veto and advance notification.

1. Legislative Veto

Beginning in 1932, Congress delegated authority to the executive branch with the condition that proposed executive actions would be first submitted to Congress and subjected to disapproval by either house or disapproval by both houses acting through a concurrent resolution. Over the years, other types of legislative veto were added, allowing Congress to control executive branch actions without having to enact a law. In 1983, the Supreme Court ruled that the legislative veto was unconstitutional on the ground that all exercises of legislative power that affect the rights, duties, and relations of persons outside the legislative branch must satisfy the constitutional requirements of bicameralism and presentment of a bill or resolution to the President for his signature or veto. *INS v. Chadha*, 462 U.S. 919 (1983). Despite this ruling, Congress has continued to enact proscribed legislative vetoes and it has also relied on informal arrangements to provide comparable controls.

a. Legislative Vetoes in Statute

Congress responded to *Chadha* by converting some of the one-house and two-house legislative vetoes to joint resolutions of approval or disapproval, thus satisfying the requirements of bicameralism and presentment. However, Congress continues to rely on legislative vetoes. Since the *Chadha* decision, more than 400 legislative vetoes have been enacted into public law, usually in appropriations acts. These legislative vetoes are exercised by the Appropriations Committees. Typically, funds may not be used or an executive action may not begin until the Appropriations Committees have approved or, at least, not disapproved the planned action, often within a specified time limit (see box).

For the appropriation account "Transportation Administrative Service Center," no assessments may be levied against any program, budget activity, subactivity or project funded by this statute "unless notice of such assessments and the basis therefore are presented to the House and Senate Committees on Appropriations and are approved by such Committees." Department of Transportation and Related Agencies Appropriations Act 2001, 114 Stat. 1356A-2 (2000).

b. Informal Legislative Vetoes

Unlike a formal legislative veto, where the arrangement is spelled out in the law, the informal legislative veto occurs where an executive official pledges not to proceed with an activity until Congress or certain committees agree to it. An example of this appeared during the 101st Congress; in the "bipartisan accord" on funding the contras in Nicaragua, the Administration pledged that no funds would be obligated beyond November 30, 1989, unless affirmed by letter from the relevant authorization and appropriations committees and the bipartisan leadership of Congress.

2. Advance Notification or Report-and-Wait

Statutory provisions may stipulate that before a particular activity can be undertaken by the executive branch or funds obligated, Congress must first be advised or informed, ordinarily through a full written statement, of what is being proposed. These statutory provisions usually provide for a period of time during which action by the executive must be deferred, giving Congress an opportunity to pass legislation prohibiting the pending action or using political pressure to cause executive officials to retract or modify the proposed action. This type of "report and wait" provision has been upheld by the Supreme Court. The Court noted: "The value of the reservation of the power to examine proposed rules, laws and regulations before they become effective is well understood by Congress. It is frequently, as here, employed to make sure that the action under the delegation squares with the Congressional purpose." *Sibbach* v. *Wilson*, 312 U.S. 1 (1941). An example appeared in the Comprehensive Anti-Apartheid Act of 1986, which was directed toward South Africa's political persecution of Nelson Mandela and other dissidents (see box).

"The President may suspend or modify any of the measures required by this title or section 501(c) or section 504(b) thirty days after he determines, and so reports to the Speaker of the House of Representatives and the chairman of the Committee on Foreign Relations of the Senate, that the Government of South Africa has [taken certain actions] unless the Congress enacts within such 30-day period, in accordance with section 602 of this Act, a joint resolution disapproving the determination of the President under this subsection." 100 Stat. 103, sec. 311 (1986).

M. Independent Counsel

The statutory provisions for the appointment of an independent counsel (formerly called "special prosecutor") were originally enacted as Title VI of the Ethics in Government Act of 1978, and codified at 28 U.S.C. §§ 591-599. The independent counsel was reauthorized in 1983, 1987, and 1994. It expired on June 30, 1999. The mechanisms of the independent counsel law were triggered by the receipt of information by the Attorney General that alleged a violation of any federal criminal law (other than certain misdemeanors or "infractions") by a person covered by the act. Certain high-level federal officials, including the President, Vice President, and heads of departments, were automatically covered by the law. In addition, the Attorney General had discretion to seek an independent counsel for any person for whom there may exist a personal, financial or political conflict of interest for Justice Department personnel to investigate; and the Attorney General could seek an independent counsel for any Member of Congress when the Attorney General deemed it to be in the "public interest."

After conducting a limited review of the matter (a 30-day threshold review of the credibility and specificity of the charges, and a subsequent 90-day preliminary investigation, with a possible 60-day extension), the Attorney General, if he or she believed that "further investigation is warranted", would apply to a special "division of the court," a federal three-judge panel appointed by the Chief Justice of the Supreme Court, requesting that the division appoint an independent counsel. The Attorney General of the United States was the *only* officer in the government authorized to apply for the appointment of an independent counsel. The special division of the court selected and appointed the independent counsel, and designated his or her prosecutorial jurisdiction, based on the information provided the court by the Attorney General. The independent counsel had the full range of investigatory and prosecutorial powers and functions of the Attorney General or other Department of Justice employees.

COLLISIONS BETWEEN CONGRESS AND INDEPENDENT COUNSELS

"The Congress' role here is terribly important. It is for them to present to the public as soon as possible a picture of the actual facts as to the Iran/Contra matter. This is so because there has been so much exposed without sufficient clarity to clear up the questions. There is a general apprehension that this is damaging. Congress properly wants to bring this to an end soon and that gives them a real feeling of urgency for their investigation.

"[The House and Senate Iran-Contra Committees] are trying to provide a factual predicate which will enable Congress to decide intelligently whether there is a need for a statutory amendment or for a closer oversight over covert activities and other matters . . . As they quite properly point out, they cannot wait for Independent Counsel to satisfy himself as to whether a crime may or may not have been committed. They have a problem of their own.

". . . We are proceeding with much greater detail than Congress would think necessary for their purposes. We come into collision when the question of immunity arises.

> ". . . There is a greater pressure on Congress to grant immunity to central figures than there is for Independent Counsel. Over the last three months, we have had long negotiations over this question of immunity . . .
>
> "If the Congress decides to grant immunity, there is no way that it can be avoided. They have the last word and that is a proper distribution of power. . . .
>
> ". . .The reason why Congress must have this power to confer immunity is because of the importance of their role. The legislative branch has the power to decide whether it is more important perhaps even to destroy a prosecution than to hold back testimony they need."
>
> Lawrence E. Walsh, "The Independent Counsel and the Separation of Powers," Houston Law Review, v. 25 (1988):1.

There was no specific term of appointment for independent counsels. They could serve for as long as it took to complete their duties concerning that specific matter within their defined and limited jurisdiction. Once a matter was completed, the independent counsel filed a final report. The special division of the court could also find that the independent counsel's work was completed and terminate the office. A periodic review of an independent counsel for such determination was to be made by the special division of the court. An independent counsel, *prior* to the completion of his or her duties, could be removed from office (other than by impeachment and conviction) only by the Attorney General of the United States for good cause, physical or mental disability, or other impairing condition, and such removal could be appealed to the court. The procedures for appointing and removing the independent counsel were upheld by the Supreme Court in *Morrison* v. *Olson*, 487 U.S. 654 (1988).

Investigation by the independent counsel could compete with parallel efforts by congressional committees to examine the same issue. Congress could decide to accommodate the needs of the independent counsel, such as delaying a legislative investigation until the independent counsel completed certain phases of an inquiry (see box on previous page).

Although Congress could call on the Attorney General to apply for an independent counsel by a written request from the House or Senate Judiciary Committee, or a majority of members of either party of those committees, the Attorney General is not required to begin a preliminary investigation or to apply for an independent counsel in response to such a request. However, in such cases the Justice Department was required to provide certain information to the requesting committee.

The independent counsel was directed by statutory language to submit to Congress an annual report on the activities of such independent counsel, including the progress of investigations and any prosecutions. Although it was recognized that certain information would have to be kept confidential, the statute stated that "information adequate to justify the expenditures that the office of the independent counsel has made" should be provided. 28 U.S.C. § 595(a)(2).

The conduct of an independent counsel was subject to congressional oversight and an independent counsel was required to cooperate with that oversight. 28 U.S.C. § 595(a)(1). In addition, the independent counsel was required to report to the House of Representatives any "substantial and credible" information that may constitute grounds for any impeachment. 28 U.S.C. § 595(c). On September 11, 1998, Independent Counsel Kenneth W. Starr forwarded to the House a report concluding that President Clinton may have committed impeachable offenses. The House passed two articles of impeachment (perjury and obstruction of justice), but the Senate voted only 45 to 55 on the perjury charge and 50 to 50 on the obstruction of justice charge, both votes short of the two-thirds majority required under the Constitution.

The independent counsel statute expired in 1992, partly because of criticism directed at Lawrence Walsh's investigation of Iran-Contra. The statute was reauthorized in 1994, but objections to the investigations conducted by Kenneth Starr into Whitewater, Monica Lewinsky, and other matters, put Congress under pressure to let the statute lapse on June 30, 1999.

Unless Congress in the future reauthorizes the independent counsel, the only available option for an independent counsel is to have the Attorney General invoke existing authority to appoint a special prosecutor to investigate a particular matter. For example, when the independent counsel statute expired in 1992 and was not reauthorized until 1994, Attorney General Janet Reno appointed Robert Fiske in 1993 to investigate the Clintons' involvement in Whitewater and the death of White House aide Vincent Foster. On July 9, 1999 Attorney General Reno promulgated regulations concerning the appointment of outside, temporary counsels, to be called "Special Counsels," in certain circumstances to conduct investigations and possible prosecutions of certain sensitive matters, or matters which may raise a conflict for the Justice Department (28 C.F.R. Part 600). Such special counsels will have substantially less independence than the statutory independent General, including removal for "misconduct, dereliction of duty, incapacity, conflict of interest, or for other good cause, including violation of Department policies."

SELECTED READINGS

Statutory Offices of Inspector General

Hendricks, Michael, et al. Inspectors General: A New Force in Evaluation. San Francisco: Jossey-Bass, Inc., 1990.

Kaiser, Frederick M. Statutory Offices of Inspector General: Establishment and Evolution. CRS Report 98-379 GOV, Regularly Updated.

——. "The Watchers' Watchdog: The CIA Inspector General." International Journal of Intelligence and Counterintelligence, v.3, 1989. pp. 55-75.

Light, Paul C. Monitoring Government: Inspectors General and the Search for Accountability. Washington: Brookings, 1993. HJ9801.L54

Newcomer, Kathryn E. The Changing Nature of Accountability: The Role of the Inspectors General in Federal Agencies. Public Administration Review, vol. 58, March/April, 1998.

U.S. Congress. House Subcommittee on Government Efficiency. 25th Anniversary of the Inspector General Act. Hearings, 108th Congress, 1st session. Washington: GPO, 2003.

U.S. Congress. Senate Committee on Governmental Affairs. The Inspector General Act: 20 Years Later. Hearings, 105th Congress, 2nd session. Washington: GPO, 1998.

U.S. General Accounting Office. Inspectors General: Office Consolidation and Related Issues. GAO Report GAO-02-575, Washington: GAO, 2002.

——. Highlights of the Comptroller General's Panel on Federal Oversight and the Inspectors General. GAO Report GAO-06-931SP, Washington: GAO, 2006.

Reporting, Consultation, and Other Sources of Information

Beth, Richard S. Disapproval of Regulations by Congress: Procedure Under the Congressional Review Act. CRS Report RL31160, October 10, 2001.

Brass, Clinton T., coordinator. General Management Laws: A Compendium. CRS Report RL30795, May 19, 2004.

Copeland, Curtis W. Federal Regulations: Efforts to Estimate Total Costs and Benefits of Rules. CRS Report RL32339, May 14, 2004.

Collier, Ellen C. "Reporting Requirements." In Joint Committee on the Organization of Congress. Congressional Reorganization: Proposals for Change. Senate Print 103-19, 103rd Congress, 1st session. Washington: GPO, 1993. p. 135.

——. "Foreign Policy by Reporting Requirement." The Washington Quarterly, vol. 11, Winter 1988.

Johannes, John. "Statutory Reporting Requirements: Information and Influence for Congress." In Abdo Baaklini, ed., Comparative Legislative Reforms and Innovations. New York: SUNY Press, 1977. pp. 33-60.

Kerwin Cornelius. Rulemaking: How Government Agencies Write Laws and Make Policy, 2nd ed. Washington, D.C.: CQ Press, 1999.

Rosenberg, Morton. Congressional Review of Agency Rulemaking: A Brief Overview and Assessment After Five Years. CRS Report RL30116, March 6, 2001.

U.S. General Accounting Office. Investigators' Guide to Sources of Information. GAO Report OSI-97-2. Washington: GAO, 1997.

U.S. General Accounting Office. A Systematic Management Approach Is Needed for Congressional Reporting Requirements. GAO Report PAD-82-12. Washington: GAO, 1981.

U.S. House of Representatives. Clerk. Reports To Be Made to Congress. House Document 108-14, 108th Congress, 1st session. Washington: GPO, 2003.

U.S. Vice President Al Gore. National Performance Review. Creating a Government That Works Better & Costs Less: Streamlining Management Control. Washington: Office of the Vice President, 1993 (Reduce the Burden of Congressionally Mandated Reports, pp. 33-36).

Resolutions of Inquiry

Fisher, Louis. House Resolutions of Inquiry. CRS Report RL31909, May 12, 2003.

History of the United States House of Representatives, 1789-1994, H. Doc. 103-324, 103rd Congress, 2nd session. Washington: GPO, 1994 (Resolutions of Inquiry, pp. 260-262).

Methods and Techniques

Art, Robert J. "Congress and the Defense Budget: Enhancing Policy Oversight," Political Science Quarterly, v. 100, Summer 1985: 227-248.

Bowers, James R. Regulating the Regulators: An Introduction to the Legislative Oversight of Administrative Rulemaking. New York: Praeger, 1990. 140p. KF5411.B69

Hill, James P. "The Third House of Congress Versus the Fourth Branch of Government: The Impact of Congressional Committee Staff on Agency Regulatory Decision-Making," John Marshall Law Review, v. 19, Winter 1986: 247-273.

Kaiser, Frederick M. "Congressional Oversight of the Presidency," Annals of the American Academy of Political and Social Science, v. 499, September 1988: 75-89.

U.S. Congress. Senate. Committee on Government Operations [now titled Homeland Security and Government Affairs]. Subcommittee on Oversight Procedures. Committee Print. Congressional Oversight: Methods and Techniques. 94th Congress, 2nd session, July 1976. Washington: GPO, 1976. 254p.

Special Studies and Investigations by Staff and Others

Johannes, John R. To Serve the People: Congress and Constituency Service. Lincoln, University of Nebraska Press, 1984. JK1071.J63

Kaiser, Frederick M. A Congressional Office of Constituent Assistance: Proposals, Rationales, and Possible Objections. CRS Report 91-893 GOV, December 18, 1991.

Pontius, John S. Casework in a Congressional Office. CRS Report 98-878, September 9, 2004.

The Press and Media

Cook, Timothy E. Making Laws and Making News. Washington. The Brookings Institution, 1989. 210 p. JK1447.C66

Hess, Stephen. Live From Capitol Hill. Washington: The Brookings Institution, 1991. 178 p. PN4888.P6H48

Mann, Thomas and Norman Ornstein, eds. Congress, the Press, and the Public. Washington: The American Enterprise Institute and The Brookings Institution, 1994. 212 p JK1140.C62

Ritchie, Donald A. Press Gallery: Congress and the Washington Correspondents. Cambridge, Mass.: Harvard University Press, 1991. PN4899.W3R58

Specialized Investigations

Congressional Quarterly. Guide to Congress. Washington: Congressional Quarterly, Inc., 2000, 5th ed. Vol. I, pp. 249-280.

Dimock, Marshall E. Congressional Investigating Committees. Baltimore: Johns Hopkins Press, 1929. KF4942.D5

Eberling, Ernest J. Congressional Investigations. New York: Columbia University Press, 1929. JK1123.A2E2

Fisher, Louis. Constitutional Conflicts between Congress and the President. Lawrence, Kansas: University Press of Kansas, 1997, 4th revised ed. pp. 160-195. KF4565.F57

——. Congressional Access to Executive Branch Information: Legislative Tools. CRS Report RL30966, May 17, 2001.

——. Congressional Investigations: Subpoenas and Contempt Power. CRS Report RL31836, April 2, 2003.

Hamilton, James. The Power To Probe: A Study of Congressional Investigations. New York: Vintage Books, 1976. KF4942.H34

Kaiser, Frederick M. "Impact and Implications of the Iran-contra Affair on Congressional Oversight of the Executive." International Journal of Intelligence and Counterintelligence, vol. 7, Summer 1994, pp. 205-234.

Mayhew, David R. Divided We Govern: Party Control, Lawmaking, and Investigations, 1946-1990. New Haven: Yale University Press, 1991. JK2261.M36

Schlesinger, Arthur M. Jr. and Roger Bruns. Congress Investigates: A Documented History. New York: Chelsea House, 1975 (5 vols.). JK1123.A2S34

Taylor, Telford. The Grand Inquest: The Story of Congressional Investigations New York: Simon and Schuster, 1955. KF4942.T38

Appropriations Limitations and Riders

Banks, William C. and Peter Raven-Hansen. National Security Law and the Power of the Purse. New York, Oxford University Press, 1994. 260 p. KF4651.B36

Devins, Neal. "Regulation of Government Agencies Through Limitation Riders," Duke Law Journal, v. 1987: 456.

Fisher, Louis. "The Authorization-Appropriation Process in Congress: Formal Rules and Informal Practices," Catholic University Law Review, v. 29, 1979:5.

LeBoeuf, Jacques B. "Limitations on the Use of Appropriations Riders by Congress to Effectuate Substantive Policy Changes," Hastings Constitutional Law Quarterly, v. 19, 1992: 457.

The Legislative Veto

Biden, Joseph R., Jr. "Who Needs the Legislative Veto?" Syracuse Law Review, v. 35, 1984: 685.

Breyer, Stephen. "The Legislative Veto After *Chadha*." Georgetown Law Journal, v. 72, 1984: 785.

Craig, Barbara Hinson. Chadha: The Story of an Epic Constitutional Struggle. New York: Oxford University Press, 1988. KF228.C43C73

Fisher, Louis. "The Legislative Veto: Invalidated, It Survives," Law & Contemporary Problems, v. 56, 1993: 273.

Gibson, Martha Liebler. Weapons of Influence: the Legislative Veto, American Foreign Policy, and the Irony of Reform. Boulder, Colo., Westview Press, 1992. 188p. JX1706.G53

Kaiser, Frederick M. "Congressional Action to Overturn Agency Rules: Alternatives to the # legislative veto.'" Administrative Law Review, v. 32, 1980: 667.

Korn, Jessica. The Power of Separation: American Constitutionalism and the Myth of the Legislative Veto. Princeton, N.J.: Princeton University Press, 1996. 178p. JK305.K67

Independent Counsel

Eastland, Terry. Ethics, Politics and the Independent Counsel. Washington, National Legal Center for the Public Interest, 1989. 180 p. KF4568.E17 1989

Harriger, Katy J. The Special Prosecutor in American Politics, 2d ed. revised. Lawrence: University Press of Kansas, 2000. 325 p. KF4568.H37

Jost, Kenneth. "Independent Counsels: Should Congress make major changes in the law?" CQ Researcher, v. 7, no. 7, February 21, 1997: 145-167.

Koukoutchos, Brian Stuart. Constitutional Kinetics: the Independent Counsel Case and the Separation of Powers. Wake Forest law review, v. 23, 1988: 635.

Maskell, Jack. The Independent Counsel Law. The Federal Lawyer, July 1998: 28-39.

Nolan, Beth. " Removing Conflicts from the Administration of Justice: Conflicts of Interest and Independent Counsels Under the Ethics in Government Act." Georgetown Law Journal, v. 79, 1990: 1-80.

Walsh, Lawrence E. The Independent Counsel and the Separation of Powers. Houston Law Review, v. 25, 1988: 1.

V. Oversight Information Sources and Consultant Services

Congress calls upon a variety of sources for information and analysis to support its oversight activities. Most of this assistance is provided by legislative support agencies: The Congressional Research Service, the Congressional Budget Office, and the Government Accountability Office. In addition, the Offices of Senate Legal Counsel and House General Counsel are valuable oversight resources. A range of outside interest groups and research organizations also provide rich sources of information.

A. Congressional Research Service (CRS)

1. CRS Mission Statement

"The Congressional Research Service provides the Congress, throughout the legislative process, comprehensive and reliable legislative research, analysis, and information services that are timely, objective, nonpartisan, and confidential, thereby contributing to an informed national legislature."

2. Organization

CRS is organized into five interdisciplinary research divisions: American Law; Domestic Social Policy; Foreign Affairs, Defense and Trade; Government and Finance; and Resources,

Science and Industry. The Knowledge Services Group provides research support services to CRS analysts and attorneys in providing authoritative and reliable information research and policy analysis to the Congress.

3. Staff of CRS

CRS has about 700 employees on its permanent staff. The professional staff are diverse, including, among others, attorneys, economists, engineers, social science analysts, information scientists, librarians, defense and foreign affairs analysts, political scientists, public administrators, and physical and biological scientists.

4. CRS Work for Congress

CRS provides the following services:

Analytical and Research Services

a. Policy analysis and research

CRS staff anticipates and responds to congressional needs for policy analysis, research and information in an interdisciplinary, integrated manner. CRS provides timely and objective responses to congressional inquiries for policy analysis, research and information at every stage of the legislative process.

Legislative attorneys and paralegal staff respond to congressional needs for legal information and analysis to support the legislative, oversight, and representational functions of Congress.

b. Information research

Information research specialists and resource specialists are available to provide information research and reference assistance. The staff also provides copies of articles in newspapers, journals, legal and legislative documents and offers assistance with a wide variety of electronic files.

c. Briefings, seminars, and workshops

CRS conducts briefings, seminars, and workshops for Members of Congress and their staffs. On these occasions CRS analysts and other experts discuss public policy issues, international concerns, and the legislative process.

Briefings. CRS analysts and specialists are available to give one-on-one briefings to Members and staff on public policy issues, the legislative process, congressional office operations, committee matters, or a general orientation to CRS.

Issue seminars and workshops. In anticipation of congressional interest or at the request of a Member or committee, CRS organizes and conducts seminars and workshops on issues of current interest to Members and staff of Congress. CRS and outside experts participate in these events with Members and staff.

Federal Law Update. This series, offered twice yearly by the American Law Division, focuses on developments on important issues of law directly related to the legislative business of the Congress. The series can meet continuing legal education (CLE) requirements in some states.

CRS Legislative Institutes. This three-part series provides training in the work of Congress and the legislative process. Topics include the federal budget process, committee system and procedures, floor procedures, amendments, and resolutions. In the Graduate Legislative Institute, participants simulate congressional proceedings as "members of the CRS Congress" and gain experience in procedures by moving bills through the legislative process.

Public Policy Issues Institute. Held at the beginning of each session of the Congress, this program provides introductory briefings and discussions by CRS staff on issues of legislative significance to the Congress.

District and Staff Institutes. These institutes provide orientation for staff of district offices that include discussions of CRS services, the legislative and budget processes, casework, Member allowances, ethics, and franking. The program is supported by the House and Senate.

New Member Seminar. Every two years CRS offers new Members an orientation seminar on public policy issues. These sessions are held in January at the beginning of each new Congress.

For additional information about CRS seminars and events, call 7-7904.

CRS Products

a. Customized Memoranda

Confidential memoranda prepared for a specific office are a major form of CRS written communication. These memoranda are solely for the use of the requesting office and are not distributed further unless permission has been given by that office. Memoranda are often used by CRS attorneys and analysts to respond to inquiries focused on legislative and policy matters of individual Member interest.

b. CRS Reports

Reports for Congress on specific issues take many forms: policy analyses, statistical reviews, economic studies, legal analyses, historical studies, chronological reviews, and bibliographies. Reports are available on the CRS website at [http://www.crs.gov]. In addition, CRS prepares concise briefing papers on issues before the Congress.

c. Congressional Distribution Memoranda

Matters that are not suitable for treatment in a CRS Report, but that may be of interest to more than one congressional office, can be the subject of general distribution memoranda provided to a congressional office upon request. General Distribution memoranda differ from

Reports because they are tailored; are directed to a specific question or concern; or are more technical or focused in nature.

d. The La Follette Congressional Reading Room, the CRS Research Centers and the Jefferson Congressional Reading Room

Staff in the congressional reading rooms and research centers provide telephone reference assistance and in-person consultation on resources and research for congressional staff. A selected research collection, newspapers and journals, and assistance with online searching is available.

La Follette Congressional Reading Room
Rayburn Research Center
Russell Senate Research Center
Hours: Monday-Friday, 9:00 a.m.-5:30 p.m.
(Hours may change when Congress is not in session.)

The Jefferson Congressional Reading Room is a Members only facility staffed by CRS research librarians providing in-person service.

e. Electronically Accessible Products and Services

CRS Website [http://www.crs.gov]. The CRS Website provides 24-hour access to an array of CRS services including full text of reports, a weekly "Legislative Alert," updates and analyses of the annual appropriations legislation, an interactive guide to the legislative process, online registration for CRS seminars, and complete information on other CRS services. In operation since the 104th Congress, the CRS Website is accessible only to House and Senate offices and other legislative branch agencies. A linked format allows the user to move easily within a CRS online document and link to the text and summary of relevant legislation and other CRS products on the topic.

Legislative Information System [http://www.congress.gov]. The Legislative Information System (LIS) was available for the first time on Capnet at the beginning of the 105th Congress. The system provides Members of Congress and their staff with access to the most current and comprehensive legislative information available. It can be accessed only by the House and Senate and the legislative support agencies. The LIS has been developed under the policy direction of the Senate Committee on Rules and Administration and the House Committee on House Administration. It has been a collaborative project of the offices and agencies of the legislative branch, including the Secretary of the Senate and the Clerk of the House; House Information Resources and the Senate Sergeant at Arms; the Government Printing Office; the Government Accountability Office; the Congressional Budget Office; the Congressional Research Service; and the Library of Congress. CRS has responsibility for the overall coordination of the retrieval system; the Library of Congress is responsible for its technical development and operation.

Floor Agenda. The "Floor Agenda: CRS Products" page, a weekly compendium of CRS products relevant to scheduled or expected floor action in the House and Senate, was available on the CRS website and through e-mail subscription to all Members, committees, subcommittees, and congressional staff. All CRS products listed on the Floor Agenda were linked for electronic delivery to subscriber desktops.

CRS Programs Listserv. Launched in fiscal 2001, this e-mail notification system provides subscribers with descriptions of current CRS programs and links to online registration forms.

Current Legislative Issues. The Current Legislative Issues (CLI) system, accessible to the Congress from the CRS Home Page, reflects policy areas identified by CRS research staff as active and of current importance to the Congress. All products presented as CLIs are maintained to address significant policy developments. On occasion the system is used to facilitate the contribution of CRS expertise in situations requiring immediate attention of the Congress on an unanticipated basis. CRS typically develops and maintains about 150 CLIs a year.

Appropriations. The CRS Appropriations Web Page continues to provide comprehensive legislative tracking and access to legislative analysis of each of the 13 annual appropriations bills. The appropriations status table includes an online guide to the FY2003 Consolidated Appropriations Act (P.L. 108-7), which offered access and short cuts to notable sections from the end-of-session measure that combined 11 appropriations acts into one bill.

f. Audiovisual Products and Services

Audiovisual Products and Services. CRS provides a variety of audiovisual products and technical assistance in support of its service to the Congress. These include producing video or audio copies of CRS institutes and seminars that congressional staff can request for viewing in DVD format or at their desktops from the Web. The Web versions are broken out into subtopics so that individual viewers can go directly to the portions that are of greatest interest to them. In addition, CRS provides two hours of television programming each weekday for the house and Senate closed-circuit systems.

Language Support. The Foreign Affairs, Defense, and Trade Division provides limited translation services for Members and committees. For translations pertaining to legislative business into or from other languages, the division can make arrangements to contract the work to outside vendors.

5. CRS Divisional Responsibilities

CRS has adopted an interdisciplinary and integrative approach as it responds to requests from the Congress. The Service seeks to define complex issues in clear and understandable ways, identify basic causes of the problems under consideration, and highlight available policy choices and potential effects of action. CRS is organized into the following divisions and offices to support the analysis, research, and information needs of the Congress.

Divisions

American Law Division

The American Law Division provides the Congress with legal analysis and information on the range of legal questions that emerge from the congressional agenda. Division lawyers work with federal, state, and international legal resources in support of the legislative, oversight, and representational needs of Members and committees of Congress. The division's work involves the constitutional framework of separation of powers, congressional-executive relations and federalism; the legal aspects of congressional practices and procedures; and the myriad questions of administrative law, constitutional law, criminal law, civil rights, environmental law, business and tax law, and international law that are implicated by the legislative process. In addition, the division prepares *The Constitution of the United States of America — Analysis and Interpretation* (popularly known as the Constitution Annotated).

Domestic Social Policy Division

The Domestic Social Policy Division offers the Congress research and analysis in the broad area of domestic social policies and programs. Analysts use multiple disciplines in their research, including program and legislative expertise, quantitative methodologies, and economic analysis. Issue and legislative areas include education and training, health care and medicine, public health, social security, public and private pensions, welfare, nutrition, housing, immigration, civil rights, drug control, crime and criminal justice, border security and domestic intelligence, labor and occupational safety, unemployment and workers compensation, and issues related to the aging of the U.S. population, to children, persons with disabilities, the poor, veterans, and minorities.

Foreign Affairs, Defense, and Trade

The Foreign Affairs, Defense, and Trade Division is organized into seven regional and functional sections. Analysts follow worldwide political and economic and security developments for the Congress, including U.S. relations with individual countries and transnational issues such as terrorism, narcotics, refugees, international health, global economic problems, and global institutions such as the United Nations, World Bank, International Monetary Fund and the World Trade Organization. They also address U.S. foreign aid programs, strategies, and resource allocations; State Department budget and functions; international debt; public diplomacy; and legislation on foreign relations. Other work includes national security policy, military strategy, weapons systems, military compensation, the defense budget, and U.S. military bases. Trade-related legislation, policies, and programs and U.S. trade performance and investment flows are covered, as are trade negotiations and agreements, export promotion, import regulations, tariffs, and trade policy functions.

Government and Finance Division

The Government and Finance division is responsible for meeting the analytic and research needs of Congress on matters relating to government operations and oversight, intergovernmental relations, congressional organization and procedures, public finance, financial regulation, and macroeconomic policy. Issue areas related to government include the operations and history of Congress; the legislative process; the congressional budget and appropriations processes; federal executive and judicial branch organization and management; government personnel; government information policy; statehood, territories and the District of Columbia; disaster assistance and homeland security; census and reapportionment; elections and political parties; lobbying; and constitutional amendments and history. Issue areas related to finance and economics include financial institutions and market structure; financial markets and securities regulation; insurance; consumer finance, including banking, credit reporting, and financial privacy; government-sponsored enterprises and housing finance; debt and taxation; economic development; international finance, including foreign exchange and financial flows; monetary and fiscal policy; and macroeconomic conditions and indicators, such as gross domestic product, price indexes, and saving.

Knowledge Services Group

The Knowledge Services Group (KSG) is comprised of information research professionals who partner with CRS analysts and attorneys in providing authoritative and reliable information research and policy analysis to the Congress. Information professionals are clustered together by policy research area and align their work directly to the CRS analytical divisions (see listing above), providing analysis in those same policy areas. KSG members 1) write descriptive products and contribute descriptive input to analytical products in policy research areas; 2) advise CRS analysts and the Congress in finding solutions for their information needs, and make recommendations for incorporating new research strategies into their work; 3) create customized Web pages; 4) evaluate, acquire, and maintain state-of-the-art resources materials and collections for CRS staff; 5) work with the analytical divisions in ensuring the currency and accuracy of CRS products and CRS-created databases and spreadsheets; 6) maintain the currency, comprehensiveness, and integrity of CRS information resources by identifying, assessing, acquiring, organizing, preserving, and tracking materials; 7) provide authoritative information on specific policy research areas through discussions or presentations; 8) provide or coordinate customized training on information research or information resources for individuals or groups, as requested or anticipated.

Resources, Science, and Industry Division

The Resources, Science, and Industry Division covers an array of legislative issues for the Congress involving natural resources and environmental management, science and technology, and industry and infrastructure. Resources work includes policy analysis on public lands and other natural resources issues; environment; agriculture, food, and fisheries; and energy and minerals. Science coverage includes policy analysis on civilian and military research and development issues, information and telecommunications, space, earth sciences, and general science and technology. Support on industry issues includes policy analysis on transportation and transportation infrastructure issues, industrial market structure and regulation, and sector-specific industry analysis.

Offices

Office of Finance and Administration

The Office of Finance and Administration maintains oversight of the Service's planning, management controls, financial management, and administrative activities. This includes coordinating development of the Service's strategic planning goals and annual program plans and conducting quarterly performance reviews. This office directs a full range of fiscal operations to achieve the Director's program objectives, including development of long-range budgetary requirements and associated appropriations requests, budget execution, contracting, and fund-raising. The office also performs facilities management and asset control activities and co-chairs the Services Contract Review Board, conducts a business analysis of all proposals for external research capacity, and makes recommendations to the Director.

Office of Information Resources Management

The Office of Information Resources Management develops and maintains information services that support both the Congress and CRS staff. The office provides information support to CRS staff through its management of three Information Resource Centers, reference services, procurement of electronic and print resources, training in the use of electronic resources, and Intranet resource development.

Office of the Congressional Affairs and Counselor to the Director

The Office of Congressional Affairs and Counselor to the Director provides counsel to the Director and Deputy Director on matters of law and policy —planning, developing, and coordinating matters relating to internal CRS policies, particularly as they affect the Service's relationships with congressional clients and other legislative support agencies. The office provides final CRS review and clearance of all CRS products; ensures that the Service complies with applicable guidelines and directives contained in the Reorganization Act, in statements by appropriations and oversight committees, and in Library regulations and CRS policy statements. This office receives, assigns to the research divisions, and tracks congressional inquiries; works with the divisions to plan and carry out institutes, seminars, and briefings for Members, committees, and their staffs, and takes the lead in developing, strengthening, and implementing outreach to congressional offices; records, tracks, and reports data on congressional inquiries and CRS responses; and develops and refines systems designed to provide managers with statistical information needed to analyze subject coverage, client service, and the use of resources. The office also provides a co-chair of the External Research Review Board, which reviews contract proposals and makes recommendations to the Director, and provides the CRS representative to the Interagency Liaison Group of legislative support agencies.

Office of Legislative Information

The Office of Legislative Information develops and maintains information services that support both the Congress and CRS staff, including the CRS website and the congressional legislative information retrieval system (LIS); provides summaries and status information for all bills introduced each Congress; builds and maintains the technology infrastructure of the Service as a whole; develops and applies new technologies to enhance CRS research capability and productivity; develops and implements information technology to enhance communication of CRS research to its clients; edits, produces, and distributes CRS products in both print and electronic format; and represents the Director in dealing with other organizations and agencies on issues regarding legislative information technology.

The Office of Workforce Development

The Office of Workforce Development administers the Service's human resources programs and the following activities: staffing, recruitment, position classification, diversity, upward mobility, performance management, mentoring, special recognition, and training and professional development. This office represents the Director on issues involving the Service's status, role, activities, and interaction with other Library entities in relevant areas of human resources administration, management, and development. Overall the goal of the office is to enhance the Service's ability to attract and retain the human resources talent it needs to respond to the dynamic research, analysis, and information needs of the Congress.

6. Interdisciplinary Teams

a. Identification of Major Issues

As part of Service-wide planning efforts, CRS managers attempt to anticipate major congressional issues. The program identifies and defines major issues, structures them for more effective scrutiny by the Congress, and provides effective, timely, and comprehensive products and services to the Congress, that usually require multi-disciplinary and interdivisional contributions. The issues chosen are national in scope, receive widespread public attention, have significant effects on the federal budget, economy, or social fabric of the Nation, and are virtually certain to be the subject of congressional hearings and legislative action.

7. Limitations

The Legislative Reorganization Act of 1970 and specific provisions in various other Acts direct and authorize CRS to provide a great range of products and services to the Congress. However, pursuant to these statutory authorities and understandings reached over time in consultation with the relevant oversight committees, the Service has developed the following policies limiting or barring certain types of assistance. When it appears that a congressional request should be declined on these policy grounds, that decision and notification to the requestor is to be made only after consultation with the appropriate division chief or the Associate Director for Policy Compliance.

a. CRS cannot prepare reports, seminars or undisclaimed products which are of a partisan nature or advocate bills or policies. But CRS will respond to requests for "directed writing" — statement drafts, casemaking or other disclaimed products clearly identified as prepared at the direction of the client and not for attribution as CRS analysis or opinion. In no case is excessive partisanship, incorrect factual data, moral denigration of opponents, or personal research damaging to Members permissible.
b. CRS cannot provide researched information focusing on individual Members or living former Members of Congress (other than holders of, or nominees to, federal

appointive office), except at the specific request or with permission of the Member concerned.

c. Members of the CRS staff shall not appear as witnesses before committees of Congress in their capacity as CRS employees or on matters relating to their official duties without the express consent of the Director.
d. CRS does not draft bills (a function of the office of the legislative counsels), but will assist with the preparation of legislative proposals.
e. CRS cannot meet deadlines or demands that could only be met by dropping or jeopardizing the quality of responses to urgent legislative requests related to the public policy work of the Congress, but the Service will respond to all requests as rapidly as is feasible under prevailing workload conditions.
f. CRS cannot accept "rush" or priority deadlines on constituent inquiries but will respond as expeditiously as is possible without compromising the quality of responses relating to current legislative business.
g. CRS cannot undertake casework or provide translating services or briefings for constituents, but can lend assistance in responding to constituent matters, including identification of the appropriate agency or private entity to contact for further pursuit of the matter.
h. CRS cannot give personal legal or medical advice, but will assist in the provision of background information, the identification of relevant issues for further scrutiny, and advice on sources of additional assistance.
i. CRS cannot undertake scholastic or personal research for office staff, but can, on a nonpriority basis, help with bibliographic and reference services.
j. CRS assistance for former Members of Congress should be limited to use of the La Follette Reading Room and reference centers, the hotline service, the provision of readily available information and previously prepared CRS congressional distribution products. CRS cannot undertake original research for former Members, but on a nonpriority basis responds to requests for reference services and research guidance.
k. CRS is not authorized to provide congressional offices with clerical assistance (e.g., typing, duplication, maintenance of mailing lists, continuing clipping services, etc.).
l. CRS must not use its staff to index hearings or congressional documents other than those prepared by the Service itself.
m. The Library of Congress is not authorized to subscribe to or lend on a regular basis current issues of periodicals and newspapers for the purpose of furnishing them regularly to individual congressional offices.
n. CRS must not use its staff to support executive or other commissions that are not funded through the Legislative Branch Appropriations Act. In those instances where Members of Congress are official members of a commission not served by CRS, the Service may supply customary assistance to the Members, but queries should be placed through the Members' offices by their official staffs, and the replies should be sent to the Members' offices, not to the office of the commission.
o. CRS does not conduct audits or field investigations.
p. CRS is not authorized to provide its services in support of political campaign organizations.
q. While CRS reference and research specialists serve all Members and committees of Congress, the Director has the authority to assign staff to work temporarily for

particular committees on request. In current circumstances, however, no full time assignments may be approved, and staff assigned to close support of a committee must be available to serve other clients. When staff is adequate to permit the loan of subject specialists for short periods, the Director may approve formal requests without reimbursement; staff loans for periods of over 60 days must be reimbursed. No full-time assignment of staff is approved if the assignment leaves the Service unable to adequately serve the Congress.

r. As a general rule, the services of CRS are provided exclusively to the Congress and, to the extent provided by law, to other congressional support agencies. Because of the benefits derived from the exchange of information with other governmental bodies (including elected and appointed officials of foreign governments), the Service may also at the discretion of the Director exchange courtesies and services of a limited nature with such organizations, so long as such assistance benefits CRS services to Congress.

s. CRS does not provide its services to congressional member organizations and informal caucuses not funded by legislative branch appropriations but will provide its normal services to the offices of Members who belong to such entities and to formal congressional party organizations. Current lists of organizations that may place requests directly are available from the Inquiry Section.

t. CRS does not offer services to former Members of Congress, other than providing copies of current CRS publications or limited brief reference assistance.

Fast Access to all CRS services
Phone 7-5700 (Press 1-5 to speak to an information specialist)
Website [http://www.crs.gov] Fax 7-6745
TTY 7-7154

[http://www.crs.gov]
e-mail lists select Services
Navigation assistance 7-7100

CRS Experts
Phone 7-5700 (press 1-5 to request an expert)
Dial by name 7-5700 (press 1-4 and spell last name then first name)

CRS Products
Website (retrieve full text or order) [http://www.crs.gov]

In-Person Services and CRS Products
(Note: Hours may change when Congress is not in session.)
Hotline (quick facts, statistics and Web assistance) 7-7100

La Follette Congressional Reading Room Madison 204 7-7100
Monday - Thursday 8:30 a.m. - 8:00 p.m.
Friday 8:30 a.m. - 6:00 p.m.
Saturday 8:30 a.m. - 5:00 p.m.

(Closed Saturdays when Congress is not in session.)

Rayburn Research Center B3355-6958
Monday - Friday 9:00 a.m. - 5:30 p.m.

Senate Research Center Russell B074-3550
Monday - Friday 9:00 a.m. - 5:30 p.m.

Jefferson Congressional Reading Room Jefferson 159
Members of Congress Only
Monday - Friday 8:30 a.m. - 5:00 p.m.

Programs and Training
Information 7-7904 or [http://www.crs.gov] (select Events)

To borrow books from the Library of Congress Collection
Fax 7-5986
E-mail loanref@loc.gov
Phone (also to open a loan account) 7-5441
To request book pick-up 7-5717

Mailing Address
Daniel P. Mulhollan, Director
Congressional Research Service
The Library of Congress, LM 213
Washington, DC 20540-7210
(Note: Hill offices may use Inside Mail)

For questions, comments or problems about CRS services, please call Robert Newlen, Legislative Relations Office, 7-3915.

B. Congressional Budget Office (CBO)

The Congressional Budget Office (CBO) was created by the Congressional Budget and Impoundment Control Act of 1974. It began operating on February 24, 1975, with the appointment of its first director, Alice M. Rivlin. CBO's mission is to provide Congress with objective, timely, nonpartisan analyses needed for economic and budget decisions and with the information and estimates required for the congressional budget process. Compared with the missions of the Congress's other support agencies — the Congressional Research Service and the Government Accountability Office — CBO's mandate is relatively narrow. But its subject matter gives it a broad reach, reflecting the wide array of activities that the federal budget covers and the major role the budget plays in the U.S. economy.

A substantial part of what CBO does is to support the work of the House and Senate Committees on the Budget, which were also created by the 1974 act. Those committees are in charge of the process, spelled out in the act, by which the Congress sets its own targets for the federal budget, including the overall levels of revenues and spending, the surplus or deficit that results, and the distribution of federal spending by broad functional categories. Each spring Congress adopts the end result of that process, the congressional budget plan, in the form of a concurrent resolution. The resolution imposes an overall framework and discipline on the consideration of appropriations, other spending measures, and tax legislation.

The policies and principles that have shaped CBO since its inception are a key factor in its effectiveness. CBO is a professional, nonpartisan staff office, and it does not make recommendations on policy. That nonpartisan stance has been instrumental in preserving the agency's reputation for professionalism and has enhanced the credibility of its products. CBO prepares independent analyses and estimates relating to the budget and the economy and presents options and alternatives for Congress to consider. It routinely discloses the assumptions and methods it uses, which enhances the general perception of its products as objective and impartial.

Some of CBO's activities are statutory tasks; others are carried out at the request of congressional committees or individual Members. According to the Budget Act, CBO must give priority first to requests for services from the House and Senate Budget Committees; second, to requests from the two Appropriations Committees, the House Committee on Ways and Means, and the Senate Committee on Finance; and finally, to requests from all other congressional committees. CBO prepares various type of analyses for Congress, including cost estimates for bills that individual Members have introduced or plan to introduce. But, committee requests always take priority. CBO handles requests from individual Members only to the extent that its resources permit.

CBO's services can be grouped in four categories: helping Congress formulate a budget plan, helping it stay within that plan; helping it assess the impact of federal mandates, and helping it consider issues related to the budget and to economic policy.

1. Helping Congress Develop a Plan for the Budget.

The House and Senate Budget Committees prepare the annual congressional budget plan, drawing on the "views and estimates" of the other committees. A major part of CBO's role in that process is to prepare an annual report, which provides economic and budget projections for the next 10 years. Typically, it also includes a discussion of some current economic or budget policy issues, such as the effects of the federal deficit on economic growth or recent changes in the budget process. CBO customarily updates its economic and budget projections in midyear.

Economic Forecasts and Projections

CBO is the only part of the legislative branch whose mandate includes making economic forecasts and projections. Its forecasts cover 18 to 24 months and involve the major economic variables — gross domestic product (GDP), unemployment, inflation, and interest rates. CBO does not attempt to forecast cyclical fluctuations in the economy more than two years ahead; instead, its longer-term projections are based on trends in the labor force, productivity, and savings.

CBO draws the information for its forecasts from the major econometric models and commercial economic forecasting services. It also relies on the advice of a distinguished panel of advisers that meets twice a year. Usually, CBO's forecasts are fairly close to the consensus of private forecasters. CBO regularly publishes an evaluation of its economic forecasting record.

Baseline Budget Projections

The purpose of CBO's budget projections is to give Congress a baseline for measuring the effects of proposed changes in tax and spending laws. The projections show what would happen to the federal budget if current spending or revenue policies were unchanged over the projection period. The Budget Committees use the projections to develop their annual budget resolutions and directives to other committees. CBO uses them to produce cost estimates for proposed legislation and in scorekeeping tabulations.

For revenues and entitlement programs, such as Social Security or Medicare, the baseline projections generally assume that current laws will continue without change. For discretionary spending, which is controlled by annual appropriation bills, CBO bases its projections on the most recent appropriations, adjusted for the projected rate of inflation.

Analysis of the President's Budget and Other Assistance

Each year, at the request of the Senate Committee on Appropriations, CBO analyzes the President's budget to see how its revenue and spending proposals would affect CBO's baseline budget projections. In the analysis, CBO uses its own economic assumptions and estimating techniques to recast the budget the President has proposed and submitted to Congress. In addition, as Congress moves towards its annual budget resolution, CBO helps the budget and other committees estimate the effects of alternative budget plans. Frequently, CBO officials are asked to testify before congressional committees about the outlook for the economy and the budget and about other matters related to developing the annual budget plan.

Long-Term Budgetary Pressures and Policy Options

The 10-year time frame CBO uses for preparing budget projections is not sufficient to show the dramatic effects that the projected demographic changes in the U.S. population over the next three decades would have on the federal budget. The upcoming retirement of the large baby-boom generation and the continuing growth of per-enrollee health care costs would place growing pressure on the budget, largely because they would increase spending on Social Security, Medicare, and other programs that serve the elderly. Since 1996, CBO has periodically prepared a report on the long-term budgetary outlook and on some of the policy options for controlling the growth of spending in those programs.

2. Helping Congress Stay Within Its Budget Plan

Once Congress adopts the annual budget resolution, the Budget Committees take the lead in enforcing its provisions. To help them, CBO supplies estimates of the budgetary impact of bills reported by the different committees and up-to-date tabulations (referred to as scorekeeping) of the status of congressional actions on legislation that affects the budget.

Cost Estimate for Bills

CBO is required to develop a cost estimate for virtually every bill reported by congressional committees to show how it would affect spending or revenues over the next five years or more. For most tax legislation, CBO uses estimates provided by the Joint Committee on Taxation, a separate congressional analytic group that works closely with the two tax-writing committees. CBO also prepares cost estimates for use in drafting bills (especially in the early stages), formulating floor amendments, and working out the final form of legislation in conference committees. To the extent that its resources permit, CBO estimates the cost of bills at the request of individual Members. In the past, where appropriate, CBO estimates contained the projected costs to state and local governments of carrying out the proposed legislation. In March 1995, enactment of the Unfunded Mandates Reform Act greatly expanded CBO's responsibilities in that area (see below).

CBO's cost estimates have become an integral part of the legislative process and committees increasingly refer to them at every stage of drafting bills. The estimates may also have an impact on the final outcome of legislation because they are used to determine whether committees are complying with the annual budget resolutions and reconciliation instructions.

Another CBO responsibility is providing estimates to the Appropriations Committees of Congress. The numbers contained in appropriation bills usually represent budget authority, and the resulting outlays must be estimated. (Outlays are generally checks issued by the Treasury or cash-equivalent transactions that, when subtracted from receipts, are used to calculate the budget surplus or deficit.) CBO's estimates may be critical in determining whether a bill complies with allocations in the annual budget resolution.

Scorekeeping

One of CBO's most important functions is to keep track of all spending and revenue legislation considered each year so Congress can know whether it is acting within the limits set by the annual budget resolution. CBO provides the Budget and Appropriations Committees with frequent tabulations of congressional action on both spending and revenue bills — although the bulk of CBO's scorekeeping involves spending legislation. The scorekeeping systems keep track of all bills that affect the budget from the time they are reported out of committee to the time they are enacted into law.

3. Helping Congress Assess Federal Mandates

To assess better the impact of its laws on state, local, and tribal governments and the private sector, Congress passed the Unfunded Mandates Reform Act of 1995. The act amends the Congressional Budget Act to require CBO to give authorizing committees a statement about whether reported bills contain federal mandates. If the direct costs of an intergovernmental or private-sector mandate exceed specified thresholds in any of the first five years after the mandate takes effect, CBO must provide an estimate of those costs (if feasible) and the basis of the estimate.

CBO's statement must also include an assessment of what funding is authorized in the bill to cover the costs of the mandates and, for intergovernmental mandates, an estimate of the appropriations needed to fund such authorizations for up to 10 years after the mandate is effective. When requested, CBO is also required to assist committees by preparing studies of legislative proposals containing federal mandates. The law took effect on January 1, 1996.

4. Helping Congress Consider Budget and Economic Policy Issues.

CBO's responsibilities also entail analyzing specific program and policy issues that affect the federal budget and the economy. For the most part, requests for those analyses come from the chairman or ranking minority member of a full committee or subcommittee. The leadership of either party in the House or Senate may also request CBO analysis.

The analyses cover a variety of federal activities, examining current policies, suggesting other approaches, and projecting how the alternatives would affect current programs, the federal budget, and the economy. In keeping with its nonpartisan mandate, CBO does not offer recommendations on policy in those reports.

Some of the analyses take nine to 12 months, or sometimes longer, to complete. Other analyses may be conducted in a much shorter time frame, usually appearing as papers or memorandums. Many CBO reports have helped shape public discussion of the issues they address, not only on Capitol Hill but in the nation at large. A list of CBO's recent publications shows the broad range of their subject matter.

Employing Staff and Budgetary Resources

CBO's annual appropriation limits the number of staff the agency may employ. The appropriation for FY1976 authorized 193 positions. Since 1977, the agency's staffing limit has grown to the present level of 235 full-time equivalent positions. Of those, 215 are designated professional and 20 are support positions.

CBO is an agency dominated by economists and policy analysts. All of its directors have held Ph.D.'s, most in economics, and about 60 percent of its professional staff hold advanced degrees in either economics, public policy, or a related field. Nearly all of CBO's professional staff have completed four or more years of college; three out of four have graduate degrees.

CBO's FY2004 appropriation was $33.6 million. Of its total expenditures, the largest share — 88 percent — is allotted to personnel. The second largest component is computer costs. Today, those expenditures make up about six percent of total spending.

Services and offices are located on the fourth floor of the Ford House Office Building (formerly House Annex II) at Second and D Streets, SW, in Washington, DC. The building is served by the Blue and Orange Lines of the Washington Metrorail system; the Federal Center SW station is across from the Third Street side of the building. A shuttle bus service operated on Capitol Hill by the Architect of the Capitol serves the Ford Building.

How to Contact CBO

For general information, call 202-226-2600. The fax number is (202) 226-2714. CBO is open weekdays from 9:00 a.m. to 5:30 p.m.

How to Obtain CBO Products

Congressional Distribution. Members of Congress receive copies of all CBO reports and studies. The fax number is (202) 226-3040. CBO is open weekdays from 9:00 a.m. to 5:30 p.m.

Public Distribution. Single copies of CBO's reports, studies, papers, and memorandums are available to the public at no charge. Those documents are also available on CBO's website (www.cbo.gov). To request a list of publications or a specific document, call the Publications Office at (202) 226-2809 weekdays between 9:00 a.m. and 5:30 p.m. or write to the following:

CBO Publications Office
Management, Business, and Information Services Division
Ford House Office Building
Second and D Streets, SW
Washington, DC 20515

To obtain multiple copies, contact the U.S. Government Printing Office, which sells many of CBO's reports and studies. For information about availability, exact costs, and ordering, call (202) 275-3030 or write to the following:

Superintendent of Documents
U.S. Government Printing Office
Washington, DC 20402

CBO cost estimates are available to the public on the website and are generally included in Senate and House committee reports that accompany reported legislation. The Publications Office does not distribute copies of cost estimates.

C. Offices of Senate Legal Counsel and House General Counsel

For over two decades the offices of Senate Legal Counsel and House General Counsel have developed parallel yet distinctly unique and independent roles as institutional legal "voices" of the two bodies they represent. Familiarity with the structure and operation of these offices and the nature of the support they may provide committees in the context of an investigative oversight proceeding is essential.

A. Senate Legal Counsel

The Office of Senate Legal Counsel[94] was created by Title VII of the Ethics in Government Act of 1978[95] "to serve the institution of Congress rather than the partisan interests of one party or another."[96] The counsel and deputy counsel are appointed by the president pro tempore of the Senate upon the recommendation of the majority and minority leaders. The appointment of each is made effective by a resolution of the Senate, and each may be removed from office by a resolution of the Senate. The term of appointment of the counsel and deputy counsel is two Congresses. The appointment of the counsel and deputy counsel and the counsel's appointment of assistant Senate Legal Counsel are required to be made without regard to political affiliation. The office is responsible to a bipartisan Joint Leadership Group, which is comprised of the majority and minority leaders, the president pro tempore, and the chairman and ranking minority member of the Committees on the Judiciary and on Rules and Administration.[97]

The act specifies the activities of the office, two of which are of immediate interest to committee oversight concerns: representing committees of the Senate in proceedings to aid them in investigations, and advising committees and officers of the Senate.[98]

(1) Proceedings to Aid Investigations by Senate Committees

The Senate Legal Counsel may represent committees in proceedings to obtain evidence for Senate investigations. Two specific proceedings are authorized.

The first proceeding is under the law providing committees the authority to grant witness immunity (18 U.S.C. § 6005). It provides that a committee or subcommittee of either house of Congress may request an immunity order from a U.S. district court when the request has been approved by the affirmative vote of two-thirds of the members of the full committee. By the same vote, a committee may direct the Senate Legal Counsel to represent it or any of its subcommittees in an application for an immunity order.[99]

The second proceeding involves authority under the Ethics in Government Act of 1978 which permits the Senate Legal Counsel to represent a committee or subcommittee of the Senate in a civil action to enforce a subpoena. Prior to the Ethics Act, subpoenas of the Senate could be enforced only through the cumbersome method of a contempt proceeding before the bar of the Senate or by a certification to the U.S. attorney and a prosecution for criminal contempt of Congress under 2 U.S.C. §§ 192, 194. The Ethics Act authorizes the Senate to enforce its subpoenas through a civil action in the U.S. District Court for the District of Columbia.[100] The House chose not to avail itself of this procedure and this enforcement method applies only to Senate subpoenas. Senate subpoenas have been enforced in several civil actions. See, for example, proceedings to hold in contempt a recalcitrant witness in the impeachment proceedings against Judge Alcee L. Hastings[101] and proceedings to enforce a subpoena *duces tecum* for the production of diaries of Senator Bob Packwood.[102]

The statute details the procedure for directing the Senate Legal Counsel to bring a civil action to enforce a subpoena. In contrast to an application for an immunity order, which may be authorized by a committee, only the full Senate by resolution may authorize an action to enforce a subpoena.[103] The Senate may not consider a resolution to direct the counsel to bring an action unless the investigating committee reports the resolution by a majority vote. The statute specifies the required contents of the committee report; among other matters, the committee must report on the extent to which the subpoenaed party has complied with the subpoena, the objections or privileges asserted by the witness, and the comparative effectiveness of a criminal and civil proceeding.[104] A significant limitation on the civil enforcement remedy is that it excludes from its coverage actions against officers or employees of the federal government acting within their official capacities, except where the refusal to comply is based on the assertion of a personal privilege or objection and not on a governmental privilege or objection that has been authorized by the executive branch.[105] Its reach is limited to natural persons and to entities acting or purporting to act under the color of state law.[106]

(2) Advice to committees and officers of the Senate and other duties

The Ethics act details a number of advisory functions of the Office of Senate Legal Counsel. Principal among these are the responsibility of advising Members, committees, and officers of the Senate with respect to subpoenas or requests for the withdrawal of Senate documents, and the responsibility of advising committees about their promulgation and implementation of rules and procedures for congressional investigations. The office also provides advice about legal questions that arise during the course of investigations.[107]

The act also provides that the counsel shall perform such other duties consistent with the nonpartisan purposes and limitations of Title VII as the Senate may direct.[108] Thus, in 1980, the office was used in the investigation relating to President Carter's brother, Billy, and his connection to Libya. The office worked under the direction of the chairman and vice-chairman of the subcommittee charged with the conduct of that investigation.[109] Members of the office have also undertaken special assignments such as the Senate's investigation of "Abscam" and other undercover activities,[110] the impeachment proceedings of Judge Harry Claiborne,[111] Judge Walter L. Nixon, Jr.,[112] and Judge Alcee L. Hastings Jr., [113] and the confirmation hearings of Justice Clarence E. Thomas. The office was called upon to assist in the Senate's conduct of the impeachment trial of President Clinton.

In addition, the counsel's office provides information and advice to Members, officers, and employees on a wide range of legal and administrative matters relating to Senate business. Unlike the House practice, the Senate Legal Counsel plays no formal role in the review and issuance of subpoenas. However, since it may become involved in civil enforcement proceedings, it has welcomed the opportunity to review proposed subpoenas for form and substance prior to their issuance by committees. The Office of Senate Legal Counsel can be reached at 224-4435.

B. House General Counsel

The House Office of General Counsel has evolved since the mid-1970s, from its original role as a legal advisor to the Clerk of the House on a range of matters that fell within the jurisdiction of the Clerk's office, to that of counsel for the institution. At the beginning of the 103rd Congress, it was made a separate House office, reporting directly to the Speaker, charged with the responsibility "of providing legal assistance and representation to the House."[114] While the function and role of the House Office of General Counsel and Senate Legal Counsel with respect to oversight assistance to committees and protection of institutional prerogatives are similar, there are some differences that will be noted below.

The General Counsel, Deputy General Counsel, and other attorneys of the office are appointed by the Speaker and serve at his pleasure.[115] The office "function[s] pursuant to the direction of the Speaker, who shall consult with a Bipartisan Legal Advisory Group," which consists of the Speaker himself, the Majority Leader, Majority Whip, Minority Leader, and Minority Whip.[116] The office has statutory authority to appear before state or federal courts in the course of performing its functions. 2 U.S.C. § 130f. The office may appear as amicus curiae on behalf of the Speaker and the Bipartisan Legal Advisory Group in litigation involving the institutional interests of the House.[117] Where authorized by statute or resolution, the office may represent the House itself in judicial proceedings.[118] The office also represents House officers in litigation affecting the institutional interests and prerogatives of the House.[119] Finally, the office defends the House, its committees, officers, and employees in civil litigation relating to their official responsibilities, or when they have been subpoenaed to testify or to produce House records (*see* House Rule VIII).

Unlike Senate committees, House committees may only issue subpoenas under the seal of the Clerk of the House. In practice, committees often work closely with the Office of General Counsel in drafting subpoenas and every subpoena issued by a committee is reviewed by the office for substance and form. Committees frequently seek the advice and assistance of the Office of General Counsel in dealing with various asserted constitutional, statutory, and common-law privileges,[120] in responding to executive agencies and officials that resist congressional oversight,[121] and in navigating the statutory process for obtaining a contempt citation with respect to a recalcitrant witness.[122]

The Office of General Counsel represents the interests of House committees in judicial proceedings in a variety of circumstances. The office represents committees in federal court on applications for immunity orders pursuant to 18 U.S.C. § 6005; appears as amicus curiae in cases affecting House committee investigations;[123] defends against attempts to obtain direct or indirect judicial interference with congressional subpoenas or other investigatory authority;[124] represents committees seeking to prevent compelled disclosure of non-public information relating to their investigatory or other legislative activities;[125] and appears in court on behalf of committees seeking judicial assistance in obtaining access to documents or information such as documents that are under seal or materials which may be protected by Rule 6(e) of the Federal Rules of Criminal Procedure.[126]

Like the Senate Legal Counsel's office, the House General Counsel's office also devotes a large portion of its time to rendering informal advice to individual Members and committees. The office can be reached at (202) 225-9700. Its website address is [http://generalcounsel.house.gov/], which is available only to House offices.

D. Government Accountability Office (GAO)

The Government Accountability Office, formerly called the General Accounting Office (GAO), was established by the Budget and Accounting Act of 1921 (31 U.S.C. § 702) as an independent auditor of government agencies. Over the years, Congress has expanded GAO's audit authority, added new responsibilities and duties, and strengthened GAO's ability to perform independently of the executive branch. GAO is under the control and direction of the Comptroller General of the United States, who is appointed by the President with the advice and consent of the Senate for a term of 15 years.

GAO's core values define the organization and its people. These core values are accountability, integrity, and reliability.

1. Accountability

Most GAO reviews are made in response to specific congressional requests. GAO is required to do work requested by committee chairmen and, as a matter of policy, assigns equal status to requests from ranking minority members. To the extent possible, GAO also responds to individual member requests. Other assignments are initiated pursuant to standing commitments to congressional committees, and some reviews are specifically required by law. Finally, some assignments are undertaken in accordance with GAO's basic legislative responsibilities. GAO staff are located in Washington and in offices across the United States.

Types of Questions GAO Answers

Is a federal program achieving the desired results, or are changes needed in government policies or management?

Are there better ways of accomplishing the objectives of a federal program at lower costs?

Is a government program being carried out in compliance with applicable laws and regulations, and are data furnished to Congress on the program accurate?

Do opportunities exist to eliminate waste and inefficient use of public funds?

Are funds being spent legally, and is accounting for them accurate?

2. Integrity

Integrity describes the high standards that GAO sets for itself in the conduct of its work. GAO seeks to take a professional, objective, fact-based, fair and balanced approach to all of its activities. Integrity is the foundation of its reputation and GAO's approach to its work.

Products

GAO provides oral briefings, testimony, and written reports. Written reports vary in format and content depending on the complexity of the assignment. If agreements reached during early discussions differ substantially from the original request, GAO often confirms changes in writing to ensure a mutual understanding about the assignment. Sometimes, agreements need to be altered as an assignment progresses. For example, a requester's needs may change, the required data may be unavailable or unobtainable in the time allowed, or the methodology may need to be changed. In these cases, GAO works with the requester to revise the assignment. Again, substantial changes from previous agreements are often confirmed in writing.

Early communication with the requester also is important because:

Similar or duplicate requests may be received. GAO tries to consolidate assignments and provide copies of a report to each requester.

An ongoing review may address (or may be revised to address) a requester's needs. GAO works with the requester to ensure a satisfactory and prompt response.

A recently completed review may adequately address a requester's concerns and make starting a new assignment unnecessary.

GAO may not be the most appropriate agency to perform the assignment. In those cases, GAO will suggest referring the assignment to the Congressional Budget Office, the Congressional Research Service, the inspector general of a particular agency, or the agency itself. GAO remains available to help a requester if the information provided does not meet the requester's needs.

GAO strives to use its budget and staff resources effectively. On occasion, the resources required by congressional requests exceed the supply of talent available within GAO. Also, in some cases, the GAO staff most knowledgeable of a request's subject matter are engaged on other assignments and are not immediately available. In either case, GAO will do everything possible to respond to a new congressional request. However, it may be necessary to delay starting some requests. In those cases, GAO seeks the requesters' help in setting priorities.

3. Reliability

Reliability describes GAO's goal for how its work is viewed by Congress and the American public. GAO's objective is to produce high quality reports, testimony, briefings, legal opinions, and other products and services that are timely, accurate, useful, clear, and candid.

The effectiveness of GAO products derives from their quality and the way requesters and agency officials use them to improve government operations. GAO offers a range of products to communicate the results of its work. The type of product resulting from a particular assignment depends on the assignment's objectives and/or a requester's needs. In selecting a type of product, tradeoffs may be necessary in scope, detail, or time. GAO's products include written reports to Congress, committees, or individual members; testimony; and oral briefings.

4. Additional Services

In addition to its audits and evaluations, GAO offers a number of other services.

a. Office of Special Investigations.

The Office of Special Investigations (OSI) conducts investigations for Congress and the Government Accountability Office (GAO). OSI's primary mission is to support the Congress by investigating allegations of illegal and improper conduct relating to federal funds, programs, and activities. OSI typically investigates allegations of fraud, corruption, abuse, ethics violations and conflicts of interest. Additionally, OSI performs security tests and reviews to determine whether security vulnerabilities exist in federal systems and facilities. OSI conducts its work in accordance with the standards established by the President's Council on Integrity and Efficiency (PCIE).

b. Legal Services

GAO provides various legal services. For example, upon request, GAO may render a legal decision or opinion on questions involving the use of, and accountability for, public funds or on other legal issues of interest to congressional committees. In addition, under a variety of statutes, GAO (1) oversees executive branch compliance with the Impoundment Control Act of 1974 and reviews and reports to Congress on proposed rescissions and deferrals of federal funds; (2) reviews all major rules proposed by federal agencies and provides reports to Congress; and (3) receives agency reports about vacancies in Presidentially appointed, Senate confirmed positions and issues legal opinions under the Federal Vacancies Reform Act of 1998. GAO publishes Principles of Federal Appropriations Law (known as the Red Book) and teaches a class that provides an orientation to federal fiscal laws. GAO attorneys are available for informal technical assistance. Also, GAO, under the Competition in Contracting Act, provides an objective, independent, and impartial forum for the resolution of bid protests of awards of federal contracts.

c. Accounting and Financial Management Policy

GAO prescribes accounting principles and standards for the executive branch. It also advises federal agencies on fiscal and other policies and procedures and prescribe standards for auditing government programs.

d. Audit/Evaluation Community Support

GAO also provides other services to help the audit and evaluation community improve and keep abreast of current developments. For example, it publishes and distributes papers on current audit and evaluation methodologies and approaches;

assists in various training programs sponsored by these organizations; and sponsors an international auditor fellowship program to help other nations achieve an effective audit/evaluation organization.

e. **Committee Support**
Occasionally, GAO assigns staff to work directly for congressional committees. In these cases, the staff assigned represent a committee and not GAO.

5. Obtaining GAO Services

Congressional requesters are encouraged to contact GAO on an informal basis prior to submitting a written request. GAO staff are pleased to consult with requesters or their staffs and help them frame questions and issues and formulate strategies and approaches even before a request letter is written.

GAO encourages the continuation of close working relationships between requesters or their staffs and GAO. GAO's Office of Congressional Relations (512-4400) can help requesters identify an appropriate GAO point for contact. To request formally GAO assistance, write to:

The Honorable David M. Walker
Comptroller General of the United States
441 G Street NW
Washington, DC 20548

Information about GAO and the materials it produces can be obtained from its website at [http://www.gao.gov].

E. Office of Management and Budget (OMB)

The Office of Management and Budget, [http://www.omb.gov], came into existence in 1970; its predecessor agency, the Bureau of the Budget, dated back to 1921. Initially established as a unit in the Treasury Department, since 1939 the budget agency has been a part of the Executive Office of the President.

1. **Capabilities.**
   a. OMB is the *President's* agent for the management and implementation of policy, including the federal budget.
   b. OMB's *major* responsibilities include:
      1. Assisting the President in the preparation of the budget and development of a fiscal program.
      2. Supervising and controlling the administration of the budget, including transmittal to Congress of proposals for deferrals and rescissions .
      3. Keeping the President informed about agencies' activities (proposed, initiated, and completed), in order to coordinate efforts, expend appropriations economically, and minimize overlap and duplication.

4. Administering the process of review of proposed and final agency files established by Executive Order 12866.
5. Administering the process of review and approval of collections of information by federal agencies and reducing the burden of agency information collection on the public under the Paperwork Reduction Act of 1995.
6. Overseeing the manner in which agencies disseminate information to the public (including electronic dissemination); how agencies collect, maintain, and use statistics; how agencies' archives are maintained; how agencies develop systems for insuring privacy, confidentiality, security, and the sharing of information collected by the government; and how the government acquires and uses information technology, pursuant to the Paperwork Reduction Act of 1995.
7. Studying and promoting better governmental management, including making recommendations to agencies regarding their administrative organization and operations.
8. Helping the President by clearing and coordinating the advice of agencies regarding legislative proposals and making recommendations about presidential action on legislation.
9. Assisting in the preparation, consideration, and clearance of executive orders and proclamations.
10. Planning and developing information systems that provide the President with program performance data.
11. Establishing and overseeing implementation of financial management policies and requirements for the federal government as required by the Chief Financial Officers Act of 1990.
12. Assisting in development of regulatory reform proposals and programs for paperwork reduction, and then the implementation of these initiatives.
13. Improving the economy and efficiency of the federal procurement process by providing overall direction for procurement policies, regulations, procedures, and forms.
14. Establishing policies and methods that reduce fraud, waste, and abuse, and coordinating the work of the inspectors general through the President's Council on Integrity and Efficiency and the Executive Council on Integrity and Efficiency.

2. Limitations.

OMB is inevitably drawn into institutional and partisan struggles between the President and Congress. Difficulties for Congress notwithstanding, OMB is the central clearinghouse for executive agencies and is, therefore, a rich source of information for investigative and oversight committees.

F. Budget Information

Since enactment of the 1974 Budget Act, as amended, Congress has more budgetary information than ever before. Extensive budgetary materials are also available from the executive branch. Some of the major sources of budgetary information are available on and off Capitol Hill. They include (1) the President and executive agencies (recall that under the Budget and Accounting Act of 1921, the President presents annually a national budget to Congress); (2) the Congressional Budget Office; (3) the House and Senate Budget Committees; (4) the House and Senate Appropriations Committees; and (5) the House and Senate legislative committees. In addition, the Government Accountability Office and the Congressional Research Service prepare fiscal and other relevant reports for the legislative branch.

Worth mention is that discretionary spending, the component of the budget that the Appropriations Committees oversee through the appropriations process, accounts for about one-third of federal spending. Other House and Senate committees, particularly Ways and Means and Finance, oversee more than $1 trillion in spending through reauthorizations, direct spending measures, and reconciliation legislation. In addition, Ways and Means and Finance oversee a diverse set of programs, including tax collection, tax expenditures, and some user fees, through the revenue process. The oversight activities of all of these committees is enhanced through the use of the diverse range of budgetary information that is available to them.

1. Executive Branch Budget Products

Budget of the United States Government, Fiscal Year 2005 contains the Budget Message of the President and information on the President's 2005 budget proposals by budget function.

Analytical Perspectives, Budget of the United States Government, Fiscal Year 2005 contains analyses that are designed to highlight specified subject areas or provide other significant presentations of budget data that place the budget in perspective.

The *Analytical Perspectives* volume includes economic and accounting analyses; information on Federal receipts and collections; analyses of federal spending; detailed information on Federal borrowing and debt; the Budget Enforcement Act preview report; current services estimates; and other technical presentations. It also includes information on the budget system and concepts and a listing of the federal programs by agency and account.

Historical Tables, Budget of the United States Government, Fiscal Year 2005 provides data on budget receipts, outlays, surpluses or deficits, federal debt, and federal employment covering an extended time period — in most cases beginning in FY1940 or earlier and ending in FY2009. These are much longer time periods than those covered by similar tables in other budget documents. As much as possible, the data in this volume and all other historical data in the budget documents have been made consistent with the concept and presentation used in the 2001 budget, so the data series are comparable over time.

Budget of the United States Government, Fiscal Year 2005 — Appendix contains detailed information on the various appropriations and funds that constitute the budget and is designed primarily for the use of the Appropriations Committee. The Appendix contains more detailed financial information on individual programs and appropriation accounts than any of the other budget documents. It includes for each agency: the proposed text of appropriations language, budget schedules for each account, new legislative proposals, explanations of the work to be performed and the funds needed, and proposed general provisions applicable to the appropriations of entire agencies or groups of agencies. Information is also provided on certain activities whose outlays are not part of the budget totals. The *Appendix* is perhaps the most useful product in the President's initial budget submission for obtaining programmatic detail.

Automated Sources of Budget Information. The information contained in the above-listed documents is available in electronic format from the following sources: (1) CD-ROM. The CD-ROM contains all of the budget documents and software to support reading, printing, and searching for documents. The CD-ROM also has many of the tables in the budget in spreadsheet format. (2) Internet. All budget documents, including documents that are released at a future date, are to be available for downloading in several formats from the Internet. To access documents through the website, use the following address: [http://www.gpo.gov/usbudget].

Several other points about the President's budget and executive agency budget products are worth noting. First, the President's budgetary communications to Congress continue after the January/February submission and usually include a series of budget amendments and supplementals, the Mid-Session Review, Statements of Administration Policy (SAPs) on legislation, and even revised budgets on occasion. Second, most of these additional communications are issued as House documents and are available on the Web from GPO Access or the OMB homepage (in the case of SAPs). Third, the initial budget products often do not provide sufficient information on the President's budgetary recommendations to enable committees to begin developing legislation, and that further budgetary information is provided in the "justification" materials (see below) and the later submission of legislative proposals. Finally, the internal executive papers (such as agency budget submissions to OMB) often are not made available to Congress.

2. Some Other Sources of Useful Budgetary Information

a. *Committees on Appropriations.* The subcommittees of the House and Senate Appropriations Committees hold extensive hearings on the fiscal year appropriations requests of federal departments and agencies. The Appropriations Subcommittees typically print agency *justification material* with the hearing record of the federal officials concerning these requests.

Each federal department or agency submits *justification material* to the Committees on Appropriations. Their submissions can run from several hundreds of pages to over two thousand pages.

b. *Budget Committees.* House and Senate Budget Committees, in preparing to report the annual concurrent budget resolution, conduct hearings on overall federal budget policy. These hearings and other fiscal analyses made by these panels address various aspects of federal programs and funding levels which can be useful sources of information.

c. *Other Committees.* To assist the Budget Committees in developing the concurrent budget resolution, other committees are required to prepare "views and estimates" of programs in their jurisdiction. Committee views and estimates, usually packaged together and issued as a committee print, also may be a useful source of detailed budget data.

d. *Internal Agency Studies and Budget Reviews.* These agency studies and reviews are often conducted in support of budget formulation and can yield useful information about individual programs. The budgeting documents, evaluations, and priority rankings of individual agency programs can provide insights into executive branch views of the importance of individual programs.

G. Beneficiaries, Private Organizations, and Interest Groups

Committees and Members can acquire useful information about executive branch programs and performance from the beneficiaries of those programs, private organizations, and interest groups. An effective oversight device, for example, is to ask beneficiaries how well federal programs and services are working. A variety of methods might be employed to solicit the views of those on the receiving end of federal programs and services, including investigations and hearings, field and on-site meetings, surveys and opinion polls, and websites. The results of such efforts can assist committees in obtaining policy-relevant information about program performance and in evaluating the problems people might be having with federal administrators and agencies.

There are numerous think tanks, universities, or associations, for instance, that periodically conduct studies of public policy issues and advise Members and others on how well federal agencies and programs are working. Similarly, numerous interest groups are active in monitoring areas such as civil rights, education, or health and they are not reluctant to point out alleged bureaucratic failings to committees and Members. Some of these groups may also assist committees and Members in bringing about improvements in agencies and programs.

There are also scores of social, political, scientific, environmental, and humanitarian nongovernmental organizations (NGOs) located around the world. Working with governments, corporations, foundations, and other entities are such NGOs as Greeenpeace, Amnesty International, the World Resources Institute, the Red Cross, and the Save the Children Fund. Many NGOs might provide valuable assistance to congressional overseers because they "do legal, scientific, technical, and policy analysis; provide services; shape, implement, monitor, and enforce national and international commitments; and change institutions and norms."[127]

SELECTED READINGS

General

Bimber, Bruce. "Information as a Factor in Congressional Politics," Legislative Studies Quarterly, v. XVI, November 1991: 585-605.

Carnegie Commission on Science, Technology, and Government. Science, Technology, and Congress: Analysis and Advice from the Congressional Support Agencies. Washington: The Carnegie Commission, 1991. 70p.

Chubb, John E. Interest Groups and the Bureaucracy. Stanford, Calif.: Stanford University Press, 1983. 319p.

Gilmour, Robert S. and Alexis A. Halley, eds. Who Makes Public Policy? Chatham, N.J.: Chatham House Publishers, Inc., 1994. 390p. JK585.W48

Heinz, John P., et al. The Hollow Core: Private Interests in National Policy Making. Cambridge, Mass.: Harvard University Press, 1993. 450p. JK1118.H55

U.S. Congress. Joint Committee on the Organization of Congress. Support Agencies. Hearing before the Joint Committee on the Organization of Congress. 103rd Congress, 1st session, June 10, 1993, Washington: GPO, 1993. 1577p. KF25.O7

Congressional Research Service [http://www.crs.gov]

Carney, Eliza Newlin. "Billington's Book Wars," National Journal, v. 24, March 21, 1992: 695- 698.

Cole, John Y. "Jefferson's Legacy: A Brief History of the Library," Library of Congress Bulletin, v. 50, April 8, 1991: 124-130.

Dalrymple, Helen. "Congressional Research Service: Think Tank, Policy Consultant and Information Factory," Library of Congress Information Bulletin, v. 49, September 24, 1990: 319-326.

Gude, Gilbert. "Congressional Research Service: the Research and Information Arm of Congress," Government Information Quarterly, v. 2, January 1985: 5-11.

Robinson, William H. "The Congressional Research Service: Policy Consultant, Think Tank, and Information Factory," In Organizations for Policy Analysis: Helping Government Think. edited by Carol H. Weiss. Newbury Park, Calif.: Sage Publications, 1992, pp. 181-200.

Government Accountability Office (formerly the General Accounting Office) [http://www.gao.gov]

Abikoff, Kevin T. "The Role of the Comptroller General in Light of Bowsher v. Synar," Columbia Law Review, v. 87, November 1987: 1539-1563.

Kaiser, Frederick M. GAO: Government Accountability Office and General Accounting Office. CRS Report RL30349, updated regularly.

——. GAO Versus the CIA: Uphill Battles Against an Overpowering Force. International Journal of Intelligence and Counterintelligence, v. 15, 2002: 330-389.

Mosher, Frederick C. A Tale of Two Agencies: A Comparative Analysis of the General Accounting Office and the Office of Management and Budget. Baton Rouge, La.: Louisiana State University Press, 1984. 219 p. HJG802.M682

Rozell, Mark J. "The Role of General Accounting Office Evaluation in the Post Reform Congress: The Case of General Revenue Sharing," International Journal of Public Administration, v. 7, September 1985: 267-290.

U.S. Congress. House. Committee on the Budget. Addressing Government Waste, Fraud, and Abuse. 108th Congress, 1st session. Washington: GPO, 2003. 421 p.

U.S. Congress. Senate. Committee on Governmental Affairs. The Roles, Mission and Operation of the U.S. General Accounting Office. Report Prepared by the National Academy of Public Administration. Senate Print 103-87, 103 Congress, 2nd session. Washington: GPO, 1994. 106 p.

U.S. Congress. House. Committee on Rules. Congressional Oversight: A "How-To" Series of Workshops. Committee Print. 106th Congress, 1st session. Washington: GPO, 2000. See pp. 90-143.

U.S. General Accounting Office. GAO History, 1921-1991, by Roger R. Trask. GAO Report OP-3-MP. (Washington: GAO, 1991).

U.S. Government Accountability Office. Strategic Plan [http://www.GAO.GOV].

Congressional Budget Office [http://www.cbo.gov]

Howard, James A. "Government Economic Projections: A Comparison Between CBO and OMB," Public Budgeting & Finance, v. 7, Autumn 1987: 14-25.

Keith, Robert and Allen Schick. Manual on the Federal Budget Process, CRS Report 98-720. GOV, August 28, 1998.

——and Mary Francis Bley. Congressional Budget Office: Appointment and Tenure of the Director and Deputy Director. CRS Report RL31880, October 29, 2003.

Schick, Allen. Congress and Money. Washington, D.C.: The Urban Institute, 1980. 604p. HJ2051.S34

Twogood, R. Philip. "Reconciling Politics and Budget Analysis: The Case of the Congressional Budget Office," Public Budgeting and Financial Management, v. 3, no. 1, 1991: 65-87.

Offices of Senate Legal Counsel and House General Counsel

Salokar, Rebecca Mae. "Legal Counsel for Congress: Protecting Institutional Interests," Congress and the Presidency. vol. 20, No. 2, Autumn 1993: 131-155.

Tiefer, Charles. "The Senate and House Counsel Offices: Dilemmas of Representing in Court the Institutional Congressional Client," Law and Contemporary Problems, v. 61, Spring 1998: 48-63.

Appendix D. Congressional Oversight Video Series

Oversight: A Key Congressional Function. Former Representative Lee Hamilton delivered the keynote address to a 1999 series of CRS programs examining various aspects of congressional oversight. In this program, Mr. Hamilton emphasizes the importance of traditional oversight and reviews factors that contribute to successful oversight.

Program Length: 60 minutes. Product No.: MM70003.

The Constitutional Context of Oversight. Michael Stern, senior counsel with the House General Counsel's Office, and Michael Davidson, former Senate Legal Counsel, discuss the constitutional context of oversight. In addition, the two attorneys address a variety of oversight topics, including congressional investigations. Taped as part of a 1999 series of CRS programs examining various aspects of congressional oversight.

Program Length: 60 minutes. Product No.: MM70004.

The "Rules & Tools" of Oversight. This program focuses on the formal institutional rules that committees must follow to insure the legitimacy and fairness of oversight proceedings. The nature of the formidable powers of inquiry available to congressional committees and the practicalities of their effective utilization are also explored. Taped as part of a 1999 series of CRS programs examining various aspects of congressional oversight.

Program Length: 60 minutes. Product No.: MM70005.

Sources of Oversight Assistance. This session focuses on where congressional committees can obtain assistance in conducting oversight. Especially relevant are inspectors general, chief financial officers, and Congress's own support agencies, the Congressional Budget Office, Congressional Research Service, and Government Accountability Office. Taped as part of a 1999 series of CRS programs examining various aspect of congressional oversight.

Program Length: 46 minutes. Product No.: MM70006.

Fiscal Oversight: "Follow the Money." This seminar examines congressional oversight of fiscal and budgetary activities, focusing on the role of the House and Senate Appropriations Committees in the annual budget cycle and key support activities of the Congressional Budget Office to Congress on budgetary matters generally. Taped as part of a 1999 series of CRS programs examining various aspects of congressional oversight.

Program Length: 45 minutes. Product No.: MM70007.

Outside Actors in the Oversight Process. This program addresses how non-congressional individuals can assist in the investigative process and in monitoring executive branch performance. The panel includes a journalist, members of public and private interest groups, and a former counsel with the House Commerce Committee, Subcommittee on Oversight and Investigations. Taped as part of a 1999 series of CRS programs examining various aspects of congressional oversight. Program Length: 50 minutes. Product No.: MM70008.

Preparing for an Oversight Investigation. This program probes the "ins and outs" of how to prepare for Congressional Investigations from the perspective of both the investigator and those being investigated Taped as part of a 1999 series of CRS programs examining various aspects of congressional oversight.

Program Length: 59:50. Product No.: MM70009.

Congress, the President, the Courts, and the Separation of Powers. Product No.: MM70097.

VHS copies of CRS video programs are available on loan to congressional offices. The soundtracks of many television programs are also available on audio cassettes. For the schedule of CRS Programs on Channel 6 of the House and Channel 5 of the Senate, call 7-7009. For further information about any of these programs, please call 7-7547.

End Notes

[1] *McGrain v. Daugherty,* 272 U.S. 135 (1927).

[2] 421 U.S. at 504, n. 15 (quoting *Barenblatt v. United States*, 360 U.S. 109, 111).

[3] 354 U.S. 178, 187 (1957).

[4] *Id.*

[5] *Kilbourn v. Thompson,* 103 U.S. 168, 204 (1880).

[6] *Watkins v. United States*, 354 U.S. at 187.

[7] *United States v. Rumely,* 345 U.S. 41, 42, 44 (1953); *Watkins v. United States,* 354 U.S. at 198.

[8] *McGrain v. Daugherty,* 273 U.S. at 174-75.

[9] *See, e.g.,* House Committee on Government Reform Rule 18 (d); Senate Committee on Homeland Security and Governmental Affairs Rule 5.C.

[10] U.S. CONST. Art. I, Sec. 6, cl. 1.

[11] *Eastland v. United States Servicemen's Fund,* 421 U.S. 491, 503-07 (1975).

[12] 365 U.S. 399, 408-09 (1961).

[13] *In re Chapman,* 166 U.S. 661, 669 (1897).

[14] False Statements Accountability Act of 1996, P.L. 104-292. Congress acted in response to the Supreme Court's decision in *Hubbard* v. *United States*, 514 U.S. 695 (1995), holding that 18 U.S.C. § 1001 applied only to false statements made in executive branch department and agency proceedings.

[15] *See* CRS Report 95-949, *Staff Depositions in Congressional Investigations*, by Jay R. Shampansky, at notes 16 and 18.

[16] *Watkins v. United States,* 354 U.S. 178 (1957); *Quinn v. United States,* 349 U.S. 155 (1955).

[17] Lawrence E. Walsh, The Independent Counsel and the Separation of Powers, 25 HOUS. L. REV. 1, 9 (1988).

[18] *Anderson v. Dunn,* 19 U.S. (6 Wheat.) 204 (1821).

[19] A more comprehensive treatment of the history and legal development of the congressional contempt power is discussed in CRS Report 86-83, *Congress' Contempt Power*, by Jay R. Shampansky (archived; out of print).

[20] *See Anderson v. Dunn*, 19 U.S. (6 Wheat.) 204 (1821); *see also McGrain v. Daugherty*, 273 U.S. 135 (1927).

[21] The 10 officials are as follows: Secretary of State Henry Kissinger (1975); Secretary of Commerce Rogers C. B. Morton (1975); Secretary of Health, Education, and Welfare Joseph A Califano, Jr. (1978); Secretary of Energy Charles Duncan (1980); Secretary of Energy James B. Edwards (1981); Secretary of the Interior James Watt (1982); EPA Administrator Anne Gorsuch Burford (1983); Attorney General William French Smith (1983); White House Counsel John M. Quinn (1996); and Attorney General Janet Reno (1998).

[22] 2 U.S.C. § 288 d.

[23] *Christoffel v. United States,* 378 U.S. 89 (1949).

[24] House Rule XI(2)(h)(2).

[25] Senate Rule XXVI(7)(a)(2) allows its committees to set a quorum requirement at less than the normal one-third for taking sworn testimony. Almost all Senate committees have set the quorum requirement at one member.

[26] *See* Archibald Cox, *Executive Privilege,* 122 U. OF PA. L. REV. 1383, 1395-1405 (1979). *See also generally,* Mark J. Rozell, Executive Privilege: Presidential Power, Secrecy and Accountability (2 ed. Revised, 2002, University Press of Kansas); Mark J. Rozell, *Executive Privilege and Modern Presidents: In Nixon's Shadow*, 83 MINN. L. REV. 1069 (1999).

[27] *See* Neil Devins, *Congressional-Executive Information Access Disputes: A Modest Proposal-Do Nothing,* 48 ADM. L. REV. 109 (1996).

[28] *United States v. Nixon,* 418 U.S. 683 (1974); *Nixon v. Sirica,* 487 F.2d 700 (D.C. Cir. 1973); *Senate Select Committee v. Nixon,* 498 F.2d 725 (D.C. Cir. 1974); *United States v. AT&T,* 551 F.2d 384 (D.C. Cir. 1976), *appeal after remand,* 567 F.2d 121 (D.C. Cir. 1977); *United States v. House of Representatives,* 556 F.Supp. 150 (D.D.C. 1983); *In re Sealed Case,* 121 F.3d 729 (D.C. Cir. 1997); *In re Grand Jury Proceedings*, 5 F. Supp. 2d 21 (D.D.C. 1998).

[29] *Senate Select Committee, supra; United States v. House of Representatives, supra;* and *United States v. AT&T, supra.*

[30] *Senate Select Committee, supra.*

[31] *Nixon v. Administrator of General Services,* 433 U.S. 425 (1977).

[32] 121 F.3d 729 (D.C. Cir. 1997).

[33] 365 F.3d 1108 (D.C. Cir. 2004).

[34] Neither case, however, involved congressional access to information.

[35] Neal Devins, "Congressional-Executive Information Access Disputes: A Modest Proposal: Do Nothing," *Administrative Law Review*, vol. 48, 109-137: winter 1996; Joel D. Bush, Congressional-Executive Access Disputes: Legal Standards and Political Settlements, *Journal of Law and Politics*, vol. 9, 717:1993; Stephen W. Stathis, "Executive Cooperation: Presidential Recognition of the Investigatory Authority of Congress and the Courts," *Journal of Law and Politics*, vol. 3, 183:1986.

[36] The subpoena was for certain tape recordings and documents relating to the President's conversations with aides and advisors. The materials were sought for use in a criminal trial.

[37] 418 U.S. 683, 712 n. 19 (1974). In *Senate Select Committee on Presidential Campaign Activities* v. *Nixon*, 498 F. 2d 725 (D.C. Cir. 1974), decided prior to *U.S.* v. *Nixon*, the appeals court denied the Watergate Committee's access to five presidential tapes because the committee had not met its burden of showing that "the subpoenaed evidence is demonstrably critical to the responsible fulfillment of the Committee's function." The court noted that its denial was based upon the initiation of impeachment proceedings by the House Judiciary Committee, the overlap of the investigative objectives of both committees, and the fact that the impeachment committee already had the tapes in question, concluding that "The Select Committee's immediate oversight need for the subpoenaed tapes is, from a congressional perspective, merely cumulative." The unique and confining nature of the case's factual and historical context likely makes this an uncertain precedent for limiting a committee's investigatory power in the face of a presidential claim of privilege.

[38] 121 F. 3d 729 (D.C. Cir. 1997).

[39] 365 F.3d 1108 (D.C. Cir. 2004). The panel split 2-1, with Judge Rogers writing for the majority and Judge Randolph dissenting.

[40] The President has delegated the formal process of review and recommendation of his pardon authority to the Attorney General who in turn has delegated it to the Deputy Attorney General. The Deputy Attorney General oversees the work of the Office of the Pardon Attorney.

[41] 365 F.3d at 1109-12.

[42] *Id.* at 1112, 1114, 1123.

[43] *Id.* at 1114.

[44] *Id.* at 1117.

[45] *Id.* at 1121-22.

[46] *Id.* at 1116.

[47] *Id.* at 1116-117.

[48] *Id.* at 1118-24.

[49] *See Presidential Signing Statements: Constitutional and Institutional Implications*, CRS Report RL33667, by T.J. Halstead, September 20, 2006.

[50] *See* Letter dated May 21, 2004 to Hon. Alex M. Azar, II, General Counsel, Department of Health and Human Services from Jack L. Goldsmith III, Assistant Attorney General, Office of Legal Counsel, Department of Justice, *available at,* [http://www.usdoj.gov/olc/crsmemoresponsese.htm]

[51] *Id.* at 3.

[52] Glenn A. Beard, "Congress v. The Attorney-Client Privilege: A 'Full and Frank' Discussion," *American Criminal Law Review*, vol. 35, 119: 1997; CRS Report 95-464, *Investigative Oversight: An Introduction to the Law, Practice and Procedure of Congressional Inquiry*, Morton Rosenberg.

[53] *See. e.g.,* "Contempt of Congress Against Franklin L. Haney," H.Rept. 105-792, 105th Cong., 2nd sess. 11-16 (1998); "Proceedings Against John M. Quinn, David Watkins, and Matthew Moore (Pursuant to Title 2, United States Code, Sections 192 and 194)," H.Rept. 104-598, 104th Cong., 2nd sess. 50-54 (1996); "Refusal of William H. Kennedy, III, To Produce Notes Subpoenaed By The Special Committee to Investigate Whitewater Development Corporation and Related Matters," S.Rept. 104-191, 104th Cong. 1st sess. 9-19 (1995); "Proceedings Against Ralph Bernstein and Joseph Bernstein," H.Rept. 99-462, 99th Cong. 2nd sess. 13, 14 (1986); Hearings, "International Uranium Control," Before the Subcommittee on Oversight and Investigations, House Committee on Interstate and Foreign Commerce, 95th Cong., 1st sess. 60, 123 (1977).

[54] *See* CRS Report, *supra* note 28, at 44-49.

[55] *McGrain v. Daugherty*, 272 U.S. 135, 177 (1926); *Watkins v. United States*, 354 U.S. 178, 187 (1957); *Eastland v. United States Servicemen's Fund*, 421 U.S. 491, 504 n. 15 (1975).

[56] *Westinghouse Electric Corp.* v. *Republic of the Philippines*, 951 F. 2d 1414, 1423 (3d Cir. 1991) ("Because the attorney-client privilege obstructs the truth-finding process, it is narrowly construed."); *Moran v. Burbine* 475 U.S. 412, 430 (1986) (Sixth Amendment not a source for attorney-client privilege); *Fisher v. United States*, 425 U.S. 391, 396-97 (1976) (compelling on attorney to disclose client communications does not violate the client's Fifth Amendment privilege against self-incrimination); *Hannah v. Larche*, 363 U.S. 420, 425 (1960) ("Only infrequently have witnesses [in congressional hearings] been afforded rights normally associated with an adjudicative proceeding"); *United States v. Fort*, 443 U.S. 932 (1971) (rejecting contention that the constitutional right to cross-examine witnesses applied to congressional investigations); *In re Sealed Case (Espy)*, 121 F. 3d 729 (D.C. Cir. 1997) (the deliberative process privilege is a common law privilege which, when claimed by executive officials, is easily overcome, and "disappears" altogether upon the reasonable belief by an investigating body that government misconduct has occurred).

[57] *In re Grand Jury Subpoena Duces Tecum*, 112 F. 3d 910 (8th Cir. 1997), *cert. denied sub. nom. Office of the President* v. *Office of the Independent Counsel*, 521 U.S. 1105 (1997) (claims of First Lady of attorney-client and work-product privilege with respect notes taken by White House Counsel Office attorneys rejected); *In re Bruce R. Lindsey (Grand Jury Testimony)*, 158 F. 3d 1263 (D.C. Cir. 1998), *cert. denied* 525 U.S. 996 (1998) (White House attorney may not invoke attorney-client privilege in response to grand jury subpoena seeking information on possible commission of federal crimes); *In re Sealed Case (Espy)*, 121 F. 3d 729 (D. C. Cir. 1997) (deliberative process privilege is a common law agency privilege which easily overcome by showing of need by an investigating body); *In re: A Witness Before the Special Grand Jury*, 288 F. 3d 289 (7th Cir. 2002) (attorney-client privilege not applicable to communications between state government counsel and state office holder). *But see In re Grand Jury Investigation*, 399 F.3d 527 (2d Cir. 2005) (upholding a claim of attorney-client privilege with respect to communications between a former chief legal counsel to the governor of Connecticut who was under grand jury investigation. It is worth noting that the Second Circuit recognized its apparent conflict with the afore-cited cases, however, the ruling is arguably distinguishable on its facts. *See* Kerri R. Blumenauer, *Privileged or Not? How the Current Application of the Government Attorney-Client Privilege Leaves the Government Feeling Unprivileged*, 75 FORDHAM L. REV. 75 (2006)).

[58] The Supreme Court has recognized that "only infrequently have witnesses . . . [in congressional hearings] been afforded the procedural rights normally associated with an adjudicative proceeding." *Hannah* v. *Larche*, 363 U.S. 420, 425 (1960); *See also*, *United States* v. *Fort*, 443 F. 2d 670 (D.C. Cir. 1970), *cert. denied*, 403 U.S. 932 (1971) (rejecting the contention that the constitutional right to cross-examine witnesses applied to a congressional investigation); *In the Matter of Provident Life and Accident Co.*, E.D. Tenn., S.D., CIV-1-90-219, June 13, 1990 (per Edgar, J.) (Noting that the court's earlier ruling on an attorney-client privilege claim was "not of constitutional dimensions, and is certainly not binding on the Congress of the United States".).

[59] Opinion No. 288, "Compliance With Subpoena from Congressional Committee to Produce Lawyers' Files Containing Client Confidences or Secrets," Legal Ethics Committee, District of Columbia Bar, February 16, 1999. (D.C Ethics Committee Opinion).

[60] *See* H.Rept. 105-792, *supra* note 29, at 1-6, 7-8, 15-16.

[61] *See* "Meeting on Portals Investigation (Authorization of Subpoenas; Receipt of Subpoenaed Documents and Consideration of Objections; and Contempt of Congress Proceedings Against Franklin L. Haney)," H. Comm. On Commerce, 105th Cong., 2nd sess. 48-50 (1998).

[62] *Id.* at 101-105.

[63] Under Rule 1.6(d)(2)(A) a lawyer may reveal client confidences or secrets only when expressly permitted by the D.C. rules or when "required by law or court order."

[64] A direct suit to enjoin a committee from enforcing a subpoena has been foreclosed by the Supreme Court's decision in *Eastland* v. *United States Servicemen's Fund*, 421 U.S. 491, 501 (1975), but that ruling does not appear to foreclose an action against a "third party," such as the client's attorney, to test the validity of the subpoena or the power of a committee to refuse to recognize the privilege. *See. e.g.*, United States v. *AT&T*, 567 F. 2d 121 (D.C.Cir. 1977) (entertaining an action by the Justice Department to enjoin AT&T from complying with a subpoena to provide telephone records that might compromise national security matters).

[65] *See. e.g.*, W. John Moore, "First Save All The Lawyers," *National Law Journal*, July 24, 1999 at 2170.

[66] 121 F. 3d 729 (D.C. Cir. 1997).

[67] 121 F. 3d at 745, 746; *See also id.* at 737-738("[W]here there is reason to believe the documents sought may shed light on government misconduct, the [deliberative process] privilege is routinely denied on the grounds that shielding internal government deliberations in this context does not serve 'the public interest in honest, effective government'").

[68] *United States v. Reinecke*, 524 F.2d 435 (D.C. Cir. 1975)(failure to publish committee rule setting one Senator as a quorum for taking hearing testimony held a sufficient ground to reverse a perjury conviction).

[69] Senate Rule XXVI(7)(a)(1); House Rule XI(2)(m)(3).

70 *See, e.g.,* Senate Permanent Committee on Investigations Rule 8.

71 *See, e.g.,* Senate Aging Committee Rule V. 8; Senate Permanent Subcommittee on Investigations Rule 7.

72 House Rule XI 2(j)(1); *see also* House Banking Committee Rule IV. 4.

73 *Ashland Oil Co., Inc.*, v. *FTC*, 548 F. 2d 977, 979-80 (D.C. Cir. 1976), *affirming* 409 F. Supp. 297 (D.D. C. 1976); *see also Exxon* v. *Federal Trade Commission*, 589 F. 2d 582, 592-93 (D.C. Cir. 1978)(acknowledging that the "principle is important that disclosure of information can only be compelled by members . . ."); and *In re Beef Industry Antitrust Litigation*, 589 F. 2d 786, 791 (5th Cir. 1979)(refusing to permit two Congressmen from intervening in private litigation because they "failed to obtain a House Resolution or any similar authority before they sought to intervene.")

74 *Leach* v. *Resolution Trust Corporation*, 860 F. Supp. 868, 874-76 (D.D.C. 1994).

75 *Id.* at 876 note 7. 5 U.S.C. § 2954 provides: "An Executive agency, on request of the Committee on Government [Reform] of the House of Representatives, or of any seven members thereof, or on request of the Committee on Government Operations of the Senate, or any five members thereof, shall submit any information requested of it relating to any matter within the jurisdiction of the committee."

76 45 Stat. 996.

77 H.R. 1757, 70th Cong., 1st Sess., pp. 2-3 (1928). A study of the Bureau of Efficiency had recommended their elimination. H.R. 1757, at p. 2; S.Rept. 1320, 70th Cong., 1st sess., p. 1 (1928).

78 S.Rept. 1320, *supra*, at 4.

79 H.R. 1757, *supra*, at 6; *see also* 69 Cong. Rec. 9413-17, 10613-16 (1928) (House and Senate floor debates).

80 In codifying Title 5 in 1966, Congress made it clear that it was effecting no substantive changes in existing laws: "The legislative purpose in enacting sections 1-6 of this act is to restate, without substantive change, the laws replaced by those sections on the effective date of this Act." P.L. 89-544, Sec. 7(a).

81 521 U.S. 811 (1997).

82 *Waxman, et al.* v. *Evans*, Civ. Action No. 01-14530-LGB (AJWx) (C.D. Calif, May 21, 2001).

83 *Waxman* v. *Evans*, Case No. CV 01-14530-LGB (AJWx) at 3.

84 *Carter* v. *U.S. Department of Commerce*, 307 F. 3d 1084 (9th Cir. 2002).

85 *Waxman* v. *Evans*, No. 02-55825 (9th Cir. Dec. 6, 2002).

86 No. CV-04-3467 MMM (Manx) (C.D. Calif., May 17, 2004).

87 521 U.S. 811 (1997).

88 *See Congressional Standing to Sue*, CRS Report RL30280, by Jay R. Shampansky, June 19, 2001 (containing a more detailed discussion of *Raines v. Byrd*).

89 *See* CRS Report RL30850, *Minority Rights and Senate Procedures*, by Stanley Bach.

90 Senate Rules XIX and XXII.

91 *See* Bach, *supra* note 63 at pp. 8-11.

92 Lee H. Hamilton, "Constituent Service and Representation," *The Public Manager*, summer 1992, p. 12.

93 John R. Johannes, "Constituency Service," in Donald Bacon, et. al., eds., *The Encyclopedia of the United States Congress* (New York: Simon and Schuster, 1995), p. 544.

94 A full description of the Office of Senate Legal Counsel and its work may be found in Floyd M. Riddick and Alan S. Frumin, Riddick's Senate Procedure, S.Doc. 28, 101st Cong., 2nd sess. 1236 (1992). *See* Charles Tiefer, The Senate and House Counsel Offices: Dilemmas of Representing in Court the Institutional Congressional Client, Law and Contemporary Problems, vol. 61: no. 2, spring 1998:48-63 (providing a more recent discussion of the history, development and work of both the Senate and House counsels' offices).

95 P.L. 95-520, secs. 701 *et seq.*, 92 Stat. 1824, 1875 (1978), *codified principally in* 2 U.S.C. §§ 288, *et seq.*

96 S.Rept. 95-170, 95th Cong., 2nd sess. 84 (1978).

97 2 U.S.C. § 288(a) and (b), 288a.

98 In addition, the office is called upon to defend the Senate, its committees, officers and employees in civil litigation relating to their official responsibilities or when they have been subpoenaed to testify or to produce Senate records; and to appear for the Senate when it intervenes or appears as amicus curiae in a lawsuit to protect the powers or responsibilities of Congress.

99 2 U.S.C. § 288b(d)(2), 288f.

100 28 U.S.C. § 1365.

101 *See* S.Rept. 98, 101st Cong., 1st sess. (1989).

102 *See, Senate Select Committee on Ethics v. Packwood,* 845 F.Supp 17 (D.D.C. 1994), *petition for stay pending appeal denied,* 510 U.S. 1319 (1994).

103 2 U.S.C. § 288d and 28 U.S.C. § 1365.

104 2 U.S.C. § 288 d(c).

105 *See* 28 U.S.C. § 1365 (a).

106 Id.

107 2 U.S.C. § 288g(a)(5) and (6).

108 2 U.S. 288g(c).

109 *See* S.Rept. 1015, 96th Cong., 2nd sess. (1980).

110 *See* S.Rept. 682, 97th Cong., 2nd sess. (1982).

[111] *See* S.Rept. 812, 99th Cong., 2nd sess. (1986).

[112] *See* S.Rept. 164, 101st Cong., 1st sess. (1989).

[113] *See* S.Rept. 156, 101st Cong., 1st sess. (1989).

[114] *See* H. Res. 5, Sec. 11, 139 Cong. Rec. H5 (daily ed. Jan. 5, 1993).

[115] House Rule II(8) of the Rules of the 108th Congress.

[116] Id.

[117] *See. e.g., Elk Grove Unified School District v. Newdow*, 124 S. Ct. 2301 (2004); *Raines v. Byrd*, 521 U.S. 811 (1997); *Beverly Enterprises, Inc. v. Trump*, 182 F.3d 183 (3d Cir. 1999); *United States v. McDade*, 28 F.3d 283 (3d Cir. 1994); *Cano v. Davis*, No. 01-8477 (C.D. Cal. March 28, 2002) (unpublished order granting motions to quash subpoenas to Members).

[118] *See. e.g., Department of Commerce v. U.S. House of Representatives*, 525 U.S. 316 (1999) (litigation in which the General Counsel was authorized by statute, P.L. 105-119, § 209(b) (1997), to represent the House in a challenge to the legality of the Department of Commerce's plan to use statistical sampling in the 2000 census).

[119] *See. e.g., Adams v. Clinton*, 90 F. Supp. 2d 35, *aff'd sub nom. Alexander v. Mineta*, 531 U.S. 940, 941 (2000); *Schaffer v. Clinton*, 240 F.3d 878 (10th Cir. 2001); *Skaggs v. Carle*, 110 F.3d 831 (D.C. Cir. 1997); *Newdow v. Eagen*, No. 02-01704 (D.D.C. filed March 24, 2004).

[120] *See. e.g.*, H.Rep. 105-797, *In the Matter of Representative Jay Kim*, Committee on Standards of Official Conduct, 105th Cong., 2nd sess. 84-85 (Oct. 8, 1998)

[121] *See. e.g.*, Hearing, "The Attorney General's Refusal to Provide Congressional Access to 'Privileged' Inslaw Documents," before the Subcommittee on Economic and Commercial Law, Committee on the Judiciary, 101st Cong., 2nd sess. 77-104 (Dec. 5, 1990).

[122] *See. e.g.*, 132 Cong Rec. 3036-38 (1986) (floor consideration of contempt citation against two witnesses who refused to testify concerning alleged assistance provided to former Philippines President Ferdinand E. Marcos and his wife).

[123] *See. e.g., Dornan v. Sanchez*, 978 F. Supp. 1315, 1317 n.1 (C.D. Cal. 1997).

[124] *See. e.g., Harris v. Board of Governors*, 938 F.2d 720 (7th Cir. 1991); *United States v. United States House of Representatives*, 556 F. Sup.. 150 (D.D.C. 1983).

[125] *See. e.g., Pentagen Technologies Int'l, Ltd. v. Committee on Appropriations of the United States House of Representatives*, 20 F. Supp. 2d 41 (D.D.C. 1998), *aff'd* 194 F.3d 174 (D.C. Cir. 1998); *United States v. McDade*, No. 96-1508 (3d Cir. July 12, 1996) (unpublished order quashing subpoena to the Committee on Standards of Official Conduct); *Brown & Williamson Tobacco Corp. v. Williams*, 62 F.3d 408 (D.C. Cir. 1995); *United States v. Arthur Andersen, LLP*, No. 02-121 (S.D. Tex. filed May 15, 2002) (unpublished order quashing subpoena to the Committee on Energy and Commerce).

[126] *See. e.g., In re Harrisburg Grand Jury*, 638 F. Supp. 43 (M.D. Pa. 1986). *Cf. United States v. Moussaoui*, No. 01-455-A, 2002 WL 1990900 (E.D. Va. Aug. 29, 2002) (order denying the "Expedited Motion of the United States for Clarification Regarding the Applicability of the Protective Order for Unclassified But Sensitive Material and Local Rule 57 to Information That May Be Made Public in Congressional Proceedings")

[127] Jim Bencivenga, "Critical Mass," *Christian Science Monitor*, February 3, 2000, p. 15. Also see "NGOs," *The Economist*, January 29, 2000, pp. 25-27.

In: Congressional Oversight An Overview, A Manual and... ISBN: 978-1-61728-477-9
Editor: Jamie C. Howell

Chapter 3

CONGRESSIONAL OVERSIGHT OF INTELLIGENCE: CURRENT STRUCTURE AND ALTERNATIVES*

Frederick M. Kaiser

SUMMARY

Interest in congressional oversight of intelligence has risen again recently in Congresses, in part because of disputes over reporting to Congress by Intelligence Community (IC) components on sensitive matters, including developments generated by the wars in Iraq and Afghanistan. The changes in the oversight structure proposed by the 111th Congress, however, reflect long-term concerns and considerations. For instance, the House Democratic majority had pledged in the 110th Congress to enact the remaining recommendations from the U.S. National Commission on Terrorist Attacks Upon the United States, commonly known as the 9/11 Commission, which called for a transformation of Congress's oversight structure. The commission's unanimous report in 2004, covering many issues, set the stage for reconsideration of the problems affecting Congress's structure in this area. The panel concluded that congressional oversight of intelligence was "dysfunctional" and proposed two distinct solutions. These were (1) creation of a joint committee on intelligence (JCI), modeled after the defunct Joint Committee on Atomic Energy (JCAE), with authority to report legislation to each chamber; or (2) enhanced status and power for the existing select committees on intelligence, by making them standing committees and granting both authorization and appropriations power.

Proposals to create a joint committee on intelligence date to 1948 and the early years of the Cold War, when the Central Intelligence Agency (CIA) and Director of Central Intelligence (DCI) were established. Similar recommendations have emerged in the meantime, although the lion's share were made before separate Intelligence Committees were established in the House (1977) and Senate (1976). The numerous proposals for a JCI, which

---

* This is an edited, reformatted and augmented edition of a United States Congressional Research Service publication, Report RL32525, dated January 25, 2010.

would end the two existing intelligence panels, moreover, vary in their specifics and raise competing viewpoints over practical matters and matters of principle.

Although it did not adopt either of the 9/11 Commission proposals, Congress has pursued other initiatives to change its intelligence oversight structure and capabilities in the 110th and 111th Congresses. The House altered its arrangements in 2007 (via H.Res. 35, 110th Congress), when it created an advisory Select Intelligence Oversight Panel on the Appropriations Committee, a hybrid structure that combines members of the House Permanent Select Committee on Intelligence and the Committee on Appropriations. The Senate has also changed its relationship between appropriations and intelligence. Other proposals have been considered, either in the 111th Congress or before. These include clarifying the independent audit authority of the Government Accountability Office (GAO) over the intelligence community, particularly the CIA; placing the CIA expressly under the Government Performance and Results Act; increasing the coordinative capabilities and reporting of relevant inspectors general (IGs); and adding a new statutory IG covering the entire intelligence community and others for certain Defense Department entities.

This chapter first describes the current Select Committees on Intelligence and then the former Joint Committee on Atomic Energy, often cited as a model for a counterpart on intelligence. The study also sets forth proposed characteristics for a joint committee on intelligence, differences among these, and their pros and cons. The report, to be updated as events dictate, examines other actions and alternatives affecting congressional oversight in the field.

INTRODUCTION

Congress has long considered various ways to oversee intelligence, an often perplexing and always difficult responsibility because of the secrecy and sensitivity surrounding intelligence findings, conclusions, dissemination, and sources and methods.[1] The field has become more complicated and demanding in the aftermath of the 9/11 terrorist attacks, with the need for improved information sharing to overcome "foreign-domestic divide" that hampered effective intelligence gathering, evaluation, and dissemination.[2]

The current state of affairs reflects a multi-faceted phenomenon. Not only does "intelligence" overlap both foreign and domestic areas; but it also covers a diversity of subjects, agencies, and procedures within each. Oversight of intelligence, particularly in the foreign realm, is consolidated to a large degree in the House and Senate Select Committees on Intelligence. But it is not centralized there; each panel has exclusive legislative authority over only the Central Intelligence Agency (CIA) and Director of National Intelligence (DNI). A number of other committees share oversight, including the four (appropriations, armed services, foreign affairs/foreign relations, and judiciary) that have representation on their chamber's intelligence committee. Additional panels with oversight or legislative jurisdiction over parts of U.S. intelligence include those dealing with civil liberties, government-controlled information, homeland security, government organization and reorganization, or individual agencies that conduct intelligence themselves of rely on other agencies for it. Along with these organizational arrangements, oversight of intelligence is affected by formal reporting requirements[3] as well as informal agreements between Members and staff in

Congress and officials and staff in the executive branch. Finally, custom and tradition play a role in the oversight process.

The first oversight proposal—to create a joint committee on intelligence (JCI)—appeared in 1948.[4] This was just one year after the establishment of the CIA and the Office of Director of Central Intelligence (DCI), both integral parts of the most far-reaching executive reorganization in United States history.[5] Numerous initiatives to change Congress's oversight structure have materialized in the meantime, including, most importantly, the creation of parallel Select Committees on Intelligence in both chambers. Nonetheless, Congress's oversight capability in this area has been questioned. The 9/11 Commission's report, released in 2004, notably, concluded that congressional oversight of intelligence was "dysfunctional" and recommended either a merger of appropriations and authorization powers into each select committee or the creation of a Joint Committee on Intelligence.[6] Since then, the House's and Senate's actions modifying each body's own structure have followed different paths, diverging not only from the 9/11 Commission proposals but also from each other.[7]

This chapter reviews the basic characteristics of proposed joint committees on intelligence, differences among them, and perceived advantages and disadvantages.[8] It also covers the congressional panels a JCI would replace: namely, the House and Senate Select Committees on Intelligence. Along with this is a brief review of the defunct Joint Committee on Atomic Energy (JCAE)—often cited as an organizational model for a joint intelligence panel, as it has been for the 9/11 Commission.

In addition, the report looks at recent actions, such as the creation of a new (and possibly unique in the history of Congress) intelligence oversight advisory panel on the House Appropriations Committee, combining Members from both the parent committee and the Select Committee on Intelligence; the new panel would make recommendations regarding the annual intelligence community appropriations to the Defense Appropriations Subcommittee. This chapter also covers separate developments in the Senate, including a Memorandum of Agreement (MOA) in 2007, designed to improve coordination and transparency between the Intelligence Committee, which handles authorizations for the intelligence community, and the Appropriations Committee, which handles appropriations for the same. Other ways seen as strengthening oversight in this field would be to (1) clarify and expand the authority of the Government Accountability Office (GAO) over the Intelligence Community (IC), particularly the CIA; (2) remove the agency's exemption from coverage of the Government Performance and Results Act; (3) add a new statutory inspector general (IG) to encompass the whole IC, along with IGs for certain Defense Department intelligence agencies; and (4) increase coordination and strengthen reporting requirements among the relevant offices of inspector general.

House and Senate Select Committees on Intelligence

A joint committee on intelligence would replace the current House Permanent Select Committee on Intelligence, established in 1977, and the Senate Select Committee on Intelligence, created a year earlier.[9] These units emerged after extensive, detailed congressional and executive investigations revealed widespread abuses in the IC and concluded that effective congressional oversight was lacking. The panels were set up to consolidate legislative and oversight authority over the entire intelligence community, supplanting the fragmented system at the time, which relied exclusively on disparate standing committees. Although titled "Select," the intelligence panels are hybrids of standing and select committees, adopting characteristics of both types. For instance, the panels have only temporary membership, as select committees have, because they are usually short-term constructions; yet each panel holds authority to report legislation to its own chamber, a power usually reserved to standing committees.

Jurisdiction and Authority

The Intelligence Committees have broad jurisdiction over the intelligence community and report authorizations and other legislation for consideration by their respective chambers. A recent change in the House places three members of the Intelligence Committee on a new Select Intelligence Oversight Panel on the Appropriations Committee (H.Res. 35, 110th Congress). The new panel, which appears unprecedented in the history of Congress, is to study and make recommendations to relevant appropriations subcommittees. This includes the Defense Appropriations Subcommittee, which continues to prepare the annual intelligence community budget, as part of the classified annex to the bill making appropriations for the Department of Defense.

Most of the jurisdiction of the current Intelligence Committees is shared. The select committees hold exclusive authorizing and legislative powers only for the CIA, the DNI (as it had over the now-defunct Director of Central Intelligence), and the National Foreign Intelligence Program. This leaves the intelligence components in the Departments of Defense, Homeland Security, Justice, and Treasury, among other agencies, to be shared with appropriate standing committees.

The House and Senate intelligence panels have nearly identical jurisdictions for the intelligence community. The House panel's domain, however, also extends over an area that the Senate's does not: "tactical intelligence and intelligence-related activities," which covers tactical military intelligence. In another departure, the House Select Committee has been given authority to "review and study on an exclusive basis the sources and methods of entities" in the IC.[10]

Membership and Leadership

The membership of the committees has been limited in time, staggered, and connected to the standing committee system and political party system in Congress. These features, moreover, differ between the two panels. Each select committee, for instance, reserves seats for members from the chamber's committees on Appropriations, Armed Services, Foreign Affairs/Foreign Relations, and Judiciary. The specifics differ, however: the Senate requires two persons, a majority and minority Member, from each of these standing committees, while the House calls for only one Member from each standing committee with overlapping jurisdiction.

The two panels also differ in size (21 on the House panel and 15 on the Senate counterpart, plus ex officio members on each), tenure, and other membership features, including partisan composition and leadership arrangements. Since its inception, the Senate panel has had only one more Member from the majority party than the minority (an eight-to-seven ratio); and its vice chairman, who takes over if the chair is unavailable, must come from the minority party. The House select committee, in contrast, reflected the full chamber party ratio when it was established in 1977: two-to-one plus one, resulting in an initial nine-to-four majority-minority party membership on the panel. In the meantime, however, the minority party has been granted additional seats on the committee and the majority-minority party ratio in the full House has grown closer. The result is a select committee membership party ratio of 12-to-9 in the 110th Congress.

Secrecy Controls

The committees also have different secrecy arrangements regarding controls over their classified holdings. Secrecy oaths distinguish the two chambers. All Members of the House, including, of course, those on the Intelligence Committee, must swear or affirm not to disclose classified information, except as authorized by the rules of the chamber; the current oath is modeled after a previous one which had been required only for the members of the House Permanent Select Committee on Intelligence. The Senate does not impose a similar obligation on its Members.[11]

Non-member access to classified materials also separates the two panels. The House committee has a more detailed and exacting set of requirements for non-members than its Senate counterpart.

In addition, the Senate panel is authorized to disclose classified information publicly on its own (following elaborate procedures in which the President and the full Senate have an opportunity to act). By comparison, the House select committee cannot do so, if the President objects to its release; in that case, the House itself makes the determination by majority vote.

Joint Committee on Atomic Energy as a Model

The Joint Committee on Atomic Energy (JCAE)—set up by the Atomic Energy Act of 1946, along with the Atomic Energy Commission (P.L. 585, 60 Stat. 772-773)—is often cited as an appropriate organizational model for a joint committee on intelligence, a reference the 9/11 Commission also adopted.[12] The JCAE, an 18-member panel composed of an equal number of Members from each house of Congress, held authority to report legislation to the floor of both chambers, a power unique among joint committees.[13] Many reasons have been offered for considering the JCAE as a model:

- favorable record for keeping highly confidential material secret;
- largely bipartisan approach to policy-making;
- considerable unity among its members;

- close working relationship with the executive (here, the Atomic Energy Commission) in this secretive and sensitive area;
- consolidated jurisdiction for a growing field;
- explicit, comprehensive oversight mandate, supported by a then-unprecedented directive that the executive keep the joint committee "fully and currently informed"; and
- ability to streamline the legislative process in general and to act rapidly, if necessary, in particular instances.

Given these attributes, the joint committee became a formidable congressional panel. In its prime, JCAE was even considered by some as "probably the most powerful congressional committee in the history of the nation."[14] Despite this—or perhaps because of it—the JCAE was abolished in 1977, nearly 30 years after its birth. It was evidently the victim of a number of reinforcing developments: concerns inside and outside Congress about JCAE's close, some thought cozy, relationship with the executive agency it was overseeing; changing executive branch conditions, such as the breakup of the Atomic Energy Commission into the Nuclear Regulatory Commission and the Energy Research and Development Administration, now the Department of Energy; new rivals in Congress, as the expanding nature of atomic energy and nuclear power extended into the jurisdictions of a number of House and Senate committees; efforts in the Senate at the time to realign and consolidate standing committee jurisdictions and reduce the number of assignments for each Member; and a relatively high number of vacancies on the JCAE (six of the 18 seats).[15]

Proposed Joint Committee on Intelligence Characteristics

Recommendations to create a joint committee on intelligence have surfaced over nearly five decades, most predating the establishment of the two select committees on intelligence in the mid-1970s. Although many of these suggestions, including that from the 9/11 Commission, have followed the design of the Joint Committee on Atomic Energy, not all have; consequently, the specifics in the blueprints have varied in a number of fundamental ways. Differences extend to (1) the range and exclusivity of the panels' jurisdiction; (2) makeup of their membership; (3) selection and rotation of chairmen; (4) possibility of and characteristics of a vice chairmanship; (5) requirements for representation of certain other committees as well as at-large members; (6) special secrecy requirements for members and staff, including a secrecy oath and security clearances; (7) staff size, method of selection, and restrictions on activities; (8) official disclosures of classified information; (9) mechanisms for investigating suspected unauthorized disclosures of such information; and (10) access by non-members to the joint committee's classified holdings. Even suggested methods of establishment have varied.

Methods of Establishment

A joint committee on intelligence could be created by a concurrent resolution, a joint resolution, or a regular bill. The Joint Committee on Atomic Energy, for instance, was established by public law through the regular bill process (i.e., the Atomic Energy Act of 1946, P.L. 580, 60 Stat. 772-773).

A concurrent resolution has the advantage (for its proponents) of requiring only the approval of Congress, while a joint resolution or regular bill must be signed by the President or his veto overridden. A joint resolution or a bill, however, may offer certain benefits to its supporters over a concurrent resolution. A number of existing provisions in public law, especially ones dealing with intelligence reporting requirements to Congress, designates the House and Senate Select Committees on Intelligence as recipients (e.g., the intelligence oversight provisions and the reporting requirements for the CIA Inspector General, codified at 50 U.S.C. 413-415 and 50 U.S.C. 403q, respectively). A bill or joint resolution, when creating a joint committee, could amend these statutory provisions, whereas a concurrent resolution could not do so directly. But a concurrent resolution, although solely a congressional device, could have the same effect. By changing the rules of both chambers, a concurrent resolution could recognize that the powers, authority, and jurisdiction of the former select committees would be transferred to a new joint committee.

Jurisdiction and Authority

A joint Intelligence Committee could consolidate jurisdiction for the entire intelligence community, extending to all intelligence entities as well as intelligence and intelligence-related activities, including significant anticipated activities (i.e., covert operations). Legislative authority over intelligence could be shared for all entities with overlapping jurisdiction; or, as is now the case in the House and Senate, it could be held exclusively for certain specified components (e.g., CIA and DNI), while being shared for others.

Membership

A bicameral body requires equal membership from both the Senate and House. In addition to bicameralism, a joint committee on intelligence could be directed to accommodate three other criteria: bipartisanship, representation of specified standing committees, and at-large selection of members.

For example, the membership from each chamber could be required to have representatives from standing committees with overlapping jurisdiction (e.g., Appropriations, Armed Services, Foreign Affairs/Foreign Relations, and Judiciary), as both the House and Senate Intelligence Committees do now. This selection might include both a majority and a minority party member from each represented committee. A JCI could also call for a specified number of members selected at-large, as the Senate intelligence panel does now. As an illustration, an 18-member JCI could include nine Senators and nine Representatives, with five majority and four minority party members from each chamber. At least one member, but not more than two, could come from each of the four committees with overlapping jurisdiction; this option (a maximum of eight from each chamber) would still allow for one selection at large from each house. By comparison, a larger committee or a panel requiring only a single member from each of the specified standing committees would allow for more members to be selected at-large.

Provision could also be made for *ex officio* members, particularly the majority and minority party leaders from the Senate and the Speaker and minority leader from the House.

Terms and Rotation

Membership on the joint committee could have no term limits or be given a maximum length of service (six or eight years, as the House and Senate Intelligence Committees have had, or shorter or longer terms). Under term limits, the total time on the committee might be measured either by continuous service or by non-continuous service accumulated over a specified number of Congresses (e.g., a total of eight years over six Congresses). If a JCI had maximum lengths of service, it could be treated as a temporary assignment, which might not count against other standing committee assignments in each chamber. By comparison, membership on the JCI could be permanent.[16] If so, it might be treated as if it were a standing committee in each chamber, counting against other committee assignments.

Member terms could also be staggered, so that new members would arrive with each new Congress. Staggered terms, however, would mean that a portion of the original membership could not serve the maximum period, at least not as part of the original composition.

Leadership

The chair, selected at the beginning of each Congress or each session (as some proposals called for), could alternate between the two chambers and/or political parties. A vice chairmanship could also be established; this officer would replace the chair when he or she is absent (as occurs now on the Senate Intelligence Committee). The vice chair could be a member of the other body and/or the other political party.

Secrecy Controls

Various types of secrecy controls could be applied to a joint committee on intelligence to regulate access to its classified holdings by non-committee members, protect against the unauthorized disclosure of classified information, and allow its authorized release. Such controls could (1) set requirements for determining access by non-members; (2) require security clearances, oaths, and/or secrecy agreements for committee members and staff; and (3) provide for investigation of suspected security breaches, conducted by the House and Senate Ethics Committees.

Controls could also spell out procedures for disclosing classified information to which the President objects, either by a joint committee itself, by the joint committee in concert with either or both chambers, or by either or both chambers as the final arbiter. One of five distinct options might be adopted: (1) the joint committee on intelligence could act alone; (2) the panel could act only after one house responded to a request from it to release classified information; (3) the JCI could act only after both houses responded; (4) a single house could disclose the information; or (5) both chambers would have to agree to do so. Currently, disclosure procedures differ between the House and Senate intelligence panels. The House select committee does not have authority to release classified information on its own. The full House must act to disclose it, at the request of its intelligence panel, if the President objects to the release. On the Senate side, the select committee may disclose classified information on its own, after both the President and full Senate have acted.[17] It appears that this procedure has not been used by the Senate panel.

Staffing

The number of staff on a new JCI would presumably be smaller than the combined total for both the House and Senate Intelligence Committees. Hiring could be accomplished in seven different ways: (1) by the majority party on the full JCI; (2) by the majority party from each chamber on the committee; (3) by full committee vote; (4) by the majority party and minority party separately; (5) by the chair alone; (6) by the chair and vice chair/ranking minority member together; or (7) by individual members (with each legislator selecting a single staff member).

Additionally, staff could be selected by a combination of several compatible ways (e.g., individual member selections for some plus committee-wide selections for others). The staff could also be required to meet certain agreed upon criteria set by the committee, such as fitness for the duties and without regard to party affiliation.[18]

Staffers could be required to have an appropriate security clearance (for Top Secret and access to Sensitive Compartmented Information), as is now mandated by both House and Senate select committees. They could also be directed to sign a nondisclosure or secrecy agreement not to reveal classified information, again a requirement for the staff of both intelligence panels.

Budget and Funding

The budget for a joint committee on intelligence would presumably be smaller than the combined budgets of the House and Senate intelligence panels. Funding could be shared by both chambers, deriving equally from the contingent funds of the Senate and House.

Pros and Cons

Differences over the establishment of a joint committee on intelligence tie into practical matters as well as matters of principle.

Pros

Supporters of a joint committee on intelligence argue that it would make for a more effective and efficient overseer than the current arrangement, which the 9/11 Commission concluded "is now dysfunctional," because of limitations on the two select committees.[19] According to its proponents, a single joint committee, housing fewer members and staff than the two existing ones combined, would:

- Strengthen oversight of intelligence for four primary reasons. The executive would be more open and forthright with a single, small oversight body than with two with a larger combined membership; the legislators and staff on the JCI, recognizing that there is no other authorizing panel to conduct oversight, would attach a greater importance to this responsibility; a committee composed of legislators from both chambers could better integrate and take advantage of congressional expertise and experience in the field; and a JCI could be established with fewer restraints and restrictions than the separate select committees now have.
- Improve coordination, cooperation, and comity between the House and Senate and among other relevant committees (with overlapping jurisdiction) in both chambers. A joint committee could serve as a conduit of information and advice and as a facilitator for policy formulation between the two chambers as well as between the political parties; a JCI could also encourage mutual respect and trust between the chambers and parties; this could occur by treating all of its members equally in committee leadership posts and voting, by merging the stands of Members of both houses in committee deliberations and decisions, by taking a joint committee consensus on legislation, endorsed by Members of both chambers, to the floor of each house, and by providing an opportunity for House Members to be involved, if only marginally and informally, in a Senate function (i.e., confirmation of presidential nominees).
- Streamline the legislative process, because only one committee, rather than two, would have to consider and report legislative proposals and authorizations to the floors of both chambers; members from the same joint committee, moreover, might comprise all or a majority of the membership of conference committees, which might be less necessary in the first place because of the bicameral, bipartisan makeup of a joint committee.
- Respond rapidly to investigate a major development, when conditions dictated.
- Increase the stature of overseeing and legislating on intelligence matters and, thus, make serving on an intelligence panel more attractive and important than on either select committee. This could result from making the joint committee the equivalent of a standing committee, by granting it permanency and authority to report legislation to each chamber and giving the members indefinite tenure. A JCI with these characteristics would be unique in the current era, the first of its kind since 1977, and apparently one of only a few in the history of Congress, also elevating its stature.
- Make for more efficient government. A single panel, versus two, would probably reduce the amount of time that the Administration and intelligence officials would

spend on Capitol Hill testifying, briefing, notifying, and meeting with members and panels.

- Improve the protection of classified information in Congress's possession. A smaller number of legislators and staff on a joint committee would have access to it, and a single office would be easier to secure.
- Encourage trust between Congress and the Executive in this sensitive field. This could occur by reducing the number of panels, Members, and staff with access to such highly classified information and by easing the cooperative relationship between the branches by way of a single committee, instead of two.
- Pinpoint responsibility in Congress for oversight and legislation affecting intelligence, thereby avoiding any confusion or uncertainty about it.
- Cut back the total number of committee seats for legislators in the House and Senate combined, by replacing the two panels with a single committee with fewer seats; for instance, a new 18-member joint committee with nine Senators and Representatives would be half the size of the combined total of 37 on the two select committees. The replacement would modestly help reduce the number of legislators holding too many committee assignments and/or being "spread too thin." Reducing the number of seats available for Representatives and Senators would allow them to concentrate on one less committee assignment.
- Reduce costs, because of fewer staff and a single suite of offices.

Cons

Critics of proposals for replacing the current House and Senate Intelligence Committees with a single joint committee contend that it would weaken oversight and compromise a fundamental feature of the Congress, namely, two different (and sometimes competing) bodies.[20] As viewed by its opponents, a JCI would:

- Adversely affect oversight of intelligence. This would occur by reducing the number of legislators and staff who have an incentive and opportunity to conduct oversight and by reducing the number of separate panels, with different characteristics and incentive structures, to conduct it; in this regard, the number of committees to which the President reports covert action plans is now only two (the select committees on intelligence), having been reduced from eight in 1980, at the request of the executive.
- Undercut the legislative benefits (e.g. longer deliberation time and different viewpoints) of relying on two committees from separate and distinctive chambers. This usual situation allows two panels—each reflecting different chambers, types of constituencies, and electoral schedules—to examine the same legislation and authorizations and conduct oversight from different vantage points, based on their own priorities and demands; the loss of a second view would be felt not only in the initial committee deliberations but also in later conference committee action, which might be dominated by joint committee members.
- Cause a loss in continuity, stability, and experience. This would be especially evident in joint committee leadership, if the chair (and ranking member or vice chair) rotated every two years; this in turn would make membership on the joint committee less desirable than on other panels; the turnover could also extend to staff, because of the

frequent change in leadership; finally, this loss of stability and experience could hamper Congress's ability to influence public policy and compete with the executive.

- Result in a more acute impact on Congress if a joint committee develops a close and supportive relationship with the executive entities it oversees, rather than a neutral and critical one. With a single panel, Congress would have only one locus for oversight and checks on the executive, not two; if this happens, the impact on Congress, on oversight, and on legislation would be more extensive and significant, because of the absence of a possible balance from a second committee.
- Operate contrary to the long-term tendency to end reliance on joint committees, either by abolishing them or not establishing them in the first place.[21] A JCI, if authorized to report legislation to the floor of both houses, would be unique currently; it would be the only such empowered joint committee since 1977 (when the JCAE was abolished), and one of the few in the history of the Congress; a joint committee on intelligence would also raise the prospect of similar panels for other policy areas, including homeland security, which have wide-ranging jurisdictions that cross a number of executive agencies and programs along with congressional committee jurisdictions.
- Harbor uncertainty regarding confirmation of presidential nominees. It might be unclear whether House Members should play any role at all in the process or, if so, perhaps only at certain stages (e.g., initial meetings and interviews, background investigations, formal hearings).
- Artificially make the political parties equal or nearly so. This could occur, even though the differences in party ratios in each chamber could be substantial, as they have been in the past.
- Artificially make the two chambers equal on the joint committee. The number of Members from each chamber would be the same, even though the House is more than four times larger than the Senate; because of this situation, Representatives would have proportionately fewer opportunities to serve on a joint committee than Senators.
- Cut back the possibility of serving on an intelligence panel for all Members of Congress, especially if there are no term limits on JCI membership. This reduction in numbers would, in turn, reduce the diversity and representational characteristics of the membership compared to two separate committees.
- Bring about a change in the different jurisdictions that the current select committees now hold. The House panel having a broader jurisdiction than its Senate counterpart.
- Not necessarily improve protection of classified information over the current two select committees. Their controls over it are exacting and their reputations in this regard are good; a JCI could also require new procedures for the public release of classified intelligence information held by the joint committee; this would raise the prospect of (and cause disagreement over) whether the joint committee alone could do so, whether one chamber could do so, or whether both houses must act together as the final arbiter.
- Add confusion and conflict over investigations of suspected unauthorized disclosures of classified information. This could arise, for instance, if the ethics committee from

one chamber conducted investigations which involved members of the other body, even if only tangentially and in an initial inquiry.
- Raise practical difficulties in setting meeting schedules, times, and locations for panel members from two different chambers of Congress.

ALTERNATIVES TO A JOINT COMMITTEE

There are other options which might enhance and regularize congressional oversight of intelligence. These changes, both formal and informal, could have an impact not only on the structure of the current select committees on intelligence, but also on their relationship with other committees and Members in its respective chamber and its counterparts in the opposite chamber, as well as the relationship between the legislature and the executive.

Changing the Select Committees' Structure and Powers

The most direct and immediate among the options to increase and improve oversight of intelligence would be ways to enhance the status, stature, and resources of the existing select committees on intelligence or replace them with standing committees.[22] This might be accomplished through several different (and sometimes competing) means:

- Grant the current select committees status as standing committees, along with indefinite tenure for their membership, to reduce turnover; increase experience, stability, and continuity; and make membership on the panel more attractive.
- Expand the authority of such committees, giving them power to report appropriations as well as authorizations and to hold subpoena authority on their own.
- Place members of the Select Committee on Intelligence on their chamber's Appropriations Subcommittee on Defense or create a new Appropriations Subcommittee on Intelligence, possibly including Intelligence Committee members, with comprehensive jurisdiction over IC appropriations.
- Establish a special advisory and oversight body on the Appropriations Committee, combining Intelligence Committee and Appropriations Committee members, as the House has done; under this plan, the new panel would report its findings and recommendations for IC funding to the defense or other appropriate subcommittee, thereby modestly expanding the effective jurisdiction and influence of the select committee.[23]
- Add professional staff, hire temporary consultants, set up short-term task forces, and/or increase the use of congressional support agencies, especially in fields where the panels might require new or expanded expertise and skills.

Although neither the House nor the Senate adopted the 9/11 Commission recommendations for intelligence oversight, other changes have occurred through a variety of mechanisms. These include the chambers' leadership, existing committees, and a Senate bipartisan working group; these efforts have led to the Senate's restructuring its oversight panels and each chamber instituting new working arrangements between its intelligence and appropriations panels.

Senate Action

The Senate's response to the 9/11 Commission and other recommendations for oversight of intelligence has proceeded through several phases.

Initial Changes in 2004

Several of these suggestions were approved by the Senate on October 9, 2004, when it agreed to S.Res. 445 (108th Congress) affecting its oversight of intelligence. The resolution eliminated certain restrictions on serving on the select committee, reduced the number of members (from 17 to 15), and modified security procedures regarding the public disclosure of classified information. S.Res. 445, however, did not transfer authority and jurisdiction over intelligence appropriations to the Intelligence Committee.

Structural Changes Involving the Committees on Intelligence and Appropriations in 2007

Additional steps were taken in the 110th Congress. A prominent one is a Memorandum of Agreement (MOA), designed to improve coordination and transparency between the Intelligence Committee and Appropriations Committee.[24] The MOA—signed by the chairman of the select committee (but not its ranking minority member) and the chairs and ranking minority members of the Senate Appropriations Committee and its defense subcommittee—advanced several changes to accomplish this:

- notify staff and allow them to attend the intelligence hearings of the other body;
- allow each Intelligence Committee member who is also an appropriator to bring his or her intelligence staff members to Appropriations Committee hearings and markups;
- permit all Senators and cleared staff of one committee to review the bill, report, and classified annex of the other before action is taken; and
- give the chairmen and ranking minority members of each the committee the opportunity to appear before the other panel to present their views prior to the markup of either the intelligence authorization or appropriations bills.[25]

Notwithstanding the effort, the effectiveness of the new arrangements under the Memorandum of Agreement has elicited differing impressions. The chairman of the Senate Intelligence Committee emphasized that the agreement "has made great strides toward bringing our committees together in a unity of effort that was lacking before."[26] A competing interpretation was offered by the Intelligence Committee's ranking minority member, who was also an appropriator at the time. He determined that the MOA was "ineffective," adding that "in my experience I've seen more evidence of the need for a better synthesis of the two."[27]

Subsequent Proposed Changes Involving the Committees on Intelligence and Appropriations

In March 2008, 14 of the 15 members of the Senate Select Committee on Intelligence—led by Chairman Rockefeller and Vice Chairman Christopher S. Bond—offered another proposal to the Senate leadership.[28] It called for the establishment of a Subcommittee on Intelligence on the Appropriations Committee, which would include members of the Intelligence Committee and would appropriate all funds for the National Intelligence Program (NIP), as opposed to the current situation where such appropriations are divided among several appropriations subcommittees. In defense of this option, Senators Rockefeller and Bond reminded the Senate leadership that the 9/11 Commission's bolder recommendation—to consolidate authorization and appropriations authority in the SSCI—"was considered and rejected by the Senate during consideration of S.Res. 445 in October 2004."[29]

This plan for a new Appropriations Intelligence Subcommittee was opposed by the leadership of the Senate Appropriations Committee. Its chairman, Robert C. Byrd, and ranking member, Thad Cochran, noted that other changes in oversight, including those by way of the 2007 MOA, have been put into effect.[30] They argued that the proposed Intelligence Appropriations Subcommittee, "led by members of the Intelligence Committee," would prove counterproductive: "We strongly believe that consolidating authority over intelligence in a smaller group of Senators is precisely the wrong way to improve the Senate's oversight of intelligence."[31] The Senators added that the separation of authorization and appropriations functions should be maintained and that consolidating appropriations for the entire NIP in one subcommittee would have an adverse impact on other policies, such as foreign policy, that are handled by different subcommittees.[32]

Despite this opposition, a formal proposal to create a new Appropriations Subcommittee on Intelligence (S.Res. 655, 110th Congress) was sponsored initially on September 11, 2008, by the vice chairman and chairman of the Senate Intelligence Committee.[33] In addition to placing the two Intelligence Committee members from Appropriations on this new Appropriations Subcommittee on Intelligence, S.Res. 655 would also have added the chairman and ranking member of the Defense Appropriations Subcommittee and, as *ex officio* members, the chairman and vice chairman of the Intelligence Committee. In introducing the resolution, Senator Bond emphasized that "on the seventh anniversary of 9/11, it is noteworthy that there remains one unaddressed 9/11 commission recommendation, and that is to reform the legislative branch's oversight of intelligence and terrorism activities which the commission rightly described as 'dysfunctional'."[34] As an alternative to the "bolder" 9/11 commission recommendations, which had been rejected, the Senator argued that "many of us believe there is a better, less disruptive way to achieve reform through a carefully constructive intelligence appropriations subcommittee."[35] Another proposal along this line appeared in the House but would have affected both chambers. H.R. 334, 110th Congress, would have required each chamber to establish an Appropriations Subcommittee on Intelligence with jurisdiction over intelligence and intelligence-related activities.

A different proposal (S.Res. 164) has been introduced in the 111th Congress. Following the 9/11 Commission recommendation, it would transfer appropriations power to the Senate Select Committee on Intelligence. The resolution's sponsor, Senator Russell Feingold, noted that "this effort to reform and improve congressional oversight has a long bipartisan history," recognizing earlier plans to accomplish this from Senators John McCain and Richard Burr, two of the 2009 proposal's co-sponsors.[36]

House Action

In the House, the option to consolidate authority—by reserving seats for Intelligence Committee members on the Defense Appropriations Subcommittee—was raised at the end of the 109th Congress by Representative Nancy Pelosi, then House Minority Leader and presumptive Speaker of the House in the 110th Congress.[37] The final product was a variation on this theme. H.Res. 35 (110th Congress), which passed the House on January 9, 2007, created a new Select Intelligence Oversight Panel on the Appropriations Committee. It consists of 13 members, with an eight-to-five inter-party ratio; three of the members are representatives from the Intelligence Committee joining 10 from appropriations, including the chairman and ranking minority member of the full committee, the chairman and ranking minority member of the Defense Subcommittee, and six additional members from appropriations. This special panel is authorized to study and make recommendations to all appropriations subcommittees on relevant areas, specifically the annual intelligence appropriations to the Defense Subcommittee, which retains authority to report it to the full committee.

In the 110th Congress, a bill (H.R. 334) was introduced that would have taken the proposal further. Instead of an advisory panel, H.R. 334 would have required each chamber to establish by law a separate Subcommittee on Intelligence in its Appropriations Committee, with appropriations jurisdiction over intelligence and intelligence-related activities.[38] No further action occurred on the bill.

Concerns about Restructuring the Intelligence Committees

The set of changes producing a restructured and strengthened Intelligence Committee in each chamber, as called for by the 9/11 Commission, might also generate concerns and criticisms. A new standing committee—smaller than the existing select committees in each chamber (if combined), with representation from four standing committees with overlapping membership and indefinite tenure for its members—would substantially reduce (1) the number of Members in each chamber serving on an intelligence panel at any one time; (2) the number of at-large seats available; (3) the number of vacancies available over time; and, thus, (4) the likelihood of a Member finding a seat on the committee. These changes in tandem would also lead to fewer former members from the committee, thus, reducing the ability of the full chamber and nonmembers to be knowledgeable about how the intelligence community operates and intelligence policy; and it could result in a decline of the ability to question if not challenge the committee (as well as the executive). Arguably, this could result in the prospect of a closed system, making it easier for the intelligence panels to dominate the agenda and debate in their respective chambers and in the full Congress.

A second set of cautions might surround the proposed new authority, particularly, adding appropriations to its authorizing control and independent subpoena power. Such subpoena authority, which could cover either or both materials and individual testimony, would be held (and used) without needing approval in each instance by the chamber. This might be seen as infringing on an important full-chamber power and removing a check on this particular committee, which would be already subject to fewer constraints than the current select committees have.

The addition of appropriations approval would apparently produce a unique situation in the contemporary Congress and a rarity in its entire history. A reversal of this plan—placing

Intelligence Committee members on the defense appropriations subcommittee—also appears to be a rare, if not unprecedented action; this revamped panel could better coordinate and complement the actions of both committees. This change, moreover, could indirectly increase the power of the select committee. By reserving seats for its members on the relevant appropriations subcommittee, the Intelligence Committee would play a more direct and influential role in appropriating IC funds than it does now. At this time, no other committee has a comparable guarantee of seats on a relevant appropriations subcommittee. Consequently, the left-out authorizing committees, particularly those dealing with sensitive national security matters, might make the same appeal as intelligence: that is, to have seats reserved on the appropriate appropriations subcommittee. Following either avenue, the intelligence panel's power would be enhanced if it held both appropriations and authorization authority, either directly or indirectly (via its members on the defense appropriations subcommittee).

In either event, however, the intelligence panel might be perceived as too powerful. It would hold two impressive and reinforcing authorities and would no longer be subject to a check and competition from a significant outside source (i.e., the Appropriations Committee in its chamber). At the same time, the transfer of appropriations would remove an important part of the Appropriations Committees' jurisdiction. Reserving seats for Intelligence Committee members on defense appropriations could also reduce competing viewpoints and an independent check on IC appropriations. Either change might encourage other authorizing committees to request the same treatment, that is, to control both appropriations and authorizations. Although the appropriations and authorization processes are parallel to one another, they are not identical and not always reinforcing or complementary. The combined authority could result in substantially more work for the Intelligence Committee in each session, with the need to "scrub" the intelligence budget twice each year. Or, alternatively, the transfer could lessen its examination of the appropriations and authorization, if each were to occur only in alternate sessions within a single Congress. The potential increase in the panel's workload could have two adverse ramifications: (1) short-change either the appropriations or authorization process, or both; or (2) reduce the panel's time for other legislative and oversight efforts.

By comparison to these two proposed changes—consolidating authorization and appropriations in the Intelligence Committee or reserving seats on the Defense Appropriations Subcommittee for Intelligence Committee members—the establishment of the special intelligence oversight panel on the House Appropriations Committee is more limited in its impact. Only three of its 13 seats are reserved for Intelligence Committee members; and the new panel can only make recommendations to the Defense Appropriations Subcommittee, which continues to report the annual intelligence community appropriations.

Improving Coordination between the Two Intelligence Panels

Such changes would affect the Intelligence Committees' individual structure and powers. Others could be designed to increase coordination and shared responsibility between the two intelligence panels—so as to avoid duplication, encourage cooperation, develop working relationships across chambers, enhance understanding, and share expertise, information, and knowledge—while at the same time, maintaining the distinct characteristics of each panel. These might include joint hearings and cross-committee leadership meetings, which may already exist on a regular basis.

Joint Hearings

One option along these lines is to schedule joint hearings for relatively routine and regular matters, such as the initial annual authorization briefings from the Executive. Another opportunity for a joint session would occur when the inspectors general in the intelligence community, especially at the CIA, submit their semiannual reports to Congress. These shared enterprises could allow the combined membership to receive the same information and data as each panel would individually, establish working relationships among the two groups of members, encourage cross-fertilization among them, and reduce duplication for the Executive. Of course, follow-up hearings could be handled separately by the two panels and may even be stimulated by such joint efforts. The shared experience over the initial budget submission could also help to avoid duplication of effort over some modest matters, while helping to set priorities for more significant ones.

Joint hearings could also be conducted into critical events, as they were with the select Intelligence Committees combined inquiry into 9/11 attacks.[39] Another example of an inquiry with panels from both chambers was the Iran-contra affair, an investigation conducted by two temporary committees working together and issuing a joint report.[40]

Leadership Meetings

Another means of encouraging inter-chamber cooperation is for the leadership of the two panels to meet regularly to discuss issues, concerns, and priorities (recognizing, of course, the practical and political limitations on such exchanges). These efforts might include only the full committee chairs or might extend to subcommittee heads and majority and minority members. These sessions could be supplemented by meetings of senior staff on both panels, at the direction of the leadership. Whatever the arrangement, a number of different opportunities exist to enhance awareness of common concerns and cooperation in examining them between the two panels.

Constraints on Coordination

Coordination between two panels from different chambers may encounter practical and political problems. Scheduling meetings and hearings, especially if a large number of members is involved, for instance, runs into several hindrances. These include (1) different priorities and meeting arrangements for each committee; (2) competing chamber and committee responsibilities for Members, especially Senators, each of whom serve on more committees than Representatives; and (3) different electoral and campaign requirements, which affect the demands on Members and the time they spend in the capital. In addition, rival political affiliations and policy stands, along with competition between the chambers for influence over public policy, might make cooperative ventures few and far between.

Enhancing Interchanges with Other Panels and Members

Other approaches to increasing the powers of each panel and their cooperative ventures might be considered: ease the exchange of information with non-committee members, allow for more oversight by other committees, and/or increase contacts among members of the appropriations and authorizing panels. Along these lines, the 9/11 Commission wrote: the "new committee or committees should conduct studies of the activities of the intelligence agencies and report problems relating to the development and use of intelligence to all members of the House and Senate."[41]

Placing Intelligence Committee members on the defense appropriations subcommittee or on a special appropriations intelligence oversight panel, as the House has done, also eases interchanges between these two committees. Other ways of increasing coordination between the appropriations and authorizing committees—through formalized member and staff involvement in the other panel's hearings, for instance—have been advanced in the Senate, as noted above.

Goals

This type of change could reduce the challenge of intelligence oversight on the select committees, bring different viewpoints to bear on intelligence matters, expand the knowledge of Members not on the panels, and allow for their informed judgments on intelligence policy and programs as well as on committee activities and operations. Strict controls over the classified information would have to be maintained. The current committee rules—which on the House side are more stringent than on any other committee—might be modified to accommodate additional sources for review and oversight. Such a revision could begin with a comparison of access controls by other panels, particularly the committees with overlapping membership. In addition, House and Senate chamber rules authorizing secret or closed sessions might be used more often to allow for an open exchange of information between the Intelligence Committees and all the Members of a particular chamber. Along with this, committee members might be allowed to present "declassified" versions of sensitive or otherwise classified reports to their colleagues, in secret or open sessions.

Techniques

Several potential techniques to expand non-committee involvement and non-member access to information follow:

- Ensure that relevant information is appropriately and expeditiously shared with committees with overlapping membership.
- Give greater allowance for other committees to conduct oversight of intelligence components, activities, and programs, including standing committees without overlapping membership.[42]
- Ease access for non-members to Intelligence Committee holdings, by reducing the exacting requirements over the availability of the classified.
- Encourage the Intelligence Committees, on their own initiative, to share information as appropriate with the full membership of their house.

- Make more information available to non-members by securing declassification of certain intelligence reports or by providing classified and declassified versions of IC reports (for the committees and for the general membership, respectively); the agencies proper or their inspectors general (charged with preventing and detecting waste, fraud, and abuse) might do either or both, possibly at the request or directive of the Intelligence Committees.

Limitations

Interchanges between the Intelligence Committees, on the one hand, and other panels and Members, on the other, might be limited for several reasons. Concerns about the unauthorized disclosures of classified information might be raised as the possibility of leaks rises, because of the increased number of individuals with access to sensitive information. Along with this, intelligence agencies would likely be reluctant to respond to congressional requests for sensitive and classified information, even from the Intelligence Committees, if the agencies anticipate that all or some of it will be disclosed outside the sequestered Intelligence Committee rooms, possibly to the floors of both houses.

Another possibility, which might retard information-sharing by the Intelligence Committees, could be a concern about a reduction in their control over the intelligence agenda and debate. As more Members and panels became familiar with the relevant information and policies, more questions might arise relating to the committees' policy positions. This development might be seen as weakening the committees, a condition that might reduce their (and, in turn, Congress's) influence over intelligence agencies and policies in dealings with the Executive.

Other Options

Several other options could enhance congressional oversight over the Intelligence Community.

Using Congressional Support Agencies

Increase Their Use

One approach is to increase the use of the legislative support agencies—Congressional Budget Office, Congressional Research Service, and Government Accountability Office (GAO), formerly the General Accounting Office—where appropriate.[43]

Clarified Authority for GAO to Audit the IC

A supplemental proposal would be to clarify and expand GAO's authority to audit, evaluate, or investigate components of the Intelligence Community, including the CIA. This concept was incorporated in both the House and Senate versions of the FY2010 Intelligence Authorization Act, building on proposals in its predecessor to accomplish this.[44] The House and Senate versions differ, however. The House provision calls on GAO to respond to requests from the select committees on intelligence in conducting audits or investigations, while the Senate version extends the coverage to any congressional committee with jurisdiction over an IC component and for certain specified purposes, such as financial management, information technology, and information sharing.

The Obama Administration has opposed the proposal for enhanced GAO audit powers, however, insisting that

> Section 335 would fundamentally shift the long-standing relationship and information flow between the IC and intelligence committee members and staff .... The Administration would welcome the opportunity to more fully address this matter before fundamental changes to the oversight process are legislated.[45]

These and similar proposals, which date to the mid-1970s, are the result of a fundamental disagreement between GAO and the IC with regard to the office's authority and jurisdiction over all of them. GAO possesses nearly unfettered jurisdiction to audit and investigate the federal government. GAO's access, however, may be precluded in certain situations: by the President, if it involves sensitive or classified records, such as foreign intelligence and counterintelligence activities; in instances where records are statutorily exempted from disclosure; or in cases where an executive agency holds competing powers which are used to prevent GAO access.[46]

The last of these obstacles to full access has led to conflicts between GAO and the IC, particularly the CIA.[47] The CIA views its own statutory authority as keeping it off-limits to independent GAO audits and investigations. Under this interpretation, the CIA has declined to participate in GAO reviews (as well as in some congressional oversight hearings held by panels other than the Select Committees on Intelligence); and the Agency has, on occasion, attempted to enlist other components to do the same.[48] In contrast to the CIA's position, however, other IC entities have not asserted the same proscription against GAO audits. For instance, the Department of Defense, which houses the largest number of intelligence units, has issued the following instructions:

> It is DoD policy that the Department of Defense cooperate fully with the GAO and respond constructively to, and take appropriate corrective action on the basis of, GAO reports .... [But DoD is also to] be alert to identify errors of fact or erroneous interpretation in GAO reports, and to articulate the DoD position in such matters, as appropriate.[49]

GAO has taken exception to the CIA's position, emphasizing that the Office has authority to audit the Agency independently but lacks enforcement power.[50] If enacted, the new provision would change this situation.

Applying GPRA Requirements to the CIA

A different scheme would affect the executive directly: place the CIA expressly under the requirements of the Government Performance and Results Act, commonly referred to by its initials (GPRA) or as the Results Act. This 1993 enactment emphasizes assessing agencies based on outcomes (that is, their performance and results) rather than outputs (for instance, meeting certain deadlines, quotas for issuing grants, or expenditure levels).[51] The CIA remains the only significant explicit exemption to GPRA's mandates. These include developing a broad mission statement; a five-year strategic plan flowing from it; an annual performance plan, setting specific objectives and ways to carry out the strategic plan; and a follow-up evaluation of the agency's accomplishments, failures to meet expectations, and reasons for both. These GPRA reports from the CIA could be submitted to the House and Senate Intelligence Committees in a classified version.

Enhancing the Inspectors General

A different set of alternatives would bring about changes in offices of inspector general (OIGs). These are statutorily created in executive "establishments" (all the cabinet departments and larger federal agencies) and "designated federal entities" (the usually smaller boards, commissions, foundations, and government corporations) to combat waste, fraud, and abuse and to keep the agency head and Congress fully and currently informed about these matters.[52] One change occurred through passage of the Inspector General Reform Act of 2008; it eases and increases coordination among the IGs through a new Council of the Inspectors General on Integrity and Efficiency, which includes the IGs from the CIA and the Departments of Defense, Justice, and State, among more than sixty agencies.[53]

Another proposal would establish a new post of inspector general with comprehensive jurisdiction over the IC. Located in the ODNI, the new IG would be appointed by the President, with Senate confirmation, and could be removed only by the President.[54] The IG's powers would be comparable—but not identical—to the establishment IGs. Notwithstanding its overarching jurisdiction, the new office would not replace the existing counterparts in various departments and agencies, except for the one currently in the ODNI. The IC inspector general, however, would have authority to resolve jurisdictional conflicts among them and otherwise coordinate their reviews, audits, and investigations.[55] The Obama Administration issued the following statement about the addition of an IC-wide IG.:

> The Administration supports the important work undertaken by Inspectors General .... and would like to work with the Congress on the optimal approach and authorities for carrying out the important functions of Inspectors General in the context of the IC.[56]

Other recommendations involving IGs have been advanced in the past. These would have added statutory IG in four DOD agencies, not just in NSA,[57] and would have augmented the authority, jurisdiction, independence, and reporting requirements of the IG in the ODNI.[58]

Observations on Oversight of Intelligence

Obstacles to Oversight

Congressional oversight of intelligence meets obstacles that are not usually present in other areas.[59]

Secrecy Constraints

The most significant constraint is the high degree and pervasiveness of secrecy surrounding intelligence policy, information, activities, operations, resources, and personnel. For Congress, this means that the legislature, its committees, and its Members are circumscribed in a number of ways: what they know; who receives the information, how, and in what form and forum; who provides it; what information can be shared with other Members and panels, how, and in what detail; and what non-governmental sources can contribute to legislators' knowledge, to what degree, and in what ways.

The secrecy imperative results in a system that is often closed to outsiders—not just the general public but also Representatives and Senators who do not have seats on the select committees on intelligence. The impact of official secrecy is evident in the restrictions on access to and disclosure of classified information in the panels' custody as well as on restraints covering what the select committee members themselves can discuss outside its confines.[60] These restrictions and their demanding requirements not only slow down or prevent access by non-members, because of an anticipated lengthy delay in complying with the procedures, but might also harbor a "chilling effect" for some, because of the strict limitations on disclosure and use of the information among colleagues outside the Intelligence Committees. As noted above, moreover, other access controls adopted by the executive set limits on the Government Accountability Office, Congress's chief audit and investigative agency.

The impacts and implications of secrecy are extensive and burdensome. The 9/11 Commission summarized the effects this way: "Secrecy stifles oversight, accountability, and information sharing."[61]

Perceived Limited Appeal of Intelligence Oversight

Along with this is the perceived limited appeal of overseeing intelligence and making intelligence policy, including authorizing the budget. This view appears because congressional efforts in overseeing and authorizing intelligence activities remain largely hidden and may have only marginal direct effects on Members' constituencies, districts, or states.[62]

Overcoming the Obstacles

Objectives and Goals

The impact of these limitations on Congress's oversight of intelligence is that it is significantly more difficult than in other fields. And the usual incentives for Members to serve on certain committees and conduct oversight appear to be more modest or even non-existent for intelligence.

Steps have been taken, however, to increase Congress's ability to overcome these hurdles. Prospects along this line include (1) heightening the appeal of serving on the intelligence panel; (2) enhancing the expertise and knowledge of Members (both on and off the panels); (3) reinforcing the shared responsibilities between an Intelligence Committee, on the one hand, and panels with overlapping memberships, on the other; (4) expanding the contacts and coordination between the intelligence authorizers and appropriators; (5) changing the relationship between the two chambers on intelligence matters, through, for instance, a joint committee or increased contacts between the existing committees; and (6) developing new connections between Congress and the executive that could lend themselves to more effective oversight.

A Joint Committee on Intelligence and Alternatives

Growing out of these goals are a number of recommendations to strengthen oversight of intelligence, which have arisen since the genesis of the modern intelligence community six decades ago. Recent ones have come from the 9/11 Commission, which proposed two distinct alternatives. One was to create a joint committee on intelligence. Yet over the years, the drafts for a JCI have differed in important respects: membership, leadership, jurisdiction, authority, staffing, and controls over classified information, among other matters. Moreover, rationales for a JCI have met with competing objections and concerns.

A second major option advanced by the 9/11 Commission was to enhance the powers and status of the Intelligence Committee in each house, along with realigning committee jurisdiction over intelligence appropriations, with the prospect of merging authorizing and appropriations in one committee in each chamber: namely, the Select Committees on Intelligence. The Senate—in S.Res. 445 (108th Congress), approved October 9, 2004—followed this path, but only part of the way, when it removed the term limits on serving on its intelligence panel and reduced the number of members. In separate action, leaders on the Senate Intelligence and Appropriations Committees issued a Memorandum of Agreement in 2006, designed to improve coordination and transparency between the two panels. In the meantime, the Senate Intelligence Committee leaders advanced a proposal to create an Appropriations Intelligence Subcommittee. It would have comprehensive jurisdiction for the intelligence budget and its membership would include Intelligence Committee members who are already on Appropriations, the chairman and ranking minority member of the Defense Appropriations Subcommittee, and the chairman and vice chairman of the Intelligence Committee as *ex officio* members. The Senate Appropriations Committee leaders, however, opposed this plan. The House has traveled a different route. It created a Select Intelligence Oversight Panel on its Appropriations Committee, to serve as an advisory body, which includes members of the Intelligence Committee.

Other Proposals

Other approaches to change legislative oversight of intelligence have been proposed, including several that would affect the executive directly as well as Congress's own capabilities. Among these are proposals to increase the use of congressional support agencies; clarify access for GAO to audit intelligence community elements, particularly the CIA; require the CIA to meet the GPRA planning and reporting obligations, as other IC components must do; and establish a new IG with jurisdiction over the entire IC as well as ones in certain Defense Department intelligence agencies.

End Notes

[1] Among many other sources examining congressional oversight of intelligence and executive-legislative relations in the area, see Loch K. Johnson and James J. Wirtz, eds., *Strategic Intelligence: Windows Into a Secret World* (An Anthology) (Los Angeles, Roxbury Publishing Co., 2004), Part VII, Accountability and Civil Liberties, pp. 345-427; L. Britt Snider, *The Agency and the Hill: CIA's Relationship with Congress, 1946-2004* (Washington, Center for the Study of Intelligence, Central Intelligence Agency, 2008), and *Sharing Secrets with Lawmakers: Congress as a User of Intelligence* (Washington, Center for the Study of Intelligence, CIA, 1997); Frank J. Smist, *Congress Oversees the United States Intelligence Community, 1947-1994* (Knoxville, University of Tennessee Press, 1994); John M. Oseth, *Regulating U.S. Intelligence Operations: A Study in the Definition of the National Interest* (Lexington, University of Kentucky Press, 1985); David M. Barrett, *The*

CIA and Congress: The Untold Story from Truman to Kennedy (Lawrence, University Press of Kansas, 2005); and U.S. Senate Select Committee on Intelligence, *Legislative Oversight of Intelligence Activities: The U.S. Experience*, Senate Print, 103-88, 103rd Congress, 2nd sess. (Washington, GPO, 1994). Several CRS Reports, dealing with the areas, include CRS Report RL33742, *9/11 Commission Recommendations: Implementation Status*, by Richard F. Grimmett; CRS Report R40240, *Intelligence Authorization Legislation: Status and Challenges*, by Richard A. Best Jr.; CRS Report R40136, *Congress as a Consumer of Intelligence Information*, by Alfred Cumming; CRS Report R40698, *"Gang of Four" Congressional Intelligence Notifications*, by Alfred Cumming; CRS Report R40602, *The Department of Homeland Security Intelligence Enterprise: Operational Overview and Oversight Challenges for Congress*, by Mark A. Randol; and CRS Report RL33616, *Homeland Security Intelligence: Perceptions, Statutory Definitions, and Approaches*, by Mark A. Randol. A broad overview of oversight is available in CRS Report RL30240, *Congressional Oversight Manual*, by Frederick M. Kaiser et al.

[2] Masse, *Homeland Security Intelligence*, p. 1.

[3] Such requirements are dealt with in two CRS reports: CRS Report R40698, *"Gang of Four" Congressional Intelligence Notifications*, and CRS Report R40691, *Sensitive Covert Action Notifications: Oversight Options for Congress*, both by Alfred Cumming.

[4] H.Con.Res. 186, 80th Cong., 2nd sess., introduced by Rep. Devitt, April 21, 1948.

[5] The monumental National Security Act of 1947 also gave birth to the National Security Council and National Military Establishment, later re-designated as the Department of Defense, among other organizational and procedural transformations (61 Stat. 496 et seq.).

[6] U.S. National Commission on Terrorist Attacks Upon the United States, *The 9/11 Commission Report: Final Report* (Washington: GPO, 2004), p. 420.

[7] The House and Senate have considered proposals in this broad area through their existing committees as well as a bipartisan working group in the Senate, which has recommended enhancing the powers and status of the current Intelligence Committee. Sen. Mitch McConnell, "Senators Reid and McConnell Convene Meeting of Bipartisan Working Group to Reform Congressional Oversight of Intelligence," Press Release, October 4, 2004; Sen. Bill Frist, "Frist, Daschle Appoint Members to Working Group Evaluating 9/11 Commission Proposals," Press Release, August 25, 2004.

[8] Additional coverage of JCI recommendations, characteristics, and perceived advantages and disadvantages, which are detailed below, is available in U.S. House Committee on Rules, Subcommittee on Rules of the House, *House Rule XLVIII*, hearing, 101st Cong., 2nd sess. (Washington: GPO, 1990); Frederick M. Kaiser, "A Proposed Joint Committee on Intelligence: New Wine in an Old Bottle," *Journal of Law and Politics*, vol.5, fall 1988, pp. 127-186; and Independent Task Force, Council on Foreign Relations, *Making Intelligence Smarter: The Future of U.S. Intelligence* (New York: Council on Foreign Relations, 1996), pp. 32-33.

[9] In addition to the citations in notes 1, 5, and 6 above, the development of and proposals for congressional oversight of intelligence are examined in, among many other sources: U.S. House Select Committee on Intelligence, *Recommendations of the Final Report*, H.Rept. 94-833, 94th Cong., 2nd sess. (Washington, GPO, 1976), pp. 1-4; U.S. Senate Select Committee to Study Governmental Activities with respect to Intelligence Activities, S.Rept. 94-755, 94th Cong., 2nd sess., Book II, *Intelligence Activities and the Rights of Americans* (Washington, GPO, 1976), p. 339; Frederick M. Kaiser, "Congress and the Intelligence Community," in Roger Davidson, ed., *The Postreform Congress* (New York, St. Martins Press, 1992), pp. 279-300; Loch K. Johnson, "Accountability and America's Secret Foreign Policy: Keeping a Legislative Eye on the Central Intelligence Agency," *Foreign Policy Analysis*, 2005, vol. 1, pp. 99-120, Mark M. Lowenthal, *Intelligence: From Secrets to Policy* (Washington, CQ Press, 2006), Chapter 10; "Oversight and Accountability;" Center for Strategic and International Studies, *Congressional Oversight of National Security: A Mandate for Change* (Washington, CSIS, 1992); and Center for the Study of the Presidency, Project on National Security Reform, *Ensuring Security in an Unpredictable World: Preliminary Findings, July 2008*, pp. v-vii, 60-63, and 87-90, available at http://www.pnsr.org.

[10] House Rule 3(l), added by H.Res. 5, 107th Cong., January 3, 2001.

[11] CRS Report RS20748, *Protection of Classified Information by Congress: Practices and Proposals*, by Frederick M. Kaiser.

[12] For background and further citations on the JCAE, see CRS Report RL32538, *9/11 Commission Recommendations: Joint Committee on Atomic Energy—A Model for Congressional Oversight?*, by Christopher M. Davis; Harold P. Green and Allen Rosenthal, *Government of the Atom: The Integration of Powers* (New York: Atherton Press, 1963); and Kaiser, "A Proposed Joint Committee on Intelligence," pp. 138-141.

[13] One caveat to the unique status of the JCAE is the Temporary Joint Committee on Deficit Reduction; it was authorized to report legislation but only on a narrow subject and on a case-by-case basis. In contrast to the JCAE, this joint panel was a short-term, periodic addition to Congress, set up by the Gramm-Rudman-Hollings Act of 1985. The panel could come into existence only when legislation on budget sequestration was needed and was empowered to report only a joint resolution setting forth specified reports from the Directors of the

Office of Management and Budget and the Congressional Budget Office. P.L. 99-177, 99 Stat. 1037, 1100 (1985). This provision apparently was never activated and was not included in the 1987 revision of GRH.

[14] Green and Rosenthal, *Government of the Atom*, p. 266.

[15] Kaiser, "A Proposed Joint Committee on Intelligence," pp. 140-141.

[16] The 9/11 Commission—referring to both a joint committee on intelligence and a new standing committee in each house—recommended that "Members should serve indefinitely on the committees, without set terms, thereby letting them accumulate expertise." 9/11 Commission, *Report*, p. 421.

[17] The select committee's charter provides for three responses from the full Senate to an Intelligence Committee request to release classified information, if the President objects to it. The chamber can (1) approve the disclosure; (2) disapprove the disclosure; or (3) "refer all or any portion of the matter back to the committee, in which case the committee shall make the final determination with respect to the public disclosure of the information in question" (Sec. 8(b)(5), S.Res. 400, 94th Cong., 2nd sess.).

[18] The 9/11 Commission, for instance, recommended that the "staff of this committee should be nonpartisan and work for the entire committee and not for individual members." 9/11 Commission, *Report*, p. 420.

[19] Competing views on a joint committee on intelligence are available from Members and committees of Congress, among other sources. Supportive arguments are included in: U.S. Senate Temporary Select Committee to Study the Senate Committee System, *Report* (Washington: GPO, 1984), pp. 13-14; Sen. Howard Baker and Rep. Henry Hyde, statements before the Temporary Select Committee, *Senate Resolution 127, To Study the Senate Committee System* (Washington: GPO, 1984), part 1, pp. 5-11 and part 2, pp. 83-85; Rep. Henry Hyde, statement before the Joint Committee on the Organization of Congress, *Committee Structure*, hearings, 103rd Cong., 1st sess. (Washington: GPO, 1993), pp. 832-841; and Minority, Senate Select Committee on Secret Military Assistance to Iran and the Nicaraguan Opposition and House Select Committee to Investigate Covert Arms Transactions with Iran, *Report,* S.Rept. 100-216 and H.Rept. 100-433, 100th Cong., 1st sess. (Washington: GPO, 1987), p. 583.

[20] Criticisms and concerns are voiced by Rep. Dan Glickman, Rep. Larry Combest, and Sen. Dennis DeConcini, statements before the Joint Committee on the Organization of Congress, *Committee Structure*, hearings, 103rd Cong., 1st sess., pp. 64-79 and 406-412; Rep. Larry Combest, Chairman of the House Permanent Select Committee on Intelligence, *IC21—The Intelligence Community in the 21st Century, The Intelligence Community Act of 1996*, Mar. 4, 1996, p. 7; U.S. House Permanent Select Committee on Intelligence. *IC21: Intelligence Community in the 21st Century* (staff study), committee print, 104th Cong., 2nd sess. (Washington: GPO, 1966), pp. 316-318 and 328; House Select Committee on Committees, *Final Report* (Washington: GPO, 1980), p. 416; and Majority, Senate and House Select Committees Investigating the Iran-Contra Affair, *Report*, p. 427.

[21] The 9/11 Commission (p. 421), for instance, did not advocate a joint committee for homeland security. Instead, it called for consolidating jurisdiction in a permanent standing committee in each chamber. For additional discussion on such a transformation, see CRS Report RS21901, *House Select Committee on Homeland Security: Possible Questions Raised If the Panel Were to Be Reconstituted as a Standing Committee*, by Judy Schneider.

[22] The 9/11 Commission emphasized the need for "substantial change" in congressional oversight, either by establishing a joint committee or by creating "a single committee in each house of Congress, combining authorization and appropriating authorities .... " Each panel would be a standing committee and hold subpoena authority. The membership would be relatively small and serve without term limits. Its composition would be nearly equal between the parties, with the majority having only one more member than the minority, and representing four panels with overlapping jurisdiction (i.e., Armed Services, Judiciary, Foreign Affairs, and the Defense Appropriations Subcommittee) with one seat each on the new committee. 9/11 Commission, *Report*, p. 420-421. For further information and analysis, see CRS Report RS21908, *Senate Select Committee on Intelligence: Term Limits and Assignment Limitations*, by Judy Schneider.

[23] This proposal materialized in 2007 in the House with members of the Intelligence Committee serving on a special oversight panel on the Appropriations Committee (H.Res. 35, 110th Congress). The concept was raised in late 2006 by Rep. Nancy Pelosi, then House Minority Leader and prospective Speaker of the House. Tim Starks, "Pelosi Wants Intelligence Appropriations Oversight Panel," *CQ.com*, December 14, 2006; David Rogers, "Pelosi Plans Panel to Oversee Spy-Agency Funds," *Wall Street Journal*, Dec. 14, 2006, p. A3; and "Pelosi Looks to Boost Oversight of Intelligence and Ethics," *Washington Post*, December 15, 2006.

[24] Hon. John D. Rockefeller, Chairman, Opening Statement, in U.S. Congress, Senate Select Committee on Intelligence, *Congressional Oversight*, hearing, 110th Cong., 1st sess., November 13, 2007, p. 2. See also, letter to Hon. Harry Reid, Senate Majority Leader, and Hon. Mitch McConnell, Senate Minority Leader, on changes in Senate oversight of intelligence, by Hon. John D. Rockefeller, Chairman, Senate Select Committee on Intelligence, and others, February 28, 2007.

[25] Senator Rockefeller, Opening Statement, *Congressional Oversight*, pp. 2-3.

[26] Ibid., p. 3.

[27] Hon. Christopher S. Bond, Opening Statement, in Senate Intelligence Committee, *Congressional Oversight*, pp. 4-5.

[28] Hon. John D. Rockefeller, Chairman, and Hon. Christopher S. Bond, Vice Chairman, Senate Select Committee on Intelligence, and others; letter to Hon. Harry Reid, Senate Majority Leader, and Hon. Mitch McConnell, Senate Minority Leader, on proposals to change Senate oversight of intelligence, March 6, 2008, pp. 2-3. Reprinted in *Congressional Record*, vol. 154, Sept. 11, 2008, pp. S8419-S8420.

[29] Senators Rockefeller and Bond, letter on proposed changes, 2008, p. 1.

[30] Hon. Robert C. Byrd, Chairman, and Hon. Thad Cochran, Ranking Member, Senate Committee on Appropriations, Letter to Hon. Harry Reid, Senate Majority Leader, and Hon. Mitch McConnell, Senate Minority Leader, in response the proposal from the Senate Select Committee on Intelligence, April 5, 2008, p. 1.

[31] Ibid., p. 2.

[32] Ibid.

[33] S.Res. 655, 110th Cong., 2nd sess., introduced by Hon. Christopher S. Bond, for himself, and Hon. John D. Rockefeller and Hon. Sheldon Whitehouse, "Senate Resolution 655—To Improve Congressional Oversight of the Intelligence Activities of the United States," *Congressional Record*, vol. 154, September 11, 2008, pp. S8416-S8417.

[34] Ibid., p. S8418.

[35] Ibid., p. S8419.

[36] Hon. Russell Feingold, Statement on behalf of S.Res. 164, 111th Congress, 1st sess., June 2, 2009, *Congressional Record*, vol. 155, pp. S5950-S5951.

[37] Sources in footnote 23.

[38] See Honorable Michael Castle, *2009 Intelligence Authorization Act Needs More Oversight*, Press release, July 17, 2008, available at http://www.castle.house.gov/News/DocumentSingle.aspx?DocumentID=106799.

[39] U.S. Senate Select Committee on Intelligence and U.S. House Permanent Select Committee on Intelligence, *Joint Inquiry into Intelligence Community Activities Before and After the Terrorist Attacks of September 11, 2001*, S.Rept. 107-351 and H.Rept. 107-792, 107th Cong., 2nd sess. (Washington: GPO, 2002).

[40] U.S. Senate Select Committee on Secret Military Assistance to Iran and the Nicaraguan Opposition, and U.S. House Select Committee to Investigate Covert Arms Transactions with Iran, *Report on the Iran-Contra Affair*, S.Rept. 100-216 and H.Rept. 100-433, 100th Cong., 1st sess. (Washington: GPO, 1987).

[41] 9/11 Commission, *Report*, p. 420.

[42] See especially House Subcommittees on Efficiency and on National Security, *CIA Refusal*, 2001.

[43] The oversight roles of the support agencies are spelled out in CRS Report RL30240, *Congressional Oversight Manual*, by Frederick M. Kaiser et al.

[44] H.R. 2701 and S. 1494, 111th Congress, 1st sess. See also U.S. House Permanent Select Committee on Intelligence, *Intelligence Authorization Act for Fiscal Year 2010*, H.Rept. 111-186, 111th Congress, 1st sess., sec. 335 (Washington, GPO, 2009); and U.S. Senate Select Committee on Intelligence, *Intelligence Authorization Act for Fiscal Year 2010*, S.Rept. 111-55, 111th Congress, 1st sess., sec. 335 (Washington, GPO, 2009). For action in the 110th Congress on similar plans, see the Intelligence Community Audit Act, H.R. 978 and S. 82, 110th Congress. Hearings and press coverage include U.S. Senate Subcommittee on Oversight of Government Management, the Federal Workforce, and the District of Columbia, *Government-wide Intelligence Community Reform*, hearing, 110th Congress, 2nd sess., Feb. 29, 2008 (Washington, GPO, 2008); Chris Strom, "Panel witnesses press for GAO audits of intelligence agencies," *Government Executive*, available at http://www.govexec.com/story_page.cfm?filepath=/dailyfed/0208/ 022908cdpm2.htm, February 29, 2008; and Paul Kane, "GAO Seeks Review of Spy Agencies," *Washington Post*, Mar. 7, 2008, p. A15.

[45] U.S. Office of Management and Budget, *Statement of Administration Policy: H.R. 2701—Intelligence Authorization Act for Fiscal Year 2010*, July 8, 2009, p. 2.

[46] Statutory citations for such restrictions include Central Intelligence Agency Act of 1949, 63 Stat. 213; General Accounting Office Act of 1980, 94 Stat. 311; 31 U.S.C. 716(d); and 31 U.S.C. 716(b) and 3524(c).

[47] GAO is limited in its independent authority to audit and investigate the CIA, because of provisions in public law and congressional rules as well as tradition and precedents. The CIA, however, is the only intelligence component which makes such an across-the-board claim. See GAO, *Central Intelligence Agency: Observations on GAO Access to Information on CIA Programs and Activities*, statement by Henry J. Hinton, GAO-01-975T (Washington: GAO, 2001); *Information Sharing*, GAO-06-385, (Washington: GAO, 2006), pp. 6-7;and *DOD Personnel Security Clearances*, Letter to Hon. George V. Voinovich, Chairman, Senate Subcommittee on Oversight of Government Management, June 14, 2006, p. 1. See also U.S. House Government Reform Subcommittees on Government Efficiency and on National Security, *Is the CIA's Refusal to Cooperate with Congressional Inquiries a Threat to Effective Oversight of the Federal Government*, hearings, 107th Cong., 1st sess (Washington: GPO, 2001); Frederick M. Kaiser, "GAO Versus the CIA: Uphill Battles Against an Overpowering Force," *International Journal of Intelligence and Counterintelligence*, vol. 15 (2002), pp. 330-389; and CRS Report RL30349, *GAO: Government Accountability Office and General Accounting Office*, by Frederick M. Kaiser.

[48] See House Government Reform Subcommittees on Government Efficiency and National Security, *CIA's Refusal to Cooperate*, pp. 1-8. The subcommittee chairmen emphasized that the CIA had initially agreed to participate

in a GAO survey of computer security programs but later declined. The Agency also attempted, unsuccessfully as it turned out, to have other IC entities follow suit. Finally, the CIA declined to participate in any of the subcommittees' hearings or meetings, even if held in executive or secret session.

[49] Department of Defense Instruction 7650.02, November 20, 2006.

[50] Elaboration of GAO's support for such new authority and the DNI's (and the previous DCI's) opposition appears in letter from David M. Walker, Comptroller General, to Hon. John D. Rockefeller, Chairman, and Hon. Christopher S. Bond, Vice Chairman, Senate Select Committee on Intelligence, March 1, 2007; and letter from J. M. McConnell, Director of National Intelligence, to Hon. John D. Rockefeller, Chairman, and Christopher S. Bond, Vice Chairman, Senate Select Committee on Intelligence, March 7, 2007. See M.Z. Hemingway, "GAO wants more muscle," *Federal Times*, March 26, 2007, p. 1; and "GAO Seeks Greater Role in Oversight of Intelligence," *Secrecy News*, October 3, 2007, available at http://www.fas.org. For the competing views of the disputes over independent GAO access, which date to the earliest days of the CIA, see U.S. Central Intelligence Agency, *DCI Affirmation of Policy for Dealing with the General Accounting Office (GAO)*, Memorandum for the Director of Central Intelligence, from Stanley L. Moskowitz, Director of Congressional Affairs, 7 July 1994; GAO, *Central Intelligence Agency: Observations on GAO Access to Information on CIA Programs and Activities*, statement of Henry J. Hinton, GAO-01-975T (2001); letters from the Comptroller General to the Director of National Intelligence (DNI), April 27, 2006, and to the Chairman and Ranking Minority Member of the Senate Committee on Homeland Security and Governmental Affairs, May 15, 2006, disputing the DNI's position that the "review of intelligence activities is beyond the GAO's purview," as stated in *Information Sharing*, GAO-06-385 (2006), pp. 6 and 71.

[51] P.L. 103-62, 107 Stat. 285.

[52] Inspector General Act of 1978, as amended; 5 U.S.C. Appendix.

[53] P.L. 110-409; 122 Stat. 4305-4313.

[54] Intelligence Authorization Act for Fiscal Year 2010, H.R. 2701, sec. 406, and S. 1494, sec. 407. The current proposal mirrors ones offered in the two previous congresses. The FY 2008 Intelligence Authorization Act (H.R. 2082, 110th Cong.) was vetoed by President Bush and his veto sustained. *Congressional Record*, vol. 154, March 11, 2008, pp. H1503-H1514. A similar recommendation was included in the FY2009 Intelligence Authorization Act (H.R. 5959, 110th Cong.), also meeting objections from the Bush Administration. See U.S. Office of Management and Budget, *Statement of Administration Policy: H.R. 5959—Intelligence Authorization Act for FY 2009*, July 6, 2008.

[55] H.R. 2701, sec. 406, and S. 1494, sec. 407.

[56] OMB, *Statement of Administration Policy: H.R. 2701* (2009), p. 2.

[57] The FY 2009 Intelligence Authorization Act (H.R. 5959, 110th Cong.), reiterating sections of the (vetoed) FY2008 bill, would place four DOD intelligence entities—the National Reconnaissance Office, Defense Intelligence Agency, National Security Agency, and the National Geospatial-Intelligence Agency—under the Inspector General Act of 1978, as amended (5 U.S.C. Appendix). These agencies would be the equivalent of "designated federal entities," that is, entities whose IGs are appointed by and removed by the agency head. In addition, the Secretary of Defense would be able to prevent or halt an audit or investigation, if the Secretary or DNI determined that such a prohibition would be necessary to protect vital U.S. national security interests. The House and Senate Committees on Armed Services and on Intelligence would have to be notified of such an exercise by the Secretary of Defense.

[58] The DNI, under authority establishing the post and office (P.L. 108-458), has complete discretion to create and construct an OIG in his Office, based on provisions he selects from the Inspector General Act of 1978, as amended. In 2006, the director established an inspector general post in his office. U.S. Office of the Director of National Intelligence, *Report on the Progress of the DNI in Implementing the Intelligence Reform Act of 2004*, May 2006. In the meantime, however, the House and Senate Intelligence Committees have raised questions about the IG's independence, capabilities, jurisdiction, and reporting to Congress. U.S. Congress, House Permanent Select Committee on Intelligence, *Intelligence Authorization Act for 2007*, H.Rept. 109-411, 109th Cong., 2nd sess.

[59] See CRS Report R40240, *Intelligence Authorization Legislation: Status and Challenges*, by Richard A. Best Jr.; and CRS Report RL32617, *A Perspective on Congress's Oversight Function*, by Walter J. Oleszek.

[60] CRS Report R40691, *Sensitive Covert Action Notifications: Oversight Options for Congress*, and CRS Report R40698, *"Gang of Four" Congressional Intelligence Notifications*, both by Alfred Cumming.

[61] 9/11 Commission, *Report*, p. 24.

[62] Ibid., pp. 420-421.

In: Congressional Oversight An Overview, A Manual and... ISBN: 978-1-61728-477-9
Editor: Jamie C. Howell

Chapter 4

SENSITIVE COVERT ACTION NOTIFICATIONS: OVERSIGHT OPTIONS FOR CONGRESS*

Alfred Cumming

SUMMARY

Legislation enacted in 1980 gave the executive branch authority to limit advance notification of especially sensitive covert actions to eight Members of Congress—the "Gang of Eight"—when the President determines that it is essential to limit prior notice in order to meet extraordinary circumstances affecting U.S. vital interests. In such cases, the executive branch is permitted by statute to limit notification to the chairmen and ranking minority members of the two congressional intelligence committees, the Speaker and minority leader of the House, and Senate majority and minority leaders, rather than to notify the full intelligence committees, as is required in cases involving covert actions determined to be less sensitive.

Congress, in approving this new procedure in 1980, during the Iran hostage crisis, said it intended to preserve operational secrecy in those "rare" cases involving especially sensitive covert actions while providing the President with advance consultation with the leaders in Congress and the leadership of the intelligence committees who have special expertise and responsibility in intelligence matters. The intent appeared to some to be to provide the President, on a short-term basis, a greater degree of operational security as long as sensitive operations were underway. In 1991, in a further elaboration of its intent following the Iran-Contra Affair, congressional report language stated that limiting notification to the Gang of Eight should occur only in situations involving covert actions of such extraordinary sensitivity or risk to life that knowledge of such activity should be restricted to as few individuals as possible.

In its mark-up of H.R. 2701, the FY2010 Intelligence Authorization Act, the House Permanent Select Committee on Intelligence (HPSCI) replaced the Gang of Eight statutory

* This is an edited, reformatted and augmented edition of a United States Congressional Research Service publication, Report R40691, dated January 29, 2010.

provision, adopting in its place a statutory requirement that each of the intelligence committees establish written procedures as may be necessary to govern such notifications. According to committee report language, the adopted provision vests the authority to limit such briefings with the committees, rather than the President.

On July 8, 2009, the executive branch issued a Statement of Administration Policy (SAP) in which it stated that it strongly objected to the House Committee's action to replace the Gang of Eight statutory provision, and that the President's senior advisors would recommend that the President veto the FY2010 Intelligence Authorization Act if the committee's language was retained in the final bill.

The Senate Intelligence Committee, in its version of the FY2010 Intelligence Authorization Act, left unchanged the Gang of Eight statutory structure, but approved several changes that would tighten certain aspects of current covert action reporting requirements. Although the executive branch has not issued a Statement of Administration Policy with regard to the Senate's bill, Director of National Intelligence Admiral Dennis Blair has indicated that he would recommend that the President veto the bill if the covert action notification changes contained in the bill remained in final legislation. Congress has not acted on the FY2010 Intelligence Authorization bill.

With Congress considering possible changes in covert action congressional notifications, this chapter describes the statutory provision authorizing Gang of Eight notifications, reviews the legislative history of the provision, and examines both the impact of such notifications on congressional oversight as well as options that Congress might consider to possibly improve oversight.

REQUIREMENTS FOR NOTIFICATIONS OF SENSITIVE COVERT ACTIONS TO CONGRESS

Under current statute, the President generally is required keep the congressional intelligence committees fully and currently informed of all covert actions[1] and that any covert action[2] "finding" [3] shall be reported to the committees as soon as possible after such approval and before the initiation of the covert action authorized by the finding.

If, however, the President determines that it is essential to limit access to a covert action finding in order to "meet extraordinary circumstances affecting vital interests of the United States,"[4] then rather than providing advanced notification to the full congressional intelligence committees, as is generally required, the President may limit such notification to the "Gang of Eight," and any other congressional leaders he may choose to inform. The statute defines the "Gang of Eight" as being comprised of the chairmen and ranking members of the two congressional intelligence committees and the House and Senate majority and minority leadership.[5]

In report language accompanying the 1980 enactment, Congress established its intent to preserve the secrecy necessary for very sensitive covert actions, while providing the President with a process for consulting in advance with congressional leaders, including the intelligence committee chairmen and ranking minority members, "who have special expertise and responsibility in intelligence matters."[6] Such consultation, according to Congress, would ensure strong oversight, while at the same time, "share the President's burden on difficult decisions concerning significant activities."[7]

In 1991, following the Iran-Contra Affair,[8] Intelligence Conference Committee Conferees more specifically stated that Gang of Eight notifications should be used only when "the President is faced with a covert action of such extraordinary sensitivity *or risk to life* that knowledge of the covert action should be restricted to as few individuals as possible."[9] Congressional Conferees also indicated that they expected the executive branch to hold itself to the same standard by similarly limiting knowledge of such sensitive covert actions within the executive.[10]

ADDITIONAL GANG OF EIGHT REQUIREMENTS

In addition to having to determine that vital interests are implicated, the President must comply with four additional statutory conditions in notifying the Gang of Eight. First, the President is required to provide a statement setting out the reasons for limiting notification to the Gang of Eight, rather than the full intelligence committees.[11] The two intelligence committee chairmen, both Gang of Eight Members, also must be provided signed copies of the covert action finding in question.[12] Third, the President is required to provide the Gang of Eight advance notice of the covert action in question.[13] And, lastly, Gang of Eight Members must be notified of any significant changes in a previously approved covert action, or any significant undertaking pursuant to a previously approved finding.[14]

WHEN PRIOR NOTICE TO THE GANG OF EIGHT IS WITHHELD

Although the statute requires that the President provide the Gang of Eight advance notice of certain covert actions, it also recognizes the President's constitutional authority to withhold such prior notice altogether by imposing certain additional conditions on the President should the decision be made to withhold. If prior notice is withheld, the President must "fully inform" the congressional intelligence committees[15] in a "timely fashion"[16] after the commencement of the covert action. The President also is required to provide a statement of the reasons for withholding prior notice to the Gang of Eight.[17] In other words, a decision by the executive branch to withhold prior notice from the Gang of Eight would appear to effectively prevent the executive branch from limiting an-after-the-fact notification to the Gang of Eight, even if the President had determined initially that the covert action in question warranted Gang of Eight treatment. Rather, barring prior notice to the Gang of Eight, the executive branch would then be required to inform the full intelligence committees of the covert action in "timely fashion." In doing so, Congress appeared to envision a covert action, the initiation of which would require a short-term period of heightened operational security.

Congress Signaled Its Intent That the Gang of Eight Would Decide When To Inform the Intelligence Committees

During the Senate's 1980 debate of the Gang of Eight provision, congressional sponsors said their intent was that the Gang of Eight would reserve the right to determine the appropriate time to inform the full intelligence committees of the covert action of which they had been notified.[18]

The position of sponsors that the Gang of Eight would determine when to notify the full intelligence committees underscores the point that while the statute provides the President this limited notification option, it appears to be largely silent on what happens after the President exercises this particular option. Sponsors thus made it clear that they expected the intelligence committees to establish certain procedures to govern how the Gang of Eight was to notify the full intelligence committees. Senator Walter Huddleston, Senate floor manager for the legislation, said "the intent is that the full oversight committees will be fully informed at such time the eight leaders determine is appropriate. The committees will establish the procedures for the discharge of this responsibility."[19]

Senator Huddleston's comments referred to Sec. 501(c) of Title V of the National Security Act which stipulates that "The President and the congressional intelligence committees shall each establish such procedures as may be necessary to carry out the provisions of this title."

With regard to Sec. 501(c), Senate report language stated:

> The authority for procedures established by the Select Committees is based on the current practices of the committees in establishing their own rules. One or both committees may, for example, adopt procedures under which designated members are assigned responsibility on behalf of the committee to receive information in particular types of circumstances, such as when all members cannot attend a meeting or when certain highly sensitive information is involved.[20]

Congressional intent thus appeared to be that the collective membership of each intelligence committee, rather than the committee leadership, would develop such procedures.[21] Moreover, the rules that each committee have subsequently adopted, while they deal in detail as to how the committees are to conduct their business, do not appear to address any procedures that might guide Gang of Eight notifications generally. Rather, to the extent that any such procedures have been adopted, those procedures appear to have been put into place at the executive branch's insistence, according to congressional participants.[22]

Congress Approved Gang of Eight Notifications in 1980, Following the Iran Hostage Rescue Attempt

Congress approved the Gang of Eight notification provision in 1980 as part of a broader package of statutory intelligence oversight measures generally aimed at tightening intelligence oversight while also providing the Central Intelligence Agency (CIA) greater leeway to carry out covert operations,[23] following a failed covert operation to rescue American embassy hostages in Iran.[24]

Congressional approval came after President Jimmy Carter decided not to notify the intelligence committees of the operation in advance because of concerns over operational security and the risk of disclosure. Director of Central Intelligence Stansfield Turner briefed the congressional intelligence committees only after the operations had been conducted. Although most members reportedly expressed their understanding of the demands for secrecy and thus the Administration's decision to withhold prior notification,[25] Senate Intelligence Committee Chairman Birch Bayh expressed concern that the executive branch's action reflected a distrust of the committees. He suggested that future administrations could address disclosure concerns by notifying a more limited number of Members "so that at least somebody in the oversight mechanism would know.... If oversight is to function better, you first need it to function [at all]."[26] Such sentiments appear to have contributed to the subsequent decision by Congress to permit the executive branch to notify the Gang of Eight in such cases.[27]

AUTHORITY OF GANG OF EIGHT TO AFFECT COVERT ACTION

Even with statutory arrangements governing covert action, including Gang of Eight covert actions, Congress does not have the authority under statute to veto outright a covert action. Indeed, former Senator Howard Baker successfully pushed the inclusion in the 1980 legislative package of a provision making clear that Congress did not have approval authority over the initiation of any particular covert action.[28]

Nonetheless, the Gang of Eight Members, as do the intelligence committees, arguably have the authority to influence whether and how such covert actions are conducted over time. For example, Members could express opposition to the initiation of a particular covert action. Some observers assert that in the absence of Members' agreement to the initiation of the covert action involved, barring such agreement, an administration would have to think carefully before proceeding with such a covert action as planned.[29]

The Gang of Eight over time could also influence funding for such operations. Initial funding for a covert action generally comes from the CIA's Reserve for Contingency Fund, for which Congress provides an annual appropriation. Once appropriated, the CIA can fund a covert action using money from this fund, without having to seek congressional approval. But the executive branch generally must seek additional funds to replenish the reserve on an annual basis. If the Gang of Eight, including the two committee chairmen and ranking members, were to agree not to continue funding for a certain covert action, they arguably could impress on the membership of the two committees not to replenish the reserve fund, providing they informed the committees of the covert action, a decision which the congressional sponsors said they intended to be left to the discretion of the Gang of Eight in any case.

Thus, the Gang of Eight could influence the intelligence committees to increase, decrease or eliminate authorized funding of a particular covert action. Some observers point out, however, that the leaders' overall effectiveness in influencing a particular covert action turns at least as much on their capability to conduct effective oversight of covert action as it does on their legal authority.

Impact on Congressional Intelligence Oversight

The impact of Gang of Eight notifications on the effectiveness of congressional intelligence oversight continues to be debated.

Supporters of the Gang of Eight process contend that such notifications continue to serve their original purpose, which, they assert, is to protect operational security of particularly sensitive covert actions that involve vital U.S. interests while still involving Congress in oversight. Further, they point out that although Members receiving these notifications may be constrained in sharing detailed information about the notifications with other intelligence committee members and staff, these same Members can raise concerns directly with the President and the congressional leadership and thereby seek to have any concerns addressed.[30] Supporters also argue that Members receiving these restricted briefings have at their disposal a number of legislative remedies if they decide to oppose a particular covert action program, including the capability to use the appropriations process to withhold funding until the executive branch behaves according to Congress's will.[31]

Critics counter with the following points. First, they say, Gang of Eight notifications do not provide for effective congressional oversight because participating Members "cannot take notes, seek the advice of their counsel, or even discuss the issues raised with their committee colleagues."[32] Second, they contend that Gang of Eight notifications have been "overused."[33] Third, they assert that, in certain instances, the executive branch did not provide an opportunity to Gang of Eight Members to approve or disapprove of the program being briefed to them.[34] And fourth, they contend that the "limited information provided Congress was so overly restricted that it prevented members of Congress from conducting meaningful oversight."[35]

Directors of National Intelligence and Central Intelligence Agency Critical of Gang of Eight Notifications For Non-Covert Actions

During their respective Senate confirmation hearings, Director of National Intelligence (DNI) Dennis Blair and CIA Director Leon Panetta criticized the use of the Gang of Eight notification procedure to notify Congress of the National Security Agency's (NSA) electronic communications surveillance program—often referred to as the Terrorist Surveillance Program, or TSP—and the CIA's detention, interrogation and rendition program. DNI Blair said both programs "involved sensitive collection activities rather than covert actions. The 'Gang of 8' notice is available ... only where notice of covert action is concerned, and its use in these programs was not expressly allowed."[36] Director Panetta said "the NSA surveillance program was not a covert action program, and, therefore, limiting notification to the 'gang of eight' was inappropriate."[37] DNI Blair said that, because of the restrictive nature of Gang of

Eight notifications in these two instances, "the intelligence committees were prevented from carrying out their oversight responsibilities."[38] Director Panetta, expressing similar sentiments, said that such limited notifications "restrict the ability of the intelligence committees to conduct oversight."[39]

House Intelligence Committee Replaces Gang of Eight Procedure in FY2010 Intelligence Authorization Act

In marking up its version of the FY2010 Intelligence Authorization Act, the House Intelligence Committee replaced the Gang of Eight statutory provision, adopting in its place a statutory requirement that each of the intelligence committees establish written procedures as may be necessary to govern such notifications.

The current Gang of Eight statutory provision stipulates:

> If the President determines that it is essential to limit access to the finding to meet extraordinary circumstances affecting vital interest of the United States, the finding may be reported to the chairmen and ranking minority members of the congressional intelligence committees, the Speaker and the minority leader of the House of Representatives, the majority and minority leaders of the Senate, and such other member or members of the congressional leadership as may be included by the President[40]

The substitute language approved by the House Intelligence Committee stipulates:

> If, pursuant to the procedures established by each of the congressional intelligence committees under Section 501(c), one of the congressional intelligence committees determines that not all members of that committee are required to have access to a finding under this subsection, the President may limit access to such findings or such notice as provided in such procedures.[41]

According to committee report language, the provision:

> requires the President to brief all members of the congressional intelligence committees, but implicitly provides for the possibility of more restricted briefings pursuant to the written procedures established by the congressional intelligence committees, pursuant to the revised Section 501 (c). This language vests the authority to limit the briefings with the committees, rather than the President.[42]

The Report's reference to a revision of Sec. 501 of the National Security Act pertained to the committee's approval of statutory language requiring that the President and the congressional intelligence committees each establish such "written" procedures as may be necessary to carry out the statutes provisions.[43] Current statute does require that any such procedures be in writing.

In approving the new provision, the committee rejected an amendment that would have authorized the committee's chairman and ranking member to decide whether to comply with a presidential request to limit access to certain intelligence information, including covert actions.

The rejected amendment stipulated that if the chairman and ranking member were unable to agree on whether or how to limit such access, access to the information would be limited if so requested by the President.[44]

According to the views of the minority contained in the report, the provision adopted by the committee:

> nowhere creates a statutory presumption that all Members of the Committee should be briefed. Instead, it would require the Committee to unilaterally develop procedures for the handling of reporting on sensitive matters, even though the President has significant constitutional authorities in the area of national security that Courts have repeatedly said must be considered with and balanced against the authorities of Congress. The provision nowhere provides a mechanism for ensuring that decisions within the Committee are made on a bipartisan basis or for reconciling any dispute between the branches with respect to such reporting, which is a receipt for Constitutional gridlock that could be disastrous with respect to such sensitive matters.[45]

THE HOUSE INTELLIGENCE COMMITTEE ADOPTED SEVERAL OTHER COVERT ACTION-RELATED MEASURES AS PART OF FY2010 INTELLIGENCE BILL

The House Intelligence Committee adopted several additional statutory changes with regard to covert action notifications. One such change would require that the information or material concerning covert actions include any information or material relating to the legal authority under which a covert action is being or was conducted, and any information or material relating to legal issues upon which guidance was sought in carrying out or planning the covert action, including dissenting legal views.[46]

Another change would require that the President provide Members who are not notified of a particular covert action, pursuant to the procedures established by the each of the committees, with general information on the content of the covert action.[47]

The committee also adopted a provision that would permit a member who objects to a particular covert action that has been notified to submit an objection to the Director of National Intelligence. The DNI is required to notify the President of the objection no later than 48 hours after the objection has been submitted.[48]

Finally, the committee approved covert action-related provisions that would

- require that the CIA inspector general audit each covert action every three years;[49]
- require that the President maintain a record of the Members of Congress notified of a covert action and to provide such record within 30 days after the notification is provided;[50] and
- define the current statutory phrase "significant undertaking" to mean an activity involving the potential for loss of life; requiring an expansion of existing authorities, including authorities relating to research, development, or operations; resulting in the expenditure of significant funds or other resources; requiring notification under section 504; giving rise to a significant risk of disclosing intelligence sources or

methods; or possibly causing serious damage to the diplomatic relations if the activity were to be disclosed without authorization.[51]

SENATE INTELLIGENCE COMMITTEE TIGHTENED CERTAIN COVERT ACTION REPORTING REQUIREMENTS

In its version of the FY2010 Intelligence Authorization Act, the Senate Intelligence Committee left unchanged the Gang of Eight statutory structure, but approved several changes that would tighten certain aspects of current covert action reporting requirements.

The committee adopted language stating that there shall be no exception to the requirements of Title V off the National Security Act to inform the intelligence committees of all covert actions.[52] The committee voted to require that all members of the intelligence committees be notified when the executive branch does not provide information "in full" to all members.[53] In such cases, the Director of National Intelligence would be required to provide in writing to the committees in a "timely manner" a statement explaining the reasons for withholding certain information from the full membership and a description of the main features of the covert action in question. The executive branch also would be required to include in reports to Congress on covert actions an explanation of the significance of the covert action and report any change to a covert action,[54] rather than any "significant" change,[55] as is currently required under statute.

Finally, the committee approved language that would require that the executive branch provide to the intelligence committees any information or material regarding the legal authority under which a covert action is or was conducted,[56] and that funding for an intelligence activity would be provided only if the intelligence committees had been fully and currently informed of that activity, or had been notified when the executive branch did not provide information in full to all members.[57]

In additional views accompanying the committee's report[58] on the legislation, Senators John Rockefeller and Olympia Snowe said they supported the committee-adopted language because, they wrote, it would improve the notification processes, while not eliminating the Gang of Eight procedure, "which many of us believe can serve an important purpose for quick and timely notifications on extraordinarily sensitive covert actions."[59]

A small number of the committee members opposed the notification provision contained in the bill that would require the executive branch to notify the full membership of the intelligence committees when a covert action notification does not disclose all information regarding such an activity to all members of the committees. In additional views, they stated that the adopted provision would modify the current balance in the National Security Act with respect to the congressional notification procedures and that such a provision "will unnecessarily increase the tension between the Legislative and Executive branches over information access."[60]

Executive Branch Threatens Veto of House and Senate Versions of 2010 Intelligence Authorization Act

On July 8, 2009, the executive branch issued a Statement of Administration Policy (SAP)[61] in which it stated that it strongly objected to the House committee's action to replace the Gang of Eight statutory provision, and that the President's senior advisors would recommend that the President veto the FY2010 Intelligence Authorization Act if the committee's language was retained in the final bill. According to the executive branch's statement, the committee's new statutory language "would run afoul of tradition by restricting an important established means by which the President protects the most sensitive intelligence activities that are carried out in the Nation's vital national security interests."[62]

Although the executive branch has not issued a Statement of Administration Policy with regard to the Senate's bill, Director of National Intelligence Admiral Dennis Blair has indicated that he would recommend that the President veto the bill if the covert action notification changes it contained remained in final legislation.[63]

Gang of Eight Notifications: The Historic Record

Notwithstanding the continuing debate over the merits of such notifications, what remains less clear is the historic record of compliance with Gang of Eight provisions set out in statute. Questions include: have such notifications generally been limited to covert actions, ones that conform to congressional intent that such covert actions be highly sensitive and involve the risk to life? When prior notification is limited to the Gang of Eight, has the executive branch provided an explanatory statement as to why it limited notification to the Gang of Eight? If the Gang of Eight is not provided prior notice, has the executive branch then informed the intelligence committees at a later date and provided a reason why prior notification was not provided? Has the Gang of Eight, once notified, ever then made a determination to notify the intelligence committees, a prerogative envisioned by its congressional sponsors? Have the congressional intelligence committees, at any time since they were established, attempted to develop procedures to guide Gang of Eight notifications, as envisioned by the sponsors of the Gang of Eight provision?

Possible Gang of Eight Options

The 111th Congress, in its assessment, could deem that the Gang of Eight notification procedure, as currently provided for in statute and by practice, continues to strike a reasonable balance between the twin objectives of operational security and congressional oversight. If, however, changes are sought, Congress could consider the following options.

Alternative One

Congress could adopt the approach approved by the House Intelligence Committee during its markup of the FY2010 Intelligence Authorization Act. This approach would eliminate the Gang of Eight statutory provision, according to its sponsors, substituting instead a provision that its sponsors said would require that the President brief all members of the congressional intelligence committees, while implicitly providing for the possibility of more restricted briefings pursuant to the written procedures that would be established by the congressional intelligence committees as may be necessary to carry out the statute's provisions.

Alternative Two

Congress could adopt the approach approved by the Senate Intelligence Committee during its markup of the FY2010 Intelligence Authorization Act. Rather than eliminating the current Gang of Eight statutory provision, the Senate language would make no exception to the requirement that the intelligence committees be notified of all covert actions. The language also would require that all members of the intelligence committees be notified when the executive branch did not provide information "in full" to all members about a particular covert action. In such cases, the Director of National Intelligence would be required to provide in writing to the committees in a "timely manner" a statement explaining the reasons for withholding certain information from the full membership and a description of the main features of the covert action in question. The executive branch also would be required to include in reports to Congress on covert actions an explanation of the significance of the covert action being considered and report any change to a covert action, rather than any "significant" change, as is currently required under statute. Finally, under the Senate Committee's provisions, the executive branch would be required to provide any information or material regarding the legal authority under which a covert action is or was conducted, and funding for a particular covert action would be provided only if the intelligence committees had been fully and currently informed of that activity, or had been notified if the executive branch had not provided information in full to all members of the two intelligence committees.

Alternative Three

Congress could adopt the provision supported by some members of the House Intelligence Committee but ultimately rejected by a majority of the committee membership that would have authorized the chairmen and ranking members of the intelligence committees to decide whether to comply with a presidential request to limit access to certain intelligence information, including covert actions. The amendment stipulated that if the chairman and ranking member were unable to agree on whether or how to limit such access, access to the information would be limited, if so requested by the President.

Alternative Four

If Congress were to decide to preserve the Gang of Eight notification procedure, but were to consider modifying the process, such modifications could include specifying explicitly in statute that

- Gang of Eight notifications are permitted only in situations involving covert action, rather than in those situations involving non-covert action programs, including sensitive intelligence collection programs;
- a Gang of Eight notification remain in place as long as sensitive operations are underway. Once such operational sensitivities no longer prevail, however, the full membership of the intelligence committees would be informed;
- Gang of Eight Members, rather than the executive branch, will decide when to notify the full membership of the intelligence committees.
- the executive branch be required to provide a statement of the reasons, *in writing*, for limiting notification to the Gang of Eight, and that the executive branch provide a *written* statement to the congressional intelligence committees in a timely fashion when it does not provide prior notice of a covert action to the Gang of Eight.
- Pursuant to Sec. 501(c) of the National Security Act, which requires the establishment of procedures as may be necessary to carry out the provisions of the statute, Congress could require that the congressional intelligence committees establish certain procedures that would govern Gang of Eight notifications, as the sponsors of the Gang of Eight provision apparently originally intended. Such procedures could include permitting Gang of Eight Members to take notes as such briefings and establishing a process of more formal consultation between Gang of Eight Members.[64]

Alternative Five

Congress statutorily could eliminate the Gang of Eight procedure and bring sensitive covert actions notifications back within the intelligence committee structure by permitting the President to limit initial briefings of such operations to the chairmen and ranking members of the two intelligence committees, the so-called "Gang of Four" formulation. Under this change, committee leadership could be permitted to consult with House and Senate leaders, and staff, and inform the full intelligence committees when they determine it to be appropriate.

Alternative Six

Congress statutorily could require that the executive branch inform the full membership of the intelligence committees of all covert actions, irrespective of their perceived sensitivity.

CONCLUSION: STRIKING A BALANCE

Striking the proper balance between effective oversight and security remains a challenge to Congress and the executive. Doing so in cases involving particularly sensitive covert actions presents a special challenge. Success turns on a number of factors, not the least of which is the degree of comity and trust that defines the relationship between the legislative and executive branches. More trust can lead to greater flexibility in notification procedures. When trust in the relationship is lacking, however, the legislative branch may see a need to tighten and make more precise the notification architecture, so as to assure what it views as being an appropriate flow of information, thus enabling effective oversight.

End Notes

[1] National Security Act as amended, Sec. 503 [50 U.S.C. 413b] (b) and (c).

[2] A covert action is defined in statute as an activity or activities of the United States Government to influence political, economic, or military conditions abroad, where it is intended that the role of the United States Government will not be apparent or acknowledged publicly. See the National Security Act of 1947, Sec. 503(e), 50 U.S.C. 413b(e).

[3] A Finding is a presidential determination that an activity is necessary to "support identifiable foreign policy objectives" and "is important to he national security of the Untied States." See Intelligence Authorization Act for FY1991, P.L. 102-88, Title VI, Sec. 602 (a) (2), 50 U.S.C. 413b (a).

[4] National Security Act of 1947 as amended, Sec. 503 [50 U.S.C. 413b] (c) (2). See Addendum A, Title V of the National Security Act as amended. The authorization for Gang of Eight notification also permits the President to notify "such other Member or Members of the congressional leadership as may be included by the President."

[5] Ibid.

[6] Addendum A, S.Rept. 96-730, 96th Cong., 2nd sess. (1980), p. 10. This chapter accompanied S. 2284, from which Title V of P.L. 96-450 is derived. Gang of Eight notification was included in a new Title V, Sec. 501, Sec. 501 (a) (1) added to the National Security Act of 1947 as amended by Sec. 407 (a) (3) of P.L. 96-450.

[7] Ibid.

[8] The Iran-Contra affair was a secret initiative by the administration of President Ronald Reagan in the 1980s to provide funds to the Nicaraguan Democratic Resistance from profits gained by selling arms to Iran. The purpose was at least two-fold: to financially support the Nicaraguan Democratic Resistance and to secure the release of American hostages held by pro-Iranian groups in Lebanon.

[9] Joint Explanatory Statement of the Committee of Conference, accompanying Conf.Rept. 102-166, 102nd Congress, 1st sess. (1991), p. 28. The Joint Explanatory Statement accompanied H.R. 1455, the FY1991 Intelligence Authorization Act, which was subsequently signed into law (P.L. 102-88). The "risk to life" language is not repeated in statute.

[10] Ibid.

[11] National Security Act of 1947 as amended, Sec. 503 [50 U.S.C. 413b] (c) (4). The statute does not explicitly specify whether such a statement should be in writing, nor specifically to whom such a statement should be provided.

[12] Ibid.

[13] National Security Act of 1947 as amended, Sec. 503 [50 U.S.C. 413b] (c) (2). The President must comply with these last two requirements—providing signed copies of the covert action and providing advance notification—when notifying the full committees of covert action operations that are determined to be less sensitive than "Gang of Eight" covert actions. Sec. 503 [50 U.S.C. 413b] (a) (1) requires a written finding unless immediate action by the U.S. is required and time does not permit preparation of a written finding. In the latter situation, a contemporaneous written record must be immediately reduced to a written finding as soon as possible within 48 hours.

[14] Ibid, (d).

[15] National Security Act of 1947 as amended, Sec. 503 [50 U.S.C. 413b] (c) (3).

[16] Ibid. What constitutes "timely fashion" was the subject of intense debate between the congressional intelligence committees and the executive branch during the consideration of the fiscal year 1991 Intelligence Authorization Act. At that time, House and Senate intelligence committee conferees noted that the executive

branch had asserted that the President's constitutional authorities "permit the President to withhold notice of covert actions from the committees for as long as he deems necessary." The conferees disputed the President's assertion, claiming that the appropriate meaning of "timely fashion" is "within a few days." Specifically, conferees stated, "While the conferees recognize that they cannot foreclose by statute the possibility that the President may assert a constitutional basis for withholding notice of covert actions for periods longer than 'a few days,' they believe that the President's stated intention to act under the 'timely notice' requirement of existing law to make a notification 'within a few days' is the appropriate manner to proceed under this provision, and is consistent with what the conferees believe is its meaning and intent." The conference report included the text of a letter sent to the chairman of the House Intelligence Committee, in which President George H.W. Bush stated: "In those rare instances where prior notice is not provided, I anticipate that notice will be provided within a few days. Any withholding beyond this period will be based upon my assertion of authorities granted this office by the Constitution..." See H.Conf.Rept. 102-166, 102nd Cong., 1st sess., pp. 27-28 (1991). Despite President George H.W. Bush's refusal to commit to either "timely" notification as defined by Congress, or any notification at all, Robert M. Gates, President George H.W. Bush's nominee as Director of Central Intelligence, said he believed that non-notification should be withheld for no more than a few days at the most, and that he would contemplate resignation if it extended beyond that time period. See Congressional Quarterly Almanac, 102nd Cong., 1st sess., 1991, Vol. XLVII, p. 482.

[17] Ibid.

[18] See Addendum B, copy of the Senate debate as recorded in the Congressional Record, 96th Congress, 2nd Session, Volume 126—Part 20, September 17, 1980 to September 24, 1980. See p. 17693.

[19] Ibid, p. 17693.

[20] See addendum B, S.Rept. 96-730, 96th Cong, 2nd sess. See p. 13 of the report.

[21] Ibid, p. 12.

[22] Letter from Representative Jane Harman to President George W. Bush, January 4, 2006. Another example of the informality which sometimes informs the intelligence notification process involves so-called Gang of Four notifications. The Gang of Four consists of the chairmen of the congressional intelligence committees, the Vice Chairman of the Senate Intelligence Committee and the Ranking Member of the House Intelligence Committee. The executive branch frequently limits certain intelligence notifications to these four Members, sometimes including committee staff directors, even though neither statute, or committee rules, appear to make provision for such notifications.

[23] Congressional Quarterly Almanac, Vol. XXXVI, 1980, p. 66.

[24] There actually were two separate operations — both of which constituted covert actions, since neither was undertaken to collect intelligence — to rescue U.S. embassy personnel after Iranian "students" overran the U.S. Embassy in Tehran on Nov. 4, 1979. The failed operation involved an attempted airborne rescue of U.S. hostages which was aborted when three of the rescue helicopters experienced mechanical difficulties. A subsequent collision of one of the helicopters and a refueling plane left seven American rescuers dead. An earlier effort resulted in the successful extrication of six Americans who had been working at the U.S. embassy but had avoided capture by taking refuge in the residences of the Canadian ambassador and deputy chief of mission.

[25] At the time, the Hughes-Ryan Amendment of 1974 requiring that the executive branch report on Central Intelligence Agency covert operations to as many as eight congressional committees, including the intelligence committees, was still the law.

[26] See L. Britt Snider, *The Agency and the Hill, CIA's Relationship With Congress, 1946-2004*, (Washington, D.C.: Center For the Study of Intelligence, Central Intelligence Agency, 2008), p. 283.

[27] Ibid.

[28] National Security Act of 1947 as amended, Sec. 501[50 U.S.C. 413] (a) (2).

[29] L. Britt Snider, *The Agency and the Hill, CIA's Relationship With Congress, 1946-2004*, (Washington, D.C.: Center For the Study of Intelligence, Central Intelligence Agency, 2008), p. 311. See also Mike Soraghan, "Reyes Backs Pelosi On Intel Briefings," *The Hill*, May 1, 2009. House Intelligence Committee Ranking Member Peter Hoekstra reportedly stated that Members of Congress are able to challenge policies they disagree with. "This is nuts, this saying, 'I couldn't do anything,'" Hoekstra told the Hill, adding that he at least once complained to then President Bush and got a policy changed, according to the newspaper.

[30] See Congressional Quarterly transcript of press conference given by Representative Peter Hoekstra, December 21, 2005.

[31] See Tim Starks, "Pelosi Controversy Suggests Changes to Congressional Briefings Are Due," *Congressional Quarterly*, May 14, 2009.

[32] See letter from Representative Jane Harman to President George W. Bush, January 4, 2006, regarding the National Security Agency (NSA) electronic communications surveillance program, often referred to as the Terrorist Surveillance Program, or TSP.

[33] See Tim Starks, "Pelosi Controversy Suggests Changes to Congressional Briefings Are Due," *Congressional Quarterly*, May 14, 2009.

[34] Press release from Senator John D. (Jay) Rockefeller, December 19, 2005, commenting on the Terrorist Surveillance Program initiated by the George W. Bush Administration. As discussed earlier in this memorandum, under Sec. 501(a)(2), nothing in Title V "shall be construed as requiring the approval of the congressional intelligence committees as a condition precedent to the initiation of any significant anticipated intelligence activity.

[35] Ibid.

[36] See "Additional Pre-hearing Questions for Dennis C. Blair upon nomination to be Director of National Intelligence," Question/Answer 4(C), at http://intelligence.senate.gov/090122/blairresponses.pdf.

[37] See "Additional Pre-hearing Questions for the Record For the Honorable Leon E. Panetta upon his selection to be the Director of The Central Intelligence Agency," Question/Answer 23 at http://intelligence.senate.gov/090205/answers.pdf. In his response, Director Panetta did not address whether the CIA's detention, interrogation and rendition program was an intelligence collection program, or a covert action program. Former CIA Director Michael Hayden, has said that the program "... began life as a covert action ... " See Australian Broadcasting Corporation, *AM*, April 17, 2009.
Before the notification briefings were subsequently expanded to include more Members, the executive treated both programs as particularly sensitive collection programs insofar as notification was concerned, in that it limited its initial notification to the Gang of Four. See letter from Representative Jane Harman to President George W. Bush, December 21, 2005, in which she makes reference to the Administration's use of the Gang of Four notification process, used initially to notify Congress. The Bush Administration also employed the Gang of Four notification procedure to notify Congress of the CIA's detention, interrogation and rendition program. See "Members Briefings on Enhanced Interrogation Techniques (EITs)," released by the CIA on May 6, 2009. A listing of the briefings can be found at http://www.humanevents.com/downloads-pdfs/EIT%20Briefings.pdf.

[38] See "Additional Pre-hearing Questions for Dennis C. Blair upon nomination to be Director of National Intelligence," Question/Answer 4(C), at http://intelligence.senate.gov/090122/blairresponses.pdf.

[39] See "Additional Pre-hearing Questions for the Record For the Honorable Leon E. Panetta upon his selection to be the Director of The Central Intelligence Agency," Question/Answer 23 at http://intelligence. gov/090205/answers.pdf.

[40] Sec. 503 of the National Security Act [50 U.S.C. 413b] (c)(2).

[41] See Intelligence Authorization Act for Fiscal Year 2010, H.R. 2701, Sec. 321 [111th Congress, 1st sess.].

[42] See H.Rept. 111-186, accompanying the Intelligence Authorization Act for Fiscal Year 2010, pp. 21-22 [111th Congress, 1st sess.].

[43] See Intelligence Authorization Act for 2010, H.R. 2701, Sec. 321 (b).

[44] See Intelligence Authorization Act For 2009, H.R. 5959, Sec. 502 (b). This language applied to reports of intelligence activities other than covert action. The amendment offered to the FY2010 Intelligence Authorization Act during the Committee's markup was extended to include reporting of covert actions.

[45] See H.Rept. 111-186, accompanying the Intelligence Authorization Act for Fiscal Year 2010, *Minority Views*, p. 3 [111th Congress, 1st sess.].

[46] See H.R. 2701, Intelligence Authorization Act for Fiscal Year 2010, Sec. 321 (d).

[47] Ibid, (g) (2).

[48] Ibid, (g) (1).

[49] Ibid, Sec. 411.

[50] Ibid, Sec. 321 (g) (3).

[51] Ibid, Sec. 321 (d) (2).

[52] S. 1494, Intelligence Authorization Act For Fiscal Year 2010, Sec. 331.

[53] Ibid, Sec. 332.

[54] Ibid.

[55] National Security Act of 1947 as amended, Sec. 503 (d).

[56] Ibid, Sec. 333.

[57] Ibid, Sec. 334.

[58] S.Rept. 111-55, accompanying S. 1494, the Intelligence Authorization Act For Fiscal Year 2010 (111th Congress, 1st Sess.), pp. 76-77.

[59] Ibid, p. 76.

[60] Ibid, p. 75.

[61] See Statement of Administration Policy on H.R. 2701, the Intelligence Authorization Act for Fiscal Year 2010, July 8, 2009.

[62] Ibid.

[63] See Ellen Nakashima, "Intelligence Oversight Bill Faces Obstacles," *Washington Post*, September 18, 2009, p. A-3.

[64] Given the demands of timing and scheduling, according to former executive branch officials, in the interest of time, Gang of Eight Members are sometimes notified by secure phone. If scheduling permits, briefings are provided to Gang of Eight Members, often on an individual basis. It is unclear whether Gang of Eight

Members ever have requested to be briefed as a group, or whether certain time and scheduling constraints would make such a request practical.

In: Congressional Oversight An Overview, A Manual and... ISBN: 978-1-61728-477-9
Editor: Jamie C. Howell

Chapter 5

CONGRESSIONAL OVERSIGHT AND RELATED ISSUES CONCERNING INTERNATIONAL SECURITY AGREEMENTS CONCLUDED BY THE UNITED STATES*

Michael John Garcia and R. Chuck Mason

SUMMARY

The United States is a party to numerous security agreements with other nations. The topics covered, along with the significance of the obligations imposed upon agreement parties, may vary. Some international security agreements entered by the United States, such as those obliging parties to come to the defense of another in the event of an attack, involve substantial commitments and have traditionally been entered as treaties, ratified with the advice and consent of the Senate. Other agreements dealing with more technical matters, such as military basing rights or the application of a host country's laws to U.S. forces stationed within, are entered more routinely and usually take a form other than treaty (i.e., as an executive agreement or a nonlegal political commitment).

Occasionally, the substance and form of a proposed security agreement may become a source of dispute between Congress and the executive branch. In November 2007, the Bush Administration announced its intention to negotiate a long-term security agreement with Iraq that would have committed the United States to provide security assurances to Iraq, and contemplated a long-term presence by U.S. forces in Iraq. This announcement became a source of congressional interest, in part because of statements by Administration officials that such an agreement would not be submitted to the legislative branch for approval. Congressional concern appeared to dissipate when U.S.-Iraq negotiations culminated in an agreement that did not contain a long-term binding security commitment by the United States, but instead called for the withdrawal of U.S. forces from Iraq by December 31, 2011.

---

* This is an edited, reformatted and augmented edition of a United States Congressional Research Service publication, Report R40614, dated October 1, 2009.

It is likely that future disputes will arise between the political branches regarding the entering or implementation of international security agreements. Regardless of the form a security arrangement may take, Congress has several tools to exercise oversight regarding the negotiation, form, conclusion, and implementation of the agreement by the United States. This chapter begins by providing a general background on the types of international agreements that are binding upon the United States, as well as considerations affecting whether they take the form of a treaty or an executive agreement. Next, the report discusses historical precedents as to the role that security agreements have taken, with specific attention paid to past agreements entered with Afghanistan, Germany, Japan, South Korea, the Philippines, and Iraq. The report discusses the oversight role that Congress exercises with respect to entering and implementing international agreements involving the United States. For more information regarding the U.S.-Iraq security agreements, see CRS Report R40011, *U.S.-Iraq Withdrawal/Status of Forces Agreement: Issues for Congressional Oversight*, by R. Chuck Mason, and CRS Report RL34568, *U.S.-Iraq Agreements: Congressional Oversight Activities and Legislative Response*, by Matthew C. Weed.

The United States is a party to numerous security agreements with other nations. The topics covered, along with the significance of the obligations imposed upon agreement parties, Tmay vary. Some international security agreements entered by the United States, such as those obliging parties to come to the defense of another in the event of an attack, involve substantial commitments and have traditionally been entered as treaties, ratified with the advice and consent of the Senate. Other agreements dealing with more technical matters, such as military basing rights or the application of a host country's laws to U.S. forces stationed within, are entered more routinely and usually take a form other than treaty.

Regardless of the form of a security arrangement, Congress has several tools to exercise oversight regarding the negotiation, form, conclusion, and implementation of the agreement by the United States. This chapter begins by providing a general background as to the types of international agreements that are binding upon the United States, as well as considerations affecting whether they take the form of a treaty or an executive agreement. Next, the report examines historical precedents, with specific attention paid to past agreements entered with Afghanistan, Iraq, Germany, Japan, South Korea, and the Philippines. The report discusses the oversight role that Congress exercises with respect to entering and implementing international agreements involving the United States.

I. International Agreements under U.S. Law

Under U.S. law, a legally binding international agreement can be entered into pursuant to either a treaty or an executive agreement. The Constitution allocates primary responsibility for entering such agreements to the executive branch, but Congress also plays an essential role. First, in order for a treaty (but not an executive agreement) to become the "Law of the Land,"[1] the Senate must provide its advice and consent to treaty ratification by a two-thirds majority. Alternatively, Congress may authorize congressional-executive agreements. Many treaties and executive agreements are not "self-executing," meaning that in order for them to take effect domestically, implementing legislation is required to provide U.S. bodies with the authority necessary to enforce and comply with the agreements' provisions. While some executive agreements do not require congressional approval, adherence to them may nonetheless be dependent upon Congress appropriating necessary funds or authorizing the activities to be carried out (where compliance with the agreement would contravene some statutory provision).

Treaties

Under U.S. law, a treaty is an agreement negotiated and signed[2] by the executive branch, which enters into force if it is approved by a two-thirds majority in the Senate and is subsequently ratified following Presidential signature.[3] The Senate may, in considering a treaty, condition its consent on certain reservations,[4] declarations[5] and understandings[6] concerning treaty application. If accepted, these reservations, declarations, and understandings may limit and/or define U.S. obligations under the treaty.[7]

Executive Agreements

The great majority of international agreements that the United States enters into are not treaties but executive agreements[8]—agreements made by the executive branch that are not submitted to the Senate for its advice and consent. There are three types of *prima facie* legal executive agreements: (1) *congressional-executive agreements*, in which Congress has previously or retroactively authorized an international agreement entered into by the Executive; (2) *executive agreements made pursuant to an earlier treaty*, in which the agreement is authorized by a ratified treaty; and (3) *sole executive agreements*, in which an agreement is made pursuant to the President's constitutional authority without further congressional authorization. The Executive's authority to promulgate the agreement is different in each case.

Although executive agreements are not specifically discussed in the Constitution, they nonetheless have been considered valid international compacts under Supreme Court jurisprudence and as a matter of historical practice.[9] Starting in the World War II era, reliance on executive agreements has grown significantly.[10] Whereas 27 executive agreements (compared to 60 treaties) were concluded by the United States during the first 50 years of the Republic,[11] between 1939 and 2009 the United States concluded roughly 16,500 executive agreements (compared to approximately 1,100 treaties).[12]

Although some have argued that certain agreements may only be concluded as treaties, subject to the advice and consent of the Senate,[13] this view has generally been rejected by scholarly opinion.[14] Adjudication of the propriety of executive agreements has been rare, in significant part because plaintiffs often cannot demonstrate that they have suffered a redressable injury giving them standing to challenge an agreement,[15] or fail to make a justiciable claim. In 2001, the Eleventh Circuit Court of Appeals held that the issue of whether the North American Free Trade Agreement (NAFTA) was a treaty requiring approval by two-thirds of the Senate presented a nonjusticiable political question.[16] It does not appear that an executive agreement has ever been held invalid by the courts on the grounds that it was in contravention of the Treaty Clause.[17]

Nonetheless, as a matter of historical practice, some types of agreements have been concluded as treaties, while others have been concluded as executive agreements.[18]

Congressional-Executive Agreements

In the case of congressional-executive agreements, the "constitutionality ... seems well established."[19] Unlike treaties, where only the Senate plays a role in authorization, both Houses of Congress are involved in the authorizing process for congressional-executive agreements. Congressional authorization takes the form of a statute passed by a majority of both Houses of Congress. Historically, congressional-executive agreements cover a wide variety of topics, ranging from postal conventions to bilateral trade to military assistance.[20] NAFTA and the General Agreement on Tariffs and Trade (GATT) are notable examples of congressional-executive agreements.

Congressional-executive agreements also may take different forms. Congress may enact legislation authorizing the Executive to negotiate and enter agreements with other countries on a specific matter.[21] A congressional-executive agreement may also take the form of a statute passed following the negotiation of an agreement which incorporates the terms or requirements of the agreement into U.S. law.[22] Such authorization may be either explicit or implied by the terms of the congressional enactment.[23]

Executive Agreements Made Pursuant to Treaties

The legitimacy of agreements made pursuant to treaties is also well established, though controversy occasionally arises as to whether the agreement was actually imputed by the treaty in question.[24] Since the earlier treaty is the "Law of the Land,"[25] the power to enter into an agreement required or contemplated by the treaty lies fairly clearly within the President's executive function. However, the Senate occasionally conditions its approval of a treaty upon a requirement that any subsequent agreement made pursuant to the treaty also be submitted to the Senate as a treaty.[26]

Sole Executive Agreements

Sole executive agreements rely on neither treaty nor congressional authority for their legal basis. There are a number of provisions in the Constitution that may confer limited authority upon the President to promulgate such agreements on the basis of his power to conduct foreign affairs.[27] The Litvinov Assignment, under which the Soviet Union purported to transfer claims against American assets previously nationalized by the Soviet Union, is an example of a sole executive agreement.

If the President enters into an executive agreement pursuant to and dealing with an area where he has clear, exclusive constitutional authority—such as an agreement to recognize a particular State for diplomatic purposes—the agreement is legally permissible regardless of Congress's opinion on the matter.[28] If, however, the President enters into an agreement and his constitutional authority over the subject matter is unclear, or if Congress also has constitutional authority over the subject matter, a reviewing court may consider Congress's position in determining whether the agreement is enforceable as U.S. law.[29] If Congress has given implicit approval to the President to enter into the agreement, or is silent on the matter, it is more likely that the agreement will be deemed valid. When Congress opposes the agreement and the President's constitutional authority to enter the agreement is ambiguous, it is unclear if or under what circumstances a court would recognize such an agreement as controlling.

Because sole executive agreements do not rely on treaty or congressional authority to support their legality, they do not require congressional approval to become binding, at least as a matter of international law. Courts have recognized, however, that if a sole executive agreement conflicts with preexisting federal law, the earlier law will remain controlling in most circumstances.[30]

Even if a sole executive agreement does not conflict with prior federal law, Congress may still act to limit the agreement's effect through a subsequent legislative enactment, so long as it has constitutional authority to regulate the matter covered by the agreement.[31] In the security context, Congress has clear constitutional authority to enact measures that would limit the effect of sole executive agreements involving military commitments. Article I, § 8 of the Constitution accords Congress the power "To lay and collect Taxes ... to ... pay the Debts and provide for the common Defence," "To declare War, grant letters of Marque and Reprisal, and make Rules concerning Captures on Land and Water," "To raise and support Armies," "To provide and maintain a Navy," "To make Rules for the Government and Regulation of the land and naval Forces," as well as "To provide for calling forth the Militia to execute the Laws of the Union, suppress Insurrections and repel Invasions" and "To provide for organizing, arming, and disciplining, the Militia, and for governing such Part of them as may be employed in the Service of the United States."[32] Further, Congress is empowered "To make all Laws which shall be necessary and proper for carrying into Execution the foregoing Powers ..." as well as "all other Powers vested by this Constitution in the Government of the United States, or in any Department or Officer thereof."[33]

In addition to the constitutional provisions that provide Congress with authority to legislate on matters concerning military affairs,[34] Congress also has virtual plenary power over appropriations—authority not qualified with reference to Congress's enumerated powers under Article I, § 8. The Appropriations Clause provides that "[n]o money can be paid out of the Treasury unless it has been appropriated by an act of Congress."[35] Accordingly, adherence to pledges made in sole executive agreements may be dependent upon the availability of appropriations authorized by Congress. Congress may specify the terms and conditions under which appropriations may be used, so long as it does not impose unconstitutional conditions upon the use of appropriated funds.[36]

Nonlegal Agreements

Not every pledge, assurance, or arrangement made between the United States and a foreign party constitutes a legally binding international agreement. In some cases, the United States makes "political commitments" or "gentlemen's agreements" with foreign States. Although these commitments are nonlegal, they may nonetheless carry significant moral and political weight. The Executive has long claimed the authority to enter such agreements on behalf of the United States without congressional authorization, asserting that the entering of political commitments by the Executive is not subject to the same constitutional constraints as the entering of legally binding international agreements.[37] An example of a nonlegal agreement is the 1975 Helsinki Accords, a Cold War agreement signed by 35 nations, which contains provisions concerning territorial integrity, human rights, scientific and economic cooperation, peaceful settlement of disputes, and the implementation of confidence-building measures.

An international agreement is generally presumed to be legally binding in the absence of an express provision indicating its nonlegal nature. State Department regulations recognize that this presumption may be overcome when there is "clear evidence, in the negotiating history of the agreement or otherwise, that the parties intended the arrangement to be governed by another legal system."[38] Other factors that may be relevant in determining whether an agreement is nonlegal in nature include the form of the agreement and the specificity of its provisions.[39]

Choosing Between a Treaty and Executive Agreement

A recurring concern for the executive and legislative branches is whether an international commitment should be entered into as a treaty or an executive agreement. The Senate may prefer that significant international commitments be entered as treaties, and fear that reliance on executive agreements will lead to an erosion of the treaty power. The House may want an international compact to take the form of congressional-executive agreement, so that it may play a greater role in the consideration. In cases where congressional action is necessary for an agreement to be implemented, the Executive may prefer to submit an international compact as a congressional-executive agreement, so that approval of the agreement and the enactment of necessary implementing legislation may be accomplished in a single step. The Executive's preference as to whether an international compact takes the form of a treaty or executive agreement may also be influenced by the agreement's prospects for approval by a two-thirds majority of the Senate or a simple majority of both Houses.

State Department regulations prescribing the process for coordination and approval of international agreements (commonly known as the "Circular 175 procedure"[40]) include criteria for determining whether an international agreement should take the form of a treaty or an executive agreement. Congressional preference is one of several factors considered when determining the form that an international agreement should take. According to State Department regulations,

> In determining a question as to the procedure which should be followed for any particular international agreement, due consideration is given to the following factors:
>
> (1) The extent to which the agreement involves commitments or risks affecting the nation as a whole;
>
> (2) Whether the agreement is intended to affect state laws;
>
> (3) Whether the agreement can be given effect without the enactment of subsequent legislation by the Congress;
>
> (4) Past U.S. practice as to similar agreements;
>
> (5) The preference of the Congress as to a particular type of agreement;
>
> (6) The degree of formality desired for an agreement;
>
> (7) The proposed duration of the agreement, the need for prompt conclusion of an agreement, and the desirability of concluding a routine or short-term agreement; and
>
> (8) The general international practice as to similar agreements.
>
> In determining whether any international agreement should be brought into force as a treaty or as an international agreement other than a treaty, the utmost care is to be exercised to avoid any invasion or compromise of the constitutional powers of the President, the Senate, and the Congress as a whole.[41]

In 1978, the Senate passed a resolution expressing its sense that the President seek the advice of the Senate Committee on Foreign Relations in determining whether an international agreement should be submitted as a treaty.[42] The State Department subsequently modified the Circular 175 procedure to provide for consultation with appropriate congressional leaders and committees concerning significant international agreements.[43] Consultations are to be held "as appropriate."[44] Congressional consultation on the substance and form of international agreements is discussed in more detail later in this chapter.[45]

II. HISTORICAL PRACTICE REGARDING SECURITY AGREEMENTS

The following sections provide a general overview of the categories of security agreements entered into by the United States of a legally binding nature. Such categories of security agreements predominantly take the form of a treaty, while others typically take the form of an executive agreement.

Categories of Security Agreements

Although some categories of security agreements have historically been concluded as treaties and others as executive agreements, this does not necessarily mean that future arrangements must follow the same pattern. An arrangement that has typically been entered into as a treaty might instead be concluded as a congressional-executive agreement, and vice versa.[46] Similarly, while some security arrangements have historically been entered as sole executive agreements, Congress might effectively limit such agreements in the future via statutory enactment[47]—e.g., limiting the availability of appropriations to carry out commitments made in a sole executive agreement.[48]

Collective Defense Agreements/"Security Commitments"

The State Department currently lists the United States as being party to seven collective defense agreements, under which members are obligated to assist in the defense of a party to the agreement in the event of an attack upon it: the Inter-American Treaty of Reciprocal Assistance; the North Atlantic Treaty; the Australia, New Zealand, and United States Security Treaty; the Southeast Asian Treaty; and bilateral security treaties with Japan, the Philippines, and South Korea.[49] All seven agreements take the form of treaties that were ratified by the United States between 1947 and 1960.[50] Each of these agreements, with the exception of the Inter-American Treaty of Reciprocal Assistance (the first to be ratified by the United States), includes a provision specifying that the agreement's requirements are to be carried out in accordance with the parties' respective constitutional processes. These provisions were included to assuage congressional concerns the agreements could be interpreted as sanctioning the President to engage in military hostilities in defense of treaty parties without further congressional authorization (i.e., a declaration of war or resolution authorizing the use of military force).[51]

In addition to these defense treaties, the United States has also adopted security commitments with respect to several former territories and possessions,[52] including pursuant to congressional-executive agreement. Congress has approved compacts changing the status of certain territories to Freely Associated States (FAS), while also imposing upon the United States "the obligation to defend the [FAS] ... from attack or threats thereof as the United States and its citizens are defended."[53] Arguably, these security commitments are distinct from other international defense arrangements, as they concern commitments to newly sovereign entities over whom the United States formerly exercised extensive and long-standing control.[54]

Consultation Requirements/"Security Arrangements"

The United States also has established security arrangements with other countries in which the U.S. pledges to take some action in the event that the other country's security is threatened. In a 1992 report to Congress listing U.S. security commitments and arrangements, President George H.W. Bush claimed that unlike "security commitments," which oblige the United States to act in the common defense of a country in case of an armed attack, "security arrangements" generally

> oblige the United States to consult with a country in the event of a threat to its security. They may appear in legally binding agreements, such as treaties or executive agreements, or in political documents, such as policy declarations by the President, Secretary of State or Secretary of Defense.[55]

Most legally binding "security arrangements" listed in the President's report constitute sole executive agreements, including agreements with Israel, Egypt, Pakistan, and Liberia.[56] Only one arrangement, committing the United States to the establishment of the Multinational Force and Observers in the Sinai, could clearly be described as a congressional-executive agreement.[57]

Although some scholars and government officials have characterized the terms "security commitment" and "security arrangement" as having distinct and particular meanings, this practice is by no means uniform. Indeed, the question of what constitutes a "security commitment" has long been a subject of dialogue and dispute by the executive and legislative branches.[58]

Other Types of Military Agreements

The United States is also a party to a significant number of defense agreements that do not obligate the United States to take action when another country is attacked, but nonetheless involve military affairs. Categories of such agreements include

- military basing agreements, permitting the United States to build or use permanent facilities, station forces, and conduct certain military activities within a host country;[59]
- access and pre-positioning agreements, permitting the stationing of equipment in a host country and the improvement and use of the country's military or civilian facilities, without establishing a permanent military presence;[60]
- Status of Forces Agreements (SOFAs), defining the legal status of U.S. forces within a host country and typically according them with certain privileges and immunities from the host country's jurisdiction;[61]

- burden-sharing agreements, permitting a host country to assume some of the financial obligations incurred by the stationing of U.S. forces within its territory;[62] and
- agreements providing for arms transfers, military training, and joint military exercises.[63]

Historically, almost all such agreements have taken a form other than treaty. Sometimes these arrangements have been concluded as sole executive agreements; others could be deemed executive agreements pursuant to treaty (e.g., military stationing agreements concluded with other NATO parties); still others have been explicitly or implicitly authorized by statute and may be considered congressional-executive agreements.

As a matter of historical practice, the types of agreements described above have not directly authorized the United States to engage in significant military operations in defense of the host country, though such agreements may supplement separate agreements or U.N. mandates that do. For example, although U.S. basing agreements with Germany, Japan, and South Korea do not expressly authorize the United States to use military force to defend those countries in case of attack, they assist the United States in fulfilling security commitments owed to those countries under separate defense treaties. Arguably, an exception to this practice occurred in 2008, when the United States and Iraq concluded a security agreement, sometimes characterized as a SOFA, which authorizes U.S. forces to engage in military operations within Iraq. The agreement is discussed in more detail *infra.*[64]

Agreements Granting the Legal Right to Military Intervention

Besides the categories of agreements described above, the United States has, on occasion, entered into long-term agreements that grant the United States the legal right to intervene militarily within the territory of another party to defend it against internal or external threats. Unlike collective defense agreements, these security agreements provide the United States with the right, but not the duty, to militarily intervene when the security of the other country is threatened. Such agreements may also be distinguished from the authority to intervene recognized under the United Nations Charter. Whereas military intervention agreements discussed below provide the United States with the *positive* legal right to intervene in a country, the U.N. Charter merely provides that its provisions do not "*impair* the inherent right of individual or collective self-defense if an armed attack occurs against a Member of the United Nations, until the Security Council has taken measures necessary to maintain international peace and security."[65]

In the early part of the 20th Century, the United States entered into legal agreements with several Latin American countries which granted the United States the right to use military force either to defend those countries from external threat or to preserve domestic tranquility.[66] All of these agreements were concluded as treaties. In 1903, following the Spanish-American War, the United States concluded a treaty with the newly independent Republic of Cuba under which the United States was expressly given "the right to intervene for the preservation of Cuban independence, the maintenance of a government adequate for the protection of life, property, and individual liberty."[67] Similarly, in the aftermath of the U.S. invasion and occupation of Haiti in 1915, a treaty between the two countries was concluded that provided the United States with the right to intervene in Haiti when the United

States deemed it necessary.[68] In 1904, the United States ratified a treaty with Panama that provided the United States "the right, at all times and in its discretion" to employ its armed forces for the safety and protection of the Panama Canal and the shipping occurring therein.[69] In 1907, the United States concluded a treaty with the Dominican Republic establishing plans for the financial rehabilitation of that country, and authorizing the United States to use military force necessary to effectuate the carrying out of those plans.[70]

There have been numerous instances where a country has permitted or invited the United States to use military force within its territory,[71] but authority to intervene has not been given via treaty. When the Senate initially opted not to approve a treaty authorizing U.S. military and financial involvement in the Dominican Republic, President Theodore Roosevelt entered a temporary "*modus vivendi*" executive agreement adopting similar policies as the unapproved treaty. This agreement, which elicited significant opposition from many Members of Congress as an unconstitutional usurpation of the Senate's treaty power, was terminated following Senate approval of a modified version of the treaty in 1907.[72] Another example of a significant security agreement taking a form other than treaty occurred in 1941 when, prior to the United States entering World War II, President Franklin D. Roosevelt concluded sole executive agreements concerning the stationing of U.S. troops in Iceland and Greenland to protect those territories from attack.[73]

Although publicly available agreements expressly granting the United States the legal right to intervene militarily in another country generally take the form of a treaty, this chapter does not consider comparable authority pursuant to classified agreements.

Non-Binding Security Arrangements

Some security arrangements are not legally binding; though they may nonetheless carry significant political or moral weight. While executive practice of extending political defense commitments to foreign countries can be traced back to the Monroe Doctrine, in which the United States proclaimed its opposition to further colonization of the Americas by European powers, U.S. pledges to assist foreign States in security matters have become more commonplace in the post-World War II era. Such commitments may take several forms, including a unilateral pledge or policy statement by the Executive or a joint declaration between U.S. and foreign officials.

For example, bilateral arrangements authorizing U.S. military intervention, when not concluded as treaties, generally have not taken the form of a legally binding, permanent agreement.[74] Instead, in non-treaty arrangements authorizing U.S. intervention, the host country often retains full discretion as to the degree and duration of U.S. presence within its territory. In 1962, for instance, U.S. Secretary of State Dean Rusk and Thai Foreign Minister Thanat Khoman issued a joint declaration in which Secretary Rusk expressed "the firm intention of the United States to aid Thailand, its ally and historic friend, in resisting Communist aggression and subversion."[75] The United States thereafter deployed armed forces to Thailand to assist the government in combating communist forces.

The Executive's authority to enter such arrangements, and, more broadly, to engage in military operations in other countries without congressional approval, has been the subject of longstanding dispute between the Congress and the Executive.[76] In 1969, the Senate passed the National Commitments Resolution, stating the sense of the Senate that "a national commitment by the United States results only from affirmative action taken by the executive and legislative branches of the United States government by means of a treaty [or legislative enactment] ... specifically providing for such commitment."[77] The Resolution defined a "national commitment" as including "the use of the armed forces of the United States on foreign territory, or a promise to assist a foreign country ... by the use of armed forces ... either immediately or upon the happening of certain events."[78]

According to the committee report accompanying the Resolution, the motivation for the Resolution was concern over the growing development of "constitutional imbalance" in matters of foreign relations, with Presidents frequently making significant foreign commitments on behalf of the United States without congressional action. Among other things, the report criticized a practice it described as "commitment by accretion," by which a

> sense of binding commitment arises out of a series of executive declarations, no one of which in itself would be thought of as constituting a binding obligation. Simply repeating something often enough with regard to our relations with some particular country, we come to support that our honor is involved in an engagement no less solemn than a duly ratified treaty.[79]

The National Commitments Resolution took the form of a sense of the Senate resolution, and accordingly had no legal effect. Although Congress has occasionally considered legislation that would bar the adoption of significant military commitments without congressional action,[80] no such measure has been enacted. The executive branch regularly makes unilateral security pledges or enters non-binding arrangements with foreign countries concerning security matters.[81] The primary means Congress uses to exercise oversight authority over such non-binding arrangements is its appropriations power, by which it may limit or condition actions the United States may take in furtherance of the arrangement.

Examples of Bilateral Security Agreements

The following sections discuss in greater detail the form, nature, and content of bilateral security agreements made by the United States with Afghanistan, Germany, Japan, South Korea, the Philippines, and Iraq.

Afghanistan

Following the terrorist attacks of September 11, 2001, the United States initiated Operation Enduring Freedom to combat al Qaeda and prevent the Taliban regime in Afghanistan from providing them with safe harbor. Shortly thereafter, the Taliban regime was ousted by U.S. and allied forces, and the United States thereafter concluded a number of security agreements with the new Afghan government. In 2002, the United States and Afghanistan, by an exchange of notes,[82] entered into an agreement regarding economic grants under the Foreign Assistance Act of 1961,[83] as amended. Additionally, the agreement allows for the furnishing of defense articles, defense services and related training, pursuant to the United States International Military and Education Training Program (IMET),[84] from the U.S. Government to the Afghanistan Interim Administration (AIA).

The Foreign Assistance Act of 1961 is "an act to promote the foreign policy, security, and general welfare of the United States by assisting peoples of the world in their efforts toward economic development and internal and external security, and for other purposes."[85] Part I of the act, addressing international development, established policy "to make assistance available, upon request, under this part in scope and on a basis of long-range continuity essential to the creation of an environment in which the energies of the peoples of the world can be devoted to constructive purposes, free of pressure and erosion by the adversaries of freedom."[86] Part II of the act, addressing international peace and security, authorizes "measures in the common defense against internal and external aggression, including the furnishing of military assistance, upon request, to friendly countries and international organizations."[87] The act authorizes the President "to furnish military assistance on such terms and conditions as he may determine, to any friendly country or international organization, the assisting of which the President finds will strengthen the security of the United States and promote world peace and which is otherwise eligible to receive such assistance.... "[88] The authorization to provide defense articles and services, noncombatant personnel, and the transfer of funds is codified at 22 U.S.C. § 2311. While this authorization permits the President to provide military assistance, it limits it to "assigning or detailing members of the Armed Forces of the United States and other personnel of the Department of Defense to perform *duties of a noncombatant nature*."[89]

An agreement exists regarding the status of military and civilian personnel of the U.S. Department of Defense present in Afghanistan in connection with cooperative efforts in response to terrorism, humanitarian and civic assistance, military training and exercises, and other activities.[90] Such personnel are to be accorded "a status equivalent to that accorded to the administrative and technical staff" of the U.S. Embassy under the Vienna Convention on Diplomatic Relations of 1961.[91] Accordingly, U.S. personnel are immune from criminal prosecution by Afghan authorities, and are immune from civil and administrative jurisdiction except with respect to acts performed outside the course of their duties.[92] In the agreement, the Islamic Transitional Government of Afghanistan (ITGA)[93] explicitly authorizes the U.S. government to exercise criminal jurisdiction over U.S. personnel, and the Government of Afghanistan is not permitted to surrender U.S. personnel to the custody of another State, international tribunal, or any other entity without consent of the U.S. government. Although the agreement was signed by the ITGA, the subsequently elected Government of the Islamic Republic of Afghanistan assumed responsibility for ITGA's legal obligations and the agreement remains in force. The agreement does not appear to provide immunity for contract personnel.

The agreement with Afghanistan does not expressly authorize the United States to carry out military operations within Afghanistan, but it recognizes that such operations are "ongoing." Congress authorized the use of military force there (and elsewhere) by joint resolution in 2001, for targeting "those nations, organizations, or persons [who] planned, authorized, committed, or aided the terrorist attacks that occurred on September 11, 2001...."[94] The U.N. Security Council implicitly recognized that the use of force was appropriate in response to the September 11, 2001, terrorist attacks,[95] and subsequently authorized the deployment of an International Security Assistance Force (ISAF) to Afghanistan.[96] Subsequent U.N. Security Council resolutions provide a continuing mandate for ISAF ,[97] calling upon it to "work in close consultation with" Operation Enduring Freedom (OEF—the U.S.-led coalition conducting military operations in Afghanistan) in carrying out the mandate.[98] While there is no explicit U.N. mandate authorizing the OEF, Security Council resolutions appear to provide ample recognition of the legitimacy of its operations, most recently by calling upon the Afghan Government, "with the assistance of the international community, including the International Security Assistance Force and Operation Enduring Freedom coalition, in accordance with their respective designated responsibilities as they evolve, to continue to address the threat to the security and stability of Afghanistan posed by the Taliban, Al-Qaida, other extremist groups and criminal activities.... "[99]

In 2004, the United States and Afghanistan entered an acquisition and cross-servicing agreement, with annexes.[100] An acquisition and cross-servicing agreement (ACSA) is an agreement providing logistic support, supplies, and services to foreign militaries on a cash-reimbursement, replacement-in-kind, or exchange of equal value basis.[101] After consultation with the Secretary of State, the Secretary of Defense is authorized to enter into an ACSA with a government of a NATO country, a subsidiary body of NATO, or the United Nations Organization or any regional international organization of which the United States is a member.[102] Additionally, the Secretary of Defense may enter into an ACSA with a country not included in the above categories, if after consultation with the Secretary of State, a determination is made that it is in the best interests of the national security of the United States.[103] If the country is not a member of NATO, the Secretary of Defense must submit notice, at least 30 days prior to designation, to the Committee on Armed Services and the Committee on Foreign Relations of the Senate and the Committee on Armed Services and the Committee on Foreign Affairs of the House of Representatives.[104]

Since at least 2003, the United States has entered into several accommodation assignment agreements with Afghanistan regarding the use of land and facilities at the Bagram Airfield.[105] The United States and its coalition partners have utilized the Bagram Airfield for military purposes in the conflict against the Taliban and al Qaeda since late 2001, and it is presently the primary facility used to detain suspected enemy belligerents captured in the conflict.[106] The most recent accommodation assignment agreement concerning Bagram was entered in 2006.[107] The agreement provides exclusive use and possession of the airfield to the United States, free of rent, during the existence of the agreement.[108] The preamble of the agreement states that the consignment of the Bagram Airfield is "for use by the United States and Coalition Forces for military purposes." The United States has the right to assign the agreement to a successor nation or organization.[109] The agreement terminates when the United States or its successor determines that usage of the Bagram Airfield is no longer required; however, the agreement does not provide Afghanistan with the same option.

On May 23, 2005, President Hamid Karzai and President Bush issued a "joint declaration" outlining a prospective future agreement between the two countries.[110] It envisions a role for U.S. military troops in Afghanistan to "help organize, train, equip, and sustain Afghan security forces" until Afghanistan has developed its own capacity, and to "consult with respect to taking appropriate measures in the event that Afghanistan perceives that its territorial integrity, independence, or security is threatened or at risk." The declaration does not mention the status of U.S. forces in Afghanistan, but if an agreement is concluded pursuant to the declaration, it can be expected that a status of forces agreement would be included. In August 2008, shortly after U.S. airstrikes apparently resulted in civilian casualties, President Karzai called for a review of the presence of all foreign forces in Afghanistan and the conclusion of formal SOFAs with the respective countries.[111] However, to date, the United States and Afghanistan have not concluded such an agreement.

Iraq[112]

Since March 2003, the United States has been engaged in military operations in Iraq, first to remove the Saddam Hussein regime from power, and then to combat remnants of the former regime and other threats to the stability of Iraq and its post-Saddam government. In late 2007, the United States and Iraq signed a Declaration of Principles for a Long-Term Relationship of Cooperation and Friendship Between the Republic of Iraq and the United States of America.[113] The strategic arrangement contemplated in the Declaration was intended to ultimately replace the United Nations mandate under which the United States and allied forces are responsible for contributing to the security of Iraq, which terminated on December 31, 2008.[114] The Declaration was rooted in an August 26, 2007, communiqué, signed by five top political leaders in Iraq, which called for a long-term relationship with the United States. Pursuant to the Declaration, the parties pledged to "begin as soon as possible, with the aim to achieve, before July 31, 2008, agreements between the two governments with respect to the political, cultural, economic, and security spheres."[115] Among other things, the Declaration proclaimed the parties' intention to negotiate a security agreement:

> To support the Iraqi government in training, equipping, and arming the Iraqi Security Forces so they can provide security and stability to all Iraqis; support the Iraqi government in contributing to the international fight against terrorism by confronting terrorists such as Al-Qaeda, its affiliates, other terrorist groups, as well as all other outlaw groups, such as criminal remnants of the former regime; and to provide security assurances to the Iraqi Government to deter any external aggression and to ensure the integrity of Iraq's territory.[116]

This announcement became a source of congressional interest,[117] in part because of statements by Bush Administration officials that such an agreement would not be submitted to the legislative branch for approval, despite potentially obliging the United States to provide "security assurances" to Iraq.[118] In the 110th Congress, multiple hearings were held which addressed the proposed security agreement. In late 2007, Congress passed the Emergency Supplemental Appropriations Act for Defense, 2008, which contained a provision limiting the funds it made available from being used by U.S. authorities to enter into an agreement with Iraq that subjected members of the U.S. Armed Forces to the criminal jurisdiction of Iraq.[119] In October 2008, Congress passed the Duncan Hunter National Defense Authorization Act for Fiscal Year 2009, which requires a report from the President to the House Foreign Affairs and Armed Services Committees, and the Senate Foreign Relations and Armed Services Committees, on any completed U.S.-Iraq agreement addressing specified subjects, including security assurances or commitments by the United States, basing rights, and the status of U.S. forces in Iraq.[120] Several legislative proposals were introduced which would have required any such agreement to either be submitted to the Senate for its advice and consent as a treaty or authorized by a statutory enactment.

On November 17, 2008, after months of negotiations, U.S. Ambassador to Iraq Ryan Crocker and Iraq Foreign Minister Hoshyar Zebari signed two documents: (1) the Strategic Framework Agreement for a Relationship of Friendship and Cooperation between the United States and the Republic of Iraq (Strategic Framework Agreement), and (2) the Agreement Between the United States of America and Republic of Iraq On the Withdrawal of United States Forces from Iraq and the Organization of Their Activities during Their Temporary Presence in Iraq (Security Agreement). In some ways, the concluded agreements differ from the long-term security arrangement originally contemplated by the Declaration of Principles. Perhaps most significantly, the concluded agreements require the withdrawal of U.S. forces from Iraq by December 31, 2011.

The concluded agreements cover different issues and are intended by the parties to have different legal significance. The Strategic Framework Agreement is a legally binding agreement under which the parties pledge to work cooperatively in a number of fields, including on diplomatic, security, economic, cultural, and law enforcement matters. In the area of security, the Agreement provides that the United States and Iraq shall "continue to foster close cooperation concerning defense and security arrangements," which are to be undertaken pursuant to the terms of the Security Agreement.[121] The Strategic Framework Agreement also states that "the temporary presence of U.S. forces in Iraq is at the request and invitation of the sovereign government of Iraq," and that the United States may not "use Iraqi land, sea, or air as a launching or transit point for attacks against other countries[,] nor seek or request permanent bases or a permanent military presence in Iraq."

The Security Agreement is a legally binding agreement that terminates within three years, unless terminated at an earlier date by either Party. The Security Agreement contains provisions addressing a variety of military matters. As previously mentioned, it establishes a deadline for the withdrawal of all U.S. forces from Iraq by December 31, 2011. The Agreement also contains numerous provisions resembling those regularly contained in SOFAs concluded by the United States.[122] Specifically, the Agreement contains provisions concerning the parties' right to assert civil and criminal jurisdiction over U.S. forces, as well as provisions which establish rules and procedures applicable to U.S. forces relating to the carrying of weapons, the wearing of uniforms, entry and exit into Iraq, taxes, customs, and claims.

The Security Agreement contains other rules and requirements which have traditionally not been found in SOFAs concluded by the United States, including provisions addressing combat operations by U.S. forces. Operations by U.S. forces pursuant to the Agreement must be approved by the Iraqi government and coordinated with Iraqi authorities through a Joint Military Operations Coordination Committee. U.S. forces are also permitted to arrest or detain persons in the course of operations under the Agreement. More broadly, the Security Agreement provides for "strategic deliberations" between the parties in the event of external or internal threat or aggression against Iraq, and provides that, as mutually agreed by the parties, the United States "shall take appropriate measures, including diplomatic, economic, or military measures" to deter the threat.

The Security and Strategic Framework Agreements entered into force on January 1, 2009, following an exchange of diplomatic notes between the United States and Iraq. Although the agreements required approval on multiple levels by the Iraqi government, the Bush Administration did not submit the agreements to the Senate for its advice and consent as a treaty or request statutory authorization for the agreements by Congress.

There has been some controversy regarding whether these agreements could properly be entered on behalf of the United States by the Executive without the participation of Congress.[123] As previously discussed, security agreements authorizing the United States to take military action in defense of another country have typically been ratified as treaties.[124] It could be argued that the Security Agreement, which contemplates the United States engaging in military operations in Iraq and potentially defending the Iraqi government from external or internal security threats, requires congressional authorization for it to be legally binding under U.S. law. On the other hand, because Congress has authorized the President to engage in military operations in Iraq, both pursuant to the 2002 Authorization to Use Military Force

Against Iraq and subsequent appropriations measures, it has impliedly authorized the President to enter short-term agreements with Iraq which facilitate these operations.[125]

It is unclear what types of agreements, if any, may be concluded with Iraq upon the expiration of the current Security Agreement, or whether the parties will seek to amend the existing Agreement to extend its duration.[126] Legislation may be introduced in the 111th Congress which clarifies the legal status of the current U.S.-Iraq agreements or establishes requirements for the entering of any future agreements with Iraq.[127]

Prior to concluding the agreements above, the United States entered into two defense-related agreements with the Interim Government of Iraq: (1) an agreement regarding grants under the Foreign Assistance Act of 1961, or successor legislation, and other items provided to the Government of Iraq,[128] and (2) an agreement regarding the bilateral end use, retransfer, and security assurances of materials supplied by the United States.[129]

Germany

In 1951, the United States and Germany entered into an agreement[130] related to the assurances required under the Mutual Security Act of 1951.[131] This act is "an act to maintain the security and promote the foreign policy and provide for the general welfare of the United States by furnishing [material] assistance to friendly nations in the interest of international peace and security."[132] Specifically, the agreement references the "statement of purpose contained in Section 2 of the Mutual Security Act of 1951, and reaffirms that ... [Germany] is firmly committed to join in promoting international understanding and good will and in maintaining world peace and to take such action as may be mutually agreed upon to eliminate causes of international tension."[133] The statement of purpose in Section 2 of the act is

> to maintain the security and to promote the foreign policy of the United States by authorizing military, economic, and technical assistance to friendly countries to strengthen the mutual security and individual and collective defense of the free world, to develop their resources in the interest of their security and independence and the national interest of the United States and to facilitate the effective participation of those countries in the United Nations system for collective security.[134]

In 1955, the United States and Germany, both parties to the North Atlantic Treaty, entered into an agreement on mutual defense assistance,[135] obligating the United States to provide for "such equipment, materials, services, or other assistance as may be agreed" to Germany.[136] The agreement reflected the

> desire to foster international peace and security through measures which further the ability of nations dedicated to the purposes and principles of the Charter of the United Nations to participate effectively in arrangements for collective self-defense in support of those purposes and principles, and conscious of the determination to give their full cooperation to United Nations collective security arrangements and measures and efforts to obtain agreement on universal regulation of armaments under adequate guarantees against violation or evasion; [and] considering the support which the Government of the United States of America has brought to these principles by enacting the Mutual Security Act of 1954,[137] which authorizes the furnishing of military assistance to certain nations[.][138]

Germany guarantees that it "will not use such assistance for any act inconsistent with the strictly defensive character of the North Atlantic Treaty, or, without the prior consent of the [United States], for any other purpose."[139] The mutual defense assistance agreement is the basis for numerous subsequent agreements between the United States and Germany.[140]

In 1959, the countries entered into an agreement implementing the NATO SOFA of 1953.[141] The agreement provided additional supplemental agreements, beyond those contained in the NATO SOFA, specific to the relationship between the United States and Germany.

Japan

In 1954, the United States and Japan entered into a mutual defense assistance agreement with annexes.[142] The agreement was amended on April 18 and June 23, 2006. The agreement references the Treaty of Peace signed between the countries in San Francisco, California in 1951.[143] The Mutual Defense Assistance Act of 1949[144] and the Mutual Security Act of 1951[145] are also referenced in the agreement as they provide for the furnishing of defense assistance by the United States.[146] The agreement provides that the United States and Japan "will make available to the other and to such other governments as the two Governments signatory to the present Agreement may in each case agree upon, such equipment, materials, services, or other assistance as the Government furnishing such assistance may authorize" subject to the conditions and provisions of the Mutual Defense Assistance Act of 1949, the Mutual Security Act of 1951, and appropriation acts which may affect the furnishing of assistance.[147]

In 1960, the countries entered into the Treaty of Mutual Cooperation and Security Between the United States of America and Japan.[148] The treaty was amended on December 26, 1990.[149] Article III of the Treaty provides that the countries, "individually and in cooperation with each other, by means of continuous and effective self-help and mutual aid will maintain and develop, subject to their constitutional provisions, their capacities to resist armed attack."[150] Article V provides that the countries recognize "that an armed attack against either party in the territories under the administration of Japan would be dangerous to its own peace and safety and declares that it would act to meet the common danger in accordance with its constitutional provisions and processes."[151] Under Article VI of the Treaty, the United States is granted "the use by its land, air and naval forces of facilities and areas in Japan" in order to contribute "to the security of Japan and maintenance of international peace and security in the Far East[.]"[152] Article VI provides further that the use of facilities and the status of U.S. armed forces will be governed under a separate agreement.[153]

Under Article VI of the Treaty of Mutual Cooperation and Security Between the United States of America and Japan, the countries entered into a SOFA in 1960.[154] The SOFA addresses the use of facilities by the U.S. armed forces, as well as the status of U.S. forces in Japan. The agreement has been modified at least four times since the original agreement.[155]

South Korea

In 1948, the United States and South Korea entered into an agreement related to the transfer of authority to the Government of South Korea and the withdrawal of U.S. occupation forces.[156] Shortly after the initial agreement, the United States and Korea entered into a second agreement concerning interim military and security matters during a transitional period.[157] This executive agreement was between the President of the Republic of Korea and the Commanding General, U.S. Army Forces in Korea.[158] The agreement calls for the "Commanding General, United States Army Forces in Korea, pursuant to directives from his government and within his capabilities" to "organize, train and equip the Security forces of the Republic of Korea" with the obligation to train and equip ceasing "upon the completion of withdrawal from Korea of forces under his command."[159] The agreement also requires the Commanding General, U.S. Army Forces in Korea, to retain authority to exercise over-all operational control of security forces of Korea until withdrawal, as contemplated by Resolution No. II passed by the United Nations General Assembly on November 14, 1948.[160]

Article III of the Agreement contains provisions related to the status of U.S. forces during the transition period. The Commanding General, U.S. Army Forces in Korea, "shall retain exclusive jurisdiction over the personnel of his command, both military and civilian, including their dependents, whose conduct as individuals shall be in keeping with pertinent laws of the Republic of Korea."[161] The agreement provides that any individuals under the jurisdiction of the Commanding General who is apprehended by law enforcement agencies of South Korea shall be immediately turned over to the custody and control of the Commanding General. Individuals not under jurisdiction of the Commanding General, but apprehended in acts detrimental to the security of personnel or property under his jurisdiction, shall be turned over to the custody and control of the government of South Korea.[162]

In 1950, the countries entered into a mutual defense assistance agreement.[163] The mutual defense agreement references the Military Defense Act of 1949, [164] which provides for the furnishing of military assistance by the United States to South Korea. The mutual defense assistance agreement provides that each country "will make or continue to make available to the other, and to other Governments, such equipment, materials, services, or other military assistance" in support of economic recovery that is essential to international peace and security.[165]

The United States and South Korea entered into a mutual security agreement in 1952.[166] The mutual security agreement references the Mutual Security Act of 1951,[167] which provides for military, economic, and technical assistance in order to strengthen the mutual security of the free world. The mutual security agreement provides that South Korea agrees to promote international understanding and good will and to take action, that is mutually agreed upon, to eliminate causes of international tensions.[168]

In 1954, the countries entered into a mutual defense treaty.[169] As part of the treaty the countries agree to attempt to settle international disputes peacefully, consult whenever the political independence or security of either party is threatened by external armed attack, and that either party would act to meet the common danger in accordance with their respective constitutional processes.[170] Article IV of the treaty grants the United States "the right to dispose ... land, air and sea forces in and about the territory" of South Korea.[171] Pursuant to the treaty, specifically Article IV, in 1966, the countries entered into a SOFA with agreed minutes and an exchange of notes.[172] It was subsequently amended January 18, 2001.

Philippines

In 1947, the United States and the Republic of the Philippines entered into an agreement on military assistance.[173] The agreement was for a term of five years, starting July 4, 1946, and provided that the United States would furnish military assistance to the Philippines for the training and development of armed forces. The agreement further created an advisory group to provide advice and assistance to the Philippines as had been authorized by the U.S. Congress.[174] The agreement was extended, and amended, for an additional five years in 1953.[175]

A mutual defense treaty was entered into by the United States and the Philippines in 1951.[176] The treaty publicly declares "their sense of unity and their common determination to defend themselves against external armed attack, so that no potential aggressor could be under the illusion that either of them stands alone in the Pacific Area[.]"[177] The Treaty does not address or provide for a SOFA.

The countries entered into a mutual security agreement in 1952,[178] as related to the assurances required by the Mutual Security Act of 1951. The assurances required under the Mutual Security Act of 1951 included a commitment to accounting procedures for monies, equipment and materials furnished by the United States to the Philippines.[179]

In 1993, the countries entered into a SOFA.[180] The agreement was subsequently extended on September 19, 1994, April 28, 1995, and November 29, December 1 and 8, 1995. The countries entered into an agreement regarding the treatment of U.S. armed forces visiting the Philippines in 1998.[181] This agreement was amended on April 11 and 12, 2006. The distinction between this agreement and the SOFA originally entered into in 1993 is that this agreement applies to U.S. armed forces visiting, not stationed in the Philippines. The countries also entered into an agreement regarding the treatment of Republic of Philippines personnel visiting the United States.[182]

III. Congressional Oversight

Congress has several tools at its disposal to exercise oversight regarding the negotiation, conclusion, and implementation of international security agreements concluded by the United States.

Notification

One manner in which Congress exercises oversight of international agreements is via notification requirements. Obviously, in cases where an agreement requires action from one or both Houses of Congress to take effect, notification is a requisite. Before a treaty may become binding U.S. law, the President must submit it to the Senate for its advice and consent. Likewise, the Executive must inform Congress when it seeks to conclude an executive agreement that requires congressional authorization and/or implementing legislation to become U.S. law, so that appropriate legislation may be considered.

While constitutional considerations necessitate congressional notification in many circumstances, it has historically been more difficult for Congress to keep informed regarding international agreements or pledges made by the Executive that did not require additional legislative action to take effect—i.e., sole executive agreements and executive agreements made pursuant to a treaty. Additionally, even in cases where congressional action is necessary for an agreement to take effect, the Executive has sometimes opted not to inform Congress about an agreement until it has already been drafted and signed by the parties. In response to these concerns, Congress has enacted legislation and the State Department has implemented regulations to ensure that Congress is informed of the conclusion (and in some cases, the negotiation) of legally binding international agreements.

Notification Pursuant to the Case-Zablocki Act

The Case-Zablocki Act[183] was enacted in 1972 in response to congressional concern that a number of secret agreements had been entered by the Executive imposing significant commitments upon the United States.[184] It is the primary statutory mechanism used to ensure that Congress is informed of international agreements entered by the United States. Pursuant to the act, all executive agreements are required to be transmitted to Congress within 60 days of their *entry into force*.[185] If the President deems the immediate public disclosure of an agreement to be prejudicial to national security, the agreement may instead be transmitted to the House Committee on Foreign Affairs and the Senate Committee on Foreign Relations. The President is also required to annually submit a report regarding international agreements that were transmitted after the expiration of the 60-day period, describing the reasons for the delay.[186]

Although the Case-Zablocki Act originally only imposed reporting requirements with respect to executive agreements that had *entered into force*, the act was amended in 2004 to ensure that Congress was regularly notified regarding the status of *proposed* agreements, as well. The Secretary of State is required to annually report to Congress a list of executive agreements that have not yet entered into force, which (1) have not been published in the United States Treaties and Other International Agreements compilation and (2) the United States has "signed, proclaimed, or with reference to which any other final formality has been executed, or that has been extended or otherwise modified, during the preceding calendar year."[187]

The Case-Zablocki Act does not define what sort of arrangements constitute "international agreements" falling under its purview, though the legislative history suggests that Congress "did not want to be inundated with trivia ... [but wished] to have transmitted all agreements of any significance."[188] In its implementing regulations, the State Department has established criteria for determining whether an arrangement constitutes a legally binding "international agreement" requiring congressional notification. These include

- the identity of the parties, and whether they intended to create a legally binding agreement;
- the significance of the agreed-upon arrangement, with "[m]inor or trivial undertakings, even if couched in legal language and form," not considered to fall under the purview of the Case-Zablocki Act;
- the specificity of the arrangement;
- the necessity that the arrangement constitute an agreement by two or more parties; and
- the form of the arrangement, to the extent that it helps to determine whether the parties intended to enter a legally binding agreement.[189]

Notification Pursuant to Circular 175 Procedures

The State Department's Circular 175 procedure also contemplates that Congress will be notified of developments in the *negotiation* of "significant" international agreements. Specifically, Department regulations provide that

> With the advice and assistance of the Assistant Secretary for Legislative Affairs, the appropriate congressional leaders and committees are advised of the intention to negotiate significant new international agreements, consulted concerning such agreements, and kept informed of developments affecting them, including especially whether any legislation is considered necessary or desirable for the implementation of the new treaty or agreement.[190]

Annual Reporting of Security Arrangements Required by the National Defense Authorization Act of 1991

In addition to the Case-Zablocki Act, Congress has enacted legislation designed to ensure that it remains informed about existing U.S. security arrangements. Section 1457 of the National Defense Authorization Act for FY1991 (P.L. 101-510) requires the President to submit an annual report to specified congressional committees regarding "United States security arrangements with, and commitments to, other nations."[191] The report, produced in classified and unclassified form, is to be submitted by February 1 each year to the Committee on Armed Services and the Committee on Foreign Relations of the Senate, and the Committee on Armed Services and the Committee on Foreign Affairs of the House of Representatives.[192] In addition to legally binding security arrangements or commitments (e.g., mutual defense treaties and pre-positioning agreements), the report must describe non-binding commitments, such as expressed U.S. policy formulated by the executive branch. It must also include, among other things, "[a]n assessment of the need to continue, modify, or discontinue each of those arrangements and commitments in view of the changing international security situation."[193]

Although reports were submitted to the appropriate committees pursuant to this statutory requirement in 1991 and 1992, it does not appear that any subsequent reports have been issued. The Federal Reports Elimination and Sunset Act of 1995 (Sunset Act, P.L. 104-66) terminated many reporting requirements existing prior to its enactment. The act eliminated or modified several specific reporting requirements, and also generally terminated any reporting requirement that had been listed in House Doc. 103-7, unless such a requirement was specifically exempted. However, the reporting requirement contained in § 1457 of the FY1991 National Defense Authorization Act was neither specifically terminated by the Sunset Act nor listed in House Doc. 103-7. Accordingly, it does not appear that this requirement has been terminated.

Consultation

State Department regulations requiring consultation with Congress regarding significant international agreements may provide a means for congressional oversight as to the negotiation of security arrangements. One of the stated objectives of the Circular 175 procedure is to ensure that "timely and appropriate consultation is had with congressional leaders and committees on treaties and other international agreements."[194] To that end, State

Department regulations contemplate congressional consultation regarding the conduct of negotiations to secure significant international agreements.[195]

Circular 175 procedures may also provide for congressional consultation concerning the form that a legally binding international agreement should take. When there is question as to whether an international agreement should be concluded as a treaty or an executive agreement, the matter is first brought to the attention of the State Department's Legal Adviser for Treaty Affairs. If the Assistant Legal Adviser for Treaty Affairs believes the issue to be "a serious one that may warrant formal congressional consultation,"[196] consultations are to be held with appropriate congressional leaders and committees. State Department regulations specify that "Every practicable effort will be made to identify such questions at the earliest possible date so that consultations may be completed in sufficient time to avoid last minute consideration."[197]

Approval, Rejection, or Conditional Approval of International Agreements

Perhaps the clearest example of congressional oversight in the agreement-making context is through its consideration of treaties and congressional-executive agreements. For a treaty to become binding U.S. law, it must first be approved by a two-thirds majority in the Senate. The Senate may, in considering a treaty, condition its consent on certain reservations, declarations and understandings concerning treaty application. For example, it may make its acceptance contingent upon the treaty being interpreted as requiring implementing legislation to take effect, or condition approval on an amended version of the treaty being accepted by other treaty parties. If accepted, these reservations, declarations, and understandings may limit and/or define U.S. obligations under the treaty.

As previously discussed, a congressional-executive agreement requires congressional authorization via a statute passed by both Houses of Congress. Here, too, approval may be conditional. Congress may opt to authorize only certain types of agreements, or may choose to approve only some provisions of a particular agreement. In authorizing an agreement, Congress may impose additional statutory requirements upon the Executive (e.g., reporting requirements). Congress may also include a statutory deadline for its authorization of an agreement to begin or expire.

Because sole executive agreements do not require congressional authorization to take effect, they need not be approved by Congress to become binding, at least as a matter of international law. Nonetheless, as discussed earlier, Congress may limit a sole executive agreement through a subsequent legislative enactment or through the conditioning of appropriations necessary for the agreement's commitment to be implemented.[198] Similar measures could also be taken to limit or condition U.S. adherence to a non-binding security arrangement.

Implementation of an Agreement That Is Not Self-Executing

Congress may exercise oversight regarding international agreements via legislation implementing the agreements' requirements. Certain international treaties or executive agreements are considered "self-executing," meaning that they have the force of law without the need for subsequent congressional action.[199] However, many other treaties and agreements are not considered self-executing, and are understood to require implementing legislation to take effect, as enforcing U.S. agencies otherwise lack authority to conduct the actions required to ensure compliance with the international agreement.[200]

Treaties and executive agreements have, in part or in whole, been found to be non-self-executing for at least three reasons: (1) implementing legislation is constitutionally required; (2) the Senate, in giving consent to a treaty, or Congress, by resolution, requires implementing legislation for the agreement to be given force;[201] or (3) the agreement manifests an intention that it shall not become effective as domestic law without the enactment of implementing legislation.[202]

Until implementing legislation is enacted, existing domestic law concerning a matter covered by an international agreement that is not self-executing remains unchanged and is controlling law in the United States. However, when a treaty is ratified or an executive agreement is entered, the United States acquires obligations under international law and may be in default of those obligations unless implementing legislation is enacted.[203] Perhaps for this reason, Congress typically appropriates funds necessary to carry out U.S. obligations under international agreements.[204]

Continuing Oversight

After an international agreement has taken effect, Congress may still exercise oversight over executive implementation. It may require the Executive to submit information to Congress or congressional committees regarding U.S. implementation of its international commitments. It may enact new legislation that modifies or repudiates U.S. adherence or implementation of an international agreement. It may limit or prohibit appropriations necessary for the Executive to implement the provisions of the agreement, or condition such appropriations upon the Executive implementing the agreement in a particular manner.

End Notes

[1] U.S. CONST., art. VI, § 2. In this regard, it is important to distinguish "treaty" in the context of international law, in which "treaty" and "international agreement" are synonymous terms for all binding agreements, and "treaty" in the context of domestic American law, in which "treaty" more narrowly refers to a particular subcategory of binding international agreements. It should be noted, however, that the term "treaty" is not always interpreted under U.S. law to refer only to those agreements described in Article II, § 2 of the Constitution. *See Weinberger v. Rossi*, 456 U.S. 25 (1982) (interpreting statute barring discrimination except where permitted by "treaty" to refer to both treaties and executive agreements); *B. Altman & Co. v. United States*, 224 U.S. 583 (1912) (construing the term "treaty," as used in statute conferring appellate jurisdiction, to also refer to executive agreements).

[2] Under international law, States that have signed but not ratified treaties have the obligation to refrain from acts that would defeat the object or purpose of the treaty. Vienna Convention on the Law of Treaties, entered into force January 27, 1980, 1155 U.N.T.S. 331 [hereinafter "Vienna Convention"], art. 18. Although the United States has not ratified the Vienna Convention, it recognizes it as generally expressing customary international law. *See, e.g., Fujitsu Ltd. v. Federal Exp. Corp.*, 247 F.3d 423, 433 (2nd Cir. 2001) ("we rely upon the Vienna Convention here as an authoritative guide to the customary international law of treaties ... [b]ecause the United States recognizes the Vienna Convention as a codification of customary international law ... and [it]

acknowledges the Vienna Convention as, in large part, the authoritative guide to current treaty law and practice") (internal citations omitted).

[3] Oftentimes, a bilateral treaty will only come into effect after the parties exchange instruments of ratification. In the case of multilateral treaties, ratification typically occurs only after the treaty's instruments of ratification are submitted to the appropriate body in accordance with the terms of the agreement.

[4] A "reservation" is "a unilateral statement ... made by a State, when signing, ratifying, accepting, approving or acceding to a treaty, whereby it purports to exclude or to modify the legal effect of certain provisions of the treaty in their application to that State." Vienna Convention, art. 2(1)(d). In practice, "[r]eservations change U.S. obligations without necessarily changing the text, and they require the acceptance of the other party." CONGRESSIONAL RESEARCH SERVICE, TREATIES AND OTHER INTERNATIONAL AGREEMENTS: THE ROLE OF THE UNITED STATES SENATE, A STUDY PREPARED FOR THE SENATE COMM. ON FOREIGN RELATIONS 11 (Comm. Print 2001); Vienna Convention, arts. 19-23.

[5] Declarations are "statements expressing the Senate's position or opinion on matters relating to issues raised by the treaty rather than to specific provisions." TREATIES AND OTHER INTERNATIONAL AGREEMENTS, *supra* note 4, at 11.

[6] Understandings are "interpretive statements that clarify or elaborate provisions but do not alter them." *Id.*

[7] As a matter of customary international law, States are "obliged to refrain from acts which would defeat the object and purpose of a treaty," including entering reservations that are incompatible with a treaty's purposes. Vienna Convention, arts. 18-19.

[8] LOUIS HENKIN, FOREIGN AFFAIRS AND THE U.S. CONSTITUTION 215 (2nd ed. 1996).

[9] *E.g., American Ins. Ass'n v. Garamendi*, 539 U.S. 396, 415 (2003) ("our cases have recognized that the President has authority to make 'executive agreements' with other countries, requiring no ratification by the Senate ... this power having been exercised since the early years of the Republic"); *United States v. Belmont*, 301 U.S. 324, 330 ("an international compact ... is not always a treaty which requires the participation of the Senate").

[10] TREATIES AND OTHER INTERNATIONAL AGREEMENTS, *supra* note 4, at 38-40.

[11] WILLIAM R. SLOMANSON, FUNDAMENTAL PERSPECTIVES ON INTERNATIONAL LAW 376 (5th ed. 2007).

[12] This estimate is based on numbers obtained via SLOMANSON, *supra* note 11, at 376 (discussing executive agreements and treaties that the United States has concluded between 1789 and 2004) and CRS research regarding treaties and executive agreements concluded from 2005 to 2009. Between 1789 and 2004, the United States entered 1,834 treaties and 16,704 executive agreements, meaning that roughly 10% of agreements concluded by the United States during that period took the form of treaties. SLOMANSON, *supra* note 11, at 376. The percentage of agreements entered as treaties has decreased further since 2004.

[13] *E.g.*, Edwin Borchard, *Treaties and Executive Agreements: A Reply*, 54 YALE L. J. 616 (1945) (arguing that the congressional-executive agreement is not a constitutionally permissible alternative to a treaty, and that sole executive agreements are permissible in limited circumstances); Laurence H. Tribe, *Taking Text and Structure Seriously: Reflections on Free-Form Method in Constitutional Interpretation*, 108 HARV. L. REV. 1221 (1995) (arguing that the Treaty Clause is the exclusive means for Congress to approve significant international agreements); John C. Yoo, *Laws as Treaties?: the Constitutionality of Congressional-Executive Agreements*, 99 MICH. L. REV. 757 (2001) (arguing that treaties are the constitutionally required form for congressional approval of an international agreement concerning action lying outside of Congress's constitutional powers, including matters with respect to human rights, political/military alliances, and arms control, but are not required for agreements concerning action falling within Congress's powers under Art. I of the Constitution, such as agreements concerning international commerce).

[14] RESTATEMENT (THIRD) OF FOREIGN RELATIONS, § 303 n.8 (1987) ("At one time it was argued that some agreements can be made only as treaties, by the procedure designated in the Constitution.... Scholarly opinion has rejected that view."); HENKIN, *supra* note 8, at 217 ("Whatever their theoretical merits, it is now widely accepted that the Congressional-Executive agreement is available for wide use, even general use, and is a complete alternative to a treaty.... "); YOO, *supra* note 13, at 759 (noting that "a broad intellectual consensus exists that congressional-executive agreements may serve as full substitutes for treaties"); Oona A. Hathaway, *Treaties' End: The Past, Present, And Future Of International Lawmaking In The United States*, 117 YALE L.J. 1236, 1244 (2008) (noting that "weight of scholarly opinion" since the 1940s has been in favor of the view that treaties and congressional-executive agreements are interchangeable). *Cf.* Bruce Ackerman & David Golove, *Is NAFTA Constitutional?*, 108 HARV. L. REV. 799 (1995) (arguing that developments in the World War II era altered historical understanding of the Constitution's allocation of power between government branches so as to make congressional-executive agreement a complete alternative to a treaty); Myres S. McDougal and Asher Lans, *Treaties and Congressional-Executive or Presidential Agreements: Interchangeable Instruments of National Policy* (parts I and II), 54 YALE L. J. 181, 534 (1945) (arguing that historical practice supports the interchangeability of congressional-executive agreements and treaties).

[15] RESTATEMENT, *supra* note 14, at § 302, n. 5; HENKIN, *supra* note 8, at 142-148. *See also Greater Tampa Chamber of Commerce v. Goldschmidt*, 627 F.2d 258 (D.C. Cir. 1980) (finding that plaintiffs lacked standing to challenge the propriety of the form taken by an international agreement between the United States and United Kingdom). Executive agreements dealing with matters having no direct impact upon private interests in

the United States (e.g., agreements concerning military matters or foreign relations) are rarely the subject of domestic litigation, in part because persons typically cannot demonstrate that they have suffered an actual, redressable injury and therefore lack standing to challenge such agreements. RESTATEMENT, *supra* note 14, at § 303, n. 11.

[16] *Made in the USA Foundation v. United States*, 242 F.3d 1300 (11th Cir. 2001), cert. denied by *United Steelworkers of America, AFL-CIO, CLC v. United States*, 534 U.S. 1039 (2001).

[17] In 1997, a federal district court in Texas ruled petitioner was not extraditable pursuant to a federal statute implementing an executive agreement, and held that extradition requires an extradition treaty ratified by the President and approved by two-thirds of the Senate. *In re* Surrender of Ntakirutimana, 988 F.Supp. 1038 (S.D.Tex. 1997). The Fifth Circuit Court of Appeals overturned the district court's finding and held that a person could be extradited by statute rather than treaty. *Ntakirutimana v. Reno*, 184 F.3d 419 (5th Cir. 1999), *cert. denied by* 528 U.S. 1135 (2000).

[18] *See* YOO, *supra* note 13 (discussing the kinds of agreements historically taking the form of treaties in contrast to those taking the form of executive agreements). *See also infra* pp. 9-15 (discussing form that different types of U.S. security agreements have historically taken).

[19] TREATIES AND OTHER INTERNATIONAL AGREEMENTS, *supra* note 4, at 5. *See also* HENKIN, *supra* note 8, at 215-18.

[20] TREATIES AND OTHER INTERNATIONAL AGREEMENTS,, *supra* note 4, at 5. Reciprocal trade agreements which were once concluded as treaties now typically take the form of congressional-executive agreements. RESTATEMENT, *supra* note 14, at § 303, n. 9. *See also* 19 U.S.C. § 2111 (conditionally authorizing the President to enter trade agreements with other nations); CRS Report 97-896, *Why Certain Trade Agreements Are Approved as Congressional-Executive Agreements Rather Than as Treaties*, by Jeanne J. Grimmett.

[21] *See, e.g.*, 16 U.S.C. § 1822(a) (authorizing the Secretary of State to negotiate international fishery agreements); 22 U.S.C. § 6445(c) (authorizing the President to enter binding agreements with other nations pledging to end practices violating religious freedom).

[22] *See, e.g.*, 19 U.S.C. § 3511 (approving agreements resulting from the Uruguay Round of multilateral trade negotiations under the auspices of GATT).

[23] *See, e.g.*, 19 U.S.C. § 3471 (authorizing U.S. participation in and appropriations for Commission on Labor Cooperation, established by a supplemental NAFTA agreement not expressly approved by Congress).

[24] TREATIES AND OTHER INTERNATIONAL AGREEMENTS,, *supra* note 4, at 5.

[25] U.S. CONST. art. VI, § 2 ("the laws of the United States ... [and] all treaties made, or which shall be made, under the authority of the United States, shall be the supreme Law of the Land").

[26] *See* RESTATEMENT, *supra* note 26, § 303 cmt. d.

[27] U.S. CONST. art. II, § 1 ("The executive power shall be vested in a President of the United States of America... "), § 2 ("The President shall be commander in chief of the Army and Navy of the United States ... "), § 3 ("he shall receive ambassadors and other public ministers ... "). Courts have recognized foreign affairs as an area of very strong executive authority. *See United States v. Curtiss-Wright Export Corp.*, 299 U.S. 304 (1936).

[28] *See* RESTATEMENT, *supra* note 14, § 303 (4).

[29] *See Dames & Moore v. Regan*, 453 U.S. 654 (1981) (establishing that Congress's implicit approval of executive action, such as historical practice of yielding authority in a particular area, may legitimize an agreement); *Youngstown Sheet & Tube Co. v. Sawyer*, 343 U.S. 579 (1952) ("When the President acts pursuant to an express or implied authorization of Congress, his powers are at their maximum.... Congressional inertia, indifference or quiescence may ... invite, measures of independent Presidential responsibility.... When the President takes measures incompatible with the expressed or implied will of Congress, his power is at its lowest ebb, for then he can rely only upon his own constitutional powers minus any constitutional powers of Congress over the matter.") (Jackson, J., concurring).

[30] Executive agreements have been held to be inferior to conflicting federal law when the agreement concerns matters expressly within the constitutional authority of Congress. *See, e.g., United States v. Guy W. Capps, Inc.*, 204 F.2d 655 (4th Cir. 1953) (finding that executive agreement contravening provisions of import statute was unenforceable); RESTATEMENT, *supra* note 14, § 115, n.5. However, an executive agreement might trump preexisting federal law if it concerns an enumerated or inherent executive power under the Constitution, or if Congress has historically acquiesced to the President entering agreements in the relevant area. *See id.*; *United States v. Pink*, 315 U.S. 203, 230 (1942) ("[a]ll Constitutional acts of power, whether in the executive or in the judicial department, have as much legal validity and obligation as if they proceeded from the legislature") (quoting THE FEDERALIST NO. 64 (John Jay)); *Dames & Moore*, 453 U.S. at 654 (upholding sole executive agreement concerning the handling of Iranian assets in the United States, despite the existence of a potentially conflicting statute, given Congress's historical acquiescence to these types of agreements).

[31] The "last in time" rule establishes that a more recent statute trumps an earlier, inconsistent international agreement, while a more recent self-executing agreement may trump an earlier, inconsistent statute. *Whitney v. Robertson*, 124 U.S. 190 (1888).

[32] U.S. CONST. art. I, § 8.

[33] *Id.*

[34] For additional discussion, see CRS Report RL33837, *Congressional Authority to Limit U.S. Military Operations in Iraq*, by Jennifer K. Elsea, Michael John Garcia, and Thomas J. Nicola.

[35] U.S. CONST. art. I, § 9. Congress may specify the terms and conditions under which appropriations may be used, so long as it does not impose unconstitutional conditions on the use of appropriated funds.

[36] *See United States v. Klein*, 80 U.S. (8 Wall.) 128 (1872) (holding invalid an appropriations proviso that effectively nullified some effects of a presidential pardon and that appeared to prescribe a rule of decision in court cases); *United States v. Lovett*, 328 U.S. 303 (1946)(invalidating as a bill of attainder an appropriations provision denying money to pay salaries of named officials). For further discussion of Congress's ability to use its appropriations power to limit the deployment or use of U.S. military forces, see CRS Report RL33837, *Congressional Authority to Limit U.S. Military Operations in Iraq*, *supra* note 34, at 23-29, 34-36.

[37] *See generally* Robert E. Dalton, Asst. Legal Adviser for Treaty Affairs, *International Documents of a Non-Legally Binding Character*, State Department, Memorandum, March 18, 1994, available at http://www.state.gov/documents/ organization/65728.pdf (discussing U.S. and international practice with respect to nonlegal, political agreements); Duncan B. Hollis and Joshua J. Newcomer, *"Political" Commitments and the Constitution*, 49 VA. J. INT'L L. 507 (2009) (discussing U.S. political commitments made to foreign States and the constitutional implications of the practice).

[38] 22 C.F.R. § 181.2(a).

[39] *Id. See also infra* at "Notification Pursuant to the Case-Zablocki Act"; State Department Office of the Legal Adviser, *Guidance on Non-Binding Documents*, at http://www.state.gov/s/l/treaty/guidance/.

[40] Circular 175 initially referred to a 1955 Department of State Circular which established a process for the coordination and approval of international agreements. These procedures, as modified, are now found in 22 CFR part 181 and 11 Foreign Affairs Manual (F.A.M.) chapter 720.

[41] 11 F.A.M. § 723.3 (2006).

[42] S.Res. 536, S.Rept. 95-1171, 95th Cong. (1977).

[43] 11 F.A.M. § 724.4(b)-(c) (2006).

[44] *Id.* at § 724.4(c).

[45] *See infra* at 27.

[46] *But see* YOO, *supra* note 13, at 830 (arguing the military commitments like NATO can only be effectuated by treaty, and not a congressional-executive agreement).

[47] Legislation proposing to limit the usage of sole executive agreements has periodically been introduced, but thus far no bill has been enacted. *See, e.g.*, S.Res. 85, 91st Cong. (1969) (non-binding resolution passed by the Senate expressing its sense that national commitments should be entered pursuant to treaty or executive agreement specifically authorized by Congress); H.R. 4438, 94th Cong. (1976) (proposing to require the President to transmit any agreement involving a national commitment to Congress, and allowing the agreement to take effect only if Congress did not pass a measure disapproving it within 60 days).

[48] The Constitution provides that "No money shall be drawn from the Treasury, but in Consequence of Appropriations made by Law." U.S. CONST., art. I, § 9, cl. 7.

[49] State Department, Office of the Legal Adviser, *U.S. Collective Defense Arrangements*, at http://www.state.gov/s/ l/ treaty/collectivedefense/.

[50] Inter-American Treaty of Reciprocal Assistance, 62 Stat. 1681, entered into force December 3, 1948; North Atlantic Treaty, 63 Stat. 2241, entered into force August 24, 1949; Security Treaty Between Australia, New Zealand and the United States of America, 3 U.S.T. 3420, entered into force April 29, 1952; Mutual Defense Treaty Between the United States of America and the Republic of the Philippines, 3 U.S.T. 3947, entered into force August 27, 1952; Mutual Defense Treaty Between the United States of America and the Republic of Korea, 5 U.S.T. 2368, entered into force November 17, 1954; Southeast Asia Collective Defense Treaty, 6 U.S.T. 81, entered into force February 19, 1955; Treaty of Mutual Cooperation and Security Between the United States of America and Japan, 11 U.S.T. 1632, entered into force June 23, 1960 (replacing Security Treaty Between the United States of America and Japan, 3 U.S.T. 3329, entered into force April 28, 1952). In 1954, the United States entered a mutual defense treaty with the Republic of China (Taiwan), 6 U.S.T. 433, but this agreement was terminated by President Carter in 1979.

[51] For background, *see* S.Rept. 797, 90th Cong., at 14-15 (1967) (describing ratification history of North Atlantic Treaty); Louis Fisher, PRESIDENTIAL WAR POWER 105-111 (2004) (describing Senate deliberations on North Atlantic Treaty).

[52] For example, the Panama Canal treaties provided that the United States and Panama would, in accordance with their respective constitutional processes, defend the Canal from attack. Treaty Concerning the Permanent Neutrality and Operation of the Panama Canal, with Annexes and Protocol, 33 U.S.T. 1, entered into force October 1, 1979.

[53] Act Approving Compacts of Free Association with the Republic of the Marshall Islands and the Federated States of Micronesia, P.L. 99-239, § 311 (1986). *See also* Act approving Compact of Free Association between the United States and the Government of Palau, P.L. 99-658, § 352 (1986) (recognizing an attack on Palau as a danger to the United States, and pledging that the United States "would take action to meet the danger to the United States and Palau in accordance with its constitutional processes").

[54] Some have argued that these agreements are "more akin to the Texas and Hawaii annexation resolutions than to international defense arrangements," given the historical status of the FAS. Peter J. Spiro, *Treaties, Executive Agreements, and Constitutional Method*, 79 TEX. L. REV. 961, n. 184 (2001).

[55] TREATIES AND OTHER INTERNATIONAL AGREEMENTS, *supra* note 4, at 248 (quoting A Report on United States Security Arrangements and Commitments with Other Nations, Submitted to the Congress in accordance with Section 1457 of P.L. 101-510, the National Defense Authorization Act of 1991, August 17, 1992).

[56] *Id. See also* Memorandum of Agreement Between the Governments of Israel and the United States Concerning Assurances, Consultations, and United States Policy on Middle East Peace, 32 U.S.T. 2160, entered into force February 27, 1976; Agreement Between the United States and Egypt Concerning Implementation of the Egyptian-Israeli Peace Treaty of March 26, 1979, 32 U.S.T. 2148, entered into force March 26, 1979; Agreement of Cooperation Between the Government of the United States of America and the Government of Pakistan, 10 U.S.T. 317, entered into force May 19, 1959; Agreement of Cooperation Between the Government of the United States of America and the Government of Liberia, 10 U.S.T. 1598, entered into force July 8, 1959.

[57] TREATIES AND OTHER INTERNATIONAL AGREEMENTS, *supra* note 4, at 248. *See also* Multinational Force and Observers Participation Resolution, P.L. 97-132 (1981).

[58] *See* The Proposed U.S. Security Commitment to Iraq: What Will Be In It and Should It Be a Treaty?: Hearing Before the Subcomm. on International Organizations, Human Rights, and Oversight & Subcomm. on the Middle East and South Asia of the House Comm. on Foreign Affairs, January 23, 2008 (statement by Prof. Michael J. Matheson) (recognizing distinction between "security commitment" and "security arrangement," while acknowledging that the "question of what constitutes a 'security commitment'... has been the subject of dialogue between the executive branch and Congress for decades"). *See also* TREATIES AND OTHER INTERNATIONAL AGREEMENTS, *supra* note 4, at 213-215, 247-250 (discussing legislation considered and enacted by Congress in response to concerns that the Executive had entered agreements imposing national commitments upon the United States without congressional notification or approval).

[59] *See, e.g.*, Agreement Between the United States of America and the Kingdom of Greece Concerning Military Facilities, 4 U.S.T. 2189, entered into force October 12, 1953.

[60] An example of such an agreement is the 2005 memorandum of understanding between the United States and Norway, discussed in more detail at American Forces Press Service, *Rumsfeld Signs Pre-positioning Agreement With Norway*, June 8, 2005, at http://www.defenselink.mil/news/newsarticle.aspx?id=16458.

[61] *See, e.g.*, Agreement under Article VI of the Treaty of Mutual Cooperation and Security Regarding Facilities and Areas and the Status of United States Armed Forces in Japan, 11 U.S.T. 1652, entered into force June 23, 1960. The only SOFA agreement to which the United States is a party that was concluded as a treaty is the North Atlantic Treaty Status of Forces Agreement (NATO SOFA), 4 U.S.T. 1792, entered into force August 23, 1953. All supplementary agreements to the NATO SOFA have been executive agreements.

[62] *See, e.g.*, Memorandum of Agreement Between The Ministry of National Defense Republic of Korea and the United States Forces in Korea Regarding The Construction of Facilities at 2nd ID USA To Improve Combined Defense Capabilities, 34 U.S.T. 125, entered into force February 2, 1982.

[63] *See, e.g.*, Agreement for Cooperation on Defense and Economy Between the Governments of the United States of America and of the Republic of Turkey in Accordance with Articles II and III of the North Atlantic Treaty, 32 U.S.T. 3323, entered into force December 18, 1980.

[64] *See infra* at "Iraq."

[65] Charter of the United Nations, 59 Stat. 1031, entered into force October 24, 1945, art. 51 (italics added).

[66] *See generally* Charles Henry Hyde, 1 International Law: Chiefly As Interpreted and Applied by the United States 27-36 (1922).

[67] Treaty on Relations Between the United States and Cuba, May 22, 1903, 33 Stat. 2248, at art. III. In 1906, acting pursuant to this authority, the United States intervened in Cuba following serious revolutionary activity in order to establish a stable government there.

[68] Treaty on Administration of Haiti: Finances and Development, entered into force November 15, 1915, T.S. 623, 1915 U.S.T. LEXIS 29, at art. XIV (providing that "The high contracting parties shall have authority to take such steps as may be necessary to insure the complete attainment of any of the objects comprehended in this treaty; and, should the necessity occur, the United States will lend an efficient aid for the preservation of Haitian Independence and the maintenance of a government adequate for the protection of life, property and individual liberty.").

[69] Isthmian Canal Convention with the Republic of Panama, entered into force February 26, 1904, 33 Stat. 2234, at art. XXIII. More generally, the agreement provided that the United States "guarantees and will maintain the independence of Panama." *Id.* at art. I. The agreement also provided the United States with authority to ensure public order in the cities of Panama City and Colon if, in the opinion of the United States, the government of Panama was unable to maintain order. *Id.* at art. VII.

[70] Treaty Between the United States and Dominican Republic Concerning the Collection and Application of Dominican Customs Revenues, proclaimed July 25, 1907, 35 Stat. 1880.

[71] For example, in 1958, President Dwight Eisenhower deployed U.S. troops to Lebanon at the invitation of its government to help protect against a threatened insurrection. Congress had passed legislation in 1957 that authorized such action. *See* P.L. 85-7 (1957). Specifically, the legislation permitted the President to "undertake, in the general area of the Middle East, military assistance programs with any nation or group of nations of that area desiring such assistance." The enactment further provided that "if the President determines the necessity thereof, the United States is prepared to use armed forces to assist any such nation or group of such nations requesting assistance against armed aggression from any country controlled by international communism: *Provided*, that such employment shall be consonant with the treaty obligations of the United States and with the Constitution of the United States."

[72] For further discussion, see W. Stull Holt, TREATIES DEFEATED BY THE SENATE 212-229 (1933) (discussing events leading to the ratification of the 1907 treaty with the Dominican Republic). In his autobiography, Roosevelt suggested that a treaty was preferable to the executive agreement he entered with the Dominican Republic, because "a treaty ... was the law of the land and not merely ... a direction of the Chief Executive which would lapse when that particular executive left office." ACKERMAN & GOLOVE, *supra* note 14, at 819 (italics omitted) (quoting THEODORE ROOSEVELT, AN AUTOBIOGRAPHY 510 (1920)).

[73] Agreement Between the United States and Denmark Concerning the Defense of Greenland, signed April 9, 1941, 55 Stat. 1245; Agreement Concerning Defense of Iceland By United States Forces, July 1, 1941, 55 Stat. 1547.

[74] *See supra* note 71 (discussing U.S. intervention in Lebanon in 1958).

[75] For text of the joint declaration, see Dept. of State, American Foreign Policy: Current Documents, 1962, pp. 1091-1093.

[76] *See* S.Rept. 91-129 (1969) (Senate Committee on Foreign Relations report in favor of the National Commitments Resolution, S.Res. 85, criticizing the undertaking of "national commitments" by the Executive, either through international agreements or unilateral pledges to other countries, without congressional involvement) [hereinafter "Committee Report"]. The vast majority of U.S. military interventions in other countries have been to protect U.S. persons, property, or interests. *See* CRS Report RL32170, *Instances of Use of United States Armed Forces Abroad, 1798-2008*, by Richard F. Grimmett. The Executive has historically claimed broad authority to deploy armed forces to protect these interests, even in the absence of clear congressional authorization. *See, e.g.*, Dept. of Justice, Office of Legal Counsel (OLC), 4A U.S. OP. OFF. LEGAL COUNSEL 185, *Presidential Power to Use the Armed Forces Abroad Without Statutory Authorization* (1980) (alleging presidential authority to deploy forces to protect, and retaliate for injuries suffered by U.S. persons and property); OLC, *The President's Constitutional Authority To Conduct Military Operations Against Terrorists And Nations Supporting Them*, 2001 OLC LEXIS 14 , September 25, 2001 (asserting presidential authority, even in the absence of congressional action, to take military action against entities responsible for the 9/11 terrorist attacks, as well authority to preemptively use force against entities that "pose a similar threat to the security of the United States and the lives of its people, whether at home or overseas").

[77] S.Res. 85, 91st Congress, 1st Sess. (1969).

[78] *Id.*

[79] Committee Report, *supra* note 76, at 26.

[80] *See, e.g.*, H.R. 4438, Executive Agreements Review Act, 94th Cong., 1st Sess. (proposing to establish legislative veto over executive agreements involving national commitments); S.Res. 24, Treaty Powers Resolution, 95th Cong., 1st Sess. (proposing that it would not be in order for the Senate to consider any legislation authorizing funds to implement any international agreement which the Senate has found to constitute a treaty, unless the Senate has given its advice and consent to treaty ratification).

[81] *See generally* The November 26 Declaration of Principles: Implications for UN Resolutions on Iraq and for Congressional Oversight: Hearing of the Subcommittee on International Organizations, Human Rights, and Oversight, February 8, 2008 (statement of Prof. Michael J. Glennon discussing presidential practice of entering non-binding security arrangements).

[82] Exchange of notes at Kabul April 6 and 13, 2002. Entered into force April 13, 2002. Not printed in *Treaties and Other International Acts Series (T.I.A.S.).*

[83] P.L. 87-195, 75 Stat. 424 (September 4 1961).

[84] 22 U.S.C. § 2347 *et seq.*

[85] 75 Stat. 424.

[86] *Id.* at 425.

[87] *Id.* at 434.

[88] *Id.* at 435.

[89] 22 U.S.C. § 2311(a)(2) (italics added).

[90] T.I.A.S. Exchange of notes September 26 and December 12, 2002 and May 28, 2003. Entered into force May 28, 2003.

[91] *Id.*

[92] Vienna Convention on Diplomatic Relations of April 18, 1961, T.I.A.S. 7502; 23 U.S.T. 3227.

[93] The transitional government has since been replaced by the fully elected Government of the Islamic Republic of Afghanistan. For information about the political development of Afghanistan since 2001, see CRS Report RS21922, *Afghanistan: Politics, Elections, and Government Performance*, by Kenneth Katzman.

[94] P.L. 107-40 (September 18, 2001); 115 Stat. 224.

[95] U.N.S.C. Res. 1368 (September 12, 2001) ("Recognizing the inherent right of individual or collective self-defence in accordance with the [UN] Charter," and expressing its "readiness to take all necessary steps to respond to the terrorist attacks").

[96] U.N.S.C. Res. 1386 (December 20, 2001).

[97] ISAF has its own status of forces agreement with the Afghan government in the form of an annex to a Military Technical Agreement entitled "Arrangements Regarding the Status of the International Security Assistance Force." The agreement provides that all ISAF and supporting personnel are subject to the exclusive jurisdiction of their respective national elements for criminal or disciplinary matters, and that such personnel are immune from arrest or detention by Afghan authorities and may not be turned over to any international tribunal or any other entity or State without the express consent of the contributing nation. In 2003, NATO assumed command of ISAF in Afghanistan.

[98] *See* U.N.S.C. Res. 1776 § 5 (September 19, 2007); U.N.S.C. Res. 1707 § 4 (2007).

[99] U.N.S.C. Res. 1746 § 25 (2007). For additional information on the war in Afghanistan, see CRS Report R40156, *War in Afghanistan: Strategy, Military Operations, and Issues for Congress*, by Catherine Dale.

[100] T.I.A.S. Signed at Doha and Kabul January 22 and February 16, 2004. Entered into force February 16, 2004.

[101] 10 U.S.C. §§ 2341-2350.

[102] *Id.* at § 2342(a)(1).

[103] *Id.* at § 2342(b)(1).

[104] *Id.* at § 2342(b)(2).

[105] Declaration of Colonel James W. Gray, filed March 5, 2007, Al Maqaleh v. Gates, 06-CV-01669 (U.S. D.D.C.), available at http://graphics8.nytimes.com/packages/pdf/topics/bagram/Affidavit.pdf [hereinafter "Gray Declaration"].

[106] Detainees are held in the Bagram Theater Internment Facility within the Airfield.

[107] Accommodation Consignment Agreement for Lands and Facilities at Bagram Airfield Between the Islamic Republic of Afghanistan Represented by His Excellency General Abdul Rahim Wardak Minister of Defense of the Office of the Ministry of Defense and the United States of America. Entered into force September 28, 2006 [hereinafter "Bagram Agreement"]. A copy of the agreement may be found as an exhibit attached to Gray Declaration, *supra* footnote 105.

[108] Bagram Agreement, at arts. 1, 5, 9.

[109] *Id.* at art. 2.

[110] http://www.mfa.gov.af/Documents/ImportantDoc/US-Afghanistan %20 Declaration. pdf.

[111] Karen DeYoung, "Only a Two-Page 'Note' Governs U.S. Military in Afghanistan," *Washington Post*, August 28, 2008, p. A07.

[112] In the 1950's, almost 40 years prior to the 1991 Persian Gulf War, the United States entered into a series of agreements with Iraq, including: (1) a military assistance agreement (T.I.A.S. 3108. Agreement of April 21, 1954); (2) an agreement relating to the disposition of military equipment and materials provided under the military assistance agreement (T.I.A.S. 3289. Agreement of July 25, 1955); and (3) an economic assistance agreement (T.I.A.S. 3835. Agreement of May 18 and 22, 1957). However, in response to the Revolution of July 14, 1958 and the subsequent change in the government of Iraq, the United States agreed to a termination of the above agreements (10 U.S.T. 1415; T.I.A.S. 4289; 357 U.N.T.S. 153. Exchange of notes at Baghdad May 30 and July 7, 1959. Entered into force July 21, 1959).

[113] The text of this agreement is available at http://georgewbush-whitehouse.archives.gov/news/releases/2007/11/20071126-11.html [hereinafter "*Declaration of Principles*"]. For a historical perspective of U.S. operations in Iraq and issues related to Iraqi governance and security, see CRS Report RL31339, *Iraq: Post-Saddam Governance and Security*, by Kenneth Katzman, and CRS Report RL33793, *Iraq: Regional Perspectives and U.S. Policy*, by Christopher M. Blanchard et al.

[114] U.N.S.C. Res. 1790 (December 18, 2007).

[115] Declaration of Principles, *supra* note 113.

[116] *Id.*

[117] For further discussion, see CRS Report RL34568, *U.S.-Iraq Agreements: Congressional Oversight Activities and Legislative Response*, by Matthew C. Weed.

[118] In a November 26, 2007 press briefing regarding the Declaration, General Douglas Lute, Assistant to the President for Iraq and Afghanistan, stated that the Administration did not foresee a prospective agreement with Iraq having "the status of a formal treaty which would then bring us to formal negotiations or formal inputs from the Congress." White House Office of the Press Secretary, *Press Gaggle by Dana Perino and General Douglas Lute*, Assistant to the President for Iraq and Afghanistan, November 26, 2007, available at http://georgewbush-whitehouse.archives.gov/ news/releases/2007/11/20071126-6.html.

[119] P.L. 110-161, Div. L, § 612 (2007).

[120] P.L. 110-417, § 1212 (2008).

[121] Initially, the Bush Administration expected any negotiated strategic framework agreement with Iraq to take the form of a political, rather than a legally binding agreement. *Hearing of the Subcommittee on the Middle East and South Asia, and the Subcommittee on International Organizations, Human Rights, and Oversight of the House Foreign Affairs Committee; Declaration and Principles: Future U.S. Commitments to Iraq*, March 4, 2008 (statement by Ambassador David M. Satterfield in response to question by Representative William Delahunt). Subsequent developments, including pressure from the Iraqi parliament that the negotiated U.S.-Iraq security agreements be submitted to it for approval before they could go into effect for Iraq, resulted in the agreements taking the form of legally binding instruments. *See also* STATE DEPT, TREATIES IN FORCE, A LIST OF TREATIES AND OTHER INTERNATIONAL AGREEMENTS OF THE UNITED STATES IN FORCE (2009) (listing both the U.S.-Iraq Security and Strategic Framework Agreements as legal agreements).

[122] For further discussion, see CRS Report R40011, *U.S.-Iraq Withdrawal/Status of Forces Agreement: Issues for Congressional Oversight*, by R. Chuck Mason.

[123] *See* CRS Report RL34568, *U.S.-Iraq Agreements: Congressional Oversight Activities and Legislative Response*, *supra* note 117 (discussing congressional hearings and proposed legislation addressing the U.S.-Iraq security arrangement).

[124] *See supra* at "Collective Defense Agreements/"Security Commitments".

[125] The 2002 Authorization to Use Military Force Against Iraq (2002 AUMF, P.L. 107-243) authorized the President to use military force as he deemed necessary and appropriate to "(1)defend the national security of the United States against the continuing threat posed by Iraq; and (2) enforce all relevant United Nations Security Council resolutions regarding Iraq." It could be argued that the removal of Saddam Hussein's regime from power in Iraq and the termination of the U.N. Security Council mandate mean that the 2002 AUMF no longer serves as a legal basis for U.S. operations in Iraq. Regardless of the continuing viability of the 2002 AUMF, Congress's appropriation of funds in support of ongoing military operations may be viewed as legal authorization for those operations. For further discussion, see CRS Report RL33837, *Congressional Authority to Limit U.S. Military Operations in Iraq*, *supra* note 34.

[126] For additional background on the Iraq war, see CRS Report RL34387, *Operation Iraqi Freedom: Strategies, Approaches, Results, and Issues for Congress*, by Catherine Dale.

[127] *See* H.R. 335, 111th Cong., 1st Sess. (2009) (A bill introduced by Representative Barbara Lee that if enacted would require the President to report annually to Congress regarding U.S. security commitments to, and arrangements with, other countries. Also, directs the Secretary of State and the Secretary of Defense to consult Congress with respect to any agreements concluded pursuant to the Strategic Framework Agreement. Additionally, prohibits any agreement (or the obligation of implementing funds) containing a security commitment to, or security arrangement with, the Republic of Iraq, from entering into force except pursuant to Article II, section 2, clause 2 (relating to treaties) or Article I, section 7, clause 2 (relating to enactment of laws) of the Constitution of the United States.).

[128] T.I.A.S. Exchange of notes at Baghdad July 24 and August 14, 2004. Entered into force August 14, 2004.

[129] T.I.A.S. Exchange of notes at Baghdad July 28 and August 14, 2004. Entered into force August 14, 2004.

[130] 3 U.S.T. 4564; T.I.A.S. 2607; 181 U.N.T.S. 45. Exchange of letters at Bonn December 19 and 28, 1951.

[131] P.L. 82-165, 65 Stat. 373 (October 10, 1951).

[132] *Id.*

[133] 3 U.S.T. 4564; T.I.A.S. 2607; 181 U.N.T.S. 45.

[134] 65 Stat. 373.

[135] 6 U.S.T. 5999; T.I.A.S. 3443; 240 U.N.T.S. 47. Signed at Bonn June 30, 1955. Entered into force December 27, 1955.

[136] *Id.*

[137] P.L. 83-665, 68 Stat. 832 (August 26, 1954).

[138] 6 U.S.T. 5999; T.I.A.S. 3443; 240 U.N.T.S. 47.

[139] *Id.*

[140] *See, e.g.,* Mutual Defense Assistance: Disposition of Military Equipment and Materials. 6 U.S.T. 6005; T.I.A.S. 3444; 240 U.N.T.S. 69. Exchange of notes at Bonn June 30, 1955. Entered into force December 27, 1955. Mutual Defense Assistance: Purchase of Certain Military Equipment, Materials, and Services. 7 U.S.T. 2787; T.I.A.S. 3660; 278 U.N.T.S. 9. Exchange of notes at Washington October 8, 1956. Entered into force December 12, 1956. Defense: Training of German Army Personnel. 8 U.S.T. 149; T.I.A.S. 3753; 280 U.N.T.S. 63. Exchange of notes at Bonn December 12, 1956. Entered into force December 12, 1956.

[141] 14 U.S.T. 689; T.I.A.S. 5352; 490 U.N.T.S. 30. Signed at Bonn August 3, 1959. Entered into force July 1, 1963.

[142] 5 U.S.T. 661; T.I.A.S. 2957; 232 U.N.T.S. 169. Signed at Tokyo March 8, 1954. Entered into force May 1, 1954.

[143] 3 U.S.T. 3169; T.I.A.S. 2490. Signed at San Francisco September, 8, 1951. Entered into force April 28, 1952.

[144] 63 Stat. 714.

[145] 65 Stat. 373.

[146] 5 U.S.T. 661; T.I.A.S. 2957; 232 U.N.T.S. 169.

[147] *Id.*

[148] 11 U.S.T. 1632; T.I.A.S. 4509; 373 U.N.T.S. 186. Signed at Washington January 19, 1960. Entered into force June 23, 1960.
[149] T.I.A.S. 12335.
[150] 11 U.S.T. 1632; T.I.A.S. 4509; 373 U.N.T.S. 186.
[151] *Id.*
[152] *Id.*
[153] *Id.*
[154] 11 U.S.T. 1652; T.I.A.S. 4510; 373 U.N.T.S. 248. Signed at Washington January 19, 1960. Entered into force June 23, 1960.
[155] Agreements concerning new special measures relating to Article XXIV (related to costs of maintenance of U.S. forces in Japan and furnishment of rights of way related to facilities used by U.S. forces in Japan) of the agreement of January 19, 1960, have been signed in 1991, 1995, 2000, and 2006.
[156] Exchange of letters at Seoul August 9 and 11, 1948. Entered into force August 11, 1948.
[157] 62 Stat. 3817; T.I.A.S. 1918; 9 Bevans 477; 79 U.N.T.S. 57. Signed at Seoul August 24, 1948. Entered into force August 24, 1948.
[158] *Id.*
[159] 62 Stat. 3818.
[160] *Id.*
[161] *Id.* at 3819.
[162] *Id.*
[163] 1 U.S.T. 137; T.I.A.S. 2019; 80 U.N.T.S. 205. Signed at Seoul January 26, 1950. Entered into force January 26, 1950.
[164] P.L. 81-329, 63 Stat. 714 (October 6, 1949).
[165] 1 U.S.T. 137; T.I.A.S. 2019; 80 U.N.T.S. 205.
[166] 3 U.S.T. 4619; T.I.A.S. 2612; 179 U.N.T.S. 105. Exchange of notes at Pusan January 4 and 7, 1952. Entered into force January 7, 1952.
[167] P.L. 82-165, 65 Stat. 373 (October 10, 1951).
[168] 3 U.S.T. 4619; T.I.A.S. 2612; 179 U.N.T.S. 105.
[169] 5 U.S.T. 2368; T.I.A.S. 3097; 238 U.N.T.S. 199. Signed at Washington October 1, 1953. Entered into force November 17, 1954.
[170] *Id.*
[171] *Id.*

[172] 17 U.S.T. 1677; T.I.A.S. 6127; 674 U.N.T.S. 163. Signed at Seoul July 9, 1966. Entered into force February 9, 1967.

[173] 61 Stat. 3283; T.I.A.S. 1662. Signed at Manila March 21, 1947. Entered into force March 21, 1947.

[174] 61 Stat. 3284.

[175] 4 U.S.T. 1682; T.I.A.S. 2834; 2163 U.N.T.S. 77. Exchange of notes at Manila June 26, 1953. Entered into force July 5, 1953.

[176] 3 U.S.T. 3947; T.I.A.S. 2529; 177 U.N.T.S. 133. Signed at Washington August 30, 1951. Entered into force August 27, 1952.

[177] *Id.*

[178] 3 U.S.T. 4644; T.I.A.S. 2617; 179 U.N.T.S. 193. Exchange of notes at Manila January 4 and 7, 1952. Entered into force January 7, 1952.

[179] *Id.*

[180] T.I.A.S. Exchange of notes at Manila April 2, June 11 and 21, 1993. Entered into force June 21, 1993.

[181] T.I.A.S. Signed at Manila February 10, 1998. Entered into force June 1, 1999.

[182] T.I.A.S. Signed at Manila October 9, 1998. Entered into force June 1, 1999.

[183] 1 U.S.C. § 112b

[184] *See* H.Rept. 92-1301, 92nd Cong. (1972).

[185] 1 U.S.C. § 112b(a).

[186] *Id.* at §112b(b).

[187] *Id.* at § 112b(d).

[188] H.Rept. 92-1301, 92nd Cong. (1972).

[189] 22 C.F.R. § 181.2(a).

[190] 11 F.A.M. § 725.1(5).

[191] 50 U.S.C. § 404c(a).

[192] *Id.* at § 404c(c)-(d).

[193] *Id.*

[194] 11 F.A.M. § 722(4).

[195] *Id.* at § 725.1(5).

[196] 11 F.A.M. § 724.4(b)-(c).

[197] *Id.* at § 724.4(b).

[198] In the 110th Congress, legislation introduced would have prohibited appropriations from being used to carry out any U.S.-Iraqi security agreement that was not approved by the Senate as a treaty or authorized by legislation passed by both Houses of Congress. (*See, e.g.*, S. 2426 (Congressional Oversight of Iraq Agreements Act of 2007); H.R. 4959 (Iraq Strategic Agreement Review Act of 2008); H.R. 5626 (the Protect Our Troops and Our Constitution Act of 2008)).

[199] For purposes of domestic law, a self-executing agreement may be superseded by either a subsequently enacted statute or a new self-executing agreement. *Whitney*, 124 U.S. at 194.

[200] *See generally* RESTATEMENT, *supra* note 14, § 111(4)(a) & cmt. h.

[201] For example, in the case of the United Nations Convention Against Torture and Other Cruel, Inhuman or Degrading Treatment or Punishment, G.A. Res. 39/46, Annex, 39 U.N. GAOR Supp. No. 51, U.N. Doc. A/39/51 (1984), the Senate gave advice and consent subject to a declaration that the treaty was not self-executing. U.S. Reservations, Declarations, and Understandings to the Convention Against Torture and Other Cruel, Inhuman or Degrading Treatment or Punishment, 136 CONG. REC. S17486-01 (daily ed., October 27, 1990).

[202] RESTATEMENT, *supra* note 14, § 111(4)(a) & n. 5-6.

[203] *See id.*, § 111, cmt. h.

[204] *See* TREATIES AND OTHER INTERNATIONAL AGREEMENTS, *supra* note 4, at 166-170 (discussing congressional use of the appropriations power to influence the implementation of international agreements by the United States).

INDEX

9

9/11, viii, 35, 42, 145, 146, 147, 149, 150, 154, 157, 158, 159, 160, 162, 163, 167, 168, 169, 170, 171, 172, 216
9/11 Commission, viii, 42, 145, 146, 147, 149, 150, 154, 157, 158, 159, 160, 163, 167, 168, 169, 170, 171, 172

A

Abraham, 3
abuse, 6, 9, 10, 13, 14, 25, 44, 55, 56, 79, 86, 88, 94, 95, 130, 132, 164, 166
access, 50, 62, 63, 64, 70, 80, 86, 92, 93, 112, 113, 128, 134, 140, 149, 150, 152, 153, 155, 163, 164, 165, 167, 168, 172, 174, 179, 180, 181, 183, 196
accommodation, 50, 53, 75, 77, 201
accountability, 12, 21, 28, 85, 128, 130, 167
accounting, 7, 12, 72, 80, 81, 88, 94, 95, 129, 130, 133, 207
accounting standards, 12
accuracy, 82, 95, 115
achievement, 21
adjustment, 31
administrators, 21, 23, 88, 110, 135
Advice and Consent, 12, 39, 42
advisory body, 168
affirmative action, 198
Afghanistan, viii, 11, 145, 190, 199, 200, 201, 217
aggression, 198, 200, 202, 203, 216
Alexander Hamilton, 3
alternatives, 121, 124, 146, 166, 168
ambassadors, 54, 213
applications, 51, 128
appointees, 39, 54, 86, 94
Appointments Clause, 41
appropriations, viii, 9, 11, 20, 21, 23, 35, 36, 37, 38, 87, 99, 102, 112, 113, 115, 116, 119, 121, 122, 123, 131, 133, 134, 145, 146, 147, 148, 157, 158, 159, 160, 161, 163, 168, 178, 193, 195, 199, 204, 210, 211, 213, 214, 220
armed forces, 23, 198, 199, 205, 206, 207, 216
arrest, 203, 217
assessment, 37, 100, 101, 123, 182, 209
assets, 2, 39, 72, 95, 192, 213
assignment, 4, 84, 119, 129, 130, 152, 155, 201
assumptions, 121, 122
AT&T, 140, 141
attacks, 162, 200, 203
Attorney General, 11, 51, 52, 53, 60, 75, 76, 87, 93, 103, 104, 105, 139, 140, 143
auditing, 11, 72, 80, 81, 88, 130
audits, 11, 12, 80, 81, 82, 86, 87, 118, 130, 164, 165, 166, 171
Australia, 195, 214
authorities, 26, 60, 61, 117, 161, 166, 170, 180, 186, 200, 202, 203, 217
availability, 37, 95, 125, 163, 193, 195

B

background, 78, 79, 84, 118, 156, 169, 190, 214, 218
background information, 78, 84, 118
banking, 115
basing rights, ix, 189, 190, 202
behavior, 5, 31, 59
binding, x, 141, 189, 190, 193, 194, 195, 196, 198, 199, 203, 207, 208, 209, 210, 211, 213, 214, 216, 218
blogosphere, 16
border security, 114
borrowing, 36, 133
Budget Committee, 27, 121, 122, 133, 134, 135
budget deficit, 20
budget resolution, 36, 37, 122, 123, 134, 135

budget surplus, 123
bureaucracy, 15, 21, 24, 79

C

Cabinet, 2, 43, 52, 94
campaign organizations, 118
Capitol Hill, 5, 14, 43, 92, 107, 124, 133, 155
case law, 44
cast, 54, 55
chain of command, 51, 52
challenges, 4, 15, 16
channels, 20, 84
character, 205
checks and balances, 6, 21
cheese, 8
Chief Justice, 92, 103
Chief of Staff, 72
children, 114
China, 214
CIA, viii, 11, 87, 88, 89, 91, 105, 136, 145, 146, 147, 148, 151, 162, 164, 165, 166, 168, 171, 172, 176, 177, 178, 180, 186, 187
circulation, 83
City, 17, 215
civil action, 126
civil liberties, 146
civil rights, 4, 114, 135
civil service, 24, 25
clarity, 103
classification, 117
clients, 56, 116, 117, 119
Cold War, viii, 4, 145, 193
colonization, 198
color, 126
commerce, 23, 101, 212
common law, 44, 54, 55, 56, 141
communication, 25, 54, 70, 71, 82, 85, 87, 111, 117, 129
communism, 216
community, 4, 60, 130, 146, 147, 148, 151, 160, 161, 162, 168, 200
compensation, 114
competence, 10
competency, 40
competition, 84, 161, 162
compilation, 71, 78, 208
complaints, 22, 31, 32, 86
complement, 8, 161
complexity, 20, 129
compliance, 6, 45, 47, 48, 49, 55, 56, 58, 63, 70, 75, 80, 88, 96, 97, 101, 129, 130, 182, 191, 211
components, viii, 5, 90, 97, 145, 148, 151, 163, 164, 165, 168
composition, 36, 149, 152, 170
conference, 38, 84, 85, 123, 154, 155, 186
conference committees, 123, 154
confidence, 60, 193
confidentiality, 49, 51, 56, 75, 76, 86, 132
conflict, 6, 20, 25, 35, 103, 105, 141, 156, 193, 201
conflict of interest, 103, 105
confusion, 155, 156
congressional budget, 11, 115, 120, 121
Congressional Budget Office, viii, 20, 27, 33, 36, 78, 109, 112, 120, 129, 133, 137, 138, 164, 170
congressional hearings, 39, 87, 117, 141, 218
congressional interests, 39
consensus, 5, 122, 154, 212
consent, ix, 12, 21, 40, 62, 118, 128, 189, 190, 191, 200, 202, 203, 205, 207, 210, 211, 216, 217, 220
Consolidated Appropriations Act, 113
conspiracy, 47
Constitution, 6, 12, 13, 20, 22, 23, 38, 39, 41, 44, 46, 99, 105, 114, 186, 190, 191, 192, 193, 211, 212, 213, 214, 216, 218, 220
constitutional amendment, 115
constitutional law, 114
consultants, 22, 27, 32, 82, 157
consulting, 174
continuity, 155, 157, 199
control, 3, 15, 23, 25, 28, 36, 54, 58, 65, 70, 80, 95, 99, 101, 114, 116, 128, 160, 161, 164, 196, 206
conviction, 14, 41, 104, 141
coordination, 5, 29, 30, 32, 34, 35, 86, 88, 112, 147, 154, 158, 161, 163, 166, 167, 168, 194, 214
copyright, iv
Copyright, iv
Corporation for Public Broadcasting, 90
corporations, 28, 88, 92, 135, 166
corruption, 21, 44, 73, 130
cost, viii, 6, 8, 13, 19, 21, 27, 28, 64, 80, 85, 96, 121, 122, 123, 125
costs, 27, 80, 96, 97, 123, 124, 125, 128, 155, 219
counsel, 46, 47, 51, 53, 56, 58, 61, 75, 103, 104, 105, 116, 125, 126, 127, 138, 141, 178
Court of Appeals, 50, 191, 213
covering, viii, 96, 133, 145, 146, 167
credibility, 103, 121
credit, 36, 74, 115
crime, 103, 114
criticism, 105
cross-fertilization, 162
Cuba, 197, 215
currency, 3, 98, 115
current balance, 181

D

damages, 65
danger, 99, 205, 206, 214
data collection, 95
DCI, viii, 145, 147, 172
death, 99, 105
debt, 36, 114, 115, 133
decision making, 51, 53
decision-making process, 75
decisions, 4, 7, 14, 17, 36, 37, 38, 44, 47, 50, 97, 120, 154, 175, 180
defence, 217
defense, ix, 3, 5, 11, 17, 36, 45, 88, 110, 114, 157, 158, 159, 161, 163, 189, 190, 195, 196, 197, 198, 199, 200, 203, 204, 205, 206, 207, 209, 214, 215
deficiencies, 7, 32, 82, 86, 97, 101
deficit, 121, 123
definition, vii, 4, 5
delegates, 57
delivery, 21, 22, 71, 113
democratization, 16
demographic change, 122
denial, 140
Denmark, 216
Department of Agriculture, 8
Department of Commerce, 142, 143
Department of Defense, 100, 148, 165, 169, 172, 200
Department of Energy, 100, 150
Department of Health and Human Services, 64, 140
Department of Homeland Security, vii, 1, 2, 90, 101, 169
Department of Justice, 24, 48, 50, 51, 53, 77, 103, 140
deposition, 46, 49, 60, 62
depression, 2
destination, viii, 20
detention, 178, 187, 217
diplomacy, 114
direct cost, 123
direct costs, 123
directives, 10, 24, 37, 53, 116, 122, 206
directors, 124, 186
disability, 104
disaster, 13, 115
disaster relief, 13
disbursement, 26
discipline, 121
disclosure, 25, 51, 53, 55, 56, 62, 71, 75, 100, 128, 142, 152, 153, 158, 165, 167, 170, 177, 208
disposition, 217
disseminate, 132
dissidents, 102
distribution, 84, 101, 104, 111, 118, 121
District of Columbia, 50, 51, 55, 115, 126, 141, 171
divergence, 15
diversity, 117, 146, 156
division, 103, 104, 113, 114, 117
Doha, 217
domestic issues, 4
Domestic Policy Council, 72
Dominican Republic, 198, 215, 216
draft, 71, 118
drawing, 121
drug abuse, 94
drug trafficking, 4
drugs, 94
duplication, 8, 35, 118, 131, 161, 162
duration, 29, 194, 198, 204
duties, 24, 26, 28, 30, 40, 51, 55, 75, 86, 97, 101, 104, 118, 126, 127, 128, 153, 200

E

economic assistance, 217
economic cooperation, 193
economic crisis, 2
economic development, 115, 199
economic growth, 121
economic policy, 121
economic problem, 114
economics, 115, 124
economy, 2, 6, 11, 28, 30, 78, 86, 98, 117, 121, 122, 124, 132
Education, 89, 139, 199
Egypt, 196, 215
elaboration, ix, 78, 173
elderly, 122
election, 59, 74
electronic communications, 178, 186
e-mail, 81, 85, 113, 119
embargo, 85
Emergency Economic Stabilization Act, 2
employees, 2, 12, 20, 24, 50, 53, 64, 70, 82, 86, 92, 103, 110, 118, 126, 127, 142
employment, 50, 133, 216
energy, 9, 14, 115, 150
enforcement, 9, 47, 49, 63, 64, 126, 127, 165
engagement, 199
England, 34
environment, 4, 115, 200
environmental protection, 9
Environmental Protection Agency, 38, 89, 94
EPA, 48, 139
epidemic, 4
equipment, 38, 196, 204, 205, 206, 207, 217
equity, 28, 96

ergonomics, 8
erosion, 194, 200
estimating, 122
ethics, 58, 73, 111, 130, 156
evening news, 83
execution, 3, 22, 26, 29, 30, 55, 79, 116
executive function, 192
Executive Order, 132
executive orders, 24, 81, 132
exercise, x, 7, 20, 23, 26, 36, 37, 51, 53, 62, 75, 76, 79, 99, 172, 190, 199, 200, 206, 207, 210, 211
expenditures, 16, 20, 21, 23, 36, 72, 74, 81, 99, 104, 124, 133
expertise, ix, 32, 60, 96, 113, 114, 154, 157, 161, 167, 170, 173, 174
experts, 13, 110
export promotion, 114
exposure, 44, 82

F

failure, 4, 38, 48, 57, 62, 95, 141
fairness, 138
faith, 50, 75, 77
FAS, 196, 215
FCC, 10, 42
fear, 52, 194
Federal Communications Commission, 10, 35, 55, 90
federal courts, 127
federal criminal law, 11, 56, 87, 103
Federal Election Commission, 74, 90
federal funds, 130
federal law, 193, 213
Federal Reserve Board, 87
federalism, 114
FEMA, 90
Fifth Amendment, 46, 58, 66, 141
finance, 72, 115
financial institutions, 115
financial market, 115
financial markets, 115
financial regulation, 115
financial system, 98
financing, 36, 94, 99
firms, 81, 83
First Amendment, 58
first responders, 100
fiscal policy, 115
fisheries, 115
fitness, 153
flexibility, 38, 49, 185
fluctuations, 121
focusing, 14, 59, 117, 138
food, 4, 8, 17, 30, 115
food safety, 4, 8
Ford, 124, 125
forecasting, 29, 121
foreign affairs, 98, 110, 146, 192, 213
foreign aid, 114
foreign exchange, 115
foreign intelligence, 88, 165
foreign policy, 12, 15, 159, 185, 199, 204
foundations, 135, 166
Fourth Amendment, 59
fraud, 5, 6, 9, 10, 11, 13, 21, 25, 31, 44, 55, 56, 79, 86, 88, 94, 95, 130, 132, 164, 166
free world, 204, 206
freedom, 58, 200, 213
fulfillment, 140
funding, 23, 36, 37, 39, 86, 88, 97, 102, 123, 135, 157, 177, 178, 181, 183
funds, 11, 21, 22, 25, 26, 28, 37, 38, 59, 80, 96, 97, 99, 102, 129, 130, 134, 153, 159, 161, 177, 180, 185, 191, 193, 200, 202, 211, 214, 216, 218

G

GATT, 192, 213
GDP, 121
General Accounting Office, 12, 25, 33, 34, 42, 105, 106, 128, 136, 137, 164, 171, 172
General Agreement on Tariffs and Trade, 192
generation, 122
Germany, 190, 197, 199, 204, 205
globalization, 4
goals, vii, 1, 2, 8, 13, 21, 65, 80, 94, 116, 168
government spending, 16
GPRA, 8, 94, 165, 168
grand jury, 48, 51, 54, 55, 141
grants, vii, 1, 2, 23, 26, 44, 46, 47, 51, 91, 97, 165, 199, 204, 206
Great Britain, 98
Great Depression, 2
Greece, 215
gross domestic product, 115, 121
groups, 6, 16, 62, 115, 134, 135, 162, 185, 201, 202
growth, viii, 2, 4, 19, 122
guidance, 10, 118, 180, 214
guidelines, 38, 96, 116
Gulf Coast, 91

H

Haiti, 197, 215
Hamiltonian, 3
Hawaii, 215
health, 114, 122, 135
health care, 114, 122

health care costs, 122
Help America Vote Act, 91
hiring, 27
homeland security, 9, 15, 115, 146, 156, 170
Homeland Security Act, 86
housing, 114, 115, 154
human resources, 117
human rights, 193, 212
Hurricane Katrina, 10, 59, 91

I

ICC, 91
Iceland, 198, 216
identification, 70, 118
identity, 208
illusion, 207
immigration, 4, 114
immunity, 44, 46, 47, 56, 58, 103, 104, 126, 128, 200
impacts, 167
impeachment, 6, 13, 40, 41, 59, 104, 126, 127, 140
implementation, vii, viii, x, 1, 2, 4, 5, 8, 9, 12, 14, 16, 19, 20, 31, 54, 79, 100, 127, 131, 132, 190, 193, 207, 209, 211, 220
imprisonment, 48, 49, 55
incentives, vii, 1, 3, 14, 15, 167
inclusion, 83, 177
independence, 11, 39, 86, 92, 105, 166, 172, 197, 201, 204, 206, 215
Independence, 87, 215
indicators, 115
industrialization, 4
industry, 3, 115
inefficiency, 15, 31, 44, 79
inertia, 213
inflation, 121, 122
information retrieval, 116
information sharing, 146, 165, 167
information technology, 28, 96, 117, 132, 165
infrastructure, 115, 116
initiation, 48, 93, 140, 174, 175, 177, 187
injuries, 64, 216
injury, 55, 64, 65, 99, 191, 213
INS, 101
inspections, 87, 90
inspectors, 11, 16, 25, 86, 88, 91, 132, 138, 146, 162, 164
institutions, 114, 135
instruments, 212, 218
insurance, 115
integrity, 44, 56, 80, 88, 115, 128, 193, 201, 202
intelligence gathering, 146
Intelligence Identities Protection Act, 25
interaction, 32, 117
interest groups, 109, 135, 138
interest rates, 121
interference, 45, 87, 128
interim regulations, 100
internal controls, 94
Internal Revenue Service, 13
international law, 114, 193, 210, 211, 212
International Monetary Fund, 114
internationalization, 4
Internet, 85, 134
Interstate Commerce Commission, 90
intervention, 2, 197, 198, 216
interview, 84
investment, 114
Iran, ix, 10, 17, 35, 43, 46, 47, 59, 61, 66, 67, 103, 105, 108, 162, 170, 171, 173, 175, 176, 177, 185
Iraq, viii, ix, 11, 59, 88, 90, 145, 189, 190, 197, 199, 201, 202, 203, 204, 214, 215, 216, 217, 218, 220
Israel, 196, 215
issues, viii, 4, 7, 9, 10, 15, 31, 32, 35, 36, 41, 44, 46, 49, 50, 51, 53, 64, 73, 77, 79, 81, 84, 96, 110, 111, 113, 114, 115, 117, 118, 121, 124, 130, 131, 135, 145, 162, 178, 203, 212, 217

J

Japan, 190, 195, 197, 199, 205, 214, 215, 219
judges, 14, 41
judgment, 40, 41
judicial branch, 115
judiciary, 40, 92, 146
Judiciary Committee, 93, 104, 140
jurisdiction, 4, 5, 9, 13, 15, 20, 26, 27, 29, 30, 31, 32, 35, 36, 45, 55, 57, 63, 64, 78, 79, 90, 91, 98, 103, 104, 127, 135, 142, 146, 148, 150, 151, 154, 156, 157, 158, 159, 160, 161, 165, 166, 168, 170, 172, 196, 200, 202, 203, 206, 211, 217
justice, 105, 114
justification, 23, 44, 134

K

kidney, 79
kidney dialysis, 79
Korea, 205, 206, 214, 215

L

labor, 3, 114, 121
labor force, 121
land, 193, 201, 203, 205, 206, 216
language, ix, 26, 38, 41, 63, 99, 104, 134, 173, 174, 176, 179, 181, 182, 183, 185, 187, 208
languages, 113
Latin America, 197

law enforcement, 2, 44, 86, 90, 92, 100, 203, 206
laws, vii, viii, ix, 1, 2, 6, 7, 8, 9, 12, 16, 17, 20, 21, 23, 24, 26, 29, 30, 31, 35, 37, 38, 39, 44, 54, 55, 78, 79, 80, 82, 86, 94, 100, 102, 122, 123, 129, 130, 142, 189, 190, 206, 213, 218
lawyers, 114
leadership, vii, ix, 10, 19, 29, 39, 86, 93, 102, 124, 149, 154, 155, 157, 159, 162, 168, 173, 174, 176, 178, 179, 184, 185
leaks, 164
learning, 81
Lebanon, 185, 216
legal issues, 130, 180
legality, 143, 193
legislative proposals, 86, 118, 124, 132, 134, 154, 202
Liberia, 196, 215
librarians, 110, 112
life span, 60
likelihood, 37, 50, 160
limitation, 38, 52, 71, 72, 99, 126
line, 7, 11, 52, 85, 87, 159, 167
links, 113
litigation, 50, 127, 142, 143, 213
loans, 13, 97, 119
lobbying, 115
local authorities, 100
local government, 28, 81, 86, 97, 100, 123
locus, 156
Louisiana, 3, 72, 137
lying, 212

M

machinery, 13
macroeconomic policy, 115
maintenance, 23, 118, 197, 205, 215, 219
majority, viii, ix, 8, 14, 15, 17, 24, 29, 40, 49, 50, 52, 53, 57, 62, 65, 93, 99, 104, 105, 125, 126, 140, 145, 148, 149, 151, 152, 153, 154, 162, 170, 173, 174, 179, 183, 190, 191, 192, 194, 210, 216
management, 13, 21, 26, 80, 88, 94, 95, 96, 97, 115, 116, 117, 128, 131, 132, 165
mandates, 7, 95, 97, 121, 123, 165, 197
market, 98, 115
market structure, 115
Marshall Islands, 214
meanings, 4, 5, 196
measures, 9, 11, 26, 28, 29, 36, 38, 64, 94, 99, 100, 102, 121, 133, 176, 193, 197, 200, 201, 203, 204, 210, 213, 219
media, 2, 14, 15, 22, 60, 82, 83, 84, 85
Medicaid, 99
Medicare, 13, 64, 79, 122
membership, 63, 72, 96, 148, 149, 150, 151, 152, 154, 155, 156, 157, 160, 162, 163, 164, 168, 170, 176, 177, 181, 183, 184
methodology, 13, 129
Mexico, 98
Middle East, 215, 216, 218
military, ix, 2, 4, 50, 114, 115, 148, 185, 189, 190, 192, 193, 195, 196, 197, 198, 199, 200, 201, 203, 204, 205, 206, 212, 213, 214, 216, 217, 218
military exercises, 197
minorities, 114
minority, ix, 27, 29, 44, 45, 62, 63, 65, 93, 124, 125, 128, 148, 149, 151, 152, 153, 158, 160, 162, 168, 170, 173, 174, 179, 180
minority groups, 65
missions, 8, 94, 120
model, 45, 146, 147, 149
models, 16, 57, 121
money, 11, 12, 15, 16, 23, 99, 177, 193, 214

N

NAFTA, 73, 191, 192, 212, 213
narcotics, 114
nation, 3, 4, 15, 16, 17, 31, 56, 124, 150, 194, 201, 216, 217
National Aeronautics and Space Administration, 89, 94
National Defense Authorization Act, 202, 209, 215
National Economic Council, 72
National Science Foundation, 90, 94
national security, 59, 60, 75, 87, 114, 141, 161, 172, 180, 182, 185, 201, 208, 218
National Security Council, vii, 1, 2, 59, 72, 169
NATO, 197, 201, 205, 214, 215, 217
natural resources, 115
negotiating, 194
negotiation, x, 3, 50, 98, 190, 192, 207, 208, 209
Nelson Mandela, 102
network, 84
New Zealand, 195, 214
newspapers, 71, 82, 110, 112, 118
NGOs, 135, 143
Nicaragua, 59, 102
North America, 191
North American Free Trade Agreement, 191
Norway, 215
nuclear power, 150
nutrition, 9, 30, 114

O

Obama Administration, 165, 166

objectives, 6, 8, 21, 26, 65, 80, 94, 116, 128, 130, 140, 165, 182, 185, 209
obligate, 196
obligation, 6, 7, 25, 37, 75, 76, 149, 196, 199, 206, 211, 213, 218
observations, vii, 1, 3
obstacles, 45, 165, 166
obstruction, 47, 105
Office of Management and Budget, vii, 1, 2, 13, 72, 95, 96, 131, 137, 170, 171, 172
openness, 52
Operation Enduring Freedom, 199, 200
Operation Iraqi Freedom, 218
operator, 101
opinion polls, 135
opportunities, 65, 129, 156, 162
order, ix, 9, 10, 46, 47, 49, 54, 55, 58, 64, 95, 99, 100, 101, 119, 126, 131, 141, 143, 173, 174, 190, 205, 206, 215, 216
orientation, 110, 111, 130
overlap, 4, 8, 10, 22, 35, 131, 140, 146
Overseas Private Investment Corporation, 90

P

Pacific, 207
Pakistan, 196, 215
Panama, 90, 91, 198, 214, 215
pandemic, 4
parallel, 88, 89, 104, 125, 147, 161
parameters, 51, 63
Parliament, 38
Pension Benefit Guaranty Corporation, 90
pensions, 114
performance, viii, 6, 8, 11, 12, 16, 19, 21, 37, 75, 79, 80, 82, 94, 96, 100, 114, 116, 117, 132, 135, 138, 165
permission, 62, 111, 118
permit, 36, 57, 80, 83, 100, 119, 121, 123, 142, 158, 177, 180, 185, 186
Persian Gulf, 217
Persian Gulf War, 217
persons with disabilities, 114
Philippines, 141, 143, 190, 195, 199, 206, 207, 214
photographs, 71
physical health, 39
planned action, 102
planning, 74, 116, 117, 168, 180
pleasure, 127
polarization, 14
policy choice, 113
policy initiative, 7
policy options, 122
political affiliations, 162
political leaders, 202
political parties, 115, 152, 154, 156
political party, 148, 152
political power, 64
poor, 114
population, 114, 122
power, viii, 3, 4, 6, 7, 11, 16, 17, 20, 23, 24, 36, 37, 38, 39, 40, 44, 45, 46, 47, 48, 49, 51, 53, 54, 57, 64, 65, 87, 88, 92, 101, 102, 104, 139, 140, 141, 145, 148, 149, 157, 159, 160, 161, 165, 192, 193, 194, 198, 199, 201, 212, 213, 214, 218, 220
precedent, 62, 64, 140, 187
precedents, 38, 41, 44, 50, 171, 190
predicate, 103
preparedness, 4, 10
president, 2, 6, 15, 74, 125
President Clinton, 41, 43, 51, 104, 127
press conferences, 83, 84
pressure, 22, 102, 104, 105, 122, 200, 218
prima facie, 191
privacy, 30, 115, 132
private sector, 2, 60, 100, 123
probe, 35, 39, 59
procedural right, 141
procurement, 5, 38, 116, 132
production, 45, 55, 63, 71, 83, 94, 126
productivity, 117, 121
professional development, 117
profits, 72, 185
program, 5, 6, 9, 10, 11, 12, 13, 14, 21, 22, 26, 27, 31, 32, 36, 70, 74, 79, 80, 82, 86, 94, 102, 111, 114, 116, 117, 124, 128, 129, 131, 132, 135, 138, 139, 178, 186, 187
programming, 113
project, 31, 102, 112
public administration, 88
public finance, 114
public health, 114
public interest, 10, 16, 21, 52, 58, 81, 85, 98, 103, 141
public policy, viii, 19, 20, 21, 54, 110, 111, 118, 124, 135, 156, 162
public support, 10
punishment, 25, 40, 48

Q

qualifications, 39, 54, 87, 92
quotas, 165

R

radio, 83, 84, 85

range, 6, 13, 16, 20, 23, 58, 78, 94, 103, 109, 114, 116, 117, 124, 127, 130, 133, 150, 199
rape, 99
reading, 112, 134
real estate, 2
reality, 4, 8, 14
reason, 52, 56, 104, 141, 182, 211
reasoning, 47
recall, 133
recess appointment, 39
recession, 2
recognition, 20, 52, 55, 56, 65, 117, 200
recollection, 10
recommendations, iv, viii, 6, 9, 11, 12, 28, 29, 30, 31, 34, 35, 37, 38, 40, 52, 59, 87, 92, 115, 116, 121, 124, 132, 134, 145, 147, 148, 157, 158, 159, 160, 161, 166, 168, 169
reconciliation, 123, 133
recovery, 91, 206
recurrence, 22
reelection, 15, 74
reformers, 37
refugees, 114
regulation, 25, 28, 94, 100, 115, 204
regulations, 7, 8, 9, 21, 81, 100, 101, 102, 105, 114, 116, 129, 132, 194, 208, 209, 210
rehabilitation, 198
rejection, 63
relationship, 6, 16, 32, 70, 146, 150, 155, 156, 157, 165, 167, 185, 202, 205
relevance, 84
reliability, 128
relief, 62, 63
rendition, 178, 187
rent, 201
Reorganization Act, 7, 20, 26, 29, 79, 82, 116, 117
replacement, 155, 201
reporters, 82, 83, 84, 85
reputation, 121, 129
Requirements, 12, 17, 87, 92, 93, 106, 165, 174, 175, 181, 196
Reservations, 220
reserves, 96, 148
resolution, 4, 8, 9, 27, 30, 45, 50, 57, 58, 77, 95, 98, 101, 102, 121, 125, 126, 127, 130, 151, 158, 159, 169, 195, 199, 200, 211, 214
resource allocation, 114
resources, 5, 8, 9, 15, 24, 27, 28, 80, 86, 94, 98, 109, 112, 114, 115, 116, 117, 121, 123, 129, 157, 166, 180, 204
respect, 30, 35, 50, 53, 54, 77, 85, 126, 127, 128, 141, 168, 169, 170, 180, 181, 190, 195, 200, 201, 202, 208, 212, 214, 218
returns, 71, 72
revenue, 36, 72, 122, 123, 133
rights, iv, 3, 22, 25, 58, 62, 65, 101, 141, 219
risk, ix, 9, 12, 13, 45, 52, 100, 173, 175, 177, 180, 182, 185, 201

S

Saddam Hussein, 201, 218
safety, 114, 198, 205
sales, 59
sampling, 143
sanctions, 37, 49, 58
SAP, 174, 182
savings, 121
scaling, 15
scandal, 24, 59
scheduling, 187
school, 2, 3
scores, 31, 135
screening, 46
searching, 112, 134
Secretary of Commerce, 63, 139
Secretary of Defense, 172, 196, 201, 218
Secretary of Homeland Security, 100, 101
Secretary of the Treasury, 93, 98
securities, 115
security, ix, x, 2, 4, 60, 88, 96, 100, 101, 114, 130, 132, 150, 152, 153, 158, 172, 173, 175, 177, 178, 182, 185, 189, 190, 193, 195, 196, 197, 198, 199, 201, 202, 203, 204, 205, 206, 207, 209, 210, 213, 215, 216, 217, 218, 220
security forces, 201, 206
selecting, 12, 15, 130, 153
seminars, vii, viii, 19, 110, 111, 112, 113, 116, 117
Senate approval, 198
sensitivity, ix, 146, 173, 175, 184
separation, 51, 114, 159
September 11, 2, 104, 159, 171, 199, 200
shape, 7, 11, 35, 124, 135
sharing, 100, 132, 164, 178, 197
Sinai, 196
skills, 5, 157
social fabric, 117
social security, 114
Social Security, 13, 79, 89, 94, 122
software, 134
South Africa, 102
South Asia, 215, 218
South Korea, 190, 195, 197, 199, 205, 206
Southeast Asia, 195, 214
Soviet Union, 4, 192
space, 115
specialists, viii, 7, 20, 110, 118

speech, 58
spreadsheets, 115
Spring, 42, 66, 67, 137
stability, 155, 157, 201, 202
staffing, 32, 117, 124, 168
stakeholders, 94
standards, 47, 80, 88, 95, 96, 97, 100, 129, 130
State Department, 90, 91, 114, 194, 195, 208, 209, 210, 214
state laws, 194
State of the Union address, 2
statehood, 115
statistics, 27, 92, 119, 132
statute, ix, 7, 36, 37, 47, 58, 64, 87, 88, 91, 96, 97, 102, 104, 105, 126, 127, 143, 173, 174, 175, 176, 177, 179, 181, 182, 183, 184, 185, 186, 192, 197, 210, 211, 213, 220
statutes, 7, 8, 9, 10, 17, 44, 53, 78, 91, 130, 179
stimulus, 16
storage, 70
strategic planning, 116
strategic position, 37
strategies, 114, 115, 131
strategy, 114
students, 186
subpoena, 6, 45, 46, 47, 49, 51, 55, 56, 58, 59, 65, 70, 71, 74, 86, 87, 92, 126, 127, 140, 141, 143, 157, 160, 170
subscribers, 113
substitutes, 212
summer, 142
supervision, viii, 4, 19, 20, 59, 80, 87
supply, 98, 118, 129
support services, 110
Supreme Court, 17, 22, 24, 38, 40, 44, 45, 47, 48, 50, 54, 55, 59, 63, 64, 75, 101, 102, 103, 104, 139, 141, 191
surging, 15
surplus, 121
surveillance, 178, 186
survey, 172
synthesis, 158

T

Taiwan, 214
talent, 117, 129
Taliban, 199, 201
tanks, 135
targets, 15, 121
tax collection, 133
taxation, 115
technical assistance, 113, 130, 204, 206
technological developments, 4
telecommunications, 115
telephone, 71, 81, 83, 85, 112, 141
television, 83, 84, 85, 113, 139
television coverage, 83
television stations, 83, 84
tenure, 88, 149, 154, 157, 160
term plans, 94
territory, 197, 198, 199, 202, 206
terrorism, 114, 159, 200, 202
terrorist attacks, 2, 4, 35, 146, 199, 200, 216, 217
terrorist groups, 202
terrorists, 202
Thailand, 198
threat, 4, 25, 40, 47, 55, 65, 196, 197, 201, 203, 216, 218
threats, 196, 197, 201, 203
threshold, 56, 103
thresholds, 123
time frame, 122, 124
time periods, 97, 133
timing, 187
Title V, 103, 125, 127, 176, 181, 185, 187
tracking, 113, 115
trade, 4, 114, 192, 213
trade agreement, 213
trade policy, 114
tradition, 75, 147, 171, 182
training, 111, 114, 115, 116, 117, 131, 197, 199, 200, 202, 206
training programs, 131
transactions, 5, 80, 123
transcripts, 29, 71
transformation, viii, 145, 170
transparency, 16, 97, 147, 158, 168
transportation, 115
transportation infrastructure, 115
treaties, ix, 54, 189, 190, 191, 192, 194, 195, 196, 197, 198, 203, 209, 210, 211, 212, 213, 214, 218
trends, 16, 36, 80, 121
trial, 14, 41, 44, 127, 140
trust, 3, 40, 154, 155, 185
Turkey, 215
turnover, 155, 157

U

U.N. Security Council, 200, 218
U.S. economy, 120
U.S. policy, 209
UN, 216, 217
uncertainty, 48, 155, 156
unemployment, 4, 114, 121
uniform, 28, 81, 95, 196
United Kingdom, 212

United Nations, 114, 197, 201, 202, 204, 206, 215, 218, 220
unreasonable searches, 59
upward mobility, 117
Uruguay, 213
Uruguay Round, 213
use of force, 200

V

vacancies, 40, 130, 150, 160
valuation, 137, 146
veto, 8, 101, 102, 109, 151, 172, 174, 177, 182, 216
video, 84, 113, 139
voting, 64, 154
vulnerability, 100, 101

W

war, 5, 21, 23, 31, 195, 217, 218
waste, 5, 6, 9, 11, 12, 13, 14, 15, 25, 31, 44, 56, 79, 86, 88, 94, 95, 129, 132, 164, 166
weapons, 114, 203
websites, 16, 85, 135
welfare, 114, 199, 204
White House, 6, 7, 11, 15, 20, 51, 52, 53, 54, 56, 59, 61, 72, 73, 75, 76, 77, 105, 139, 141, 217
winning, 6, 15
winter, 140
withdrawal, x, 126, 189, 202, 203, 205
witnesses, 6, 14, 45, 46, 49, 57, 58, 62, 79, 118, 141, 143, 171
workload, 118, 161
World Bank, 114
World Trade Organization, 114
World War I, 4, 5, 191, 198, 212
writing, viii, 20, 71, 85, 88, 93, 117, 123, 129, 140, 179, 181, 183, 184, 185
wrongdoing, 10, 76, 88